ALSO BY LOIS P. FRANKEL, PH.D.

Kindling the Spirit:
Acts of Kindness and
Words of Courage
for Women

Quit Bein' a Girl:
101 Dumb Ways
Smart Women Sabotage
Their Careers

Women, Anger and Depression:
Strategies for Self-Empowerment

"Whether you're a senior executive or entry-level professional, you'll find Overcoming Your Strengths *an invaluable addition to your business library. Not only did it help me in my pursuit of excellence, it also helped me to coach my staff toward peak performance."*
—LYNNE SEGALL, Vice President & Associate Publisher,
The Hollywood Reporter

"Powerful! [This book] points you to areas within yourself where you would never think of looking to find the missing link to the success you have been searching for. A totally different approach. A 'must read' for anyone who wants to maintain or achieve greater success in today's uncertain and changing workplace."
—CHARLES T. MARTIN, Vice President, Human Resources and Administration,
International Family Entertainment, The Family Channel

"A must-read for coaches working with corporate employees.... Each chapter is a mini-workshop, and the author's generous use of client stories and coaching examples makes for an interesting read. This is the perfect gift for the client who's ready to get back on track."
—CHERYL RICHARDSON, Founding President,
International Coach Federation

"Lois Frankel's advice is accurate and to the point. She has offered me personal counsel and has never asked me to change the way I do my job. Her advice is real time and, if added to your repertoire of skills, will increase your effectiveness."
—EDWARD F. GARNETT, Vice President
Human Resources, Amgen, Inc.

"Filled with understandable, usable suggestions. The tips contained at the end of each chapter are excellent, straightforward, and easy to do. Every manager should have this book on his or her to-read list."
—J. DOUGLAS ANDREWS, Ph.D., Assistant Dean and Chair,
Department of Business Communication,
University of Southern California

"Dr. Frankel develops organizations by focusing on the fundamentals: effective personal performance by fully functioning people. Her critical insights and tools for shaping complete capability offer personal and organizational tool kits for people and their managers. Individual inefficiency and personal barriers to success are the frightening cost issues of twenty-first-century companies. Lois offers useful means to avoid those costs beginning now!"
—JOHN HOFMEISTER, Vice President Human
Resources, Allied Signal Aerospace

Overcoming
Your
Strengths

8 Reasons Why Successful People Derail
and How to Remain on Track

Lois P. Frankel, Ph.D.

Corporate Coaching International Publications
PASADENA, CALIFORNIA

Although the author and publisher have made every effort to ensure the accuracy and completeness of information contained in this book, we assume no responsibility for errors, inaccuracies, omissions, or any inconsistency herein. Any slights of people, places, or organizations are unintentional.

First printing 2003

ISBN 0-9724662-1-5
LCCN 2002112888

ATTENTION CORPORATIONS, UNIVERSITIES, COLLEGES, AND PROFESSIONAL ORGANIZATIONS: Quantity discounts are available on bulk purchases of this book for educational, gift purposes, or as premiums for increasing magazine subscriptions or renewals. Special books or book excerpts can also be created to fit specific needs. For information, please contact Corporate Coaching International Publications, 540 El Dorado Street, Suite 102, Pasadena, CA 91101; ph. 626-405-7310.

This book would not be possible without the coaching clients who allow me to enter their personal and professional lives and trust me enough to make the leap of faith required to overcome their strengths. It is to each of you that this book is dedicated.

Contents

Acknowledgments

The most pleasant part of writing a book is when it comes time to thank those who helped and supported me through the process. My work is enhanced by my relationships with these people, and the input I receive from them. Therefore, I thank the following people:

Dr. Karen Otazo for introducing me to the concept of coaching and providing me with the opportunity to work with the staff at ARCO as I developed my own coaching philosophy.

Susan Picascia for providing me with not only insights and material used throughout this book but also with her friendship and support.

Karen Flannery, formerly with McKinsey and Booz Allen & Hamilton, for doing research and feeding me with a continual stream of relevant information from her own reading and thirst for knowledge.

Carol DiPaolo, editor of *Employment Relations Today*, for over thirty years a dear friend, active advocate of my work, and editor extraordinaire.

Shirley Trissler, for the time spent researching biographical information and tolerating my never-ending, often exhausting, pursuit of possibilities.

Tom Henschel, for his never-flagging optimism, willingness to be a sounding board, and friendship.

Dr. Kim Finger and Majella Lue Sue for your support, gentle reminders, and management of CCI during the absences I spend writing.

Dr. Pam Erhardt, for being my muse.

To each of you, and the others in my network of extended family and friends, I extend a heartfelt "thank you." I hope that each of you knows how very grateful I am for the gifts you have given me.

Introduction

Have you ever wondered why certain people move ahead steadily through their careers while others stall or fall from their career tracks entirely? Some folks always seem to do and say the right thing, while others can't quite figure out what it takes to become and, more important, remain successful. Regardless of career path or position, most of us have experienced being on the sidelines and watching as less qualified colleagues get the choice assignments, promotions, or developmental opportunities that are intended to groom them for the next rung of the corporate ladder. We may grumble about the injustice of it all, but rarely do we take the time to examine why this happens and what we can do to make ourselves more competitive.

After 25 years as a resources consultant and corporate coach, working inside corporations and organizations worldwide, I've observed what makes certain people become and remain successful while others spin their wheels in what are at times lucrative but dead-end assignments. Corporations typically don't waste their time, energy, and resources on ne'er-do-wells, but they do put considerable effort into helping bright, capable, and competent people, who are stumbling over themselves, to succeed. The cost of turn-over and finding these competent people is too high to do otherwise.

If you're reading this book, it is likely that your profile resembles the following: You are good at what you do, and may even be recognized for one or more particular strengths, but are somehow stalled or perhaps on the verge of career derailment. The term derailment was first used by researchers at the Center for Creative Leadership in Greensboro, North Carolina, to describe the process whereby fast-trackers are displaced from their successful career

1

paths. The researchers estimate that 30 percent to 50 percent of high-potential managers and executives derail. Throughout this book the term derailment is used in a broad context to refer to people at any level in their careers who are faced with the possibility of unexpected career failure. Derailment occurs among secretaries with the same regularity as it does among executives— and for the same reasons.

Derailment is a change in career momentum. Otherwise successful people begin to stall in their careers, or fail entirely, for seemingly inexplicable reasons. People who work hard and have been rewarded for their contributions to a firm through promotions, job assignments, or special perks and incentives suddenly find themselves being overlooked for further recognition for no apparent reason. Their opinions may no longer be solicited, they may not be included in meetings with key people, or they may be given more routine, low-profile assignments than in the past. People suddenly feel invisible.

In exploring why some people derail while others remain on their career paths I found that people who experienced career derailment difficulties behaved in ways consistent with childhood expectations of them and relied almost exclusively on these behaviors for continued success. Typically, these are employees who have no history of job-related performance problems. In fact, they have frequently been identified as high-potential candidates and targeted for upward mobility.

Looking inside organizations that have downsized over the past decade, it is clear that the "survivors" of ongoing layoffs are frequently not the most technically proficient, best educated, or most productive. As corporations cut more closely to the bone, there appear to be few notable differences between those who are given their pink slips and those who remain. Examining the situation more closely, what emerges is a pattern of keeping people on staff who have the widest array of technical and interpersonal capabilities, rather than those who have very specific, but more limited, ones. This is what has become known as the "best-player" approach to downsizing: keeping those people who can function in a wide variety of areas and with a diverse group of people.

Managers are forced every day to make choices between keeping and laying off people who on the surface appear to be equally qualified. How, then, do they choose one over another? The answer lies in infrequently commented on, less tangible aspects of workplace behavior. Remarks like, "Steve's a great worker, cranks out the work like no one else, but he doesn't get the big picture" or "Ann is one of our most talented engineers, but she doesn't get along with people" give us our greatest clues as to what contributes to one person's longevity and another's derailment. Derailment doesn't necessarily equate to automatic layoff or termination. People who are derailed frequently simply get overlooked again and again. Their input may be ignored or they or their departments may be overlooked for further growth opportunities. Whether they are laid off, ignored, or overlooked, the result is the same: career stagnation.

The common thread for people who derail is that they exhibit superior skill in a particular area to the exclusion of developing complementary ones. Even when a change in job assignment requires them to apply a different skill set, or when they see people around them develop in diverse areas, they fail to notice that they are limiting themselves and turn up the volume on those behaviors that they already do well, hoping that doing more of the same will save them! How do intelligent people neglect to notice something as important as their own lack of a diversified approach to other people and problem solving? The answer lies in the degree to which a strength was learned and reinforced in response to early childhood experiences.

Take for example Jamie, who comes from a home where Mom was an alcoholic and Dad, partially in response to Mom, was a workaholic. Jamie grew up knowing that her survival depended on taking good care of herself because there was no one else to do it for her. She learned to be independent and self-sufficient. Initially, she was a terrific employee. She was self-motivated and required little coaxing or direction. Eventually, however, Jamie began missing deadlines because she became overextended and failed to ask for assistance. Paradoxically, Jamie's strengths were what ultimately caused her to fail. She must learn to overcome her strengths, through the development of complementary skills, if she is to remain successful over the long term.

The truth is, we all have a little of Jamie in us. Maybe we didn't grow up in the same type of household, but we did grow up in environments that placed certain expectations and restrictions on our development. Whether we learned by word or deed that "children are to be seen and nor heard," "you must do things yourself because no one else is to be trusted," or "never disagree with authority," those internalized messages affect our present behavior in the workplace. Our subconscious tells us that if our childhood survival depended on being quiet, independent, or compliant, then our adult well-being is certainly contingent on exhibiting those same behaviors.

Employees like Jamie need to be coached on how to add complementary skills to their existing strengths to help them stay on track. Enlightened companies realize that the cost of letting talented people go is way too high. Not only is there the cost of advertising, contracting firms, or interviewing, but there is also a cost to morale, productivity, and teamwork when someone is fired. Before making the decision to terminate employees like Jamie, these companies hire coaches to give the employees every opportunity to succeed. These companies realize that their own management may not always be the best coaches for their employees.

My coaching philosophy is simple: People should not stop engaging in behaviors that work for them, but rather identify the gaps in their repertoire of skills and fill them in with complementary strengths. People should remain essentially the same while adding new skills. It's a bit like learning a sport. When the golf coach suggests that the student change her grip he isn't asking her to fundamentally change who she is. He's only giving her a hint for how to be more successful on the golf course. If the student incorporates this hint into her game, she's rewarded with better scores.

The process of learning how to avoid derailment need not involve a lot of time or money. It isn't always necessary to hire an outside coach or spend countless years in psychotherapy. You can coach yourself to success by recognizing the eight must commonly made career mistakes described in the following chapters and learning the skills needed to overcome them. *Overcoming Your Strengths: 8 Reasons Why Successful People Derail and How to Get Back on Track* is designed for anyone who ever wondered why his or her career came to a screeching halt—and everyone who wants to prevent that from happening in the future. The Derailment Inventory in the following chapter will help you to assess your current derailment status, and suggestions throughout the book offer ways of staying or getting back on track. The key to using this book effectively lies in your willingness to critically assess your background, your behavior, and the direction of your career.

Throughout this book you'll find descriptions of how real-life employees nearly derailed as well as examples of high-profile personalities and historical figures who experienced premature career failures. Specific suggestions for overcoming your strengths are contained at the end of the subsequent chapters. You may discover that you have more in common with Los Angeles Lakers coach Phil Jackson, Donald Trump, or former British Prime Minister Margaret Thatcher than you realized . . .and that even people who achieve great things need to continue to find ways to overcome their strengths.

Why Successful People Fail

Sarah was a senior accountant with an outstanding record of achievement in her midsize manufacturing firm until eight months ago, when she was promoted to manager of her department. Although she was able to produce high-quality results for the six years she was an individual contributor, she is currently floundering in her role as leader. She tries to do it all herself. Not only does she exclude others from the decision-making process, but she fails also to delegate. It appears that the skills that enabled her to accomplish so much at lower levels in the organization are the same ones that are now impeding her progress.

With only minor variations to the script, this scenario is played out daily in companies of all sizes around the globe. As a corporate coach, I'm called on to help employees like Sarah overcome obstacles to ongoing career success. My work typically begins with a phone call from a senior-level manager who wants coaching for someone who directly reports to him or her. The descriptions are similar: "I've got this employee who was outstanding when he first came on board. He was a real workhorse. We promoted him to manager, and now he's on probation. He needs help." When asked for a more detailed description of what the employee is doing wrong, the manager continues, "He's like a bull in a china shop, runs roughshod over people and embarrasses them in front of their peers. He just can't seem to understand that what it takes is a collaborative effort, not muscle."

Frequently, people like Sarah and the one this manager described fail without ever understanding why. Unfortunately, they often go on to other jobs and make the same mistakes again. They don't understand that those skills, characteristics, and qualities that contribute to success early in their careers are the same ones that ultimately serve to derail them once they reach higher levels of an organization or later stages of their careers. Paradoxically, the behaviors contributing to early career success are learned early in childhood as defense mechanisms: that is, they enabled people to survive what might have been difficult, traumatic, or demanding childhoods. In corporations, workers at every level of the business operation succeed by using the same survival skills they learned in childhood. These skills normally work, but only up to a point.

Repeating Past Behaviors

Whether the description is of someone who runs roughshod, does all the work instead of delegating, sees only the pieces of the puzzle instead of the bigger picture, has difficulty with authority, or is so easy-going that people walk all over him or her, it's a variation on the same theme: people who have not developed new skills that will provide balance to those skills that have contributed to early career success. If you are someone who continues to rely on behaviors that enabled you to survive childhood, despite the fact that *those behaviors have become counterproductive*, then you face the possibility of derailment.

Although many of Freud's theories have been questioned in recent years (and for good reason), he was right about the *repetition compulsion*: the tendency of human beings to return to past states, to repeat certain acts over and over again. And we repeat those acts over and over, even when they no longer work, until we understand what purpose they serve. We can all cite examples of people we know who marry several times, each time selecting the same type of partner and each time wondering why it doesn't work. For those of us on the outside looking in, it's abundantly clear why it doesn't work, but for the person making the choices it's Freud's repetition compulsion in action.

The choice of a partner often approximates the early childhood experience. That is, if Dad was an alcoholic, a woman may choose a husband who is either an alcoholic or in some similar way incapacitated. If Mom was depressed, her son may choose a depressed wife. This is not to say that these choices are conscious, because they most frequently are not. We make choices because they're familiar, and this familiarity enables us to know how to act in a given situation. Choosing a partner who is in some way familiar enables us to repeat the childhood behaviors we learned to survive—even though those behaviors are no longer functional!

Thus far the focus has been on developing survival skills in response to dysfunctional family behavior, but don't get the impression that people from these families are the only ones who develop such skills. Although current research suggests that nine out often people come from families of origin in which there is some type of dysfunction, these are not the only families for which survival skills are needed. You may come from that one functional family where everyone is a high achiever with advanced degrees in rocket science. Survival skills in this family may look different but still have the effect of obscuring necessary, complementary behaviors.

Defense mechanisms and survival skills aren't bad things. We all learned early on which behaviors pleased or satisfied our childhood primary caretakers, whether they were parents, nannies, grandparents, favorite teachers, or child-care workers. Even a preverbal child subconsciously knows that his or her survival depends on the caretaker. Therefore, repeating pleasing behavior was critical to survival, it is logical, then, that we would assume that those behaviors that pleased the caretaker also would please others later in our lives. Most of us want to be loved and accepted, and often our behavior is motivated by this, rather than an objective assessment of what the situation requires. Because the caretaker is also the first authority figure in our lives, we think that behaviors that pleased him or her will also please another authority figure—in the workplace that authority figure is the "boss."

What does all of this psychological jargon mean in today's corporate arena? Let's go back to Sarah for a moment. She is an outstanding individual contributor, but she can't quite empower others. Sarah's direct reports complain about her grandstanding (keeping the high-profile projects for herself), about not trusting them with an entire project, and about micromanaging their work. To understand these behaviors, we need to look at how they developed and what functional purpose they served in the past. As it turns out, Sarah was the oldest of six children. Both parents worked, and she had responsibility for taking care of her younger siblings after school, getting dinner started, baby-sitting during summer vacations, and so on. She learned early in life that her survival—approval from her parents—was dependent on taking responsibility for whatever needed to be done, without being asked. In order to juggle school and her chores at home, Sarah had to be organized, plan her activities in advance, and keep a close eye on her siblings.

In college Sarah was the ideal student. She not only had her papers done on time, she had them done in advance. She remained current with her studies while holding a part-time job from the second semester of her freshman year. As a young accountant, Sarah was every boss's dream. She showed initiative by anticipating what needed to be done and doing it thoroughly, paying close attention to detail, and with little supervision. Her performance reviews were, as might be expected, outstanding. The reward for her accomplishments as a superb worker was a promotion to a management position. As in most corporations, good individual performance in Sarah's company led to being promoted to leader of a team of employees. The problem inherent in this common practice is that the skills needed to lead a team are substantially different from those needed to succeed independently.

The repetition compulsion suggests that Sarah would naturally rely on the same skills that made her successful up to this point to ensure her success in her new assignment, and she did. What was perceived as grandstanding, not trusting others, and micromanaging was merely the repetition of the same childhood behaviors that contributed to her survival. She wasn't consciously keeping the high-profile projects to herself, nor was she intentionally trying to impede the growth of her staff by giving them only small pieces of projects. Given an assignment from upper management, she would simply plan out what had to be done and diligently go about doing it. She was more than happy to assist her direct reports with their routine tasks, in much the same way as she would help her younger siblings with their homework, but they perceived it as micromanaging. Sarah had no inkling that her behavior was unusual or inappropriate. It's almost as though she thought, "If it got me to this point, I should do more of it." And herein lies the problem for so many employees at all levels: not only doing what has worked in the past, but doing more of it.

Turning up the Volume

When faced with the prospect of failure, the child part of the adult psyche kicks into gear and *turns up the volume* on the same old behaviors, then wonders why there is static on the new station. The old station didn't have static! If controlling, planning, and doing the work herself worked for Sarah in the past, then certainly doing more of the same will work. As Sarah met with resistance from her staff, in the form of missing deadlines, withholding critical information, or doing work that wasn't up to acceptable standards, her survival instincts told her that she needed to engage more in the behaviors that contributed to her past success.

The obvious problem is that these were the same behaviors that now contributed to poor morale, low productivity, and lack of cooperation within her department. Doing more of the same only served to escalate the problem. It never occurred to Sarah that she exacerbated the problem by controlling and directing even more. In fact, because she had no alternative skills in her repertoire, she thought that she wasn't doing these things enough!

Promotions are not the only situations that can contribute to derailment; the inability to recognize and make the shift to the requirements of the organizational culture and movement from one company to another, one department to another, or one boss to another are others. Clearly, behaviors that are appropriate in one situation can become potential career derailers when applied in a different situation. If the culture of Sarah's company was more hierarchical, one in which people expected close supervision and little responsibility for entire projects, then her behavior would not have been considered problematic. In fact, she would continue to succeed using the behaviors she learned early in life.

Margaret Thatcher provides a familiar example of someone who derailed due to her failure to balance strengths with complementary skills when the situation called for it. As prime minister of England, Margaret Thatcher had a clear vision of where she wanted to take her country and how that should be accomplished. She was willing to take on rough and, at times, controversial issues. Her strengths earned her the nickname "The Iron Lady." Early in her tenure as prime minister she was welcomed by many citizens as one who stood by her convictions and who could lead the nation out of a difficult period of social and economic decline. She never faltered during the Falklands War and is characterized by her statement during the poll tax controversy, "You turn if you want to. The lady's not for turning."

So, what went wrong? Thatcher relied almost exclusively on behaviors learned early in childhood. Her independent, self-sufficient behaviors required complementary skills in consensus building and succeeding through cooperative efforts—skills that she not only never developed, but ones that she eschewed. Shortly after her election she proclaimed, "I am not a consensus politician. I am a conviction politician." And when the going got tough, Thatcher got tougher. She turned up the volume on her convictions. Throughout her tenure, she relied on the same skills she learned and relied on in childhood, and they ultimately failed her.

By all accounts Thatcher grew up in a joyless household. Outsiders report that there was never much gaiety or laughter in the home. Her mother was competent, but remote. Thatcher never really forged a relationship with her and rarely makes mention of her. It was her strict, work-oriented, and devoutly religious father with whom Thatcher aligned and to whom she credits her success. When she went to school and realized that other children actually had fun in their families, she asked him why their family never went on picnics, rode bicycles, or played games. His reply was, "Margaret, never do things or want to do things just because other people do them. Make up your own mind about what you are going to do and persuade people to go your way." Clearly, she learned that lesson well. So well that she was alienated from her peers throughout her school years and to this day claims no close friends with the exception of her husband.

In the corporate arena, an example of an employee turning up the volume is one who moves from a department that places high value on teamwork, collaboration, and consensus to another department in the same organization that requires independent decision making, quick turnaround, and minimal interaction among team members. Because the employee came from a family where harmony was the norm, it is expected that he or she would be successful in the first department; its requirements match his or her behavioral schemata. Moving to the latter department, the person will be unsure of what behaviors are expected and will, most likely, rely on the people skills that secured career success thus far. When at first they don't work, he or she will likely engage in the behaviors to an even greater degree. The employee will flounder if he or she doesn't recognize the need to engage in alternative, situationally expected behavior. As the individual tries to reach consensus and build collaborative relationships, he or she may meet with resistance from his or her new coworkers. The likely method for dealing with this resistance is to turn up the volume even further on the affiliative skills—and wonder why there is static on the line.

High Tolerance Levels

Another aspect of relying on early childhood behaviors involves the ability to tolerate bad employment situations or poor leadership. When confronted with a boss who is unreasonable (or downright impossible), employees will tolerate those behaviors that are congruent with their primary family experience. At the end of a leadership workshop, Tim took the facilitator aside and asked how to cope with a boss who made unreasonable demands, embarrassed him in front of others, and never gave any praise. When asked, "Does he remind you of anyone?" Tim hesitated for a moment while thinking and finally replied, "My father."

You may find that you have a high level of tolerance for inappropriate behaviors that are familiar to you, especially if feelings about being treated in a particular way haven't been worked through in psychotherapy or other developmental opportunities, such as attending workshops, raking classes, or reading self-help books. You may seek approval from authority, can't see when you're being treated unfairly or inappropriately and, therefore, assume responsibility for making the situation better. This is another instance in which behaviors that worked in the past to assure survival will be turned up in volume.

Rita worked for a boss who confided in her about myriad personal problems with her children, parents, and her spouse. On some occasions, the boss would go into Rita's office, close the door, and break down and sob. Rita said she was uncomfortable being used as a confidante in this manner because it prohibited her from going to the boss with her own work-related problems. She felt sorry for her boss and didn't want to burden her any more than necessary. As a result, Rita was left having to figure out for herself how to resolve problems and create programs for which she had little experience. Because she grew up with a mother who needed excessive attention and was histrionic, Rita felt as responsible for her boss as she did for her mother. She turned up the volume on her listening and care-taking behaviors in order to soothe the boss. The child in the workplace needed to make things better, never expecting that she was entitled to leadership and direction from her boss.

Tim and Rita tolerated bad employment situations because the situations were familiar and they knew how to survive them. However, their performance and self-esteem suffered from lack of mentoring and growth opportunities expected from people in management positions. Both employees eventually left their positions and their companies once they understood the dynamics and decided not to be controlled by old behaviors that had outlived their usefulness.

The Corporate Playing Field

It is sometimes helpful to draw an analogy between a sports playing field and the corporate arena. Just as in sports, there is a playing field in companies and organizations. The field has bounds that mark the area in which players must operate. When you go out of bounds in sports you are called out, foul, lose a point, or lose control of the ball. There is typically some type of penalty for going off the playing field. The same holds true in companies. You must understand the boundaries of the playing field in order to win the game.

A major difference that presents a unique problem is that the bounds of corporate playing fields change from company to company, department to department within the same company, and even from boss to boss within a company. It's easy to go out of bounds when they change so frequently. Successful corporate players scope out the playing field and adjust their behavior accordingly. In other words, they remain in bounds for each given situation.

Although the corporate playing field clearly denotes the area in which it expects employees to operate, there are a number of inherent dangers. The field may be artificially narrowed based on factors relating to gender, ethnicity, age, or other subjective factors. When the field narrows, it becomes easier to go out of bounds. For example, the playing field for men in the area of emotionality is narrower than it is for women. The range of emotions that they are permitted to express is narrower than that permitted for women. Similarly, the playing field for women in the area of assertiveness is narrower than for their male counterparts. Displaying the same assertive behavior as men may get them called out of bounds. All corporate players need to be aware of their own biases that may artificially narrow the playing field for their colleagues and make every effort to create a more even field for everyone.

There is also the danger that people will play the game too carefully, never taking the kinds of risks that might put them out of bounds. In an environment such as this, creativity is stifled. As in sports, you must take calculated risks and play the game toward the edge of the bounds, but intentionally decide when the risk of going out of bounds is worth what will potentially be gained by it.

Once again, it is about balance. If you are someone who constantly goes out of bounds, don't be surprised if you are eventually called out. On the other hand, if you always play the corporate game safely within bounds, you may not be adding the value required for long-term success. People who avoid premature career derailment are those who (1) know where the bounds are and recognize that they narrow and widen with different circumstances, (2) play the corporate game taking calculated risks, and (3) balance the risks with the eight behaviors described in this book.

The Eight Most Common Reasons Why Successful People Fail

Consider the following workplace conversation:

Al: Did you hear about Kathy's promotion?

Barbara: Did I ever. I've been here three years longer than Kathy and work twice as hard. I should have been the one given that promotion.

Al: I thought for sure this one had your name on it. Kathy's only been in her position for eighteen months. Seems like she hardly warmed up the chair. She must know people over at corporate.

Barbara: Not only does she know them, she spends more time meeting with them than doing her work. She's always going to this committee meeting and that presentation. If she spent half as much time in her office working as she does schmoozing, she could get something done.

Al: Yeah. It's people like us who keep this place going and people like her who get all the credit. Do you know that she even has time to take her staff members out to lunch for their birthdays?

Barbara: That's what I mean. She's so busy getting everyone else to do her work that of course she has time for all that stuff. The HR vice president asked me to be on the personnel review committee, and I turned him down flat. If I don't keep close tabs on my staff nothing gets done.

Al: I know what you mean. I've got my schedule just about where I want it now; and I'm not willing to change it for anyone. Those committees take up too much time.

Sound familiar? While Barbara and Al are busy micromanaging, doing the work themselves, and sticking close to their offices, behaviors that have worked for them up until now in their careers, people like Kathy are expanding their repertoires of business behavior. You may have heard people talk about the differences between "careerists" and "achievers." The former manage their careers, and the latter get the work done. In fact, both are important elements of remaining on your career track. You can't simply focus on your career to the exclusion of accomplishing your work, and you can't only accomplish your work without paying attention to your career development. It is a combination of specific behaviors that ultimately leads to career success.

It should go without saying, but I'll say it anyway to make it clear: *There is no substitute for technical competence.* It is the foundation on which all the other behaviors referred to in this book rely. Without technical competence you build a career on quicksand. The problem is that most people who derail rely on technical competence to the exclusion of all other necessary behaviors. They think that expertise in their field should be enough to maintain their careers. This may have been true in 1960 or 1970, but it is far from true in today's competitive workplace.

People who possess the technical competence but prematurely derail from their career paths do so because of the following factors. They

1. Overlook the importance of people.
2. Do not function effectively as part of a team.
3. Fail to focus on image and communication.
4. Are insensitive to the effect they have on others.
5. Have difficulty working with authority.
6. Have too broad or too narrow vision.
7. Are indifferent to customer or client needs.
8. Work in isolation.

Most derailed people fail to build skills in more than just one area. For example, the inability to function effectively as part of a team may be related to working in isolation. Or, having difficulty working with authority may cause you to be indifferent to client or customer needs. The Derailment Inventory at the end of this chapter will help you to determine which specific areas you may need to work on in order to prevent or overcome derailment. I urge you to take the inventory and to use it in determining which chapters might have the most meaning for you personally. Also, examine your workplace behaviors in light of early childhood experiences and determine which complementary skills the inventory suggests are required to be a fully functioning adult. If you look only at your scores, you miss out on the opportunity to understand your behavior in a fuller context. Here's where many career coaches fail. They focus on changing behavior, not understanding the purpose the behavior serves and *how it has contributed to success in the past.*

The chart following the Derailment Inventory ties together the eight most common reasons why successful people fail with possible early childhood experiences contributing to learned behaviors. Because people develop strength in a particular area for any number of reasons, it is impossible to list every combination of experiences contributing to every strength. Use the chart as a point of reference to begin thinking about how and why you developed in certain areas and not others. You may even want to add your own unique experiences to those listed.

Factors to Consider in Assessing and Changing Behavior

Critically examining your behavior is no easy task, but it can have immense payoff, both at work and home, over the long term. There are several key points to keep in mind before you respond to the Derailment Inventory.

● **People don't intentionally behave inappropriately or ineffectively.** To hear managers tell it, you would think that the behaviors of their employees are intentional attempts to undermine their efforts. As a result, they wind up labeling and blaming employees, and employees internalize these labels as undeniable truths—truths that impede learning alternative behaviors. I don't think that there is a person on earth who gets up in the morning, pours a cup of coffee, and says, "I think I'll go to work today and make a huge, costly mistake." My belief is that the large majority of people act with the best of intentions. If you knew how to do things differently, you would. The problem is, you can't know what you don't know!

It is crucial to separate the act from the actor. Someone who hasn't learned how to build affiliative relationships isn't a bad person simply because he or she hasn't learned this skill. Generally, the reason that a particular skill hasn't been learned is that, historically, it wasn't important in the scheme of things. As you use the Derailment Inventory to assess your current skills and those that you'd like to add to your repertoire, avoid the tendency to become your own "critical parent." Keep in mind that we all have strengths and developmental areas. There are no right or wrong answers. Praise yourself for being open to change, and allow plenty of room for initially falling short of the mark.

● **People do best the things for which they have been rewarded in the past.** What does the Derailment Inventory indicate are your greatest strengths? Think about these strengths as overdeveloped survival skills, and ask yourself these three questions:

1. Who wanted (or needed) me to act in this way?

2. How was I rewarded when I did?

3. What happened if I didn't?

Use the chart that follows the Derailment Inventory to help stimulate your thinking in this area. This exercise will help you to demystify the part that your strengths played while you were growing up and enable you to examine why other behaviors weren't as important.

● **Be willing to take calculated risks.** Examine your scores and look for the items for which you rated yourself "3" or "4." These are behaviors that may not come naturally to you or ones that you may even have been discouraged from exhibiting in childhood. Developing complementary skills may mean being uncomfortable in the beginning. As people progress through the stages of initial learning they feel inadequate, impatient, or insecure and revert back to more familiar behaviors as a means of coping. It is only through the willingness to engage in unfamiliar, uncomfortable behavior, and to stick with it, that complementary skills can be developed.

● **Don't do anything less.** Expand your skill set. Successful people don't fail because they're not good at what they do. They fail when they can't see the complementary behaviors that must be developed in response to a new challenge or situation. If you, for example, focus on being less critical or less task oriented, you'll naturally be uncomfortable with doing less of what you know best. Instead, think about the skills that you need to add to your repertoire of workplace behaviors to be more effective. It's all about having a balanced skill set.

Sarah's manager didn't want her to completely cease getting the work cranked out. He wanted her to achieve more balance in her leadership style. Employees frequently leave feedback sessions feeling more confused than when they first went in. They become fearful of engaging in what's described as the "problem behavior" at all and wind up going to the opposite extreme. Continue engaging in those behaviors where you rated yourself a "1" or "2" as you develop comfort and familiarity in those areas where you rated yourself lower.

● **Successful people are good observers of people and events.** In most cases, people change positions, companies, departments, bosses, or jobs, and no one bothers to tell them what is expected of them. It's as though they hear a tape playing over and over, telling them how to behave, and they try harder and harder to act consistently. The only problem is that the tape is usually an old one, developed in response to childhood needs, not present realities. The people who succeed at career transitions are the ones who observe how others in the new situation are acting and adjust their behavior accordingly. When in Rome, do as the Romans do.

This is not to say that people should be chameleons, giving up the essence of who they are from situation to situation. They should, however, take note of cultural customs such as how people dress, whether they have lunch with coworkers, and the kind of social interactions that go on in the office. A little bit of accommodation can go a long way toward the perception of "fitting in."

● **Assure success through a development plan and ongoing feedback.** Just as you wouldn't build a house without a plan, neither should you count on personal or professional development without one. The common theme to motivational speeches is the fact that the person had a vision of what he or she wanted and a plan for attaining it. Success isn't accidental. Based on the Derailment Inventory, decide the two or three skills that are most important to add to your repertoire and determine how you will achieve them. Be sure to identify the resources you will require in the process: people, classes, books, and experiences.

One tip you might consider is to let others know the changes you're attempting to make. This way, people will actually look for and notice the behavior change, and increase the likelihood of giving you positive feedback. Once you have your development plan, ask someone you trust to review it with you and to give you feedback as to how you're doing. Let him or her know what you're trying to accomplish and how you would like to receive your feedback. Then, on a regular basis, sit down and review progress. Discuss where you encountered difficulty, brainstorm methods for overcoming obstacles, revise the plan, and, perhaps most important, reward wins—even small ones—with a mental pat on the back, thumbs-up, or more tangible self-indulgences. Remember, you're most likely to repeat behaviors for which you've been rewarded.

The goal is not to make you an armchair psychologist, but rather to help you to look at your strengths in the context of your experiences and motives. We are not one-dimensional objects. We bring to the workplace a host of multifaceted intentions, which, when developed in light of organizational needs, can contribute significantly to work's synergistic process and the satisfaction we gain from it. When we view ineffective behaviors as overdeveloped, purposeful strengths, they no longer seem like insurmountable obstacles—and we no longer feel like failures.

Each of the following chapters fully explores the behaviors that lead to career derailment and provides a strategy for avoiding those pitfalls. Well-known historical and contemporary figures who derailed at some point in their careers are used as a means of illustrating why certain behaviors are developed early in childhood as survival skills and the effect of such behaviors on careers. Also provided are examples of behaviors based on encounters with real-life employees and suggestions for how to build complementary skills in each of these areas. At the end of each chapter is a list of ways that you can develop skill in the area on which the chapter focuses. Even if many of them may be a stretch for you, I urge you to consider each one as a simple and economical way to begin expanding your repertoire of workplace behaviors. You may come up with other suggestions for yourself based on what you have just read. The Resources, at the end of the book, contain references for many of the books, workshops, and inventories mentioned throughout. Combined, these serve to illuminate how successful people stay that way and how you can overcome your strengths.

DERAILMENT INVENTORY

To determine where you currently stand in the derailment process, use the scale below to answer each of the following questions as candidly as possible. Even if it is difficult to answer a particular item, do not leave it unanswered.

1 = Highly descriptive of me or my situation
2 = Descriptive of me or my situation
3 = Somewhat descriptive of me or my situation
4 = Not descriptive of me or my situation

1. ___   Others describe me as a real "people person."

2. ___   I prefer to work as part of a team rather than work independently of others.

3. ___   When I speak, people pay close attention to my ideas and opinions and I see them later used or implemented.

4. ___   I see myself as even-tempered.

5. ___   When I have a logical reason for it, I don't have a problem with expressing a viewpoint different from my management's.

6. ___   When working on a project, I enjoy taking time out now and then to reassess its direction and my own method of approaching it.

7. ___   I find it a challenge to overcome initial obstacles to achievement.

8. ___   I spend at least some portion of each week networking with colleagues.

9. ___   I spend at least some part of each workday engaged in small talk with coworkers.

10. ___   I enjoy working collaboratively as a member of a team.

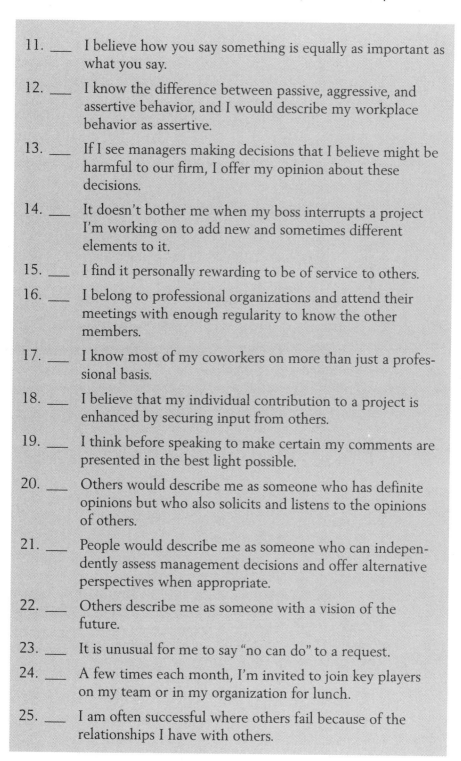

11. ___ I believe how you say something is equally as important as what you say.

12. ___ I know the difference between passive, aggressive, and assertive behavior, and I would describe my workplace behavior as assertive.

13. ___ If I see managers making decisions that I believe might be harmful to our firm, I offer my opinion about these decisions.

14. ___ It doesn't bother me when my boss interrupts a project I'm working on to add new and sometimes different elements to it.

15. ___ I find it personally rewarding to be of service to others.

16. ___ I belong to professional organizations and attend their meetings with enough regularity to know the other members.

17. ___ I know most of my coworkers on more than just a professional basis.

18. ___ I believe that my individual contribution to a project is enhanced by securing input from others.

19. ___ I think before speaking to make certain my comments are presented in the best light possible.

20. ___ Others would describe me as someone who has definite opinions but who also solicits and listens to the opinions of others.

21. ___ People would describe me as someone who can independently assess management decisions and offer alternative perspectives when appropriate.

22. ___ Others describe me as someone with a vision of the future.

23. ___ It is unusual for me to say "no can do" to a request.

24. ___ A few times each month, I'm invited to join key players on my team or in my organization for lunch.

25. ___ I am often successful where others fail because of the relationships I have with others.

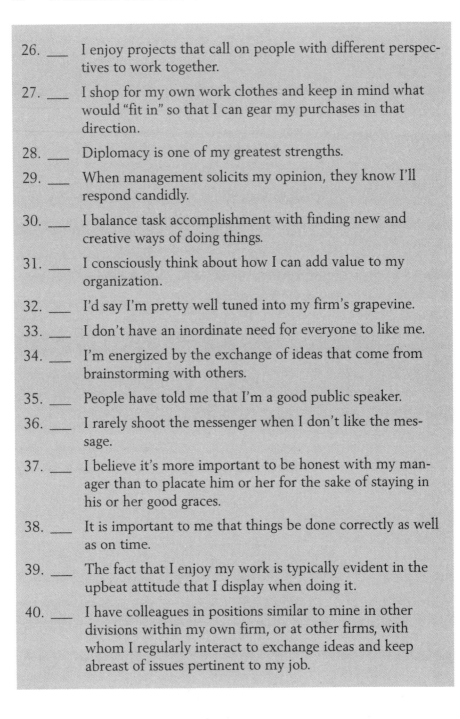

26. ___ I enjoy projects that call on people with different perspectives to work together.

27. ___ I shop for my own work clothes and keep in mind what would "fit in" so that I can gear my purchases in that direction.

28. ___ Diplomacy is one of my greatest strengths.

29. ___ When management solicits my opinion, they know I'll respond candidly.

30. ___ I balance task accomplishment with finding new and creative ways of doing things.

31. ___ I consciously think about how I can add value to my organization.

32. ___ I'd say I'm pretty well tuned into my firm's grapevine.

33. ___ I don't have an inordinate need for everyone to like me.

34. ___ I'm energized by the exchange of ideas that come from brainstorming with others.

35. ___ People have told me that I'm a good public speaker.

36. ___ I rarely shoot the messenger when I don't like the message.

37. ___ I believe it's more important to be honest with my manager than to placate him or her for the sake of staying in his or her good graces.

38. ___ It is important to me that things be done correctly as well as on time.

39. ___ The fact that I enjoy my work is typically evident in the upbeat attitude that I display when doing it.

40. ___ I have colleagues in positions similar to mine in other divisions within my own firm, or at other firms, with whom I regularly interact to exchange ideas and keep abreast of issues pertinent to my job.

DERAILMENT INVENTORY SCORE SHEET

To score your inventory, first transfer your numerical responses from the questionnaire itself to the columns below. Please notice that the item numbers within each column are not in order, so be sure to put your response next to the correct item number. After you have transferred your answers, making sure you have answered each question, tally each column separately, then add each of the column subtotals together for an overall inventory total.

I. PEOPLE SKILLS	II. TEAM- WORK	III. IMAGE/ COMMU- NICATION	IV. PERSON- ALITY	V. WORKING WITH AUTHORITY	VI. DETAIL VS. BIG PICTURE	VII. CAN-DO ATTITUDE	VIII. NET- WORKING
1.____	2.____	3.____	4.____	5.____	6.____	7.____	8.____
9.____	10.____	11.____	12.____	13.____	14.____	15.____	16.____
17.____	18.____	19.____	20.____	21.____	22.____	23.____	24.____
25.____	26.____	27.____	28.____	29.____	30.____	31.____	32.____
33.____	34.____	35.____	36.____	37.____	38.____	39.____	40.____

SUBTOTALS: ____   ____   ____   ____   ____   ____   ____   ____

INVENTORY TOTAL: _____

INTERPRETING YOUR SCORES:

The subtotal of each column tells you areas in which you need to expand your complementary skills and areas where your current strengths lie. The total score tells you how close to derailment you are. It is entirely possible to need development in one or two specific areas without being career derailed.

If each column subtotals:	or	Your total score is:	
5-8		40-75	You're right on track! Examine those areas where you rated yourself 1 or 2 and consciously try to continue engaging in those specific behaviors.
9-13		76-115	Fine-tuning may be needed to stay on track. Review those questions where you gave yourself 3 or 4 and add those complementary skills to your existing repertoire.
14-17		116-145	Warning! You're dangerously close to derailing. Time to do a serious self-assessment and expand your skill set.
18-20		146-160	Whether you know it or not, you're seriously derailed. Seek help (a career coach, a mentor) to get your career back on track.

Childhood Experiences Contributing to Strengths and Development Areas

DERAILMENT FACTOR:	PERSON/BEHAVIOR COMMONLY DESCRIBED AS:	OVERDEVELOPED SKILL/BEHAVIOR:	POSSIBLE CHILDHOOD CAUSATIVE FACTORS:
1. POOR PEOPLE SKILLS	A loner Socially inept Uncomfortable in social situations Unfriendly Lacks insight Aloof Avoids people contact Inordinate need to be liked	Technical brilliance Ability to work independently Exactness, precision, and accuracy People pleasing Tolerance for bad situations	Value placed on accomplishments Rewarded for grades, achievements Overly protective parenting Intelligent, ostracized by classmates Economic status lower than peers' Physical impairment Narcissistic parenting Conditional love and acceptance
2. INABILITY TO WORK AS PART OF A TEAM	Doesn't see interdependent linkages Grandstands Doesn't include others in decision making Hoards information Impatient	Individual contributions Ability to work unsupervised Completion orientation	Oldest in family or only child Alcoholism in family Both parents worked outside the home Rewarded for self-reliance High-achiever expectations
3. INATTENTION TO IMAGE AND COMMUNICATION STYLE	Doesn't think before speaking Wears cheap clothes Dresses as one would for a party Can't get to the point, rambles on Uncomfortable making presentations Lacks confidence	Independent thinking Straight shooting Risk taking Humility	Wasn't listened to Given little parental guidance Neglected Limited world exposure

DERAILMENT FACTOR:	PERSON/BEHAVIOR COMMONLY DESCRIBED AS:	OVERDEVELOPED SKILL/BEHAVIOR:	POSSIBLE CHILD-HOOD CAUSATIVE FACTORS:
3. INATTENTION TO IMAGE AND COMMUNICA- TION STYLE (cont.)	Like a bull in a china shop Seems insincere Not credible		
4. INSENSITIVE TO ONE'S EFFECT ON OTHERS	A bully Muscle level too high Turns people off Inconsiderate of others Too loud Knows it all Doesn't listen	Doing whatever it takes Perseverance Autonomous functioning Self-confidence	Critical parental messages Parents with emotional problems Lack of positive reinforcement Conditional love High-achiever expectations
5. DIFFICULTY WORKING WITH AUTHORITY	Argumentative with management Embarrasses management in front of others Afraid to speak up in front of superiors Doesn't point out potential problems	Independence Respect for hierarchy Support for traditional values	Overly critical or controlling parenting Narcissistic parenting Physical or emotional abuse
6. TOO BROAD OR TOO NARROW VISION	Narrowly focused One-track mind Can't juggle multiple tasks simultaneously Unable to turn ideas into reality Unrealistic	Determination Task orientation Creativity	Ritualistic family behavior Alcoholism or physical abuse Unpredictable or chaotic environment Absence of boundaries or norms
7. LACK OF CONCERN FOR CUSTOMER OR CLIENT NEEDS	A "naysayer" Fails to add value Identifies problems, not solutions Not a self-starter	Critical thinking Attention to detail Careful, deliberate behavior Compliance	Controlled environment Predetermined career path "Powerless" parental attitude

DERAILMENT FACTOR:	PERSON/BEHAVIOR COMMONLY DESCRIBED AS:	OVERDEVELOPED SKILL/BEHAVIOR:	POSSIBLE CHILD-HOOD CAUSATIVE FACTORS:
7. LACK OF CONCERN FOR CUSTOMER OR CLIENT NEEDS (cont.)	Requires inordinate supervision Risk-averse		
8. WORKS IN ISOLATION	Isn't well connected Doesn't have the contacts in place Doesn't keep up professionally	Ability to work independently High task orientation Makes good use of time	Rewarded for self-reliance Not encouraged to join clubs or teams Overly attached to primary caretaker

Reason #1:

Overlooking the
Importance of People

Strategy: *Build Strong One-on-One Relationships*

An early coaching experience involved a woman whom I'll call Diane. She was the assistant to the vice president of human resources at a large corporation. When the vice president called me about Diane, he told me that she was an outstanding assistant. He found no fault with the quality of her work. The problem was that Diane's peers didn't want to work with her. They found her stand-offish and difficult to work with. Despite the fact that she was technically competent, she would soon derail if she didn't stop creating morale problems in the department. Diane arrived at our first coaching session looking every bit the executive assistant. Trim, neatly groomed, and impeccably dressed, she appeared to be the very model of professionalism. As we became acquainted with one another through initial superficial conversation, it was noted that she spoke with a clarity and confidence that belied her age (she was in her late twenties). When she was asked what she thought the problem was for which she had been asked to receive coaching, she didn't have a clue. She said she just wanted to do the best job possible and tried to be perfect so as to make her boss look good. A light went on.

The "package" that Diane presented was indeed one of perfection. On the surface, you could find no fault with her image or communication, but my hunch was (and it later proved to be ac-

27

curate) that she overrelied on her ability to be perfect for her boss to the exclusion of other critical workplace behaviors. I explored this with her by changing tack. She was asked what she did for fun outside of work. What was she like when she wasn't being perfect? Unexpectedly, this unleashed a flood of emotion. Diane tearfully said that she didn't have much of a life outside of work. She arrived at work early, so as to be prepared for the busy day that always ensued working for this executive, and she typically didn't leave until 7:00 P.M. By the time she made the hour commute home, she was exhausted; she would have something to eat and then fall into bed.

After carefully listening to her explain that she had not had a significant relationship in a number of years, nor was there one on the horizon, I asked Diane if perhaps her need for affiliation was fulfilled at work with friends and colleagues. Her answer was no. She worked through her lunch hours and didn't want to waste the company's time and money on idle chat or gossip with her co-workers. She did notice that the other women on the floor seemed to spend time engaged in casual conversation, which was fine for them, but she herself didn't have the time to spare, nor did she think it was right.

What others interpreted as standoffishness, or being difficult to deal with, was really just Diane's need to be the perfect employee. Having grown up in a strict Norwegian household, she developed the defense mechanism of striving for perfection early in life to ward off critical comments from her parents and older siblings. The need to be perfect underscored not only her workplace relationships, but her personal ones as well. One reason for not having close friends or intimate relationships was that no one ever measured up to her high standards. Even though she never said anything to her colleagues, they picked up on the fact that she was critically assessing them. She found their personal conversations self-indulgent and didn't feel that anyone else worked as hard as she did, which was in fact true. No one else shared her compulsive need for perfection.

When Technical Expertise Ceases to Be Enough

Diane provides a wonderful example of someone who, despite technical competence, was on the verge of premature derailment. An infrequently talked about fact of business life is that at some point in most people's careers, technical expertise ceases to be the key factor contributing to success. We *build* our reputations early in our careers on competence. We *remain* successful, however, based on a combination of competence and the eight factors described in this book. Once we have proved our technical abilities in our respective fields, competence becomes a given—something that others can depend and rely on, but, after a point, not something that necessarily moves us forward. It is as though our competence reaches the point of diminishing returns. The mistake that many people make is to focus exclusively on gaining increased technical skill to the exclusion of developing other complementary workplace behaviors.

Review the following checklist to see how well you build one-on-one relationships. Ideally one would check every item (here as with each checklist contained in subsequent chapters). The fewer items checked, the greater likelihood that this is a potential developmental area for you.

_____ I know the names of the people on my floor.

_____ I can usually tell when something is troubling a colleague.

_____ I'm comfortable making small talk with coworkers.

_____ I enjoy the opportunity to meet socially with coworkers.

_____ I tend to go out of my way for colleagues—even if I see no immediate benefit.

_____ I see building relationships as equally important to accomplishing my job tasks.

_____ Others would describe me as a good listener.

_____ I make it a point to spend some part of each day engaged in casual conversation with coworkers.

_____ I know the names of the husbands, wives, significant others, and children of my coworkers.

_____ I don't consider sharing personal information or topics of common interest as a waste of company time.

_____ I know the names of my colleagues' administrative assistants.

In today's competitive job market, employers are careful to choose people for their past experience, education, and previous on-the-job success. In other words, they select people who are good at what they do. Once on the job, however, when the playing field is level with equally qualified employees, it is the more subtle behaviors that differentiate the fast-trackers from those who remain stagnant. Those with superior interpersonal skills, combined with technical capability, are perceived as a more valuable asset than those who exhibit only technical competence. Through the ability to establish positive working relationships we secure the cooperation of the people we need to accomplish our tasks and further the organization's goals. These interpersonal skills also help us to develop the goodwill of clients and customers and a network of people on whom we can rely for the skills and information required to function effectively.

In Diane's case, coaching alone wasn't sufficient to help her prevent derailment. The presence of a deep-seated need for perfection suggests intrapersonal conflicts that require professional counseling. Fortunately, when this was recommended to Diane she was open to the idea and followed up on it. Her coaching sessions focused on several specific things that she could do immediately to change the impression others had of her. She is a good example of someone who had several overlapping areas of development. Diane needed not only to do a better job of building one-on-one relationships, but also to be a better team player and begin to think about the importance of networking. My work with her addressed all three areas.

Her first assignment was to spend no less than fifteen minutes each day engaged in casual conversation with a different coworker—even if she had to force herself to do it. She was asked to get to know her colleagues personally, to find out what outside interests and hobbies they had, the names of their children, and what made them tick. This is no easy task for people like Diane. It makes them feel as if they are somehow robbing the company coffers, when in reality they are investing in relationships that have a long-term benefit to the company. Building such relationships enables the work to be done more efficiently, with less sabotage and higher team morale.

Similarly, it was recommended that Diane take a lunch break at least once a week and use the time for something she enjoyed. The adage "all work and no play makes Jill a dull girl" was certainly true in Diane's case. Part of what made it so difficult for her to talk to others was that she felt she had nothing to say. She had become so immersed in her work that she was oblivious to outside interests. Diane decided to join a nearby gym and work out. At the gym, she met several people with whom she shared common interests, eventually became friends with them, and started to have lunch and socialize with them after work.

In an effort to coach her in how to be a better team player and networker, it was recommended that Diane offer help to coworkers rather than spend time perfecting and fail-safing her already good work. She could put her compulsive work behaviors to good use by extending herself to those who needed her assistance. In other words, she could win back their regard by making not only her boss look good, but her colleagues as well. In the process, she was building what is described as network reciprocity—the exchange of services and favors within formal and informal networks. The importance of networks is discussed in detail in Reason #8, Working in Isolation, but for now suffice it to say that Diane had to identify and participate in the quid pro quo of her workplace relationships. Diane worked hard to change the perceptions of others and successfully learned how to overcome her strengths. She has been promoted to a new position, has many friends both at work and home, and reports that the quality of her life is now better than she has ever known it to be.

Understanding the Quid Pro Quo

In nearly every relationship there is something called a quid pro quo—something given in exchange for something else. Without realizing it, we are exchanging things with people all the time. Inherent to every relationship there is a quid pro quo. Many relationships fail when the quid pro quo isn't recognized or when it changes without the consent or acknowledgment of one or both of the parties involved. I remember working with one woman who was concerned with her troubled employment history. It seemed that she had no trouble getting a job. In fact, she was never without one for long. She was technically competent, physically attractive, and interpersonally capable. Clearly, she presented well in interviews and secured most of the jobs for which she interviewed. The problem was that once she was in the job, she became quickly dissatisfied and disillusioned. Her employers wouldn't give her challenging assignments or recognize her technical capability.

In an effort to uncover what the cause of the problem really was, I asked her to role-play an interview with me. Was I surprised to find that this professional woman turned into a femme fatale in the role play! Her normally assertive demeanor was replaced by what I would intentionally describe as a sweet disposition. The slight Southern accent with which she normally spoke became more pronounced. She was coy, acquiescent, and charming.

It was apparent that the woman secured the job based on one set of behaviors but unwittingly changed them once she was inside the company. In other words, the quid pro quo changed. Her employer expected one thing based on the interview and, instead, got something else. She didn't present as, nor was she selected for being, an assertive, upwardly mobile career woman in the interview. Her employers selected her for the behavior she presented, not what she became once employed. This created a chasm between what *they* wanted and what *she* wanted. There was obviously nothing wrong with what she wanted, but it was not the message she gave during her interviews. When the quid pro quo changed, unbeknownst to the parties involved, it created turmoil and unfulfilled expectations for both.

Part of building successful relationships at work involves identifying the quid pro quo between you and everyone with whom you interact, and working to assure that everyone's—including your own—needs get met. Some might say that this business of quid pro quo sounds awfully manipulative. On the contrary! It's an honest businesslike assessment of what you have to offer others and what you need from them. We trade on relationships all day long without ever realizing or discussing it. Say a month ago you asked me to cover for you at a meeting so that you could attend to a problem with one of your children, and I willingly complied. A while later, I needed some research done that only you know how to do and you gladly obliged. Neither of us was counting the chips we had collected with each trade, but they had accumulated in our accounts. The trick is to always have more chips in your account than you need—and this can't be done manipulatively; it can only be done through a generosity of spirit. To do otherwise would soil the integrity of the relationship.

The value of the quid pro quo was apparent during a training program, when a small group that was working on an assignment decided that they needed a particular piece of audiovisual equipment that projects written material directly from a laptop onto a screen. One participant said that she thought she could arrange it and excused herself to make a call. I mentally noted that there was little chance of getting the equipment on time—their presentation was just a few hours away. Ninety minutes later the equipment arrived. When I took the woman aside to ask her how she managed to get it so quickly, she smiled and said, "I've done this man many favors. We have a good relationship."

Dr. Karen Otazo, formerly manager of training and development at ARCO, once reminded me of the value of having an account full of chips. We were working together on a project and I made a mistake with some aspect of it. I called to let her know about it and indicated that I was willing to do whatever was necessary to make it right. "Not to worry," she assured me, "Your hank account is full." I knew what she meant. I could afford to make a mistake, because the positive aspects of our relationship and all of the error-free work I had done superseded this error.

Besides overlooking mistakes, covering at meetings, or conducting research, what else gets traded in the workplace? You would be surprised. Here's a list that one workshop group came up with in less than five minutes:

Information	Quality Service
Promotions	Lunch
Friendship	Quick Turnaround
Gossip	Technical Know-How
A Listening Ear	Priority
Raises	Help

Muscle/Brawn	Influence
Information on Jobs in Other Firms	Feedback
Gifts	Public Praise
Personal Concern	Heads Up (Advance Notice)
Information on Upcoming Job Openings	

It is important to remember that *once you need a relationship, it's too late to build it.* This is what makes building relationships on an ongoing basis so important. Again, it can't be done simply for the purpose of knowing that you might have to call on it at some time. It must be done because you value people and your relationships with them. Absent this, others will detect a lack of genuineness, and perhaps a bit of manipulation, and never fully engage in a relationship with you.

Every so often I hear someone claim that he or she just doesn't care about building relationships. It always strikes me as oddly incongruous. These same people who claim not to care frequently exhibit behaviors that indicate they care very much. It is their defense mechanisms speaking. After years of being hurt by others, or not having much success in building relationships, they build impenetrable walls that they dare others to break through. In other cases, people who claim not to care about others are the same ones who don't care much about themselves. They don't pay attention to their own needs and certainly don't expect others to fulfill them. Whatever the reason, it is critical to overcome real or perceived indifference to the people with whom you interact. Once technical competence has become a given, the foundation on which successful careers are built is genuine, mutually rewarding relationships.

Look at the person at the very top of your own organization. It is unlikely that he or she is a rocket scientist or could find a cure for cancer. In fact, there are probably many people smarter, and perhaps more technically capable, than this person. Despite this lack of genius, he or she found the way to the top. It is likely due to basic competence combined with the relationships that were built throughout his or her career.

Then there are those who build good relationships—but only with those at levels in the organization that are higher than their own. It is a clever move, but a mistake in the long term. You may be able to identify people like this in your own organization. They're like heat-seeking missiles. Watch them in a room full of people—they'll gravitate toward those with the most power. The only problem is, power shifts. Those in power today may be out tomorrow.

I once worked with a woman who built her career on relationships with people in power. She managed up quite successfully, but she failed to gain the commitment of her colleagues and staff. Because of her relationships with senior management, she traded favors to become exempt from the grunt work the rest of us had to do. It worked for a while, but then, as in most corporations, the power shifted. Her protectors were out, and a new wave of power brokers swept in. The new people in power had, at one time, been the woman's colleagues. They had long memories and short tolerance for her. Within months she was looking for another job.

Fear of losing your job should not be the primary reason for building relationships with people at all levels of the organization. Throughout the organization, a wealth of information resides within the rank and file, and at some point you will have a need for it. It is a lot easier to gain access to information when you already have a relationship in place at the time you need the information than to try to do so with someone with whom you never took the time to speak in the hallway or the coffee room.

Two fascinating political counterpoints related to relationship building are former President Bill Clinton and former Israeli Prime Minister Benjamin Netanyahu. Beginning with Clinton, I firmly believe that the primary reason why he wasn't run out of office for behavior that some would describe as improper and others as immoral (depending on your politics) was because he mastered the secret of building relationships. Despite his many transgressions, both before and during his term of office, Clinton reminded us of a kid brother who was always getting himself into mischief but we looked the other way. People who have met him describe him in similar ways, "makes you feel like you're the only person in the room," "talks to you in a way that draws you in," and "asks you questions about yourself and remembers the answers."

In trying to understand how such a bright guy could end up in such hot water I go back to his childhood. Young William Jefferson

Clinton grew up not knowing his biological father and watching his alcoholic stepfather abuse his beloved mother, Virginia, and younger brother, Roger. He lived on the wrong side of the tracks, a chubby yet intelligent kid. His survival depended on, in part, his ability to be charming and likeable. But it was a double-edged sword. The same charm that caused us to twice elect him President, was used to sexually exploit women. Just as he was elected through the power of his personality, his presidency was tarnished by the actions of a man acting much like an emotionally poverty-stricken little boy. Of course, the factors contributing to Clinton's, or anyone else's behavior, are far more complex than this, but it will give you an idea of how early childhood experiences contribute to career success and derailment.

Netanyahu's fate was determined by just the opposite: the failure to build relationships. Elected in 1996 by a victory margin of less than 1 percent, he served only one term before being ousted by an opposing political party. Despite the fact that his policies met with overwhelming approval from the Israeli people, he was never able to build the kinds of relationships that would support him in the longer-term. And, in retrospect, he *knew* that was one factor contributing to his downfall. In a January 1999 interview with Time magazine, when asked what he would do differently if he had a second term in office, he replied, "I wouldn't do anything differently on the political side. Where I would do things differently is in the management of egos . . . the maintenance, shall we say, of, ah, personal relationships."

Once you have achieved technical competence, building relationships is the most important thing that you can do to continue your success and avoid derailment. How do you do it? Those people who received more reinforcement for task accomplishment than for relationship building initially in their careers won't find it particularly easy or comfortable. Like Diane, who was described earlier in this chapter, you may have to take some risks and be willing to stop hiding behind your technical competence. One thing is certain, the profit will outweigh the risk in the long term.

Listening with a Third Ear

When John F. Kennedy Jr. was asked what he thought his father would most like to be remembered for, he replied, "For being a good listener." Others had shared stories about how his father could make the people who spoke with him feel as though they were the only people in the world. The President's ability to concentrate singularly on the person speaking was one of the behaviors that also endeared him to others. Anne Morrow Lindbergh, author and wife of the aviator Charles Lindbergh, underscores the importance of this trait: "It is not possible to talk wholeheartedly to more than one person at a time. You can't really talk to a person unless you surrender to them for the moment (all other talk is futile). You can't surrender to more than one person a moment."

Listening is the most important thing that you can do to build, and maintain, relationships. Most people spend the greatest part of their days hearing what others say, yet few people really listen. They don't take the time to fully understand what other people think, what problems they may be encountering, or even how they might feel. There are myriad reasons why it is difficult to surrender to another, and the reasons differ from person to person. Decide which reasons on this list are your greatest obstacles to listening.

- Rehearsing. Mentally practicing what you're going to say before the speaker stops talking is rehearsing. The moment you start rehearsing, you stop listening.
- The halo effect. This is thinking that you already know what someone is going to say, or putting a positive or negative slant on the message, based on your previous relationship with him or her. For example, if every time Bob comes into my office he gives me bad news, before long, when I see Bob, I cast a negative halo around all of his messages, regardless of actual content. Conversely, if Ingrid and I have a great relationship, then her messages tend to be perceived positively, no matter what the content.
- Pseudolistening. Pretending to listen (and even looking like you are) when in fact you're thinking about something other than the message is pseudolistening. You know that you've been

busted when the speaker asks, "So what do you think?" and you don't have a clue about what he just said.

- Distractions. When you are preoccupied with other thoughts or problems, you become distracted and unable to listen to the message. Also, interruptions or noise (phones ringing, people coming in and out of your office, noise from the hallway) that make it difficult to concentrate on the speaker's message are common workplace distractions.

- Listening for a point of disagreement. We all know people who wait for one point with which they can disagree so that they can look intelligent, one-up the speaker, or impress others in the conversation.

- Nervousness. Anxiety about the situation, the message, or upcoming responsibilities impedes being able to fully listen to the message.

- Disinterest. It is difficult to listen to the subject or the speaker if the topic is of no interest to you.

- Poor speaker. A speaker who is boring, has difficulty making his or her point, or who makes the subject dry and tedious is someone to whom you may be unlikely to listen.

You will have to ascertain for yourself the reasons why you fail to completely surrender yourself to others when they speak. Once you do, you'll be able to overcome some of your difficulties by engaging in the technique of active listening developed by the psychologist Carl Rogers. He coined the term unconditional positive regard to refer to the process by which you enter into a relationship believing the best about another person. Without strings attached or qualification, you hold another person in high esteem. In order to really listen to someone, you first must have unconditional positive regard for him or her. Otherwise, the halo effect overshadows the message. Rogers said that once you have unconditional positive regard, active listening, rather than the passive taking in of information, can help you to assure that you've actually heard not only the message, but what the speaker may **not** be saying as well.

Active listening involves these three steps:

1. Paraphrasing. This is the act of repeating (in your own words) what you think the speaker has just said. If you haven't really listened, then you can't do it. If you haven't surrendered yourself to the speaker, paraphrasing isn't as easy as it sounds. You need not worry about repeating the message verbatim. When you paraphrase, the other person will let you know whether you have heard him or her correctly. Paraphrasing also has the secondary benefit of allowing the speaker to hear his or her message played back. After a paraphrase, it's not unusual to hear someone say, "That's what I said, but it's not what I meant." It allows clarification for both the speaker and the listener.

Here's an example of a paraphrase:

Speaker: Whew! I'm glad that presentation is over. Every member of the board of directors was there, and every one of them had questions. What was supposed to be a fifteen-minute presentation turned into an hour of picking apart every last detail of the proposed new building site.

Listener: Sounds like your audience really raked you over the coals.

Speaker: And how. I never knew there could be so many differences of opinion about what I thought was a done deal. At least I was able to answer every question.

When you paraphrase, the speaker feels heard and is encouraged to continue. Paraphrasing alone, however, gives the impression of simply parroting the speaker. The next step in active listening is being able to ask questions that provide for further clarification and full understanding.

2. Asking appropriate questions. By asking questions, both you and the speaker delve more deeply into the content of the message. An appropriate question is always one that is *based on what has just been said.* All too often the listener changes conversation by asking a question unrelated to what the speaker is saying. On the surface, it may appear appropriate, but closer examination reveals that it is really just a polite way to change the subject. An example of an inappropriate question based on the above conversation would be, "What did you think about the guy from ABC

Company? I'm going to have to meet with him next week." Active listening for the purpose of building relationships is designed to help you to hear and understand another person, not get your needs met at that particular moment.

If the listener wants to build a relationship with this speaker, then the focus has to remain with the speaker. Here's how the conversation might continue:

Listener: Do you think the project might be stalled?

Speaker: Not really. It's just that everyone was trying to one-up everyone else, and the only way they could really do it was by showing how much they knew about the building site and proposal. I just got caught in the crossfire. I guess I thought that the presentation was pro firma, when in fact I see now that it was a political decision to put me on the agenda.

Now the listener has even more information about what happened, why the speaker thinks it happened, and, without directly saying it, how he or she might feel. Here is where the third part of active listening comes in: the ability to extrapolate the speaker's feelings from the spoken message by reading between the lines.

3. Reflecting feelings. This is the toughest part of active listening. It involves making a guess at how you think the other person must feel. It brings the relationship to an even deeper level of understanding. People who have difficulty expressing their own feelings have difficulty with listening to and reflecting the feelings of others. If you reflect feelings and they're ignored, or the conversation comes to a grinding halt, it's best to drop this step. Part of being an active listener and listening with a third ear includes the ability to respond to the needs of the speaker. If talking about feelings makes him or her uncomfortable, don't push. Not everyone wants his or her feelings reflected, but those who do will appreciate a well-timed reflection.

The same conversation might continue with this reflection combined with continued paraphrasing and asking questions:

Listener: You must have felt as though you were ambushed.

Speaker: Yeah, I was pretty mad. I wished that someone had let me know what the real agenda was instead of my having to figure it out for myself. I guess I felt a little foolish.

Listener: I don't blame you for feeling as you do. What are you going to do about it?

Speaker: I'm not sure yet. I do know that I don't want to be put in that situation again—or at least I want to be forewarned about it.

Listener: How do you think you might prevent it from happening in the future?

Speaker: I guess I should talk to the boss. She's usually open to hearing me out. I think I'll sleep on it and decide tomorrow what to do.

Listener: Sounds like a good idea. Let me know if I can help in any way.

Speaker: You already have.

This conversation could have gone in any number of directions—and all away from the speaker's feelings. Active listening helps you to stay focused on the topic and not be distracted by tangential issues or personal needs. As you can see, it requires surrendering to the speaker and putting your own opinion on hold for the moment. The speaker walks away feeling as if he or she has really been heard, and the listener benefits from understanding the full context of the message—both content and emotion.

Using Doorway Conversations to Build Relationships

Now that you know how to listen, the next question is, to what degree are you comfortable taking the time to do it? If relationships are the cornerstone of ongoing career success, then doorway conversations are the cornerstone of relationships. The term doorway conversations comes from a client who uses it to describe those moments when someone appears in your doorway and stands there talking about the latest headline, the previous night's baseball game, or a problem he or she is encountering with a child. In the scheme of things, it may seem trivial to spend time talking about these subjects, but in the long term, these are the very things on which relationships are built. As Dale Carnegie once said, "You can make more friends in two months by becoming interested in other people than you can in two years by trying to get other people interested in you."

Relationships that are valuable and meaningful have three essential ingredients: trust, reciprocity, and genuine caring. There's no faking these three elements. They are what distinguish a casual encounter from a real relationship. This is not to say that every workplace relationship must be of the same caliber as the relationships you have with your best friends, but rather that both relationships share common elements. People who fail to build solid workplace relationships are frequently the same ones who fail to build solid friendships. The same childhood defense mechanisms get in the way of both growing close to a friend and knowing a colleague on more than a superficial level. People who have no trouble building relationships may at this point be saying, "But all of this is so obvious!" It may be obvious for you, but for people who have never built mutually rewarding relationships, especially in the workplace, the next section is critical.

Trust

How do you develop trust? Why do we trust some people more than others? Why are certain people everyone's trusted friend whereas others have difficulty getting people to confide in them? The answer lies in the degree to which you act consistently and honestly. Consistency is the key to enabling others to know what to expect from you. Honesty lets them know that you do what you say you will. Combined, these qualities are very powerful in building trust in the workplace.

One of the more bizarre cases that I investigated when I was an equal employment opportunity specialist involved a woman who filed a sex discrimination charge with the California Department of Fair Employment and Housing claiming that her boss was rude, condescending, and treated her unfairly. She believed that this was because she was a woman and that the men in her department were not treated similarly. In interviewing both male and female coworkers it turned out that they did not share her opinion that women were treated unfairly, and, in fact, they trusted their boss very much. How could there be such disparate opinions of the same boss? Each of the people interviewed admitted that the boss was difficult and could be rude and obnoxious. He would yell at them in front of colleagues and embarrass them at meetings, but they watched him do this to everyone, not any one individual. "It's just the way he is" was a common remark.

The irony in this situation was that they trusted him because he acted consistently and honestly with everyone. They knew exactly what to expect from him, even if it was inappropriate behavior, and therefore always knew where they stood. Winning this case for the company relied on men in the department being willing to state that they were treated the same as the woman filing the claim. There was no unlawful discrimination—just poor management, which is exactly what the commission eventually determined.

It is not recommended that you show everyone the same terrible treatment that this man did, but there is a lesson here. Even in the face of adversity, people will trust if there is consistency. Now, imagine the kind of trusting relationships that could be built with positive behaviors! Think of the people that you trust. It is likely that you're willing to go the extra mile for them because you know that they are true to their words.

Reciprocity

Reciprocity involves not only the quid pro quo exchanges described earlier in this chapter, but also a mutuality of sharing. In a solid workplace relationship, each person knows that the other has similar feelings about the nature of the friendship. They know this because there is a mutual sharing of personal information, allowing the "human side" to emerge. Too many of us have been taught that there's no place at work for personal problems or personal information to be shared. However, because we spend the largest part of our day at work it is only natural to disclose personal information in the workplace. In instances in which a person may be a good listener but does not share personal information, that person will soon set himself or herself apart from everyone else.

Adults who come from narcissistic parents are particularly vulnerable to this dilemma. They learned early in life that they are merely reflections of their parents and, therefore, should not think that their own needs deserve consideration. They go through life listening, but not telling. In a workplace relationship, the person who is always doing the talking may begin to feel uncomfortable about continuing to share information when he or she knows nothing about the other person in return. In reality, it takes very little self-disclosure to create a sense of mutuality. It must simply be enough to illuminate the human side of your character.

Recently at a workshop that I was conducting, I mentioned a personal experience that demonstrated the need for paraphrasing and asking questions when engaged in a conversation. I remarked that I had initially misunderstood the person with whom I had been collaborating about the program design and had, therefore, wasted quite a bit of time designing the wrong program. After the program a woman came up to me and, somewhat critically, asked why I had the need to make myself look bad in front of the group. She felt that the comment was unnecessary. I explained that I want program participants to see me as human and that the comment was a quite intentional way to accomplish this.

Often, as with the woman mentioned above, the fear that people have that they will be seen as less competent or somehow imperfect precludes them from being genuine with others. However, honest self-disclosure can be a valuable tool in letting others see the human side of you, and most people do not take advantage of it. The willingness to be seen and heard can be quite a liberating experience.

Genuine Caring

The last of the three ingredients for successful relationships, genuine caring, is the hardest of all to coach. It is something that comes from deep inside the heart and transcends logic and intellect. The absence of caring is a lot easier to explain than how to care, because the absence suggests the lack of caring in one's own life. With the exception of perhaps sociopaths, who truly lack the ability to care about their fellow human beings, most people have a deep and profound capacity to care. Women tend to have an easier time showing that they care, but it doesn't mean that men don't care. Men have simply been socialized to hide it better. Therefore, the question is not "How can I show that I care?" but rather, "Why don't I show that I care?" When you have the answer to this, you'll have the answer for how to genuinely care.

Chris, a woman I had coached, appeared not to care at all about her staff of twenty salespeople. Chris's single-minded devotion was to provide the best service possible to the company's customers. Her natural energy and enthusiasm made her want to take every hill that she encountered. She was always coming up with unique and creative ways to better serve the customer and overcome existing obstacles to superior service. There is nothing wrong with that, but Chris failed to take into account the fact that she could successfully do this only if her staff followed her into battle. While Chris was charging up the hill, she failed to look behind her and see that her followers were lingering at the bottom, deciding whether or not to take the hill.

My first contact with Chris was through a team-building session that she requested to find ways for her staff to be more effective. When it came time to assess the team's strengths and developmental areas, the primary complaint of her staff was that Chris didn't care about them—she was so self-absorbed that she didn't care whether or not her staff had the time, resources, and interest in pursuing the projects to which she committed them. So, when it came time to deliver, Chris was often left holding the bag and trying to figure out why. Chris neglected the human needs of her team, and they responded (very humanly) by resisting her efforts.

Chris was hired because it was clear that she could bring value-added service to this company. Her past achievements in former employment situations pointed to this fact. Chris saw herself as someone who could do anything she put her mind to, and she typically did, provided that she could do it alone. When it came to gaining the cooperation of others, she couldn't quite figure out why she never really got it. Heretofore, Chris had been a tremendous individual contributor, but in order to avoid career derailment she was at the point in her career where she had to learn how to accomplish the goal through others.

Fortunately for this team, Chris did care about other people. She just had a hard time showing it. Chris told me about her military father who expected high achievement but seldom rewarded it. She realized that, in some ways, she had become her father. She expected a lot from her team, but she didn't see them as people, only as objects there to assist her with meeting her goals. When she understood how this behavior impeded her reaching the goal, she was actually distraught. She had vowed never to do to others what her father had done to her and yet now she found that she was displaying the same behavior. Chris had to learn to complement her already good task-oriented behaviors with skills for building relationships with each team member and creating a cohesive team. Chris was able to draw on her teenage experience as a member of a tennis team to remind her of the value of teamwork. It was helpful because she had a point of reference for just how interdependence works.

Chris began with doorway conversations—just dropping by to say hello to people and to find out how—not what—they were doing. At first, they regarded her with skepticism. They wondered what ulterior motives she had. This discouraged Chris initially, but she was determined to win them over. She approached building relationships in much the same way as she approached her other "projects"—with vigor and enthusiasm. Pretty soon the individuals on her team began responding to her friendly overtures and expressions of interest. Chris didn't do it to get more work out of her team, but to get to know them as unique and valuable individuals. Chris learned the true meaning of Chinese philosopher Lao-tzu's saying "Fail to honor people, they fail to honor you." It took Chris a while, but she finally succeeded in building trust, reciprocity, and caring into workplace relationships. That's what made team members work for Chris in the long term and helped her to avoid premature career derailment.

Empathy

Empathy is a bit like caring. It is pretty tough to teach someone to be empathetic, but it is another important aspect of building relationships. If you can't empathize with someone, you can't really understand them. Empathy is the ability to put yourself in the other person's shoes and feel what they feel. It differs from sympathy in that sympathy requires only that you be able to see intellectually what another person is experiencing, not necessarily understand how that person feels. Sympathy is a more cognitive process, whereas empathy is a more emotional one.

I am not even sure that I would have thought to include the importance of empathy in relationship building had I not taken the time to have a conversation with a wonderful program administrator named Andrew. As we were both waiting for participants to arrive at a one-week program being held in Prague, we discussed what made certain programs go well and others not so well for him as an administrator. He remarked that it really made a difference when participants could empathize with how difficult it was to respond to their requests in the exact time frame that they wanted. As a program administrator, his responsibility involves taking care of all of the little details that participants might require. This includes making flight arrangements, ordering special meals, scheduling ground transportation, sending or receiving faxes, and making dinner reservations. The comment that really got my attention was, "When people show a little empathy I'll go the extra mile. When they treat me as though I have no brains, I act as though I have no brains."

It was one of those aha! moments. Part of the quid pro quo involves understanding what it's like to be in another person's position. Not looking simply at the job, but at the person in the job as well—seeing the human being performing the task. It made sense. Treating someone impersonally, like a functionary, does little to secure the relationship and assure longer-term cooperation.

What does it take to be empathetic? It takes surrender, in much the same way as Anne Morrow Lindbergh described it. It takes a suspension of personal need, judgment, or urgency in an effort to connect with the person with whom you are interacting.

Empathy is what is missing from sociopaths—they cannot relate in any way to the victim. Those criminals who commit brutal murders and feel no remorse lack empathy. Those people who cry when they see pictures of the atrocities of war have empathy. Empathy in the workplace is exhibited by noticing, and commenting on, changes in mood or behavior, by talking about problems that may be inherent to a particular position, by following up on personal problems that may have been discussed in a passing moment. Empathy is one way of showing that (1) you care and (2) you understand.

You Like Me! You Really Like Me!

The "You Like Me" acceptance speech that Sally Field made when she won an Academy Award a number of years ago speaks to a unique issue in building relationships. It reveals why she was typically cast in "cute" roles rather than more mature ones. She had an inordinate need to be liked and that need was typified over and over in her behavior. So, a word of caution about building positive relationships: There is a difference between taking the time to build positive relationships and making it the focal point of every day because you're afraid people won't like you. An inordinate need to be liked interferes with your ability to make difficult decisions, be direct with people, get your own needs met, and be perceived as someone who can perform even when the chips are down.

Although both men and women suffer from this problem, it seems to be more prevalent among women—and for good reason. Women have been socialized to be the nurturers, caretakers, and accommodators in society. They are expected to be good relationship builders. When women act in a manner counter to that expectation, they are often called overly aggressive, bitchy, or some other choice terms. So, they go out of their way to be pleasant and try to win support for their ideas by making others like them.

Overutilization of this particular strength can create situations where others don't take you seriously. Ironically, it is the people, both men and women, who have established good workplace relationships who can well afford to err on the side of being more assertive or direct. Their accounts are full of chips that can be used at the appropriate time.

Maria is a good example of someone whose strength in building relationships interfered with her ability to achieve her career goals. She is the coordinator of outreach efforts for a nonprofit organization. Technically, she knows her job and is respected for her ability to perform it effectively. But when the department manager position has opened up on several occasions, she has consistently been overlooked as a viable candidate to fill it. When she has asked why, she has been told that she "isn't ready" to take this next step.

If you were to meet Maria, you would like her—as does everyone in her office. She's warm, affable, and a good listener. She makes you feel as if what you have to say is important to her. If you spend any length of time with her, however, you realize that her strength in this arena stems from the need to be liked and is not balanced with the ability to be direct and straightforward. If she has an opinion different from yours, she won't tell you. She'll embrace yours as if it were her own. She won't take a stand on any issue if she thinks it might offend you. If you correct something that she does wrong, she becomes overly apologetic and tries to make up for the mistake by bringing you home-baked cookies the next day. Maria will never be considered "management material" until she overcomes this particular strength by balancing it with more assertive behaviors.

It is understood that relationships will never take the place of technical competence; they complement and support it. The ability to see and be seen is an essential ingredient for all good relationships, workplace and otherwise. One method by which you can avoid premature career derailment is by balancing excellence in technical capability with building one-on-one relationships that help you to achieve your goals through cooperation and camaraderie.

Beyond making an individual contribution and building one-on-one relationships, you have to work effectively as part of a team. The next chapter provides suggestions for how you can be an effective team member and contribute to your team's success.

Ways to Build Strong One-On-One Relationships

1. At least once a week have lunch with one or more coworkers.

2. Drop into one person's office per day for ten minutes of casual conversation.

3. Smile at people as you walk past them in the hall.

4. Have your desk situated so that it faces out the door.

5. Keep your office door open unless you are conducting confidential business or trying to meet a tight deadline and don't want distractions (but never more than a few times each month).

6. When people talk to you, surrender yourself for the moment.

7. Open up to people to let them get to know you by disclosing personal information with which you are comfortable.

8. Read *People Skills: How to Assert Yourself, Listen to Others, and Resolve Conflicts* (see page 209).

9. Solicit input from knowledgeable coworkers about projects on which you are working.

10. Accept coworkers' invitations for lunch or dinner and extend your own.

11. Attend company-sponsored social events.

12. Learn the names of coworkers' husbands, wives, significant others, and children.

13. Remember birthdays by keeping a list or marking them on your calendar.

14. Follow up on information that has been previously shared with you, particularly personal information.

15. Learn the names of everyone on your floor and in the departments with which you interact most frequently.

16. Say thank you when someone goes out of their way for you.

17. Go out of your way for others.

18. Interact with everyone equally, regardless of level in the organization.

19. Begin conversations with small talk, unless you know the other person doesn't like it.

20. Enroll in The Dale Carnegie Course (see page 202).

21. Don't allow an inordinate need for others to like you to get in the way of being direct and straightforward.

22. Put yourself in the shoes of the other person.

23. Do favors for people even if you don't anticipate needing them returned.

24. See beyond the task to the human being who is performing it.

Inability to Function Effectively in a Work Group

Strategy: Become an Integral Member of Your Team

One by-product of building relationships is the often unexpected, but always welcomed, gift of insight provided by those who have a view of the world that is different from my own. For example, toward the end of a meeting with my client and friend Ben Hunter, controller of payroll and compensation accounting at the consulting firm McKinsey & Company, he casually inquired into what new and exciting things I was doing lately. I told him about this book, and we began discussing what made successful people derail. I happened to mention that I had decided to discuss interpersonal and team relationships in one chapter rather than discussing them separately. Ben seemed surprised. He thought that the skills required to build relationships with individuals were quite different from those used to work as an integral member of a team and deserved independent attention. We didn't have time for an in-depth discussion about it, but his comments remained with me long after our meeting ended.

As I continued thinking about it, I realized that Ben was right. I have encountered people who were terrific team players, but who were unable to forge deeper, more intimate, one-on-one relationships. Teamwork allows for anonymity, depending on the size of groups, but effective interpersonal relationships do not. It is easier to "hide" personally in a group than it is in individual relationships, provided you contribute to task accomplishment.

Conversely, people who create strong personal support systems consisting of relationships with individuals may derail due to their inability to participate as members of task forces or project teams. Their discomfort with groups precludes them from making the same contribution to a team that they might when working independently or with just one other person on a project. These people do quite well one-on-one, but somehow become lost in a group.

So, I would like to thank Ben for his insight. The ability to work effectively as a team member is not simply an extension of good interpersonal skills, but a separate and unique skill set.

Even if building relationships is one of your strengths, this checklist might reveal a very different area for potential derailment.

_____ I would describe myself as a good team player.

_____ Even when the topic doesn't interest me, isn't pertinent to my function, or I have nothing to add, I stay engaged in team discussions by looking for ways to contribute to the outcome.

_____ I believe that the final product of a group typically exceeds the quality of something that I produce alone.

_____ I freely share information with teammates without questioning their "need to know."

_____ I believe that differences of opinion on a team add value to, rather than simply delay, outcomes.

_____ I understand the difference between the task and the process of a team.

_____ I am comfortable with being a follower while someone else leads a group.

_____ I do not display impatience with the lengthy discussions that are often part of a group's process because I know that they will contribute positively to the outcome.

_____ I volunteer for team-based projects.

_____ Getting individual recognition is not as important to me as my team's success.

_____ I publicly acknowledge others who have worked with me on a successful project.

The Value of Teamwork

Because most cultures reward competition and individualism with money and recognition, there are those who question the value of developing cooperative team abilities. Some people prefer to be "individual contributors" and in fact work more effectively in this way. They tend to avoid opportunities to work collaboratively. The efficacy of teamwork, however, is well documented through sports analogies, war and peace efforts, and medical triage. The following routine training exercise for flight attendants underscores the importance and value of teamwork.

When flight attendants are trained in techniques for aircraft crash survival at sea, they are taught to look for passengers at the beginning of a flight who are most likely to survive on a raft and contribute to the survival of others. The key to ensuring successful survival is in choosing people who can play all kinds of roles at sea. A leader is needed who can remind others of the vision of being rescued. He or she can keep people optimistic about their chances of staying alive by remaining calm, having faith in and seeing the "big picture," whether this is called faith in God or a higher power. Beyond this role, technical competence is required to survive as well—to desalinate saltwater, repair a tear in the raft, read a compass, or administer first aid. In the end, survival depends not on any single skill set, but rather on taking advantage of the fact that the whole is greater than the sum of the parts. The chance of survival increases with the synergistic effect of team-work. Paradoxically, as people pool their resources, instead of focusing exclusively on their own survival, the likelihood of success increases exponentially.

The same is true in organizations. Individuals come to the workplace with unique skill sets that contribute to their own success and the success of their teams. Each of us is endowed with things that we do well and for which people rely on us. Some of these skills are learned, others are developed with practice, and still others are the result of our natural proclivity for them. We aren't expected to do everything equally well, but we are expected to use the resources around us, including the human resources, to accomplish our tasks effectively. Much like the survivors of an airplane crash, business survivors must have the ability to perform tasks not only independently or together with only one other person, but collaboratively in group settings as well.

Team-based projects have become increasingly popular and appear to be here to stay. It is important that you be able to work effectively not only with individuals, but also with entire teams of people. Whereas some people are able to forge good one-on-one workplace relationships, others excel and find satisfaction in participating as members of a group committed to a common goal.

The term good individual contributor refers to someone who does his or her job well working independently, but doesn't function effectively as a member of a team. The term is frequently used to describe someone with good technical skills but poor interpersonal ones, so don't take it as a compliment if someone tells you that you're a terrific individual contributor. The message may be that you are not perceived as a good team player. Even jobs that appear on the surface to be perfect for individual contributors later turn out to be ones that require integrated teamwork. As a matter of fact, it is difficult to think of one job in most workplaces today that doesn't require integrated teamwork. Teams accomplish significantly more through the synergistic process of sharing information, technology, or skills than would a group of individual contributors working on pieces of the same project.

The experience of one major car manufacturer is testament to this fact. The company traditionally put people into assembly-line jobs where each worker was responsible for one part of the car. The frequent occurrence of production mistakes forced management to examine the inefficiency and find ways of overcoming it. The managers discovered that by increasing the scope of each person's position and creating teams of people who had overall responsibility for the car's assembly rather than each person being responsible for only one piece, the quality of the automobiles produced actually increased.

In a different kind of business, the Ritz-Carlton hotel chain also stresses teamwork in addition to excellence in individual performance during new employee orientation at each facility. A stay at any one of the hotels is likely to make you realize that the Ritz-Carlton has redefined customer service in the broadest sense of the term. Each employee is taught that he or she is personally responsible for the satisfaction of the hotel's guests. Employees are not taught to do just one job well; they are taught to work as a part of the overall hotel team of staff members and to accept responsibility for any request that a guest might make.

During a leadership workshop at the Ritz-Carlton in Pasadena, California, the cofacilitator of the program decided to test the hotel's philosophy to see whether it worked in practice. Several times during our stay, she would ask staff members for items or services that were clearly outside the domain of their responsibility. Each time her request was promptly met. In an effort to make a point to the managers in this workshop about the value of teamwork, she asked a man from the catering staff, who came in to refresh the coffee, whether he knew where we could get some masking tape. He said that he would take care of it. Several minutes later he returned, masking tape in hand.

After she thanked him, I asked how he liked working at this hotel. He said that it was one of the best jobs that he ever had. When I asked why, he said because he was trained to do his job properly *and* felt like an important part of the hotel team. He said that each morning management held team meetings to talk about the guests and their particular needs so that everyone would have all of the information required to meet the demands. It was a valuable lesson to the participants about the efficacy of teamwork and how it can enhance customer and employee satisfaction.

Another example of the value of teamwork is provided by the restaurant chain California Pizza Kitchens. With a main fare of individual gourmet pizza and pasta, the restaurants first opened in California in the mid 1980s. Since that time they have grown significantly and have expanded to several states across the country. Besides serving good food (showing that they are technically competent), these restaurants also offer a pleasant dining experience. Their waiters and waitresses have been trained in how to treat customers and how to work as a team. There are no fixed table assignments for servers—everyone is responsible for every table. When I inquired how this worked with regard to tips, I was told by one young man that it wasn't a problem. Peer pressure essentially eliminated those staff people who brought down the tip average for the others.

An example of effective teamwork that supersedes individual team member differences can be seen among the group of lawyers assembled for what the media proclaimed as the trial of the century: *The People of the State of California v. Orenthal James Simpson*. Simpson, given his years as a professional football player, knew the value of teamwork. He was represented by a defense team on which each lawyer was, in his own right, an outstanding individual contributor but could probably not have alone saved Simpson from being convicted. Together, they successfully defended Simpson and helped him to avoid what would in all likelihood have been a lifetime prison sentence.

It wasn't until after the trial was over that the public became aware of the strong feelings of antagonism among the team members. Attorney Robert Shapiro went so far as to say that he would never again work with at least one of his trial colleagues, and similar insinuations were made by many of the key players. The outcome of the trial speaks loudly to the ability of individuals to put aside their differences for the purpose of achieving a common goal in an uncommon manner.

Perhaps the sports arena offers the greatest source for understanding the importance of teamwork. Sports teams consist of groups of outstanding individual contributors who know that they can't win the game alone—and if they think they can, they don't get the cooperation of their teammates for long. Los Angeles Lakers head coach Phil Jackson had this lesson emphasized for him the hard way. Jackson's coaching record of 612–208 is the best in NBA history. In his book *Sacred Hoops: Spiritual Lessons of a Hardwood Warrior*, Jackson shares an experience from an early stint as coach with the Albany Patroons. Despite the fact that he had no formal training as a coach, he did have a coaching vision: "to create a team in which selflessness—not the me-first mentality that had come to dominate professional basketball—was the primary driving force." Part of his method for accomplishing the vision was to assure that everyone on the team be paid the same amount and be given equal playing time.

His strategy worked. Within two years, the Patroons moved from an 8–17 season to having the second best record in the league, with Jackson being named Coach of the Year. His achievement began to unravel, however, when he allowed one player, Frankie J.

Sanders, to dominate the game and compromise his principles. Sanders first convinced Jackson to move him from second slot to starting player, then successfully lobbied management for a sizable raise. Combined with his superior playing skill, these factors gave Sanders (and his teammates) the impression that he was first among equals. Following a series of incidents that included Jackson's suspending Sanders (for what amounted to insubordination) and then implicitly supporting management's decision to reinstate him (because they felt he was needed to win games), the team was never the same. "The solidarity that had taken so long to build had suddenly evaporated," writes Jackson. "Not only did we lose the series, we were lost as a team."

Jackson then went on to show other good, but not winning, teams the same formula for success. First, with the Chicago Bulls during the 1980s and 1990s, he turned a team that was built around one outstanding player (this time Michael Jordan) into six-time NBA champions. More recently, Jackson sold the Lakers on his team-based philosophies and coached the team to its first NBA championship in more than a decade—capitalizing on but not overrelying on start players like Kobe Bryant and Shaquille O'Neal.

Clearly, teamwork pays huge dividends for both individuals and groups of people. Why, then, do so many people derail due to the inability to work as part of a team? The reason so many people resist teamwork lies partially in how jobs came into being in the first place.

Overcoming Resistance to Teamwork

The concept of working independently in a "job" is a relatively recent phenomenon born of the industrial revolution. It was during this period that individual jobs were created as a means of responding to the requirements imposed by factory assembly procedures. Throughout history, however, human beings worked much more collaboratively to assure their survival. Clans, tribes, and families can be viewed as the earliest teams. Even in prehistoric time, our predecessors pooled resources by allowing those with the best vision to sight their prey, those with the best dexterity to kill it, and those with the greatest strength to haul it back to the cave.

Consciously or otherwise, they realized that their survival depended on a collaborative effort.

Today, in an age where rugged individualism and an "everyone for themselves" attitude prevails, teamwork seems like a revolutionary concept. The irony is that people resist having to depend on others for their success when in fact they would fare so much better if they worked collaboratively. In their wonderfully written and enlightening book *The Wisdom of Teams* Jon Katzenbach and Douglas Smith recognize that there exists a natural resistance to moving from individual contributor to team player. "Our natural instincts, family upbringing, formal education, and employment experience all stress the primary importance of individual responsibility as measured by our own standards and those to whom we report," Katzenbach and Smith write. "We are more comfortable doing our own jobs and having our performance measured by our boss than we are working and jointly being assessed as peers."

The story of a man whom I met during a team-building session in Germany provides insight into how and why some people resist teamwork. Erik was raised in a small village about eighty miles outside of Berlin. Throughout the program he arrived late to each of the sessions, sat on the outside of the small groups to which he was assigned, and spoke very quietly, which led to him often being ignored, after which he would shut down completely. Combined, his behavior and body language indicated that he was resisting this team's effort to coalesce.

After one particularly intense group exercise where several members of the team received some pretty difficult feedback, Erik raised his hand and said that people never change anyway and we shouldn't expect them to. His real message being that he wasn't going to change. Whereas his teammates were doing their best to overcome cultural and personal obstacles to teamwork, Erik threw a monkey wrench into this painstaking process. Democracy in what was formerly East Germany is a relatively new system and the remnants of communism were reflected in the hesitance which many of the participants had in speaking openly and honestly. Erik's resistance wasn't making it any easier.

One evening I arrived late to dinner and found only Erik left at the table. We made small talk about our families and upbringing while I waited for my meal to arrive. Much to my surprise, he began telling me about his childhood with a cruel father and timid mother. In broken English, he conveyed perfectly that although his father was well intentioned (he wanted Erik to be more than the truck driver that he himself was), he was nonetheless abusive, both physically and emotionally. Erik's mother was ineffectual in preventing the damage he did to his children's psyches. As a result, he said, he always tried to do his best and worked hard to achieve his goals, never relying on anyone else for assistance.

Erik's lesson from childhood was to be strong and independent, always giving his personal best in an effort to deflect his father's constant criticism and verbal abuse. His survival, and the survival of all of the children in his family, was dependent on each person fending for him or herself. Neither could he rely on his mother, who had her own problems in the abusive atmosphere created by Erik's father. His resistance to my efforts to help this group become a high-performing team was now understandable to me. I no longer viewed Erik as an impediment to the process, but rather as a human being struggling for survival in an unknown and changing world. Erik had no idea that he now had to overcome his greatest strengths in order to assure ongoing success. It was a concept as alien to him as democracy once had been.

The ingredient essential to teamwork, trust, is missing from those most reluctant to embrace it. Somewhere along the line, they learned that they could rely only on themselves. To be a fully productive member of a team requires the ability to make a leap of faith that you will actually be better off by relinquishing some of the need to work independently. In order to do so you must first believe that other people have something valuable to offer and that together you can accomplish great things.

Understanding and Valuing "Gifts Differing"

One invaluable tool that I use in conjunction with individual coaching and team-building programs is the Myers Briggs Type Indicator (MBTI®) personality inventory. The title of a lovely companion book, *Gifts Differing*, helps us all to understand that we each bring unique gifts to the workplace. The challenge of working as part of a team is to understand the gifts that you bring *as well* as those brought by fellow team members. All too often we come to believe that the gift we bring is the only gift needed by the team. Success as a team member depends on your being able to value and use the gifts of others as effectively as you use your own.

The MBTI measures individual preferences on four separate scales: what energizes or takes energy away from a person, what a person likes to pay attention to, how a person makes decisions, and how a person likes to live life. On each of the four scales shown on the chart on page 62, you exhibit a preference for one set of behaviors over the other. Knowing these four things about yourself and your teammates can help you to contribute your own personal best and bring the best out in others as well. Similarly, failure to understand personality types can lead to an enormous amount of frustration and misunderstanding.

Here is an example. At a team-building session in Jakarta, Indonesia, that involved a lot of work in small groups and pairs of people, a woman, Sarinah, came up to me and whispered, "Whatever you do, don't pair me with Malu," and hurried away. Naturally, as the facilitator, this was a red flag to me that she probably *needed* to be paired with Malu. Then, a little while later, Malu came up to me and—you can already guess what she wanted—asked not to be paired with Sarinah. I was pondering how best to handle the situation when knowledge of type preferences helped me to solve this dilemma.

I typically do an exercise where people who are opposite types on the MBTI are asked to pair up together to discuss ways in which they have difficulty working as teammates and how those difficulties could be turned into opportunities. Sarinah and Malu scored as opposite profiles. Whereas Sarinah was an Extrovert / Senser / Thinker / Judger, Malu was an Introvert / Intuitor / Feeler / Perceiver. Sarinah was outgoing, practical, results-oriented, in-your-face, and Malu was more introspective, attuned to possibilities instead of reality, and sensitive to people and processes. As frequently happens when these two particular types work together without understanding how to capitalize on their differences, on-going communication problems and misunderstandings existed between them. Malu viewed Sarinah as too blunt, unconcerned with how people felt about things, and so concerned with the bottom line that new and innovative ways of doing things were ignored. Conversely, Sarinah thought Malu was too slow to reach decisions, overly concerned with people's opinions, and withheld information.

Given my instructions, they reluctantly paired up together. Once they began talking about the problems between them based on their types, each realized that she saw the world through a different set of lenses. Instead of each thinking the other was just trying to make her life miserable, both learned that these differences could be used to help each other be more effective. As a result of their discussion they decided to use each other's strengths to complement their own and as a means of learning alternative skills. Although I don't think that Malu and Sarinah will ever be best friends, they did begin to work more effectively as teammates and overcome the barriers that existed to a collaborative working relationship.

Herein lies one of the secrets to being a successful team player: the ability to move outside the scope of your own preferences and limited worldview to a broader understanding of the complementary nature of team relationships. We get so stuck in our own paradigms that we fail to see how other paradigms add value. Our way of doing things becomes the way, thereby limiting the possibilities that result from synergistic teamwork. And the more we learned in childhood that we had to be staunchly independent and self-sufficient, the harder it is to shift our paradigms.

The importance of being able to shift paradigms is made abundantly clear in the works of the futurist Joel Barker. His book *Paradigms: The Business of Discovering the Future* and his film *The Business of Paradigms* provides examples of how the failure to move from your own comfort zone to a new, different, and perhaps unexplored sphere of possibilities can limit your future and sabotage your success. I like to tell the story of one Thanksgiving when I learned a lesson about shifting paradigms and teamwork.

It was the first year that I decided to invite a large group of relatives and friends for Thanksgiving dinner. Being the independent woman that I am, I wanted to prepare and serve the meal by myself. As more people came into the kitchen to help, I became increasingly frustrated with my inability to maintain control of the situation. My mother was telling me to do one thing to the turkey, a friend was telling me to do another to the stuffing, and still someone else was telling me how to cook the vegetables. Finally, heeding my own guidance to others that the paradox of control is *the more control you have the more you give away*, I decided to let everyone do what they wanted. I was just positive, however, that this meal would wind up a disaster.

When we finally sat down to dinner I held my breath. I would assume no responsibility for how the food tasted. No one was more surprised than I was when it turned out to be one of the best Thanksgiving dinners ever to come out of my kitchen. Too many cooks hadn't spoiled the meal, they had made it even better than I would have done alone. There was no better way for me personally to learn the lesson that I already knew to be true for professional teams—collaboration yields a better product if you only allow the process to flow. In retrospect I realized that my resistance to team-work in the kitchen was no different from the resistance to team-work in the workplace. Each person came with skills different from mine, but complementary. If I had been smarter from the beginning, I would have used those skills to my advantage, rather than resisting them.

MTBI® PREFERENCES CHART

ENERGIZING (HOW A PERSON IS ENERGIZED)

EXTROVERT (E)	INTROVERT (I)
external	internal
outside thrust	inside pull
blurt it out	keep it in
breadth	depth
involved with people, things	work with ideas, thoughts
action	reflection
do-think-do	think-do-think

ATTENDING (WHAT A PERSON PAYS ATTENTION TO)

SENSING (S)	INTUITION (I)
the five senses	sixth sense, hunches
what is real	what could be
practical	theoretical
present orientation	future possibilities
facts	insights
using established skills	learning new skills
utility	novelty
step-by-step	leap around

DECIDING (HOW A PERSON DECIDES)	
THINKING (T)	FEELING (F)
head	heart
logical system	value system
objective	subjective
justice	mercy
critique	compliment
principles	harmony
reason	empathy
firm but fair	compassionate
LIVING (LIFESTYLE A PERSON ADOPTS)	
JUDGMENT (J)	PERCEPTION (P)
planful	spontaneous
regulate	flow
control	adapt
settled	tentative
run one's life	let life happen
set goals	gather information
decisive	open
organized	flexible

Copyright © 1990 by Consulting Psychologists Press, Inc.

It's been more than twenty years since Lakers coach Phil Jackson vowed to trust his instincts when it comes to team-work. During that time he's used Zen philosophy to hone his techniques for convincing individual team members about the importance and value of teamwork. In the process, he's become one of the most successful coaches in the history of the National Basketball Association. In a December 1995 interview with *Fortune* magazine he explains his approach:

> Back in the late eighties I used to remind Michael Jordan that no matter how many great scoring games he had, he still sometimes ended up coming out on the losing end, because he would try to beat the other team by himself. Even though he could pull it off occasionally, we weren't going to win consistently until the other players on our team started helping us.... Even for people who don't consider themselves spiritual in a traditional,

religious way, you need to convince them that creating any kind of team is a spiritual act. People have to surrender their own egos so that the end result is bigger than the sum of its parts.

And Jackson is right. Once you realize that you can't possibly do it all yourself, you can begin to reap the benefits that come from teamwork. Although you may be able to win a few games alone, long-term wins come from interdependent team functioning, not grandstanding. It is a leap of faith to move from individual contributor to team member, but one well worth the risk.

Team Roles

Individuals must play certain roles for a sports team or a business team to achieve its goals. The difference is that in business, groups work on two fundamental levels: the content level and the process level. The content level consists of the actual purpose of what the group is supposed to accomplish or what goals it must achieve in order to fulfill the expectations of management. The process level involves how the group achieves those goals—something which is frequently of lesser concern to management, but nonetheless important. Groups that focus exclusively on content get the job done, but at a great personal cost to team members. Groups that focus exclusively on process assure that team members' personal needs are attended to, but often at the expense of achieving their goals.

In addition to capitalizing on the gifts brought to the team by individuals, team members must fill certain roles if the content and the process are to be addressed. These roles are commonly divided into two categories, which parallel the content and process of a group: task roles and group-building and maintenance roles. Whereas task roles help the group to achieve the goals expected of them, process roles are designed to maintain the emotional health of the team so that it can function effectively over the long term. Both roles are equally important, but group-building and maintenance roles are frequently ignored in favor of task accomplishment.

Task roles include behaviors such as assuring that enough information is available to make a decision, analyzing and assessing that information, rendering opinions, and moving the group toward making a decision. Most people are fairly good at playing task roles. Teams begin to encounter problems, however, when members become so focused on the task at hand that they fail to see the ramifications of their behavior on fellow teammates. They ignore the importance of maintaining relationships in group settings. You can put a really good relationship builder into a group setting and the skills he or she is comfortably able to use one-on-one go out the window. Suddenly you see counterproductive behaviors such as competitiveness, jockeying for position, talking over people, ignoring the opinions of others, and even mentally checking out when it appears the group is going in a direction different from the direction desired. Depending on one's childhood family, it may look very much like what happened at the dinner table.

One man was sent to an interpersonal skills program because he was disruptive at team meetings, always creating more turmoil than necessary, and interfering with the team's ability to reach consensus. After a videotaped exercise where he received feedback about the specific behaviors that were contributing to potential derailment, he explained why he acted as he did. He said that both of his parents were attorneys and that arguments at the dinner table were thought of as sport. His brothers and sisters, in an effort to get parental approval, would routinely take contrary positions and shout over one another in order to "win" the argument. To an outsider, he said, it would look quite bizarre. He considered chaotic team meetings the norm and actually fun. If there wasn't controversy to begin with, he created it.

Here's where team-building and maintenance roles come in. Such roles include behaviors like gatekeeping (making certain everyone is heard before the decision is made), encouraging the team to work through difficult issues, mediating differences of opinion, and relieving tension through jokes or attempts at levity. High-functioning teams assure that equal attention is paid to the team's process and its product. Failure to do so results in hard feelings among team members, outcomes being delayed, sabotage of the ultimate decision (especially when it's made by just a few group members), and the eventual dropping out of team members with valuable input.

Team-building and maintenance roles, so called because they are designed to maintain the life of the group, are more subtle, but nonetheless critical for long-term effective team functioning. If a group of people were to come together to make only one decision or complete one task and then disband and never have to work together again, the group's dynamics would be irrelevant. Exclusive focus on the task might be appropriate. In the workplace, however, individuals move from team to team and project to project, thereby necessitating assurance that each time a group meets it will successfully carry out its explicit and implicit agenda, unhampered by past or present inappropriate individual and group behavior.

During team-building sessions, I've watched as certain members become increasingly uninvolved with the team activity. They look out the window, get up and leave the room (always for a good reason, of course), or engage in pseudolistening. When asked why they mentally "checked out," they frequently respond that they didn't have anything to add or that they didn't know enough about the subject to make a contribution. This is all well and good, except for the fact that people notice when members drop out, even if they don't say anything at the moment, and the team is no longer a team. Managers who observe the process often make a mental note of who furthers goal attainment and who hinders it from lack of participation. These observations are later used as a basis for making employment decisions.

As an effective team member your job is to decide which role you are comfortable playing, or which one needs to be filled in order for the team to move forward, and to fill that role for your team. Think of yourself as a facilitator, not simply an individual contributor. Even when team meetings have a designated leader, you can help the team to meet its goals by observing the process and filling in missing roles. For example, if it seems as if the team is becoming increasingly frustrated with its inability to overcome an impasse, you can make an observation about the current climate of the group with a comment such as, "It looks as though we've reached an impasse. Let's take a minute to make sure everyone's point has been heard and understood." On the other hand, if the team is so concerned with hurting one another's feelings that decisions are being avoided, you can say something like, "It seems as though we're being very careful with one another. I'm wondering how we can make it safe enough to speak our minds without damaging any relationships."

The role of facilitator is an especially good one to play if you don't have the technical expertise required to add value to a team project or help solve a team problem. Don't wait for the formal leader of the team to take that role; at times he or she is not particularly adept at being a facilitator and your intervention will be welcomed. If you are not quite comfortable with what may appear to be usurping his or her authority, you can say, "Since this isn't my area of expertise, perhaps I could facilitate the discussion so that those of you with the knowledge can fully participate?" Playing group-building and maintenance roles keeps you connected with the team's process, makes you clearly involved to anyone who may be observing your behavior, and enables you to help your team to accomplish its goals.

People who successfully remain on their career tracks aren't the ones checking out. They know that they can always fill group-building and maintenance roles if the subject area either isn't of interest to them or isn't their forte. By shifting roles, you stay involved with the process and help the team to meet its goals by facilitating the group's activities. For example, if you become lost on the technical aspects of some discussion, look around the room and watch what is happening with the team's dynamics. Become an observer of the event itself. Check to see whether anyone else appears confused as well. If so, you can always help the team by saying something like, "It seems to me that a number of us need more explanation before we can get on board." Or, if an argument is taking place, act as mediator by interjecting, "Clearly, there's a difference of opinion. Let's see if we can reach a mutual agreement before our time is up."

Being able to build one-on-one relationships and working as part of a team are two of the most important things that you will do to assure career longevity. They'll never take the place of hard work and technical competence, but they will complement these two performance givens. If you tend to work independently, find ways to collaborate on team projects and make contributions to team meetings. Although the ability to work independently can be viewed as a strength, it must be balanced with adding value to your team and teammates.

Strategies for Team Meetings

1. Stay involved in team meetings by consciously choosing the role that you will play.

2. Act as a facilitator at team meetings.

3. Pay as close attention to the team's process as you do to achieving the task.

4. Notice and invite quieter or more reluctant members of the team to speak up.

5. Before team meetings adjourn, assure buy-in by asking whether every-one agrees with whatever decisions have been made—and if they don't revisit the issue or schedule it for discussion at the next meeting.

6. Suggest that the last fifteen minutes of team meetings be used to talk about the team's process and what could be done differently at the next meeting to make it more productive.

7. Stay tuned in when the meeting topic isn't immediately applicable to your present work by looking for the opportunity to learn something new that may be useful to you later.

Strategies to Use Between Meetings

8. Volunteer for projects that require you to work with at least two other people.

9. Be willing to give up your way of doing things if it means the team will benefit.

10. Rather than seeing differences of opinion as obstacles, use them to reach well-rounded solutions to team problems.

11. Circulate articles that you think may be of interest to teammates.

12. Showcase the accomplishments of teammates as well as your own.

13. Move from "me" to "we" thinking.

14. Share information freely without considering whether there is the need to know.

15. Ask teammates for input into projects for which you have primary responsibility.

16. Suggest celebrating team accomplishments with a small party, public recognition, time off, token gifts, etc.

17. Volunteer to help teammates who may be under a tight deadline or experiencing a time crunch.

18. Don't be afraid to ask for help when you are experiencing a time crunch.

Personal Development

19. Take a class in group dynamics.

20. Read *Please Understand Me* (see page 209).

21. Critically assess your behavior on teams and make adjustments as needed.

22. Instead of viewing other people's strengths as a threat, use them to complement your own.

23. Read *Mining Group Gold* (see page 208).

24. Read *The Wisdom of Teams* (see page 209).

Failure to Focus on Image and Communication

Strategy: Capitalize on the
Power of Perception

During the 2000 presidential election, the late night television show, *Saturday Night Live*, skewered both Al Gore and George W. Bush with ongoing satirical skits. The writers characterized Gore as overly formal and rigid and Bush as a simplistic dolt. Of course, neither depiction is 100 percent accurate, but as with most humor, there is a kernel of truth. So what gave Bush the slight lead needed to achieve a narrow victory? It's simple. People were not as concerned with the message as they were with the ability to relate to the candidate. Bush was not a particularly strong speaker but, compared with Gore, he seemed more genuine, down-to-earth, and approachable.

And herein lies yet another factor that differentiates otherwise equally qualified people: *the power of perception.* My good friend and colleague, Tom Henschel, president of Essential Communications, a Studio City-based communications consulting firm, refers to it as the likeability quotient. We all tend to gravitate toward people who are likeable, whether we ourselves are likeable or not. Many different factors contribute to likeability—high energy, approachability and upbeat attitude to name a few—but Tom tells clients, "If you want to get ahead you've got to be the kind of person others want to have at their Thanksgiving table."

Nowhere was this more apparent than in 1995, when, for nearly a full year, the world was mesmerized by a real-life courtroom drama called *The People of the State of California v. Orenthal James Simpson*. Although many of the players on that legal stage provide us with tremendous insight into the power of perception as it relates to credibility, perhaps no two players illustrate the counterpoint more effectively than prosecutor Christopher Darden and defense attorney Johnnie Cochran. From the beginning of the trial we knew that only one of the men could prevail in his quest for justice, but we may not have realized that it would at least partially hinge on factors related to image and communication: the ability to convince a jury that he alone spoke the truth.

Both Darden and Cochran are well educated, intelligent, and articulate men. They worked hard for the career success they have achieved. In many ways they can be considered equals in the legal arena. One major difference between them, however, is their communication styles—and soon after the trial began the courtroom camera captured these differences. As Darden became frustrated with the tactics of his opponents, viewers could see and hear the change in his demeanor. He became increasingly sullen and morose. He questioned witnesses in such a low tone of voice that it was often difficult to hear him. He appeared lethargic and, at times, indifferent to the court proceedings. Sarcastic remarks and disparaging facial expressions bespoke his contempt for the court, his opponents, and the defendant. In short, Darden looked and sounded like a man defeated before the final bell.

On the other hand, with few exceptions, Cochran presented the picture of composure throughout the trial. He would vehemently argue his points, but when decisions didn't go his way he accepted them and moved forward. Throughout the trial he displayed an energy and affect that exuded self-confidence. He spoke loudly, clearly, and with animation. Despite the fact that at times he was equally as contentious as Darden, this isn't a description that would accurately characterize Cochran. He could be no surer of the final outcome than Darden, but up until the moment the verdict was announced, he looked and sounded like a winner.

These kinds of differences demonstrate the significant part that image and communication play in how we are perceived by others. Perhaps the seminal defining moment of the importance of image occurred during yet another presidential election—this time the Kennedy/Nixon debate of 1960. Although most of us can't remember the content of the debate, we do remember the physical appearance of the candidates as they sat on the platform. Despite the fact that Kennedy was in poor health, he looked youthful, tan, poised, and relaxed. Although only four years Kennedy's senior, Nixon (who refused to wear television makeup) looked wan and tired. In terms of outcome, polls of television viewers conducted after the debate gave Kennedy the edge, while polls of radio listeners reported Nixon the victor. From this point forward political candidates became constantly aware of the power of image to make or break their aspirations.

Dr. Allen Weiner, president of Communication Development Associates in Woodland Hills, California, has conducted research that suggests in day-to-day communication the impression that we make on others is based largely on how we look and sound. The following chart reveals that, in fact, a full 90 percent of that impression is based on factors related to other than what we actually say.

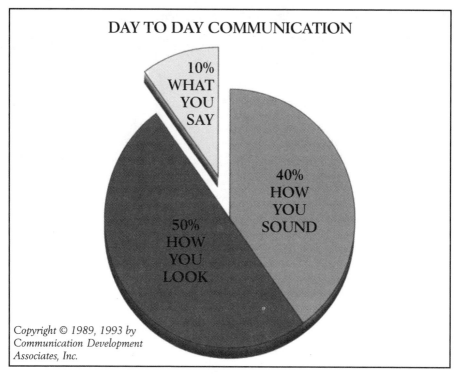

DAY TO DAY COMMUNICATION

10%
WHAT
YOU
SAY

40%
HOW
YOU
SOUND

50%
HOW
YOU
LOOK

Copyright © 1989, 1993 by
Communication Development
Associates, Inc.

Before reading further, check off the items below with which you agree. This list will help you to assess the degree to which you are aware of the importance of the image that you present and the manner in which you communicate.

_____ I know that image is important; therefore, I take special care to dress in a manner consistent with my position.

_____ I think before I speak, taking care to express my message succinctly and effectively.

_____ I pay special attention to grooming: hair, nails, skin, makeup (women), facial hair (men), hands, teeth, etc.

_____ My shoes are always shined.

_____ My body language suggests confidence and poise.

_____ I am no more than fifteen pounds over- or underweight.

_____ My clothes are always freshly pressed when I begin the day.

_____ I know what colors look best on me, and I use that to my advantage.

_____ I am practiced at making presentations in front of a group.

_____ I typically maintain my composure under pressure.

_____ My breath and body are free from unpleasant or offensive odors.

_____ I have no heavy regional accent that might detract from my message.

Image

A rule of thumb in business is that you should not dress for the job that you have, but rather dress for the one that you want. Look around your organization and make a mental note of what people at the next level up from yours are wearing. If you are in a manufacturing environment, you may need to look several levels up. Here is where you'll find your greatest clues for how you should look when you go to work. As much as you may not like it, the fact is that your credibility is, in part, determined by the degree to which you look neat, crisp, professionally attired, and well groomed.

I can recall my mother preaching during my teens that I should always iron my clothes and look in the mirror twice before I went out. After all, she would warn, you never know who you are going to run into (and heaven forbid that I should be a bad reflection on my upbringing!). Arguments always ensued about what was more important—what's on the inside or the outside? Like many teen-agers, I wanted my identity to be based on who I was, not what I was wearing. Many adults today continue to cling to that teenage opinion. They think that what's inside will supersede what's out-side. All these years later I think that Mom was right. We are judged on our appearance first, and on who we are second—if we are fortunate enough to have a second chance. Many times we never have the opportunity for a second chance because we're written off before it comes.

The issue of dress has been the topic of many discussions, of late, particularly among women (men's workplace "uniforms" have remained relatively static). Whereas it was unusual as recently as five years ago to find women dressed in pants in most corpora-tions, today it has become commonplace. When I remarked during a Leadership Skills for Women program (at which all of the par-ticipants were wearing pants) that wearing pants would not likely move them up the corporate ladder, I was met with overwhelming resistance from this group of thirty-something-aged women. Sev-eral protested that their pant outfits were just as expensive and stylish as the dresses worn by the more senior executive women. The cost of your apparel is not as important as the fact that those people in corporations who make hiring and promotion decisions *still* view dresses and skirt suits as more professional. If you are aiming at upward mobility, then you need to adopt a more conser-vative form of dress.

This same topic arose during a casual conversation with a friend who is the director of nursing at a hospital in the Los Angeles area. I commented that the professionalism of nursing seemed to have declined since staff members were no longer required to wear uniforms. Her response, and one with which I agree, is that it is tough to get this generation of employees to conform and that she would rather have a qualified and competent employee than one simply in a white uniform. But the answer isn't that simple. We are always affected by others' perceptions of us. If I had a dollar for each time I told a client, "Perception is reality," I'd be a rich woman.

People will always make assumptions about our competence based on how we look. When a nurse wearing a pair of jeans and a wrinkled blouse appears at my bedside, I somehow believe that she is less competent than someone wearing a starched white uniform. Is this true? Is one really more competent than the other? Of course not. Your image only gets you in the door. As with all of the coaching hints contained in this book, being concerned about your image is meaningless unless you back it up with the goods—capable performance. It makes a lot more sense, however, to start the interaction, whether it be between a nurse and a patient, an interviewer and a candidate, or a sales clerk and a customer, with a leg up. Remember, *you sell the sizzle, not the steak.*

Maybe a real-time example will help here. George was an accounting manager in a small division of a major apparel manufacturer. He grew up in a Pennsylvania coal mining town. He was a son of working-class parents, and the oldest of eight children. His father was the union steward of his mine. Always small for his age, George grew up knowing how to take care of himself with both his fists and his tongue. He could be described as scrappy. He put himself through college at night while working days in a coal mine and, at the same time, raising his own family.

George used to go to work casually dressed in slacks and a short-sleeved shirt—certainly a step up from his mining days. His favorite shoes were a pair of worn, black, soft-sole loafers—the kind that you can't polish (which he obviously didn't care to try). His gray hair was wiry and often unkempt. The guy was brilliant. He was, without a doubt, the most technically competent manager in his division, but a bit of a rebel. He didn't seem to care how others dressed, he didn't need to be like them, and he didn't care about what they thought of him. He knew that he knew his stuff.

When the brass from corporate visited the plant, however, they often ignored George's remarks at meetings and overlooked his valuable suggestions for how to improve bottom-line profits. No matter what he said or how he said it, he couldn't get them to take him seriously. He became increasingly frustrated, belligerent, and intolerant of others. He knew what he was saying made sense, but he couldn't get anyone to listen to him.

One day, after a trip to the corporate offices, George appeared at the office in a navy blue suit, red power tie, well-shined black leather shoes, and with hair neatly styled. He looked ten years younger and every bit the executive that he was. It was interesting to watch his staff interact with him. Although George had not fundamentally changed who he was, others treated him with more respect and deference. After a while, George actually started to act differently. Always a bit brash and too quick to speak in the past, he now weighed his words carefully and took care not to step on too many toes. He gave new meaning to the adage *clothes make the man*. Within two years, George had been promoted out of his small division and into the corporate accounting office. Within five years, he was named vice president of one of the company's up-and-coming divisions.

George is a terrific example of someone who overcame his strengths: technical expertise and staunch independence. No one knows who or what persuaded George to change his dress, and ultimately his behavior, but it prevented George from derailing from an otherwise successful career. Just as coworkers judged George, people judge us every day by how we look. Before we even open our mouths, people have made a mental judgment about us based on how we are dressed, how we carry ourselves, and the demeanor with which we present ourselves. Within thirty seconds, a first impression is formed, so you had better make that the best impression possible—it can make the difference in someone giving you the edge or simply dismissing you.

If you think this isn't right, or that's not how you judge others, think again. We are all guilty of doing the same thing. How many times have you walked up to a particularly well-dressed person in a department store and asked for help, only to be told that he or she didn't work there? Or, have you made an assumption about someone's intelligence based on his or her appearance? Which one of us would look at scientist and author Stephen Hawking, who is wheelchair bound because of his disabilities, and think that he is one of the most brilliant individuals on the face of the earth? This is the same difficult phenomenon that so many people with visible disabilities encounter. Hawking's phenomenal intellectual ability, however, is enough to eclipse his looks. Most of us don't possess such extraordinary talent, and assumptions are made based on very little information. This is why it's so important to leverage image so that the first impression is at worst a neutral one and at best a positive one.

When Less Is More

Is it possible to pay too much attention to your looks and look too good? YES! On a continuum from one to ten, with one being slovenly and ten being glamorous, your appearance should probably be around a seven or eight. Going to work is not going out on a date. Women tend to have more difficulty with this particular problem than men, although I've seen extraordinarily handsome men encounter similar problems.

It is a fine line between well dressed and provocative. Cologne or perfume should be kept to a minimum. Jewelry is meant to complement an outfit. Even though Madison Avenue may dictate pants, short skirt lengths, or garish fashions, it's better to be safe than sorry in most businesses (the fashion and entertainment industries may be the exceptions). Take a moderate approach. One woman executive says that after she's finished dressing in the morning, she stands with her back to the mirror then quickly swings around. If any one thing stands out, she removes it.

Both men and women who are blessed with outstanding looks encounter much the same difficulties. Both men and women can be thought of as dumb blonds. One businessman whom I coached, Jeff, could be described as drop-dead gorgeous. He had a George Hamilton tan, was blond, trim, and impeccably groomed. He could easily pass for a model. During the course of our coaching, Jeff revealed that as a teenager he was the classic ninety-pound weakling. Years of working out and special attention to his looks had transformed this fellow into an Adonis. He admitted that he was obsessed with his looks and never left the house without being the picture of perfection.

Jeff's good looks, combined with native intelligence, landed him in his career as a sales representative for a pharmaceutical firm. His problem was that people didn't take him seriously. They couldn't get past his looks. His colleagues tended to feel somewhat inferior in his presence and sabotaged his efforts by withholding essential information and upstaging him at sales conferences. His defense mechanism for overcoming childhood trauma was getting in his way. The coaching focused extensively on getting Jeff to grow into his adult role and not act out of childhood pain. At the same time, I gave him several suggestions for downplaying his looks in ways that would immediately change how others perceived him: trade in his colored contacts for a pair of glasses; wear plain, inexpensive ties instead of bold ones that called attention; let his hair grow slightly longer and out of its precision cut; and exchange manicures for doing his nails himself.

It wasn't easy for him, but Jeff's desire to avoid derailment gave him the courage to look different. A secondary gain for Jeff from the change in physical appearance was that he no longer needed to be a perfectionist in other ways. He tended to be less cautious in his choice of words and acted more like one of the guys. Within several months, Jeff found people responding to his messages rather than to him as the messenger, and his relationships with his peers began to improve. More important, Jeff felt better about himself.

Like many people who are coached, Jeff was fearful that he would lose his entire identity if he did anything different. In reality, however, coaching, or self-coaching, is about moving from out of bounds to back onto the playing field. It is not about terminating behavior, but rather about turning down the volume on those behaviors that are putting you out of bounds. It is about building complementary skills or behaviors.

What Does Your Body Say About You?

Another aspect of image is body language. Awareness of how you present yourself is critical to avoiding derailment. The three most important areas of which you should be aware are face, hands, and posture. Combined, these can shout that you are fearful and insecure or that you are comfortable and confident.

I once watched an interview with Secretary of State Colin Powell and was struck by how comfortable he seemed with himself, the interviewer, and the world in general. I analyzed what gave me this impression, and it came down to how he looked and sounded (the latter I'll save for a bit later in this chapter). I realized that it boiled down to his face, hands, and posture. When seated, Powell had his hands loosely interlocked in his lap, moved them when he gestured, then unobtrusively returned them to the original position. Throughout the interview, I watched him do this countless times. It gave the impression of comfortable profession-alism. Contrast this with someone who fidgets with a pen, tightly clings to the sides of a chair, or drums his or her fingers. The message somehow just isn't the same.

Then I watched as Powell listened to the interviewer's questions. His eyes stayed on the reporter, his head nodded with understanding and he sat upright, but not rigidly, in his chair. With the toughest of questions Powell remained the same, never shifting in discomfort or wincing at the deep probes. He smiled when it was appropriate and didn't when he wanted to convey that his message was serious. I turned to someone in the room who is less attuned than I am to matters pertaining to image and communication and commented that Powell seemed so comfortable with himself. The response, "I was just thinking the same thing," speaks to the fact that others do notice these things about us. Whether he was trained to do so or it comes naturally to him, Powell provides a model of confidence and ease with himself and others.

Smiling presents a unique problem for women and people of certain cultures. In another workshop on leadership skills for women, a petite woman engineer working for a major airline proclaimed that no one ever took her seriously, and she said it with a big smile on her face. Everyone in the room laughed because they could immediately see the problem. Smiles should be used to communicate happiness, levity, or joking, not serious messages. The smile totally diminished the serious nature of the woman's message. Unfortunately, women frequently use smiling as a means of softening their messages to avoid appearing too strong. Most women could smile less, choose the times when they smile more carefully, and avoid using a smile to ward off criticism.

Paradoxically, smiling can be used as a valuable tool for both men and women in their repertoires of skills—provided the feedback that you get from others is that you're too serious, staid, or intimidating. This was the case with a man I coached not long ago. The intensity with which he delivered his messages frequently overwhelmed his colleagues. He was tall, assertive, smart, and always on target, but people were intimidated by him and wouldn't respond when he asked for their opinions of his ideas. I knew that he recently became a father and asked how he talked to his child. With this, a big smile came to his face with a softness that warmed my heart. When I suggested that he think about the child when speaking with his colleagues he looked at me incredulously. Certainly I couldn't be serious. He thought that people would perceive him as being too soft. In fact, his other characteristics would overshadow this slight change in facial expression. This was another example of adding to the repertoire rather than taking something away. With this change, and some other coaching hints that he practiced, people began to describe him as more approachable and easier to talk to.

Posture is yet another means by which we reveal our self-esteem. How many times have you seen someone in a meeting slouched down in a chair or hunched over the table leaning on one elbow? Or, have you ever noted a statuesque woman who walks a bit hunched over so as not to appear too tall? Although rigidity is not the order of the day, good posture conveys the message that I am someone to contend with. Your posture increases the perception of credibility and confidence before you ever open your mouth.

One last suggestion about how you look. This one comes from communication specialist Dr. Allen Weiner, who was mentioned earlier in this chapter. When people stand in front of a room making a presentation or being introduced, they often appear uncomfortable, largely because they don't know what to do with their hands. They will put them in their pockets, fold them in front of them (Weiner calls this the fig leaf approach), or clasp them behind their backs—all the while looking none too comfortable. Weiner suggests that hands be kept with fingers loosely clasped at about the same height you would hold a glass while standing at a cocktail party. Similarly, when gesturing in front of groups, hands should be kept at about the same height and moved no wider apart than as if you were holding a basketball. The exception being when speaking before large groups where more pronounced gestures are required and would not likely detract from the message.

Communication

Let's revisit another set of debates. The first is the television debate that took place during the 1988 presidential campaign when

Dan Quayle ran for vice president as George Bush's running mate. At one point, he found himself debating his challenger, Lloyd Bentsen. In contrast to the stately and comfortable Bentsen, Quayle appeared anxious, his speaking voice was hesitant, his messages were incoherent, and his body language lacked confidence. With the sound turned off on the television, Quayle paled next to his elder colleague. With the sound on it was even worse. He looked and sounded nothing like the seasoned, statesmanlike vice presidents to whom we'd become accustomed. Regardless of your political persuasion, you must admit that Lyndon Johnson, Hubert Humphrey, Nelson Rockefeller, and George Bush all presented themselves confidently and credibly.

Four years later, Quayle was on the podium debating Al Gore and Ross Perot's running mate, Captain James B. Stockdale. After just a few minutes, I thought to myself, "This guy's been coached!" His positions on the issues were clearly stated, he used emphatic gestures to punctuate his remarks, and his body language was relaxed and controlled. Perhaps, in his role as vice president, he simply had become more comfortable in front of the cameras, but throughout his tenure he had been prone to such malapropisms and misstatements that it's doubtful that experience alone could be the reason for the transformation.

Dan Quayle provides us with a particularly poignant example of how early coaching can help to prevent derailment. Quayle was coached too late. Had he been coached early in the 1988 campaign, perhaps his term in office would have been significantly different and both he *and* Bush would have won in 1992. When it comes to communication, it is important to remember that we live in a sound-bite society. We measure people's abilities and judge their effectiveness in brief bits and pieces that we absorb during a moment in time. Once we *look* the part, the next important step is to *sound* the part.

Communication is made up of a number of components: accent or dialect, thought patterns as expressed in speech, and the actual sound of the speech itself. Each contributes to the overall impression of knowledge and credibility. Remember the pie chart at the beginning of this chapter: 50 percent of the impressions others have of you is based on how you look and 40 percent on how you sound. Only 10 percent is based on what you actually say. The importance of how you sound is embodied in a Chinese saying: "May you have a wonderful idea and not be able to convince anyone of it."

The Sexes' Differences in Communication

Before going further, I should mention that there are well-defined differences between how men and women communicate. My own experience indicates that many women tend to use words and sentence structures that are less direct than those of their male counterparts and, therefore, these women are less likely to be heard or taken seriously.

For example, I was playing tennis one morning and my ball went into the next court. I waited until the two men playing had finished their point, then said, "I think that's my ball behind you." Now, I didn't just think it was my ball, I knew full well that it was my ball because I watched it roll to a stop. Instead of just tossing it back, one of the men asked, "What are you playing with?" (referring to the brand of ball). He looked at the ball and then asked, "What number?" I realized that had I simply called over "Thank you," and nodded toward my ball, which is the custom on tennis courts, the entire scenario would have been different. By adding the words I think to my message I conveyed uncertainty, when in fact I wasn't the least bit uncertain. In essence, I caused him to doubt my credibility.

The tennis courts may be an odd place to identify differences in the sexes' communication, but the differences occur in boardrooms as well and make a significant difference in whose ideas are ultimately acknowledged and utilized. Here are five fatal errors that I've noticed that women make more frequently than men when they communicate.

1. **Asking permission.** Although this may appear on the surface to be fairly benign, it in fact puts the woman in a subservient position. In our society, we expect children to ask permission, not adults. When women ask permission, they set themselves up to hear no.

Example: Would it be all right if I took next Wednesday off for my son's graduation? In the same situation a man would say: Just thought I'd let you know, I'll be out next Wednesday.

He assumes that if there is a problem with this his boss will tell him. This very situation arose during a team building that I did in the Midwest several years ago. The women complained that they were expected to ask permission to exceed their monthly budgets, but their male colleagues just informed the boss of such an occurrence. To the boss's credit, he admitted that he did subconsciously expect women to ask permission and changed his expectations.

2. Using preambles. Words soften a message, not strengthen it. The longer you talk, the more you dilute an effective message and lose the attention of the listener. Women soften their messages by using more words when fewer will do.

Example: Would this be a good time to talk to you about something? Thanks. Well, I've been going over our accounts payable system. Did you know that this system was devised over fifteen years ago? That's an awfully long time to be using the same system. A friend of mine over at XYZ Company tells me that in the same time span they've revised their system four or five times. Ours is really antiquated. Well, maybe not antiquated, but certainly in need of looking at. Anyway, where was I? Oh, yeah, improving the accounts payable system. It would appear to me that one of the problems lies in how payables are logged when they arrive. We get so many dunning notices and even wind up paying a lot in late fees because of it. Last month alone we must have paid nearly 5 percent of the total payables in late fees. I'm not really sure why this happens, since we've got plenty of people in the department working on it....

At this point the boss wants to scream, "What's your point?"—and rightly so. Far too many words were used before ever getting to the main point, and more important, the causes of and solutions to the problem. Managers want their staff members to solve problems, not create more. This woman suffers from a serious case of the preambles. How could she strengthen her message? Perhaps like this:

I need about five minutes of your time to discuss something important. There's clearly a problem in our accounts payable system. Bills are long overdue, and we're unnecessarily paying excessive late fees. I just wanted you to know that I'm working on a system to revise the current process, so if you have any ideas for shortening the payment cycle based on your experience you might want to join our brainstorming session next Friday.

Crisp. Clear. To the point. Within thirty seconds the boss knows what the problem is, that it's going to be fixed, and that he or she is invited to be part of the process of solving the problem.

---

3. Asking questions instead of making statements. This technique was invented by our foremothers as a means of getting their two cents in without appearing too aggressive. In business, however, a woman leaves herself open to a critique of the idea, rather than a discussion of the value of it, when she couches her opinions in the form of questions.

Example: What would you think about moving toward a smorgasbord approach to employee benefits?

The savvy listener knows that this really is not a question. The speaker has an idea that she is trying to further, but by putting it as a question she obscures that fact. In contrast, this approach would be much more effective: It seems to me it's time to move in a new direction with regard to employee benefits. I think the smorgasbord approach merits examination for the following reasons....

The second example states the case, provides backup data, and expects a discussion based on merit rather than on the whim or goodwill of the boss.

---

4. Apologizing. Women apologize significantly more frequently than men, even when no apology is necessary. A woman's self-image is increasingly eroded with each apology.

Example: A boss gives his female assistant a large graphics project with very clear directions. She follows those directions to a T and presents him with the results before the deadline. He looks at the project and says it's not how he wants it. He then proceeds to change the instructions and asks that it be redone. Nine times out often, the woman will say, "I'm sorry, I didn't realize that's what you wanted. I'll redo it."

Don't get me wrong. There's a time and place for apologies. That time and place, however, is when a large, costly, or high-profile mistake is made. Even then, men are hard-pressed to get the apology through their lips. Women's apologies are frequently inappropriate and demean them. My most frequent coaching suggestion for women is stop apologizing.

5. Explaining ad nauseam. This is at the other end of the preamble. A woman has now asked permission, couched her opinion in the form of a question, used a lot of words to get to her point, perhaps apologized in the process—and now she explains some more! Now, I must admit that this is not always her fault. Especially when she's communicating with a man. Many times men will fail to use body language, such as head nods or verbal remarks, that indicate that they have heard what's been said. Therefore, the woman talks more, thinking that she hasn't been understood. She explains her point two or three times, waiting for some acknowledgment of the message. Women, take care to say it once. Let silence be a powerful tool in prodding the other person into responding; you are not responsible for the entire communication.

With very subtle modifications, women can change the manner in which they are perceived. Here are eight things that *both* men and women can do to put more power behind their messages:

1. Make certain your handshake is firm. The handshake can be the very first thing you use to convey the message "I'm someone to be contended with." Women have asked me if it's appropriate for them to extend their hand first. Absolutely! Being the first to extend your hand in greeting, combined with a firm handshake, communicates control and confidence. Use them to your advantage.

2. Dress appropriately. "Dress for the job you want, not the job you have" remains your best guide for being taken seriously.

3. Use "I" statements. Don't be afraid to begin your sentences with "I." What many of us learned in grade school about never starting a sentence with "I" (because it sounds too egotistical) doesn't hold true in business. If you are giving your own opinion, then own it with statements like "I believe," "I contend," "I would expect," or "I feel strongly."

4. Make direct eye contact. Although you don't want to stare someone down and make them uncomfortable by never averting your eyes from theirs, looking someone directly in the eye when you are giving your opinion does add a certain amount of credibility to your message. When someone is able to look us in the eye, we believe he or she is speaking the truth.

5. Know your subject. You've already heard it several times in this book: "Nothing takes the place of technical competence." When you know your subject, you speak with a certainty that is impossible to convey when you're unsure. You can build a base of technical knowledge that adds to your confidence by getting a college degree, taking classes or workshops, reading technical journals, or networking with other professionals in your field.

6. Pepper your conversation with the other person's name. When you want to get children to listen to you, you use their names when speaking to them. A similar tactic works equally well in business conversations. You don't want to sound like a used car salesperson, but you do want to keep the other person's attention.

7. Make affirmative statements. Instead of couching your comments in the form of questions, turn them into affirmative statements, beginning with an "I" message. Change "What would you think if we" to "I think that we should." The latter conveys much more certainty and influence.

8. Get to the point. Dr. Allen Weiner developed a technique that he calls "bottom-line communication." His research indicates that when you make your main point the first thing that comes out of your mouth, and support it with several key facts, you are more likely to avoid using preambles and explaining ad nauseam. Don't obscure the most important part of your message with a lot of words; give it clearly up front.

To learn more about self-defeating behaviors that contribute to the derailment of women, look for my new book, *Quit Bein' a Girl: 101 Dumb Ways Smart Women Sabotage their Careers*, to be published in 2003 by Warner Books.

Accents and Dialects

The issue of accents and dialects is a sensitive one that needs to be considered in light of our rich heritage as a melting pot, welcoming of people from all nations and backgrounds. Although some may find it offensive, or inappropriate for discussion here, the words of my friend and colleague Susan Picascia ring in my ear: *A good coach has the courage to speak the unspoken.* Therefore, I would find it an unconscionable error of omission to avoid a discussion about accents and dialects.

As the complexion of society changes, both literally and figuratively, so do our impressions about expecting others to look and sound the same in the microcosm called work. If the stereotypes of fifty years ago prevailed, the workforce would still be predominantly white and male. Similarly, if we continue to perpetuate the stereotype of how people should sound in the workplace, everyone would be accentless—sounding somewhat like newscasters who are hired partly for their ability to speak without an accent. The goal of this discussion is not to encourage homogeneity, but rather to illuminate the ways in which strong accents and dialects can be potential career derailers.

As a Jewish woman, I am all too aware of the fact that what appear to be legitimate workplace expectations can be guises for prejudice and discrimination. Likewise, I know that I must constantly be vigilant about crossing the line between expression of my individuality and being heard and seen in the most favorable light possible so that I can achieve my goals. Just as I wouldn't wear blue jeans to a meeting with a new client, in that same meeting I wouldn't use the Yiddish jargon that I learned growing up. On the other hand, even if it might in some way damage my career, I wouldn't hesitate to decline an invitation to a private club from which women or people of color are excluded. The goal is to increase the likelihood of success by playing the corporate game within commonly accepted bounds, *without compromising your principles or ethical standards.*

There are numerous examples of successful people who have strong accents. As the United States continues to establish multinational firms, those numbers will increase and bring with them greater tolerance for other than "newscaster" accents. I simply ask you to consider how your accent or dialect might be perceived by others. Can you be clearly understood? Do you use phrases or jargon that, while acceptable in your neighborhood, are not commonly used by your workplace peers? Does your accent diminish your self-confidence when speaking before groups or at meetings? Do you feel as if your vocabulary is not sufficient for fluid conversation?

If you answer yes to any of these questions, or if you believe that your manner of speaking has impeded your progress, then you may want to consider doing something about it. Accent reduction schools and elocution classes are available in most major cities. Conversely, if you believe it is too great a compromise to refrain from using certain jargon or to reduce your accent, don't do it. Like all of the other suggestions contained in this book, it is one more factor to consider in your effort to avoid derailment.

Sam was on the verge of derailment but didn't have a clue why. Neither did his boss. She asked me to coach him, saying his career was stalled despite the fact that he was a good, solid performer. Higher-ups in the European shipping company where he worked began asking that Sam be excluded from certain meetings, particularly those at which clients were present. No matter how hard she tried to find out what the problem was, people were never forthcoming with an answer.

My first meeting with Sam took place in his office in Miami Beach. When his secretary ushered me in, Sam stood and extended his hand to greet me. He was well dressed, neatly groomed, and had an engaging smile. So far so good. When he began to speak, however, the problem became readily apparent, because Sam spoke with a thick Cuban accent. He also spoke quickly and in long rambling sentences so that it was difficult to understand him and follow his train of thought. Several times during the conversation, I had to ask him to slow down.

We then proceeded to a nearby upscale restaurant for lunch. People appeared to know Sam and greeted him with friendly waves. Another point in his favor, I noted. He is a relationship builder. Over lunch I listened to Sam talk about his career, how he got to where he was, what he thought might be the problem, and how he was now working harder than ever in hopes of turning the situation around. I also observed his behavior as he ate his meal. Strike two. He began by tucking the linen napkin into his collar, then breaking and buttering a roll before the bread plates were on the table, making an awful mess in the process. During the meal, he talked with his mouth full of food, unaware of how it might appear to others.

Over the course of several coaching sessions I learned more about Sam. He was from a poor family who emigrated from Cuba in the 1950s. His parents believed in education and worked hard to make certain that their son could go to college. He was the superstar of the family, the only one to have a blossoming career. In turn, he worked long, hard hours to get where he was and to feel worthy of the efforts his parents had made on his behalf. He truly believed that working harder, turning up the volume on what he did best, was the answer to his problems.

Between sessions I spoke with Sam's boss to determine whether my assessment that productivity was not the problem was in fact true. She confirmed my hunch that he was always willing to go the extra mile and produced what was expected of him and more. Why, I wondered, was no one willing to tell him that his accent, rambling monologues, and table manners were about to derail him? Speaking with his boss a bit longer, I found out that Sam had worked for her at her previous job as well. In total, they had worked together for more than twenty years. She was so accustomed to him and his habits that she never noticed that he had reached a stage in his career where they were no longer acceptable. She was too close to the situation. As for the higher-ups, they probably were too embarrassed, or fearful of being called snobby, to help Sam to get back in bounds.

It is one of the tougher jobs of a coach to talk about behaviors as personal as accents and table manners. It's a lot easier to suggest letting your hair grow longer. Nevertheless, Sam was coached in these areas and he responded immediately. He enrolled in an accent-reduction class, followed my instructions for table manners, and took care to speak in shorter, better-defined sentences. Unfortunately, his senior management wouldn't give him a chance and directed his boss to fire Sam, which she did with great personal anguish. The coaching was not wasted, however. As often happens when individuals are *freed up to find new opportunities* (fired), they go on to find a position better suited for them. Such is the case with Sam. He is now back on his career track in another organization that highly values his abilities and appreciates his efforts. Without the coaching, he might have found himself in the same situation over and over again until he overcame his strengths.

Thought Patterns

As I mentioned in Sam's case, the ability to speak cogently and concisely contributes to others' perception of us. Except in unusual circumstances when the speaker or material being conveyed is extraordinarily compelling, people can listen to only relatively brief, clearly ordered messages and actually comprehend them. Countless messages are lost entirely when the speaker rambles on long after his or her point has been made. In videotaping workplace interactions, I'm struck by the number of times a speaker makes a point, then explains it, makes the point again, and explains it once more. As the camera pans the room, it reveals undeniably bored, uninterested faces straining to listen politely until the speaker has finished.

The person who rambles also loses his or her audience. Returning to Colin Powell for a moment, it was clear from the interview I saw that his credibility is in part due to his speech patterns. Each time he was asked a question he directly answered the question using clear, succinct sentences. If he didn't have an answer, he said so. There was no fat to be trimmed and no misunderstanding about where he stood.

Here is an example of how disorganized thought patterns ineffectively convey the message, lose the listener's interest, and diminish the speaker's credibility in the process:

Boss: Do you think we should change our marketing strategy next year?

Employee: Well, that's a good question. I guess there are a number of different ways of looking at it. If we were to continue along the same path we're on, that is if we were to not make any changes that might upset the apple cart, it's possible, maybe we might—that is, some people think that we're going along the right path now and with a few minor variations could, well, there's a chance that the numbers might increase a bit over last year's sales, but I'm not really sure my-

> self. It seems to me that we've changed the strategy a number of times in the past year or two, well actually maybe five years, and in most cases, with a few exceptions, the results were average, so you could say they were effective, but nothing really spectacular happened. On the other hand, take a look at what our competitors have done for the past few years and it looks like they're marginally edging us out. Of course, there's ABC Company, which did a lot worse than we did, but that's only because they sold off one of their cash cows. So, I guess it might be worth a try to.

Even writing this script was painful, let alone listening to it! Yet it's not so far from how people answer questions every day in corporate America. The major mistakes made by the speaker include:

- Failure to express a point of view
- Soft word choices (e.g., maybe, I guess, we might)
- Rambling thought process
- Incomplete sentences and ideas
- Too much playing "devil's advocate"

Let's replay the same scenario, this time using a more Powellesque approach:

> *Boss:* Do you think we should change our marketing strategy next year?
>
> *Employee:* [Pause to think] Definitely not. Our current strategy has only been in place for less than a year and is already yielding very promising results. There's been a 10 percent increase in sales despite a sluggish market, which forecasts well for next year when the market is expected to pick up.

Who seems more credible to you? The first or second employee? In fewer than fifty words, the second employee clearly communicated his or her opinion as well as provided a rationale for it. Sam was coached to do the same thing with four pretty darn simple steps:

1. (Pretty) Pause a moment to collect your thoughts. Don't answer immediately.
2. (Darn) Directly answer the question that was asked.

3. (Simple) Support your answer with facts or knowledge.
4. (Steps) Stop.

Getting and Keeping Audience Attention

According to Shakespeare, all the world's a stage, and we humans are merely players. The workplace can be considered just another set and scene. For most people, however, the anticipation of making a presentation, be it to a group of five people or fifty, engenders a sense of fear second only to that of dying on the list of things Americans fear most. Yet we present ourselves and our ideas all the time. The next time you have to give a public speech, think of it as actors do—as an opportunity to create a special way of sending a message and make a lasting, and positive, impression.

The following are a few simple coaching hints, recommended by Dr. Douglas Andrews, a University of Southern California professor and communications coach, to help you become an influential player on the corporate stage.

1. Never give a presentation you haven't prepared. The saying *chance favors the prepared mind* is never more true than when speaking before an audience. Unless you are one of the few gifted people who can speak extemporaneously in front of groups, you can't afford to wait until the day of your presentation to prepare. Even if you only jot down a few notes on index cards, you're more likely to remember the key points and avoid aimless rambling. When planning on speaking to a few people, mentally rehearse what you plan to say, picture people listening attentively to you, and know when to stop.

2. Practice to music. If you tend to make a monotone, slow-paced presentation, begin practicing to a tune with an up-beat tempo. Don't use a Sousa march, but choose something that will help you keep a quick pace. Try using a metronome to overcome either slow and plodding presentations or the inclination to speak too fast. Keep in mind that when you speak too fast it can be a sign of lack of confidence. It gives the impression that you don't want to take up too much of the listener's time. Tempo is an important determinant of the impression one has of your message.

3. Break up your presentation. Another way of avoiding long monologues is to break up your presentation into smaller pieces and focus on changing one aspect of each piece when it's delivered. For example, make a notation to slow down during one particular piece, to speak more quickly during the next, and to use hand gestures during the next. Alternate these behaviors throughout the presentation until they look and sound natural. Underline words that you want to emphasize and indicate when you want to look directly at the faces in the crowd.

4. Use pace to alter pitch. If your voice unnaturally goes up several octaves the moment you speak in front of a room full of people, or when the spotlight shifts to you during a meeting, try speaking a bit more slowly. As you slow down your speech, your voice tends to drop as well.

5. Use short words. Giving a presentation is not the time to impress others with your command of the English language by using long, obscure words. Not only is your audience likely to think it pretentious, you're more likely to forget or mispronounce them. Don't feel compelled to use a dollar word when a quarter one will do. It's easier for the listeners to process the message, it doesn't challenge them, and you tend to enunciate shorter words clearly.

6. Use body English. Don't forget the importance of body language. Good posture, direct eye contact, and subtle gestures combine to give the impression of confidence and credibility.

7. Use a camcorder. Here's a place to make good use of the family video camera. Videotape yourself practicing a presentation. Critically assess what you can do to be more effective, and don't be afraid to ask the family for feedback. Sometimes they'll give you better coaching hints than anyone else!

Like it or not, the image that we portray and the communication style that we use are the first two things that others notice about us—and they contribute significantly to the impression that we make. Fortunately, they are also two of the more simple factors to address when considering how to avoid premature derailment. Think of them as tools that you can use to your advantage. Develop your own unique style, but fine-tune that style so that it works for you rather than against you.

Strategies for Improving Image

1. Get a good barber or hairdresser.

2. Don't scrimp when it comes to spending money on work clothes.

3. Never leave the house before looking in the mirror twice.

4. Manicure your nails once a week.

5. Check the shine, heels, and soles of your shoes, especially before an important meeting.

6. Use smiles, head nods, and other facial expressions to soften messages.

7. Use appropriate pacing and gestures to strengthen messages.

8. Read *Letitia Baldrige's New Complete Guide to Executive Manners* (see page 208).

9. If there's something about your appearance that you're so self-conscious of that it affects your self-confidence, have it colored, cut, plugged, removed, lifted, tucked, or otherwise surgically altered!

10. If your corrected vision leaves you with Coke bottles, switch to contact lenses or high-index glasses.

11. Exercise regularly—it improves your physical health, self-image, and outlook.

12. Absent intervening medical factors, try to stay within ten to fifteen pounds of your ideal body weight.

13. Dress for the job you want, not the job you have.

14. Wear knee-length socks or other appropriate hosiery.

Strategies for Improving Communication

15. Join Toastmaster's International (see page 204) to gain composure and confidence when speaking before groups.

16. Take an acting class to increase fluidity of expression.

17. Use a firm, "I'm someone to be contended with" handshake.

18. Think about what you want to say before you say it.

19. Consider an accent-reduction or elocution class.

20. Practice important presentations in advance.

21. Use mental imagery to "see" what you're going to say and picture a positive response from the audience.

22. When using notes during a presentation, use index cards instead of sheets of paper (the cards will be less conspicuous in the event that your hands begin to shake).

23. Use simple, easy-to-understand words.

24. Use the four Pretty Darn Simple Steps to mentally prepare your responses.

Insensitivity to the Reactions of Others

Strategy: *Craft a Winning Personality*

The CEO of an internationally known manufacturing firm recently mentioned in passing that his highly competent, well-educated staff would soon need coaching and training on how to be less "technocratic." Because the company is a leader in its field and has always prided itself on choosing the cream of the crop from the most prestigious business schools, this came as somewhat of a surprise. When I probed into the CEO's sudden change of heart, he explained that his customers had begun complaining about the condescending and arrogant attitudes that his staff brought to their interactions. In fact, they were in jeopardy of losing their biggest client because of it. In spite of this senior management team's technical competence, the customer doesn't want to work with them.

If you are eccentric (but smart), difficult (but gifted), or an oddball (but a whiz), you're destined to derail. You can't stay competitive if you do not have a winning personality. This chapter is about the behaviors that comprise a winning personality. Difficult to measure and describe, personality is noticed and judged in nearly every interaction. A pleasing personality includes having self-confidence and insight into how you affect others, relating to all kinds of people and making them feel at ease around you, knowing that you don't have to control everyone and everything, striving to act with integrity at all times, treating others the way you would want to be treated, and acting graciously even in the most difficult situations.

_____ The following checklist should help you assess your own personality.

_____ I am aware of how others perceive me.

_____ I keep my personal moods out of the office.

_____ Others would describe me as even-tempered.

_____ It's more important to me that the project gets completed than for me to get credit for its completion.

_____ I generally tell people where I stand on various issues so that they're not left guessing.

_____ People have told me that they enjoy working with me.

_____ I am generally aware of other people's moods.

_____ I can laugh at my mistakes when the situation calls for it.

_____ I know the difference between being assertive and being aggressive and typically opt for the former.

_____ It's hard to recall a time when I've embarrassed someone by one of my remarks.

_____ I look waiters and waitresses in the eye when I speak to them.

_____ I give others feedback as objectively as possible and always in private.

When you think about successful people with winning personalities, television hosts Katie Couric and Oprah Winfrey come to mind, as do movie directors Ron Howard and Stephen Spielberg, Ogilvy & Mather CEO Shelly Lazarus, and British Prime Minister Tony Blair. No doubt someone on this list is one you might like to sit down and chat with. Although it is difficult to know how public figures act in private, these examples appear to share the common traits of a strong sense of self, commitment to a cause greater than themselves, and a fundamental respect for all those whom they encounter on life's path. It is what makes up what is frequently called *character*. Legendary basketball coach John Wooden once said, "Be more concerned with your character than with your reputation. Your character is what you really are, while your reputation is merely what others think you are."

Conversely, when you think about successful people with offensive or abrasive personalities, you might name radio hosts Rush

Limbaugh and Howard Stern, politicians like Newt Gingrich, and entrepreneurs Leona Helmsley and Donald Trump. Their own needs precede their deeds and the needs of others. They may espouse a philosophy of benevolence, but it fails to ring true and is contradicted by their actions. I once observed tennis legend Martina Navratilova at a fundraiser. As you might imagine, people were thrilled with the opportunity to meet her and many approached her to ask for an autograph. My high regard for her diminished with one act. When she obviously became tired of signing, she rolled her eyes and gave a disgusted look to one of her admirers who dared to ask for an autograph. The person walked away looking hurt and embarrassed. It was a reminder that it takes a lifetime to build a positive image, but only a moment to have it tarnished in the eyes of others.

The question that most frequently arises in discussions about character is, *can character be developed or is it something that you're born with?* My own position is that not only can character be developed, but most people do develop it and are not born with it. It is unlikely that Oprah Winfrey was born with character. If, anything, quite the opposite. We know that Winfrey experienced a troubled childhood, was raised by a number of different family members, and was sexually abused by male relatives. Although it could be argued that she was born with the ability to overcome adversity, it is just as likely that she *learned* how to do so. Oprah Winfrey is just one reason why I believe that a winning personality can be developed. Another reason is that I've seen people develop it— people like Joe.

To Change or Not to Change—That Is the Question

When Joe's boss told him that he had to go for coaching if he had any hope of keeping his job, Joe specifically requested that I be his coach. I had met Joe when we'd both served on the board of a non-profit agency. When I first got the call I wasn't too excited about coaching Joe. I had watched him in action, and he could be brutally indifferent to the feelings of others and intellectually snobbish. All in all, Joe was not a pleasant fellow to be around.

During our first coaching session, Joe started as he frequently did, by intellectualizing everything going on at the government agency in which he worked. He shared with me his analysis (which appeared to be correct) of this person's behavior and that person's motives until I finally asked him to stop. I looked at him and said, "I already know you're a really smart guy. You don't have to prove it to me, but I'm wondering why you have the need to prove it to yourself." Joe stopped dead in his tracks. After a split second of shock, a boyish grin came across his face. It was as if he was caught doing something wrong. 'Is it that obvious?" he replied.

Like so many smart people, Joe used his intelligence as a weapon against other people. Growing up smart isn't always easy. In fact, in many public schools, it is more socially acceptable to be developmentally slow than smart. Smart children are often the targets of ridicule and derision by their classmates. Joe's defense mechanism for childhood survival was to keep people at a distance with his carefully chosen, but cutting, words and indifferent attitude. He knew that he could survive using his intelligence, so he did not consider how he affected those around him until his personality caught up with him. He made the mistake of embarrassing his boss's boss with one of his offhand remarks in a meeting, and his intelligence was suddenly no longer the shield that protected him. It was his worst nightmare.

Luckily, Joe turned out to be ripe for coaching. His wife had recently been complaining about the same qualities of which I was making him conscious. His job and his marriage would be in jeopardy if he didn't learn to act differently, win back people he had offended, and avoid making the same mistakes in the future. Joe's coaching plan involved a few simple but specific steps, which he followed religiously.

To begin with, he was coached never to be the first one to speak in meetings. His quick responses often precluded other people from making their points and gave the impression that he was grandstanding. Instead, he was to use the techniques of active listening described in Reason #1, Overlooking the Importance of People, to hear what other people were saying.

The next step was to always tie his own ideas together with the ideas expressed by other people. In other words, he had to seek similarities between his ideas and others' ideas—something that would be impossible to do if he weren't really listening. By seeing similarities he could assure that everyone walked away from a problem-solving session feeling like a winner.

The third coaching hint was to count slowly to three before answering any questions directed to him. This would diminish the appearance of being flip or rash in his comments, give him more time to prepare a thoughtful response, and reduce the inclination toward sarcasm that often accompanied his quicker responses. In the end, his responses might contain the same content, but the moment of hesitation changed the perception of his being a "loose cannon."

Within weeks, Joe changed noticeably. When his boss was called for input about Joe's progress, he said that Joe was like a new man and that the people working with him could see the difference, although they didn't know to what to attribute it. Joe avoided derailment by adding to his skill set and, he tells me tongue in cheek, avoided divorce by practicing the same behaviors at home. Joe approached the coaching hints in much the same way as he approached intellectual challenges—with tenacity and perseverance. He didn't particularly care to know much about why he acted as he did; he only knew that he didn't want to derail and was willing to do whatever it took to avoid it—and he did.

Not all people are as successful as Joe, however, when it comes to matters of character or personality. In contrast, another fellow, George, was advised to get coaching for much the same reason as Joe. In his case, though, he had already been sued for sexual harassment by one of his subordinates. George claimed that all that he did was make some innocent jokes, at which everyone laughed. He was the proverbial bull in a china shop. George was always offending someone with his jokes or casual remarks but never noticed that people didn't like it. Sure they might have laughed, perhaps uncomfortably, at the moment, but people tended to avoid him so that they did not fall victim to his thoughtlessness.

When George was asked why he thought his boss wanted him coached, his reply was that people in his department were overly sensitive, and he supposed he should be more careful. When asked what the value of being more careful might be, he said that it would get his boss off his back. It appeared from the outset that George was not a particularly good candidate for coaching. His inability to see how his behavior affected others, and the lack of desire to correct it for that same reason, made it virtually impossible for George to change. The way he saw it, the rest of the world was against poor, innocent George, a perception that George just couldn't, or wouldn't, overcome. George will spend his life feeling persecuted, never realizing that he and the world interact, and that it is not just the world acting on George. Within a year George was "made redundant" during a corporate downsizing.

George and Joe are representative of the differences between people who respond favorably to coaching and those who don't— people who have the insight to see how their behaviors get in the way of long-term success and people who can't (or won't) admit that their own behaviors play any part in their career difficulties. It appears that 75 percent of the people who are coached are able to make significant changes in their work and their lives as the result of coaching; the other 25 percent do not. It is most likely that if you are still reading this book, you are in the 75 percent category.

Successful behavioral change, especially in the area of character or personality, requires a foundation of emotional stability. People who are so damaged by early childhood experiences that make it impossible for them to see how these experiences affect the present have a difficult time making the leap of faith that coaching requires. It is common to hear people express fear about changing. The major fear is that changing certain aspects of one's behavior will cause them to be less effective. After all, for the largest portion of their professional lives they have relied on one or two strengths, and now they are being asked to balance those strengths with complementary skills. The request evokes uncertainty and anxiety. It also brings up fears that even a single change will set off a chain of life changes. A strong foundation of emotional stability, however, enables them to have enough faith in the coaching process to at least test out the coaching hints. Absent this foundation, the request for change is just too great.

The Five Most Deadly Character Traits

There are five character traits that most often lead to career derailment. Of course, there may be others, but these are the ones that seem to trip people up most frequently. They include:

1. Condescension

2. Abrasiveness

3. Belligerence

4. Blaming

5. Insensitivity

Each one alone is bad enough, but when one person possesses all five traits (and some people do), it's deadly. You may wonder how anyone with all five characteristics could survive for long in an organization. It happens in a number of circumstances. The most common scenario is that the person possesses a unique skill set that is difficult to find or reproduce. The person usually knows this and it only serves to exacerbate the offensive behaviors. He or she has no reason to change because the behavior gets rewarded along with the valued skills. The obvious problem here is that sooner or later someone with the same skills, but not the offensive behavior, comes along and looks mighty attractive to the organization.

A second scenario is that the organizational culture actually *values* the offensive behavior. I once conducted a management skills program for a group like this. It was the sales department of a well-known manufacturing firm, and out of a group of twenty-five participants, twenty of them possessed each of the five deadly character traits. These twenty people would ignore the ground rules that the group set for itself, come to group sessions late, talk over one another, one-up each other, and, in general, act abrasive, belligerent, condescending, and insensitive. When confronted with their behavior, they blamed the other five for not being enough fun! I'd never seen anything like it. When I spoke with the department manager on the lunch break, he actually seemed proud of his team's behavior. He grinned and said that they were on their best behavior. I'd hate to see their worst behavior!

This particular organization isn't alone. There are others where specific, inappropriate behaviors are viewed as simply eccentricities of the company and its employees. Their customers and clients are aware of the behavior, as are candidates applying for jobs and others in their industry. Because of some unusual or special service or product that they provide, they can get away with it. These organizations don't thrive for long, however. The inappropriateness of their actions eventually catches up with them. At some point another company provides the same services but without the offensive behavior.

A good example of an organizational culture that condoned inappropriate behavior is the phone company. When AT&T was the only show in town for long-distance service, customers had to tolerate abrasive and condescending telephone operators. To add insult to injury, their prices were exorbitant. Once deregulation became a fact of life, the story changed. Service has improved and prices have declined in the past decade.

Here are some examples of how the five deadly character traits play out in real life and people who derailed because of them.

Condescension

Condescension is characterized by giving others the feeling that you're placating them or doing them a favor. People who are condescending hold themselves above others due to real or perceived status or privilege. Whether or not they really are of a higher status isn't the point. There are people of the highest social standing who are not condescending and people of the lowest who are.

There is a type of social clustering that occurs in the workplace that reflects the clustering in other circumstances. At work, people who have similar interests will have lunch together or do social things together. However, if common courtesy is not extended to those outside the group due to status, sex, race, ethnicity, or some other subjective variable, clustering becomes condescension. People who avoid derailment are the ones who treat the janitor with the same dignity and respect they offer to the company president. These are the people who really see the service people around them and believe that there are no worthless jobs or people.

Whether or not she actually was, the late Princess Diana gave the impression she was not the least bit condescending, whereas her ex-husband, Prince Charles, was accused of being not only condescending but also cold and aloof. It has only been since the passing of Diana that the future King has been forced to face the issue of his public image—and by all accounts seems to be doing a fairly good job of turning perceptions around.

Abrasiveness

Abrasive behaviors involve acting out against other people. Whereas condescending people are, at times, passive-aggressive (appearing benign on the surface, but subversively acting in their own best interest), abrasive people are just plain aggressive. Newt Gingrich provides an outstanding model for the term abrasive. Regardless of the value or content of his message, it is difficult to hear because it is couched in so much negativity about the opposing political party. His comments about the Democrats, whether on target or not, come across as snide remarks rather than logical, albeit critical, assessments. His behavior might also fall into the condescending category because he frequently smirks, which suggests an air of superiority or imperiousness, while he makes his abrasive remarks.

A notable business figure with an abrasive personality is hotelier Leona Helmsley. In the midst of legal problems that resulted from her failure to pay sufficient taxes, Helmsley managed to alienate a rather substantial population of would-be guests with her comment that only the "little people" pay taxes. Throughout her trial similar thoughtless and abrasive remarks (always devoid of remorse) only contributed further to her ultimate incarceration for tax evasion.

Abrasive people care more about the content of their messages and less about the impact that the messages will have on others. They choose "hard" words to get the point across rather than neutral ones. Hard words are ones that offend or attack, whereas neutral ones lean toward bridging differences of opinion and problem solving. Hard words are frequently value-laden, whereas neutral ones are more objective. The differences sound something like this:

Hard: It's obvious that you simply didn't put the time into writing the report that it required. If you had, it wouldn't have turned out so ineptly
written and blatantly filled with mistakes.

Neutral: The report isn't what I had anticipated. It contains numerous errors of fact and grammar. I'm wondering whether the time required
to do it was actually devoted to it?

You will note that the neutral statement did not attack or con-
demn, but rather presented a simple statement of fact. Additionally,
the hard word choices include "you" statements, as opposed to "I"
statements, that tend to make another person defensive and less
likely to want to work through the problem.

Belligerence

As much as I enjoy watching her antics, the behavior of television's
Judge Judy can best be described as belligerent. Her comments
from the bench are not simply opinions, they're verbally abusive.
She's mean-spirited and acts as though she's better than the show's
guests. One might say she's just doing her job to secure ratings and
further the cause of justice. I don't buy it. I've read enough about
her history and watched her during interviews to believe it's not
an act—this is who the woman is. Any of us could use the same
excuse in our jobs and it would still not make the behavior acceptable.

In the international political arena, Middle East leaders Yasser
Arafat and Saddam Hussein can't be described as anything but
belligerent. Although they verbally profess peaceful intentions, their
actions are contentious and designed to inflame the situation, not
ameliorate it. Like most belligerent people they act not in good
faith, but in ways that are good for them personally. On our own
soil, the same holds true for former presidential candidates Ross
Perot and Pat Buchanan. Fortunately, the American public recognized their belligerence (and other flaws) and declined to let them
get near the Oval Office.

Blaming

Most of us have had the great displeasure of working with a blaming or Teflon boss or coworker. When something goes wrong, watch out because someone is going to wind up the scapegoat. Their inability to admit their own mistakes goes beyond any single mistake; it is at the very core of their interactions with others. People who are unable to admit mistakes are frequently the very same people who lack insight into their own behavior.

Looking across past decades we see the phenomenon of blaming occur with late president Richard Nixon's Watergate scandal, Lieutenant Colonel Oliver North's Iran-Contra affair, Hillary and Bill Clinton's accusations blaming the "vast right wing conspiracy" for their peccadilloes, and with former Enron CEOs Jeffrey Skilling and Kenneth Lay. In each of these instances the fingers couldn't point fast enough at someone else.

As of the time this book went to press, only Nixon (resigning in the face of probable impeachment) and North (a conviction that was later overturned) have been held even remotely responsible for their actions. Despite these embarrassing failures and attempts to blame others, Nixon led a very public life until his death in 1994 and North went on to run for the U.S. Senate in Virginia in 1994. Equally notable and of interest is that as the cameras capture each "blamer" in the midst of his or her imbroglio, a cavalier, unrepentant attitude was conveyed. Like most blamers, they refused to admit they had done anything wrong.

Insensitivity

Insensitive people tend to disregard others' preferences or desires, embarrass others with thoughtless comments, and make certain that their own needs prevail. They frequently speak before they think, thereby saying things that in retrospect they wish they hadn't—but the damage is already done.

Insensitivity isn't always thoughtless—at times it is an intentionally used tactical weapon. One woman in a workshop on interpersonal skills spent the first day embarrassing and berating others. To a grossly overweight woman she made the comment,

"The food here [at the conference center] is so heavy. I must have gained ten pounds. I feel like a beached whale." During an evening of group singing and dancing, she stood up and mimicked another participant who had a heavy Asian accent and who had just led the group in a song. When I asked to speak with her privately to give her some feedback about how she was affecting the rest of the group members, she proudly admitted that she could find a person's Achilles' heel and go after it. She told me that this was her way of maintaining a competitive edge.

Insensitivity, whether intentional or otherwise, gives the impression that you are a loose cannon. People who are insensitive are frequently excluded from important client or customer meetings for fear of what they're going to say. Insensitive people wind up being avoided in the workplace because their coworkers don't particularly care to set themselves up for hurt or embarrassment. Failing to know how you affect others, being unaware that you may have hurt someone else, and neglecting to ask for feedback about your behavior are other examples of insensitivity, which may also be viewed as lacking insight. People who lack insight have huge blind spots about their own personalities because they are largely oblivious to how others respond to them. They fail to see the reactions of others because they are so absorbed in themselves. Lack of insight probably causes more career derailments than any other single factor.

William Agee, former CEO of Bendix Corporation, and more recently of Morrison Knudsen, provides us with an example of someone who derailed for, among other things, lacking insight. Agee, an honors graduate of Harvard, was chief financial officer at Boise Cascade by the time he was thirty-one and CEO at Bendix by thirty-eight. People expected great things from him and he didn't let them down.

The beginning of his derailment process began amid controversy when he was at Bendix that he was having an affair with his young executive assistant, Mary Cunningham. Although he denied the rumors, resentment against both Cunningham and Agee for his preferential treatment of her reflected poorly on his judgment. His judgment was called into question even more so when he married her. Although his business decisions certainly played a major role in his ultimate departure from Bendix, it appeared that his lack of insight about how his behavior affected others deprived him of the support from staff and management that he might otherwise have had.

What might have eventually been overlooked as simply a matter of the heart was later revisited when the pair found themselves in trouble again, this time at Morrison Knudsen. Not having learned his lesson about preferential treatment, Agee this time put his wife at the helm of the Morrison Knudsen Foundation. His attempts to turn around the declining company met with resistance as he alienated employees with his insensitive management style. Top that off with the fact that members of the community found both Agee and Cunningham standoffish and pretentious and their dismissal was inevitable.

When Too Much of a Good Thing Is a Good Thing

There are five behaviors that counter the deadly character traits: kindness, honesty, humility, genuineness, and self-awareness. Remember, when you are trying to overcome your strengths it is not particularly helpful to think about *stopping* a behavior. You only focus more on the behavior that you want most to diminish! You must add new skills to your existing repertoire. Add these five, and your personality worries will be over.

Kindness

Many of us grew up with the Golden Rule: *Do unto others as you would have others do unto you.* True kindness takes that motto a step further. In order to be truly kind, you must now *treat others as they would like to be treated.* I've already described the importance of seeing people for who they are. In order to be kind, you must now respond to who *they* are and what *they* would like, not who *you* are and what *you* would like.

Many of the behaviors inherent to kindness overlap with the relationship-building behaviors described under Reason #1. Kindness goes beyond relationship building, however, because it also encompasses what you do when there is no quid pro quo, when you have nothing to gain from the act. This concept is exemplified in the role played by Kevin Costner in the movie *The War.*

In one scene he takes the cotton candy he has just purchased for his wife and daughter at a fair and gives it to some bullies who have been beating up on his kids. When his son looks at him incredulously and asks why he did that, his response is simple: "Because it looks like they haven't been given nothing in a long time." This type of kindness stems from a sort of generosity—not a generosity of materialism, but a generosity of spirit. You are kind not because someone reminds you to be, or because you know that you will gain something tangible from it, but because you want to make a difference in the lives of those around you—even those whom you may never see again.

I can remember the exact moment in childhood when I learned my first lesson in kindness. It was on a crowded subway in Manhattan when I was five or six years old. My aunt had taken me to see her office in the city and we were returning home amid the rush-hour commuters who were packed like sardines into the train. I watched as a young professional woman stood, tapped an elderly woman on the shoulder, and motioned her to the seat she had just vacated. The older woman sat down wearily and the younger woman remained standing until she exited many stops later. A simple act of kindness that took place nearly forty years ago had such a profound effect on me that to this day I recall it nearly every time I ride the subway.

Honesty

Honesty can be looked at in a number of ways. Do you tell the truth when asked a question, or do you pass the buck and look for someone else to blame? Do you give people honest feedback, or do you say what you think people want to hear? Are you willing to speak the unspoken—even when not asked—or are you content to not rock the boat? No matter how you slice it, honesty involves having the integrity to say and do the right thing no matter how difficult.

When it comes to speaking your mind, there are different ways of being honest. It is possible to be honest without demolishing another person. Honesty does not always have to be hurtful, but it does have to meet two criteria: it must be direct and it must be kind. Once, after a lengthy explanation in the ways of being honest, someone in a workshop summarized it beautifully when she pointed out that *honesty is the ability to tell someone to go to hell so that they look forward to the trip!* Let's take a look at how you might successfully meet this challenge.

Quite often, when people are coached to be honest but with kindness, they think that they are being asked to act passively— to care more about the receiver of the message than about making their points. This is far from the case. It is just that people who are brutally honest frequently go out of bounds in terms of their direct, straightforward behavior. It becomes too much of a good thing. By following these "three Ds" of honesty, you will increase the likelihood of getting your message across without damaging the relationship:

Describe	=	Describe why you are having the conversation with this person.
Discuss	=	Discuss the situation, using active listening to fully understand the other person's position or opinion.
Determine	=	Determine outcomes suitable for both parties involved.

All too often honesty comes out sounding something like this: Bill, I can't believe that report you gave me last week. You must have been asleep when you prepared it. You made mistakes about the size of the workforce and surrounding population. You even misspelled the CEO's name. You can certainly do better than that.

Messages that sound like this one, no matter how true they are, do nothing to further the relationship, build self-esteem, or encourage creative problem solving. The receiver of this message winds up feeling small and stupid. Notice that by using the three Ds and avoiding blame through the use of the word you, the entire tone is turned around, even though the sentiment remains the same:

Describe

> *Speaker:* Bill, I'd like to talk to you about the report that you handed in last week. Is this a good time?
>
> *Receiver:* Sure.

Discuss

> *Speaker:* I noticed that, in addition to being late, it had numerous errors in both content and typing. I was wondering what happened. This doesn't seem like the quality of work that you're capable of doing.
>
> *Receiver:* Well, actually, I did it in kind of a rush and didn't have time to proof it before I gave it to you.
>
> *Speaker:* What made you so rushed?
>
> *Receiver:* The equipment that I needed to access the data was down for nearly a week. We couldn't get anyone out here to fix it.
>
> *Speaker:* Why didn't I know about it?
>
> *Receiver:* You've been so busy with the new acquisition that I didn't want to bother you.
>
> *Speaker:* I'm sorry that you felt like you couldn't come to me. It has really put me on the spot. Was there something that I could have done differently that would have made you more comfortable to let me know?
>
> *Receiver:* No, not really. I guess I just didn't want to burden you any further than you already were.

Determine

> *Speaker:* I appreciate your trying to protect me like that, but it has created a problem for me. What is most important now is to decide what to do to prevent this from happening again. I need to know when I assign something to you that I'll get it on time and that it'll be free from so many errors.
>
> *Receiver:* I'm sorry that I put you in this position. in the future, I'll let you know whether there are any extenuating circumstances that prohibit me from getting my assignments to you on time.
>
> *Speaker:* Good. That's what I need. Thanks for your cooperation.

Following the three Ds allows you to be direct and kind at the same time. The message is the same in both of the examples above, but the second scenario will assure long-term cooperation and good-will.

Humility

Humility is embodied in this paraphrase of Vince Lombardi's coaching philosophy:

> When the team loses—it's my fault.
> When the team does well—we did it together.
> When the team wins—they did it themselves.

Humility is the absence of arrogance and the presence of modesty. It is the ability to put your own achievements into a perspective that simultaneously recognizes your own limitations and the strengths of others. Humble people do not boast or require extended time in the limelight (we all need a bit). They are so self-assured that they internalize their strengths and use them as stepping-stones for future success.

One example of someone who lacks humility is financier Donald Trump. Not only does Trump exaggerate his accomplishments, but he diminishes others in the process. A number of years ago Trump took over construction of Central Park's ice skating rink from the city of New York. When the project was completed, he called a press conference to gloat over the fact that he had succeeded where the city had failed. When asked how he managed to finish the project under budget and on rime, he could have acknowledged the work of good contractors and associates, but instead Trump chose to use the opportunity to demean Mayor Ed Koch and otherwise impugn the reputation of the city.

General Norman Schwarzkopf, in contrast, exemplifies a man of humility. Despite the fact that he was instrumental in the decisive defeat of the Iraqi military during Operation Desert Storm, Schwarzkopf never took the credit for himself alone. He shared the triumph with his colleagues and troops, and, in the process, allowed everyone involved to be a hero. It's easy to see why a man like Schwarzkopf is revered while in the minds of many someone like Trump is viewed as a caricature of himself.

Ironically, those who are unable to be humble are often raised as children in households so withholding of praise and affirmation that the child must call attention to himself or herself or otherwise fade into oblivion. The behaviors that we learned to survive difficult childhoods later become the cause of derailment. Self-confident people are able to highlight their accomplishments discreetly for the purpose of furthering their goals; people lacking humility must showcase their strengths as if their lives depended on it—because they do.

It is not as if humble people don't know that they are good—or even great. They do know this, but they lack the need to receive constant praise for it. Humility should not be confused with passivity. They are two entirely different things. Whereas passivity is marked by the unwillingness or inability to be proactive, humility is characterized by the desire to downplay one's position, strengths, or contributions.

Genuineness

Being comfortable with ourselves as imperfect humans—scars, flaws, and all—is the essence of being genuine. It is not quite the same as the expression *what you see is what you get*, because implied in that maxim may be a take-it-or-leave-it attitude. It's more like *I'm not perfect, but I know that I'm not and I don't try to be anyone other than who I am.* Genuine people accept who they are, and are likely to accept others for who they are for the same reason. They can laugh at their own foibles and eccentricities without embarrassment or self-consciousness. They have relinquished the need to be perfect.

The opposite of genuineness is pretension—putting on airs or pretending to be who you are not. I knew a man once who was always showing excessive kindness to others that had nothing whatsoever to do with the recipient's needs or circumstances. One Christmas he gave each member of his staff a piece of silver from Tiffany's, a seemingly kind and generous gesture on the surface. The only problem was that this same man refused to give performance reviews, say a kind word about anyone, or provide even cost-of-living increases to his employees when they were warranted. His staff would have much preferred to be recognized for their performance throughout the year than rewarded with an extravagant gift once a year. Similarly, he would take them to the most expensive restaurants in Chicago for their birthdays but failed to say good morning to them. It was more important to him that he appear magnanimous than that he be genuine. And, in turn, he got subversive compliance from his staff. They would do only what was necessary to keep afloat in their positions and nothing more.

Self-Awareness

People who are self-aware know their strengths and flaws and act to improve their skills. They are aware of the effect they have on others. Combined with genuineness, honesty, and humility, self-awareness enables individuals to respond flexibly to different situations.

Self-awareness can be developed in a number of ways.

1. Ask for feedback. Even if there's no formal mechanism in place for it at your job, ask other people for feedback. Couch it in terms of what they think you could do more of, less of, or continue. This model provides a non-threatening way of giving, and receiving, feedback. If you ask for feedback, however, be sure that you're ready to hear it. Once given, don't argue with it or try to explain away your behavior. The best way to deal with feedback is to ask for clarification if you don't understand it, thank the giver, and then go off to think about it. Even if it's only one person's opinion, you need to consider the ramifications of the feedback and how many more people may be thinking the exact same thing but not telling you.

2. Use a 360 feedback instrument, a performance survey available to all levels of employees—professionals, supervisors, managers, and senior executives. The surveys are completed anonymously by people who know your work and returned to a third party, who then sends them off for computer processing, from which a computer profile of your strengths and needs for development emerges. In Resources you'll find the name of a reliable company that you can contact for such profiles. Because the results can at times be pretty overwhelming, it is recommended that a feedback instrument be used in conjunction with a business coach. You'll find coaching contacts listed in Resources as well.

3. Take self-awareness classes. These classes focus on behavior in a business context. Unlike EST or Wellspring, they're typically designed for businesspeople who want to examine how their behavior impedes or contributes to career success. The company I consider to be the nation's premier provider of such classes is NTL (National Training Laboratory). They've been facilitating self-awareness programs for businesspeople for nearly fifty years. You'll find a contact for them, as well as other reputable organizations, in Resources.

4. Get a business coach. Good coaches work with you to overcome specific behaviors that may contribute to potential derailment. In addition to providing you with coaching hints related to your particular situation, they can refer you to other resources in your community that may be helpful for assuring ongoing self-awareness. Many use 360 feedback instruments as part of the coaching process.

5. Enter into counseling. At times, behaviors are so ingrained and related to early childhood experiences that longer-term, in-depth professional help is required to understand and change them. Since I am a licensed psychotherapist myself, I offer this recommendation with somewhat of a bias, but even coaches with no psychological backgrounds report that from 75 to 90 percent of the people they coach are referred to counseling for treatment that goes beyond the scope of coaching.

Avoid Going for the Bait

A client I've been coaching called to tell me about a situation that he thought he handled poorly. We had been working on how to overcome the impression that others have of him of being too blunt, undiplomatic, and hurtful in his remarks to others. We discussed many of the coaching hints already provided in this chapter, and he was making some headway in winning back the regard of his staff and colleagues. He slid backward, however, when someone did the same thing to him that he was accused of doing to others.

A female coworker sent him an E-mail message berating him for being rude, slow in responding to requests, and mean-spirited at meetings. She sent it not only to him, but electronically copied all of the people reporting to him and to his boss. Furious, he responded in kind with an equally abusive letter in which he let the woman know what he thought of her. In short, he went for the bait. The woman who sent the letter wanted to get a rise out of him, and she did. The situation was now escalating, and both parties looked childish.

One technique to avoid matching the inappropriate intensity level of another person, and thereby avoid going for the bait, is called *fogging*. Although the man and I had discussed it during his coaching sessions, the importance of fogging was underscored by this encounter. Fogging is especially helpful when someone catches you unaware or off guard with their intensity or anxiety. When others are angry or abusive it is human nature to become angry and abusive back. Meeting the other person's intensity level typically only escalates a problem.

Fogging involves first putting up a visual fog between you and the other person so that his or her intensity is diffused and neither intimidates nor infuriates you. Next, you attempt to de-escalate the situation by remaining calm and using specific phrases designed to permit you to maintain your dignity and allow others to maintain theirs. Phrases like "I can see you are really upset by this. Let me check into it and get back to you" or "I had no idea you felt this way. Tell me more about it" are examples of fogging that buy you time to gather your composure or investigate the complaint, without responding in kind.

When the man asked what he could have done differently, it was suggested that he might have responded with a return E-mail message that said: *I had no idea that my behavior is being interpreted in the way that you described. Why don't we schedule a meeting within the next few days to sit down and discuss the problem so that we can remedy it as quickly as possible.* He said that this was all well and good, except that it didn't address the fact that he was embarrassed in front of his staff and boss. *His* response, on the other hand, evened the score, a fact about which he appeared to be proud.

As was explained to him, there are any number of ways of winning a battle without losing the war. The preferred response would go a long way toward assuring his ongoing success despite how his colleague chose to act. By smoothing the waters, he would allow others to see that even when provoked, he treats people with dignity and respect. He would wind up looking like a hero, rather than being seen as stooping to his colleague's level. In keeping with Lao-tzu's teaching, "Fail to honor people, they fail to honor you," honoring others over the long tenure of your career will always serve you better than acting out of malice or vindictiveness.

Strategies for Crafting a Winning Personality: Interacting with Others

1. Never embarrass anyone—ever.
2. Don't tell jokes at the expense of anyone except yourself (and think twice before you do that).
3. Publicly praise, privately criticize.
4. Know when to give up the battle so that you can win the war.
5. Remember to say please and thank you.
6. Create win-win situations by considering everyone's needs not just your own.
7. Find ways to allow people to save face—give the benefit of the doubt.
8. Be humble.
9. Be a gracious loser—and winner.

10. Be assertive (not aggressive).

11. Give other people credit when it's due (and maybe even when it's not).

12. Be honest, but be careful how you express your honesty.

13. Look people in the eye when you speak with them.

14. Stop what you are doing and pay attention to people when they come into your office.

15. Think before you speak—especially when you are angry or upset.

16. Use the lowest level of muscle possible.

17. Despite how you are treated, always treat others with dignity and respect.

Strategies for Crafting a Winning Personality: Self-Development

18. Use a 360 feedback instrument to get input into how others perceive you.

19. Attend NTL's Human Interaction Laboratory (see page 203).

20. Attend an assertive communications class.

21. Be kind to yourself...so that you can be kind to others.

22. Be who you are, but be the best you possible.

23. Take self-awareness classes.

24. Use the three Ds of honesty: *describe* your concern, *discuss* the problem, *determine* outcomes.

Difficulty Working With Authority

Strategy: *Learn How to Manage Up*

A seldom-discussed fact of business life is the need to "manage up." The concept of managing up is not to be confused with toadying or apple polishing. I'm not suggesting that you act insincere or in a way calculated to garnet favor from management. *Managing up* means that you are aware of the need to cultivate a relationship with management that produces satisfactory results for *both* parties. Managing up simply means that you understand the unspoken quid pro quo between you and your boss and consciously make an effort to keep up your end of the agreement.

People rarely refer to the men and women who supervise their work or to whom they report as "bosses." Instead, they call them leaders, facilitators, coaches, coordinators, and an array of other nonhierarchical terms in an effort to remove the traditional notion that one position is in any way more important or better than another. After all, if there is a *subordinate* then there must be a *superior*. Modern theories of motivation suggest that in order to bring out the best in people managers can no longer rely on the power of their positions, but must build relationships of mutual respect. Unlike their predecessors, who saluted authority figures simply for the authority of power they possessed, today's workers expect to actually have a relationship with their supervisors, and the new terminology is reflective of this change.

Nevertheless, a rose is still a rose, and a boss is still a boss, and here's where the necessity for *managing up* comes in. No matter what you call the boss, the fact remains that most people working in companies and organizations report to someone else who reviews their work and makes determinations about salary, promotion, assignments, and, at times, termination. You can change the term used to describe him or her, you can expect to have an amiable relationship with him or her, but you can't alter the fact that you are ultimately accountable to someone higher in the organization. From an entry-level position right on up to the CEO, everyone is accountable to someone. People who successfully avoid premature career derailment understand that, as with all other relationships, this relationship must be managed effectively.

Although the labels have become fuzzier and management techniques friendlier, the nature of the employer/employee relationship has not changed significantly. Labor attorneys are as busy as ever representing companies for their decisions to terminate employees and employees who believe they have been unjustly treated. The fact remains that you have to satisfy the expectations of the people who supervise you if you are to succeed in the workplace.

Managing up is difficult in the new employment arena because no other workplace relationship resembles one's original family experience as much as the employee-manager relationship. For the employee, this relationship may encompass all of the same frustrations, triumphs, challenges, and satisfaction that existed within the relationship with his or her father, mother, or other primary caretaker. An employee may unwittingly respond to the boss in much the same way he or she responded to the first of life's authority figures.

Because of this association between caretakers and bosses, employees' responses may vary between extraordinarily tolerant in the worst of situations, and intolerant in the best of situations. This creates a unique dilemma because derailment can come from being too submissive as well as from being too argumentative or unwilling to comply with directions. The real trick is to know (1) what the boss expects from you and (2) how to maintain your integrity as you walk the fine line between being a yes-person and being a thorn in the boss's side.

Perhaps this checklist is a place to begin thinking about how well you work with authority figures.

_____ I am able to disagree with the boss when I feel strongly about something.

_____ I see it as my duty to provide the boss with alternative viewpoints.

_____ I would rate myself high on being able to disagree without being disagreeable.

_____ I know when to disagree with the boss and when not to.

_____ I balance respect for authority with voicing a dissenting viewpoint.

_____ I know what kind of boss will listen to a differing viewpoint and which will not and act accordingly.

_____ I would never be accused of currying favor with someone in order to advance myself.

_____ I would never be accused of defying authority.

_____ I have worked through whatever issues I may have had with the type of parenting I received (either positive or negative).

_____ I am able to objectively assess my boss's strengths and developmental areas.

_____ I know when someone in authority is being unreasonable with me, and I don't usually take it personally.

_____ I see people in authority as only human.

An interesting coaching case that portrays the effect of parenting on the boss/employee relationship involved a woman, whom I'll call Carolyn. She requested coaching as a means of helping her to manage work stress. Carolyn was clearly an upwardly mobile career woman who seemed to have all the skills needed to be successful within her current organization or any other organization to which she might move. She had a good career track record with other companies and was articulate, intelligent, poised, and self-confident. Coincidentally, I knew her boss from some consulting that I had done for their company a number of years before. My recollection of him was that he was sarcastic, sexist, and a know-it-all. He saw himself as "the boss" and everyone else as merely underlings.

Throughout the first coaching session, I couldn't quite figure out what the real problem was. Carolyn never mentioned her boss (an omission I found strange), only that her job was very demanding and creating an abundance of stress for her. Without revealing my own assessment of her boss, I finally asked about her relationship with him. She skirted the issue for several minutes, and each time I gently came back to the topic. Suddenly, Carolyn started sobbing. As it turned out, she was feeling inadequate and incompetent. No matter what she did, her boss wasn't satisfied. Carolyn was certain that it was all her fault.

After exploring the situation with her a bit more, I turned the topic to her personal life. Was she married? Were her parents still alive? Did she have siblings? With this, she lit up. No, she wasn't married, but she did have a particularly close relationship with her parents. She had grown up an only child, doted on by adoring grandparents and aunts. She thought that she probably wasn't married yet because no man could measure up to her father, whom she described as a loving, considerate, and nurturing man.

Carolyn's greatest strengths—her self-confidence and talent—were now put in question by a boss who was the polar opposite of her father. Carolyn came to the job seeing the boss as her loving mother, nurturing father, and doting extended family all rolled into one. Despite all factors pointing to the contrary, she believed in the boss more than she believed in herself. She was not capable of seeing the boss for who he really was and, therefore, bought into his critical assessment of her. Her perception was that he was the all-knowing, benevolent father figure. There couldn't possibly be anything wrong with him, so it had to be her!

Subsequent coaching sessions with Carolyn focused on enabling her to assess her boss's behaviors critically vis-a-vis her own and to deal with those behaviors more objectively. She was ultimately able to separate the boss from her father in her mind, and when she did, she made the decision to find a boss who was in actuality more like her father. Carolyn realized that there were certainly some areas on which she needed to work, but that it would be better for her to leave the company. She is now happily working for a small company in Indiana that has a family-like feel to it. She vows never again to let someone take away her self-esteem.

As for Carolyn's former boss—he's an example of someone who manages up well. His own boss is a lot like him and, in fact, appreciates and rewards his hard-nosed approach to management.

Both former marines, they remain true to the marine motto *semper fidelis*—always loyal. The man is still with the company, making people's lives miserable, and no one in authority seems to be taking notice.

The opposite phenomenon—total acquiescence to the boss—can be equally damaging to one's career. A manager once asked if I would work with one of his employees. The manager's main complaint was that the employee, Dave, would never challenge anything he said. Dave would follow the boss's instructions to the letter, even if it became apparent in the process that there was a better way to do it or a more appropriate path to pursue. The particular behavior that frustrated the manager was just part of a larger problem. Someone who won't challenge authority often won't take the kinds of risks needed to explore, make mistakes, learn from those mistakes, and go on to bigger and better things. As a member of a creative services team, Dave was *expected* to take risks.

Dave's greatest strength was following instructions. He grew up in an Eastern culture where respect for authority was demonstrated by close adherence to the directions and desires of the elders. Like Carolyn, Dave had to learn to separate his early experience with authority from the business situation with the boss. His coaching sessions involved enabling him to think and act independently of his boss's desires. He was coached first to develop a weekly plan for task accomplishment that included two to three items that he could see were needed in the department but that weren't mentioned by his boss. Next, he was instructed to give his own opinion at least once at every staff meeting. The third thing he was coached to do was to speak more loudly. His quiet, somewhat flat tone of voice gave others the perception that he was someone who could be walked on. The combined coaching hints—to think more broadly, give his own opinions, and do so in a louder voice—were designed to eventually increase his self-confidence. Once this happened, he would be more likely to take more risks. The goal was to get Dave to "walk the walk" and "talk the talk." Fortunately, Dave had a boss who was very supportive of the process and not only allowed but also encouraged him to overcome his particular strengths.

The My Lai Massacre:
A Study in Deference to Authority

There is no better example of someone on the compliant side of the managing-up spectrum than that of Lieutenant William Galley Jr. In 1968 the Vietnam War was raging. Calley was in charge of a platoon that, on March 16 of the same year, was instructed to invade and destroy the Vietnamese village of My Lai, an alleged Viet Cong stronghold. When they arrived, they found no Viet Cong, but Galley and his platoon nevertheless slaughtered hundreds of innocent civilian women and children.

A fellow soldier was so disturbed by the events that he wrote letters to Congress—letters that eventually brought Calley to trial for murder and resulted in his conviction. Galley's only defense throughout the trial was that he was simply following the instructions of his superiors. His remarks at the time were, "Personally, I didn't kill any Vietnamese that day. I mean personally. I represented the United States of America. My country." These words underscore what happens when one is blindly loyal to authority.

A glimpse into his childhood gives us a few clues to help understand his actions. Galley is described as an unexceptional child and a product of a 195 Os upbringing. He was sent to the Florida Military Academy after being caught cheating on a test in the seventh grade. One can only imagine what possessed his family to send him away and what he learned about following instructions once at the academy. One man recalls young Galley being a loyal friend: "[H]is sense of loyalty was wonderful. If you had a problem at 3:30 in the morning he would be there for you." After dropping out of junior college he wandered from job to job until he wound up in the military. The same friend claims that Calley liked the regimentation and needed the discipline that the service afforded.

What he must certainly have learned at the military academy about compliance, especially after being sent there for cheating on a test, combined with the comment about his loyalty to friends, provides us with the greatest insight into his decision to follow the instructions he was given on March 16, 1968. Although Calley's strengths lay in these two factors, they became his greatest liabilities and forever changed his life. After his release from prison (most of which, at President Richard Nixon's direction, was spent in his own apartment under house arrest) after serving less than four years of a life sentence, he refused to talk about the incident and until this day will not give interviews or discuss the matter. His silence is testament to his loyalty to the service, despite the fact that he was the only person convicted of crimes related to what we now call the My Lai Massacre.

Except for the gross atrocities of his crime, Lieutenant Calley is no different from the scores of businesspeople who salute the boss and fail to add value to their positions due to their inability to confront authority when necessary or appropriate. These men and women are great followers, but the company suffers from their unwillingness to think and act independently of authority. They do as they are told, keep their noses clean, and perpetuate the status quo of their organizations.

Frank Biondi and Viacom

The story of the abrupt and surprising dismissal of Frank Biondi as CEO of entertainment giant Viacom, Inc., by his boss, chair Sumner Redstone, illustrates what can happen when a good relationship turns sour. Industry insiders say that the relationship between the two—who were initially viewed as a winning executive team—may have slowly eroded over differences in style and strategy. Just two weeks prior to the dismissal, Biondi attended a fete in honor of Redstone and sang his boss's praises. Similarly, for years Redstone publicly acknowledged Biondi's contributions to Viacom. Behind the scenes, however, a different scenario was being played out.

Redstone hired Biondi in 1987 to help him manage the company that was burdened with a debt ten times its cash flow. Together, the team whittled away the debt and expanded operations. It was widely recognized that Biondi and Redstone didn't always see eye to eye, although little was made of it at the time. Biondi was the Harvard MBA numbers man, while Redstone was the visionary who operated from instinct—a potentially lethal combination unless both parties are aware of the quid pro quo. One incident that underscores their different approaches took place in the late eighties, when on a Friday they made the decision to buy King World.

By Monday morning Redstone decided he wanted out of the deal. When Biondi asked why, Redstone said that after consulting with longtime friend Barry Diller, he decided it wasn't viable. Biondi then implied that Redstone's friend might not be the most objective person with whom to consult, since he could be negatively affected by the acquisition. The deal never went through.

There were other occasions when Biondi publicly contradicted Redstone. One such incident was when Redstone declared that acquiring a music company would be "another enormous source of software" while Biondi publicly stated that it was an "awfully small business." Some say that the real turning point came in 1993 when Redstone wanted to buy Paramount and Biondi resisted, insisting that it would overleverage the company's assets. Immediately following this event Redstone became increasingly critical of Biondi, implying that the failure of a costly Paramount film was due to Biondi's negligence. Biondi's influence dwindled to the point where his input into decisions was second-guessed by other Viacom executives who were supported behind the scenes by Redstone, and he was summarily dismissed. In the end, it appears that Biondi's greatest strength, a logical, level-headed approach to managing a business, became his greatest liability, absent the ability to manage up effectively.

Calley and Biondi, both devoted to their careers, are on opposite ends of the managing-up spectrum. Whereas one had difficulty critically assessing the decisions of his superiors, the other did so too much. The secret of successfully managing up is to be willing to take risks with regard to questioning authority, but to know when and how to do it.

Putting the Past into Perspective

Beyond the examples above, difficulties with authority affect the lives of employees in all milieus. A woman called Alice illuminates this phenomenon in a less spectacular setting. The case study is from psychotherapist and corporate coach Susan Picascia. Susan, formerly with the Employee Assistance Program at Cedars-Sinai Medical Center in Los Angeles, now has her own consulting firm in which she coaches people on how to overcome the effects of childhood experiences in the workplace. She shares with us her experience coaching Alice, the manager of information research at a high-profile, Hollywood-based entertainment firm.

As a manager, Alice is a technically proficient relationship builder who shows respect to her peers and staff and receives the same in return. She prides herself on being a compassionate, people-oriented manager with strong technical skills. Although she works independently in relation to others, Alice becomes dependent in relation to her boss, Curtis.

Unfortunately, Curtis reminds Alice of her father, who was a perfectionist and hypercritical. In Curtis's case, it isn't so much that he's a perfectionist, hut rather that he is so self-absorbed that he never takes time to notice Alice's many achievements or to give her feedback—except for negative comments on rare occasions when something isn't done as he wanted it. At those times, Alice cries in private because she feels like she can never do anything right in his eyes. In front of him, she becomes defensive, to which he reacts by saying, "Don't get your back up." She is beginning to question her ability and competence, despite the fact that she has successfully worked with bosses in other firms.

Although this is the first time in her career that Alice has experienced a situation like this one, it certainly won't be the last. The personal development that Alice must now undertake in order to avoid derailment involves developing the ability to put "little Alice" on hold while "adult Alice" takes over. She must learn to judge herself, rather than allowing the opinions of others to eclipse her self-esteem. She can successfully accomplish this with these three specific coaching hints.

---

1. Lower her antennae for tuning into feelings—both her feelings and Curtis's. As a result of her experience with her father, Alice is supersensitive to criticism, especially from men. Whereas others would take Curtis's feedback at face value, Alice interprets it as failure. She learned early in life to put extra effort into doing things perfectly in order to ward off potential criticism and has transferred this behavior to the workplace. The obvious problem is that it's impossible to ward off criticism entirely. Inevitably, we all do something differently than the boss wants it done and we must make adjustments. Alice's need to be perfect is getting in her way. No one in her present life—not even Curtis—expects her to be perfect. She must let go of this particular childhood defense mechanism and become less sensitive to Curtis's requests for change, as well as the manner in which he delivers these messages.

2. Raise her antennae for message content. Conversely, Alice should pay more attention to the content of the message, thereby avoiding overreaction to how it is delivered. By focusing on the content, she can remove herself from the role of the child who is responsible for the opinions of her father/boss.

3. Use positive self-talk and visualize success. When feelings from the past surface, Alice must say to herself, "I will attend to my feelings later, right now the focus is on content. I will respond to content in an open-minded, non-defensive way." Self-talk is a powerful tool to tape over the old messages that play in the back of our heads. By using self-talk and by visualizing successful encounters with the boss, Alice can develop new messages and images on which she can rely for support and encouragement when they are needed most.

Alice permits her past to define her present and future. The work of each of us is to be able to objectively see the authority figures in our lives as they really are and not as ghosts from the past. If you find yourself overreacting to your boss or other authority figures, ask yourself these questions:

- Whom does he or she remind me of?
- Whom or what do I act like when I am around him or her?
- Why do I give up so much of my own power to him or her?

The answers to these questions will help you to begin demystifying the boss-employee relationship. And finally, remember these wise words of Eleanor Roosevelt: "No one can make you feel inferior without your consent."

The Eight Secrets of Successfully Managing Up

Even in the most enlightened organizations, where the manager's title has been changed to team leader, coordinator, or something equally nonhierarchical, there still exist certain expectations for how followers should interact with leaders. Although on the surface there has been a shift toward the appearance of egalitarianism, the Golden Rule of Management still prevails: He or she who has the gold sets the rules. The degree to which you are able to work within the boundaries established by the boss, and to adapt to the changing expectations from one boss to another, largely determines your ultimate success in an organization.

Here are the eight secrets of successfully managing up:

1. The boss is only human, with strengths and weaknesses like everyone else. Expecting superhuman behavior from the boss, or thinking that you can aid in his or her development, is a little like trying to teach a pig to sing—it frustrates the teacher and annoys the pig. Reminding the boss about his or her weaknesses only serves to rub salt in the wound. Once you see the boss as human, you can overcome your childhood fantasies of having the perfect parent and interact with him or her on an adult-to-adult basis.

2. The boss wants you not only to do your job, but to make his or her job easy as well. This is not to be confused with threatening the boss by acting as if you want his or her job. Every reasonable request that the boss makes should be met with the implicit or explicit response: no problem. On the other hand, if you foresee a problem, let the boss know in a way that encourages problem solving as opposed to presenting obstacles. Bosses don't want to hear that it can't be done; they want to know how it can be done. Seek opportunities to help the boss with his or her workload. Not only is it appreciated, but you get the chance to learn skills that will be helpful to your career.

3. The boss never wants to be embarrassed. If you want to disagree with the boss, do it in private—even if it means calling a time-out during a meeting. If he or she decides to make a correction to course given your input, it must ultimately be his or her decision. If a project fails or loses momentum due to the failure to heed your warning, in no way indicate, "I told you so." Continue to provide relevant information that will help to guide the project back on course.

4. The boss doesn't want to have to tell you what to do. But he or she wants to know what you're doing. You add value by thinking strategically, foreseeing what has to be done, and preempting the boss from having to give you continual instructions. By planning for upcoming events, projects, or special needs, you show that you are capable of more than simply the day-to-day activities. Avoid being a loose cannon, however, by informing your boss of what you're planning and asking for his or her input into the direction (no matter how much more technically capable you think you may be).

5. The boss, whether or not he or she admits it, wants you to make him or her look good. In the long term, making him or her look good makes you look good. Rather than always looking for ways to showcase your accomplishments, find opportunities to make the team and your team leader look good. By so doing you will ultimately look like someone who is politically astute and capable of ultimately leading a team yourself.

6. The boss wants to be able to give you feedback easily. When given feedback, listen to it, ask for clarification if necessary, think about it, but don't argue with it. No one particularly likes giving feedback in the first place. Don't make it any tougher by arguing your point or trying to negate it in some way. Regardless of the veracity of the feedback, openly listening to it at least gives the impression that you're flexible and open to change. That's half the battle. The other half is making enough changes to meet the boss's expectations without feeling like you are compromising your own principles.

7. The boss, in most cases, is not capable of helping you with your personal problems. Even the most patient, enlightened, and understanding bosses have trouble with bringing personal issues to the workplace. They may be genuinely empathetic, but the bottom line is that they don't want to play amateur psychologist—nor should you expect them to. The best bosses make special allowances now and then, but, as a rule, you shouldn't dwell on personal problems unless they are so severe that you know that they will seriously affect your performance. Doing otherwise sets you up for close scrutiny and eventual feedback related to the problem.

8. The boss wants you to deliver what you promise. The easiest way to destroy credibility is to renege on your promises—especially those made to the boss. If trust is built on consistency, then lack of trust stems from broken promises. Use the fifty-fifty rule for planning your workload: once you are given an assignment, you have half the amount of time until the deadline to ask questions and the other half to actually complete the project. If the boss doesn't hear from you within the first half of the time allotted for project completion, he or she assumes it will be done on time.

Managing Up with a Difficult Boss

The process of managing up is difficult enough when you have a rational, mature boss. It is nearly impossible when you have one who isn't. Most of us have had the challenge of working with a boss who thinks employees never do anything right. This may be because he or she didn't give sufficient information, constantly changed his or her mind about how things should be done, or was so disorganized that the rules constantly changed when new information came to the forefront. Whatever the reason, and there are as many reasons as there are difficult bosses, it is still your responsibility to manage up effectively. Regardless of the difficulty, he or she who has the gold still sets the rules.

One problem inherent with difficult bosses is that they can significantly diminish your confidence and self-esteem. This is yet another situation where early childhood experiences come into play. If a difficult boss reminds you of one of your parents or some other early authority figure, the likelihood that you will remain with him or her and be demoralized by his or her inappropriate behavior is greater than if this was not your experience. Ray is a good case in point.

A very talented graphic artist working in the animated films industry, Ray consistently produces high-quality results that are admired and valued by his clients. His boss (the company's owner), however, comes from the Neanderthal school of management. Despite the fact that Ray puts in seventy to eighty hours of work a week (with no additional compensation, since he is a "salaried" employee), he is never given a word of positive reinforcement by his boss. "My boss won't say anything that will make me feel good," says Ray. "It's as if he thinks it will go to my head and I'll ask for a raise. He doesn't want me to have any sense of control. What he doesn't understand is that a compliment now and then would actually make me work even harder and I wouldn't want any more money."

Ray could go anywhere else and write his own ticket. He's that talented. His problem is that his boss is exactly like his father—who never gave him a word of encouragement and kept tight control over Ray during his childhood. When others point out to Ray that he really should be looking elsewhere for a job, he comes up with a litany of excuses. Ray is bound by his history to repeat a familiar situation because it is in some ways comfortable. To leave would be symbolically to break the tie with his father.

If Ray's boss were not the company owner, the situation might be different. The difficulties that such bosses present to their followers typically do not go unnoticed by their superiors. One of two things happens: They derail because of the behavior, or they are kept in their positions because they do get the job done—even if it's at the expense of others. In their monograph, Coping with an Intolerable Boss, authors Michael Lombardo and Morgan McCall report their findings of interviews with seventy-three managers who were asked to tell about their experiences working with intolerable bosses. Lombardo and McCall found that patience and waiting the boss out is often the best course of action. Creating an adversarial situation only yields counterproductive results. Here's what they say:

Even an intolerable boss is still the boss . . . . A few of the managers [in the study] tried to change the boss, but in only six situations did a manager report any significant change in his superior's behavior as a result of the subordinate's efforts. The far more productive strategies were to change one's own response or, as a last resort, to get out of the situation.

In the meantime, the question remains, how do you maintain your sanity and self-respect when working for an intolerable boss? Here are a few ideas for how you can maintain some semblance of control over your life in the face of a difficult situation:

● **See the boss as the boss—not as your mother or father.** As it should now be abundantly clear, you must first understand the effect that childhood experiences have on dealing with authority, then separate in your mind your boss from your parents or other authority figures. This is especially true when it comes to dealing with a difficult boss. He or she may unintentionally be pushing the same buttons that Mom or Dad did and you, therefore, react the same way as you did when you were a powerless child. When you find yourself angry or frustrated with the boss, first ask yourself whether you feel as you did when you were a child or as you feel around your parents. If so, switch gears and tell yourself that you are now an adult and give yourself permission to respond differently. Such a response may include the realization that you are not bonded by blood to this person and you can leave if you so choose.

● **Anticipate and prepare for difficult behavior.** Difficult bosses often exhibit the same behaviors over and over. If you take the time to analyze it, you can predict certain behaviors with quite a bit of accuracy. I once had a boss who, no matter how much time and effort I put into a report, would march into my office and pick it apart. It always made me feel guilty, as if I hadn't done enough work on it to begin with. In order to deal with him and my feelings about his response to my efforts, I made a game of keeping a tally of the number of things he claimed that I overlooked. I kept my little tally sheet underneath the phone in my office and whenever he left I added chit marks to the score. Anticipating his response, and making light of it without ignoring his comments, enabled me to maintain my self-confidence in the face of ongoing criticism.

● **Weigh the risks versus the benefits of telling the boss what you need.** Consider the possibility that the boss just doesn't have a clue about what he or she is doing that is creating a problem for you. Decide what could be the worst thing that would happen if you told him or her how you felt and what you needed in order to be more effective in your position. This must, of course, be done without affixing blame, but rather by giving an "I message." For example, if the boss consistently fails to give you enough information to do a project properly, you could say something like, "I think I could be more effective if I had more details at the beginning of a project. Would it be possible to go over the specific requirements and how it fits into the bigger picture?" A riskier, but potentially even more beneficial, strategy would be to give the boss direct feedback as to how his or her behavior is affecting you. Still using the "I message" technique, you could say something like, "I find it difficult to complete assignments efficiently because of the lack of information I'm given at the start of a project. I'm wondering whether it would be possible for you to be more specific when I begin rather than complete a project." If it doesn't work, you're no worse off than you were before having the conversation.

● **Remember that the best defense is a good offense.** This doesn't mean that you should be defensive with a difficult boss, even though it's easy to fall into that trap. Instead, it means that knowing what his or her hot buttons are, you should be thoroughly prepared and well organized in those particular areas. If the boss is a stickler for having a document free of typos, make certain that that's what you provide, even if it means having a colleague, or several colleagues, proofread your work for you. If it is tardiness that drives him or her up the wall, then you should be making Herculean efforts to meet deadlines and arrive to work and meetings on time. For whatever reason, what may seem like a small thing to you is a big thing to the boss. Recognize what these things are, and head him or her off at the pass.

● **Evaluate the cost of staying in your position.** There comes the time when working with a difficult boss that you must ask yourself if it's worth it to stay. If in fact you have tried all of the things suggested above and the situation gets no better, you have only three alternatives: (1) put up with it hoping that the situation will change, (2) request a transfer within the company, or (3) quit. I have heard people say that they have to stay in their position because it pays well or because good jobs are hard to find, both of which are true, but there is a psychological cost to doing so. If the benefits of the job outweigh the cost in terms of damage to your self-confidence or self-esteem, then the logical choice is to stay and hope that the situation will eventually change. I have seen people wait it out and the boss eventually quits, is fired, or is promoted to another position. However, when the cost becomes too great, you have no alternative but to request a transfer (if the company is large enough) or to seek other employment. Most people with a difficult boss find that life improves significantly once the decision is made to leave, and once they actually begin a new job they wish they had done it sooner.

The ability to manage up is simply another element that successful people include in their skill sets. They know that good followership is as important as good leadership, and they make it easy for others to lead them. However, making it easy for others to lead can be difficult if the parameters of the employee-boss relationship are not clearly understood. Be realistic about the boss's expectations as well as how and to what extent they can be met. Most important, disengage from past personal circumstances and behaviors so that they don't obscure current workplace roles and relationships.

Ways to Manage Up

1. Always remember the Golden Rule of Management: He or she who has the gold sets the rules.

2. Choose your battles carefully—not every issue needs to be a battle, and you may win the battle but lose the war.

3. Make giving feedback to you easy by asking the boss how you can improve.

4. Never confront the boss in the presence of a higher authority.

5. Never make the boss look stupid or inept (even if he or she is).

6. Deliver more than what you're asked for.

7. Make yourself look good by making the boss look good.

8. Critically assess what you are asked to do, and make suggestions for improving on the original idea.

9. Lower your antennae for tuning into feelings that may belong more in childhood than in the present.

10. Use positive self-talk when feelings from the past do arise.

11. If the boss's position interferes with your confidence, pay more attention to the task than to the relationship.

12. Separate your image of the boss from that of your mother or father.

13. Weigh the risk versus the profit of giving the boss feedback.

14. View differences with the boss as just that—differences to be discussed and not confrontations to be won or lost.

15. Read the monograph *Coping with an Intolerable Boss* (see page 208).

16. Remember that you control no one's behavior except your own.

17. Have outside interests that capture your passion so that work issues can be put into perspective.

18. Be willing to give the boss your honest opinion and make every effort to influence him or her toward a decision that is in the best interest of the organization, but remember that the decision ultimately may not be yours.

19. Once a decision is made, fully support it—even if you disagree with it.

20. Keep your boss informed about what you are planning to do and ask for input.

21. Focus on the content of the boss's message rather than on how it is delivered.

22. Add value to your department and company by thinking ahead and identifying issues that the boss may not have thought of.

23. If you are inclined to acquiesce to authority take more risks with standing up for what you believe in.

24. Consider the possibility that you may be better off in a different position or company

Too Broad or Too Narrow Vision

Strategy: Balance Detail Orientation With Strategic Thinking

An article entitled "How to Integrate Work and Deepen Expertise" (*Harvard Business Review*, Sept–Oct 1994) details a scenario that occurred when Kodak's product development group introduced the concept of a single-use, disposable camera. They envisioned that it could potentially become a popular item with people who didn't own a camera or had forgotten their own. Since they viewed the project as something involving the use of high-tech film, executives gave the idea to their film development department and asked that they work on it. The staff of the film department, however, didn't share their colleagues' enthusiasm for the project. Believing that a disposable camera would only decrease sales of the already profitable film that Kodak sold, the department dragged its feet and paid little attention to its development.

We all know how the story ends. The disposable camera was developed and has become a highly successful addition to Kodak's product line. It was developed not by the film development department, but by Kodak's camera division, who saw the value of management's original vision for the product and acted on it. Whereas the film development staff looked narrowly at the potential of the product and allowed initial skepticism to interfere with development, the camera division looked broadly at the possibilities and developed a real winner for Kodak.

The story emphasizes the importance of balancing detail orientation with strategic thinking. Most of us seem to have a natural inclination to pay attention to either the nitty-gritty details or to the bigger picture. It is what makes us choose professions in, for example, accounting, medical technology, and administration over those in research, social work, or architecture. This is not to say that there aren't people in accounting who enjoy seeing the bigger picture or people who prefer a detail orientation in research, but rather that such preferences often influence our choice of career and our ultimate success in those professions.

If you will refer back to the MBTI® Preferences Chart (Reason #2, pages 62–63), you will notice that on the Attending scale (what a person likes to pay attention to) there are two types of people: sensers and intuitors. This gives us our greatest clue to whether we prefer details or the big picture. Whereas sensers prefer to deal with what is concrete, real, and tangible, intuitors are happier operating in the realm of theory and possibility. As you peruse the two lists, think about where you fit in. One source of job dissatisfaction can arise from being in a job that is counter to your natural inclination.

Another way of understanding these preferences comes from research pertaining to the brain's functioning. We know that the left and right hemispheres of the brain each process and handle information in distinctly different ways. Betty Edwards, in her work *Drawing on the Right Side of the Brain*, explains that the left hemisphere "analyzes, abstracts, counts, marks time, plans step-by-step procedures, verbalizes, [and] makes rational statements based on logic," whereas the right hemisphere helps us to "understand metaphors, dream, [and] create new combinations of ideas." Her contention, that our culture and educational system tend to focus on and value left hemisphere activity, explains why so many of us have difficulty bringing our more creative selves to the forefront. It isn't that we don't have creative capability, it is that the capability isn't developed and languishes from lack of use.

It is no wonder, then, that so many corporations suffer from a lack of creativity. The strengths that most of us have in right-brain functioning are not balanced with left-brain activity. Long after we lose our effectiveness, we continue to do the same things in the same way. We fail to draw on our capacity to envision our products or services differently and, instead, perpetuate the status quo. We maintain, but we don't create, thereby losing the competitive edge. This becomes especially problematic when the people who are entrusted to lead organizations are saddled only with strength in right brain functioning.

People who avoid premature derailment are good at both. They don't sacrifice close attention to detail for broader, more strategic thinking and vice versa. They successfully balance detail orientation with a view of the bigger picture. Use the following checklist to see how good you are at this balancing act.

_____ I am equally good at seeing the forest through the trees as the trees through the forest.

_____ Given a project, I first think about how it fits into the overall scheme of things and then become involved in the details of making it happen.

_____ I can take a good idea and turn it into a reality.

_____ I don't get bogged down in analysis paralysis.

_____ I find it as easy to come up with better ways of doing routine tasks as it is to develop processes for implementing these ideas.

_____ I'm patient with projects that require close attention to detail.

_____ I am seldom bored during brainstorming sessions.

_____ If I had the technical ability to do both, it would be as appealing to me to design a house as it would be to actually build it.

_____ I balance my checkbook regularly, but I don't spend an inordinate amount of time trying to find where it may be off by a few cents.

_____ It is fairly easy for me to see and hear nuances in messages and interpersonal communication.

Strategic Thinking + Attention to Detail = Success

Thomas Alva Edison, possibly the most prolific inventor of the nineteenth century, is an example of a historical figure who successfully balanced attention to detail with strategic thinking. Never a particularly good student, Edison was described as "addled" by one teacher, and another teacher described his classroom behavior as "dreamy, inattentive, with a tendency to drift off during recitations." These comments motivated Edison's mother to take him out of public school and tutor him herself. Even as a child, Edison exhibited the essence of a true visionary: curiosity. In adulthood, that same curiosity and willingness to take risks made him one of the most successful inventors of our time. By the age of twenty-one Edison had invented a stock ticker-tape machine, and throughout his life he produced more than one thousand invaluable devices, such as the electric light bulb, steam-driven power stations, the alkaline storage battery, celluloid film, the movie projector, and the phonograph, the invention in which he took the most pride. Edison had vision, but he also had the technical competence and proficiency to make those visions a reality.

On the business front, Elizabeth Claiborne (better known as Liz) provides an inspirational example of someone who had a vision and developed a strategy to turn it into a billion-dollar Fortune 500 company. With a background in art, she worked her way up the ladder of fashion design, ultimately becoming chief designer for Jonathan Logan. Despite her frustration over the fact that she could not sell her fashion vision to her employer, she remained with the company for sixteen years. Like many career women, she deferred her own dream while her husband pursued his and until her children were safely through college. Finally, in 1975, at age forty-six, Claiborne invested her family's life savings ($50,000) to form the fashion giant that shares her name.

Claiborne intuitively knew what fashions should be designed and marketed to working women and at what price. When she started her business this was a largely untapped market. Her less visionary colleagues continued producing clothes designed for pencil-thin models, not the average female figure, while Claiborne saw and filled a gap in the clothes market. Her strategy was to design mix-and-match clothes, decide how much women would be willing to pay for each design, and then negotiate to have them produced in Asia at a cost consistent with the sales price.

Within six years of starting the business, Liz Claiborne clothing generated $117 million in revenues and soon thereafter went public. Within ten years Claiborne's personal net worth was estimated to be $200 million. Within fifteen years of operation sales were double those of her established competitors and the company was named the Fortune 500's most profitable firm. Today, the company dominates the field of women's better sportswear with a 33 percent market share, generating more than \$2 billion annually in revenues.

THE DETAIL/STRATEGIC THINKING CONTINUUM

ACUTE ATTENTION TO DETAIL	BALANCED ATTENTION TO DETAIL AND STRATEGIC THINKING	OVERUTILIZED STRATEGIC THINKING
Acute attention is paid to minute detail and to doing the job in a prescribed, routine way, while outside factors that affect the work are neglected, overlooked, or seen as impediments to task accomplishment. Project completion may suffer due to overconcern with detail.	A project is looked at in its entirety with all variables being considered, including the human resources that are required, innovations that would make it more valuable, and a specific plan for carrying it out in the most effecient and cost-effective manner.	Ideas and concepts are of prime importance, while practical implications for executing ideas are overlooked. Projects are stalled due to ongoing changes, revisions, and analyses.

Edison and Claiborne are quite different examples, but similar in that they are two ordinary human beings who produced extraordinary results. Countless great ideas never become reality because people can't attend to the details required to carry them through. An idea without a plan for executing it is only a dream. Close adherence to detail conceptualization maintains status quo. The ability to think broadly and act intentionally forms the core of balancing detail orientation with strategic thinking.

With a little practice, we are each capable of functioning on the dual levels of detail orientation and strategic thinking. There is a continuum that goes from highly detail-oriented to overly concerned with the big picture (see chart above).

As you move toward the center of the continuum there is an increased balance between the two extremes that provides for maximum job effectiveness. People at either extreme are limited in the value that they add to a job or project. Ideally, we would surround ourselves in the work environment with people who complement our strengths, but because this is typically not possible, the job is either done routinely, with little concern for innovation or customer needs, or is stalled entirely due to analysis paralysis.

Jim Harkins, director of business and strategic planning at AlliedSignal Aerospace, introduced me to the concept of strategic intent, which is another way to approach strategic thinking. He cites numerous examples of companies that had broad visions for what they wanted to accomplish and developed specific plans for how to achieve them—in spite of seemingly insurmountable odds. One case in point is Canon Business Machines, Inc., in Costa Mesa, California. Canon's management made the *strategic decision* to not take on the leader in the field, Xerox, but instead to develop inexpensive copiers and provide services ancillary to their use. With this strategic intent, Canon has become better than any of its competitors at building the copier's printing engine and in the process earned the respect of customers and colleagues.

Major corporations such as IBM, GM, and Sears nearly self-destructed in the 1980s because of their failure to do what Canon did—redefine their visions of the future. They were so caught up in their routines, and what worked yesterday, that they neglected to see the changes in customer needs and what was needed to be successful tomorrow. Strategic intent works for companies and for individuals who want to avoid derailment. Attention to the future helps you to focus on what's important, guide your career, and make value-added contributions to your organization.

The business world is full of individuals who have derailed due to the inability to balance detail orientation and strategic thinking. In his presentations to corporate leaders, Harvard professor John Kotter routinely mentions that the airline industry provides us with two such examples of high-profile personalities: Frank Borman, formerly president of Eastern Airlines, and Donald Burr, founder of the once wildly popular airline People Express. Clearly, both men achieved great things in their careers, but both men also prematurely derailed due to overreliance on their unique strengths.

Most of us remember Frank Borman as the commander of the first human flight around the moon. He went on to become president of Eastern Airlines in 1975, a position he held until he resigned in 1986 under less than favorable conditions. As a child, he spent hours engrossed in building model airplanes—a somewhat solitary activity. His schoolmates didn't want much to do with him because they found him to be so bossy—which left him even more isolated. Borman went on to attend West Point. He is remembered there as someone who was staunchly independent. When an upperclassman intentionally stamped on his foot as part of the traditional hazing process (where underclassmen are expected to grin and bear it), Borman instead "called him a son of a bitch and threatened to kill him." When he graduated in 1950, his training as a pilot combined with a scientific education enabled him to become an astronaut in the Gemini program.

Not surprisingly, given his character and background, Borman earned the reputation at Eastern as a command and control leader. His goal for the struggling airline was to "restore discipline and profitability." The only problem was that he wanted to accomplish this while at the same time treating his staff like functionaries. He expected them to respond in much the same way as an aircraft would to his deft maneuvering: swiftly and unquestioningly. Borman never understood that his success depended on looking at the bigger picture, seeing how people fit into strategies, and how creative problem solving would be his only salvation—not command and control. He pounded employees with letters about the problems Eastern was facing and underscored his expectation that everyone would sacrifice for the good of the whole. His training as an engineer precluded him from balancing a strong orientation toward controlling detail with creatively and strategically seeking solutions to his company's problems.

Donald Burr, on the other hand, suffered from the opposite limited skill set. From childhood he approached everything he did with passion. As a youth he was even a proselytizer for his church, traveling from city to city to recruit other teens into a fellowship program. He approached his work in much the same way. Aviation was more than just a career to him—it was a "romance." In 1981 Burr started his own airline, People Express, after walking out on former boss Frank Lorenzo at Texas International Airlines. He had a vision for a "no frills" airline where passengers benefited from low prices and friendly service and employees from an exciting and rewarding work environment. He made it a contingency of employment that all employees own stock in the company. Burr himself conducted much of new-employee training, using his proselytizing skill to generate enthusiasm and rally people behind his vision.

At the time, the concept of cheap fares was a radical one: other airlines would charge $189 to $250 or more for the same flight that would cost only $79 on People Express. In order to do this, Burr shifted outside the normal airline paradigm and expanded the scope of each job, limited services offered, and made employees partners in the business. Whereas Eastern had dozens of job categories and a terrible relationship with its unions, People Express had only three categories: the people who fly the plane, the people who fix the plane, and everyone else. A truly creative solution to rising airfares. So why did Burr derail? Because he failed to manage the details inherent to his business and listen to his advisers who tried to talk him out of expanding when there were no systems in place to manage the expansion. His staff, including top management, burned out while Burr continued hammering away at the vision. Burr was great when it came to developing a vision, but short on attention to the kinds of details that ultimately derailed him.

You may be surprised when you read that a person who successfully combined the two skill sets was a woman who worked with cosmetics and had a penchant for pink Cadillacs—the late Mary Kay Ash, founder of Mary Kay Cosmetics. She began her business with a clear strategic intent: to create a company that would enable women to be financially independent while permitting them to focus on God first, family second, and work third. Next, she had the foresight to surround herself with good people who complemented her own natural abilities. Mary Kay thought strategically and planned thoughtfully—a combination of skills that contributed significantly to her success and the success of everyone involved with Mary Kay Cosmetics. When less enlightened leaders attempted to embarrass her about the fact that she rewarded employees with pink Cadillacs, her typical response was, "What color Cadillacs do you give to your employees?"

Square Pegs in Round Holes

People with a natural inclination for either detail orientation or strategic thinking often choose jobs that enable them to rely on one or the other skill. It is not coincidence that those who are happy working for the IRS generally have an ability to pay acute attention to detail, whereas those who find job satisfaction at NASA or the Jet Propulsion Laboratory are likely to be strategic thinkers. Both types of people, however, may find themselves in a quandary when they are forced into a job or assignment that requires the complementary behavior. Just one skill or the other isn't enough to assure continued success.

A few years ago, a client of mine had a significant reduction in its workforce, entirely eliminating its public relations department. One staff member, whom I will call Amanda, had been with the company for nearly twenty years and her management wanted to reward her loyalty by finding a place for her in another department. Amanda had been a public relations coordinator and, as such, had significant contact with the media, senior executives, and esteemed guests. She was superb at finessing all of the relationships involved in her job.

Amanda's management was pleased when they found her a job as a clerk in their benefits department. Now they wouldn't have to lay her off. Amanda herself was pleased as well—at least in the beginning. After Amanda had been in the new job for several months, I called her to see how she was doing. This normally upbeat and optimistic woman was extremely unhappy in her new job and was thinking about leaving the company. When I probed into what the problem was, she said that she couldn't stand working alone day after day and paying such close attention to the most minute details that her job required.

For twenty years Amanda was used to seeing the big picture, juggling multiple tasks and people, and paying close attention to people problems. When she was put into a job that required close attention to detail and afforded little contact with people, it wasn't so much that she *couldn't* do it, but that she didn't want to do it. And herein lies the mistake that so many companies make: when people fail to succeed in their positions, they send them for training rather than assess their suitability for the job. The fact is, most of us can do whatever we put our minds to provided, of course, that we have the necessary basic skills. When we're not doing what we are capable of, it does no good to get more training. Job satisfaction comes from doing what we're good at and what we have a natural inclination toward. When we enjoy our work, we are more likely to be able to balance the big picture with the details required to do it.

A case in point is that of a woman who was sent for coaching because she "wasn't detail oriented enough and displayed poor judgment." When her boss was asked to be more specific, he gave the example of how she chose the wrong kind of furniture for the executive offices. Instead of choosing conservative, dark wood, she chose to go with a lighter, more contemporary look. Before my first meeting with the woman, I went to the executive floor to take a look at the furniture. It was a lovely choice that complemented the surroundings, but it couldn't be called conservative.

At our first meeting, I asked the woman why she thought coaching had been suggested for her. She said that she supposed it was because she didn't fit in. She had an artistic background and she had been hired as an interior decorator for the company based on her knowledge of design. Nevertheless, her management always second-guessed her decisions. She brought to our second meeting a portfolio of watercolor paintings that were incredibly beautiful. As she proudly displayed each one, she said that this was what she wanted to be doing—painting. It occurred to me as I looked at the paintings that one has to have an eye for detail in order to be able to paint on the scale of which she was clearly capable. On the other hand, she had to see the world in a way that was very different from that of her corporate counterparts. It wasn't that she didn't have derail orientation or that she lacked good judgment, she simply wasn't inclined to pay attention to the details required in her job.

Both this woman and Amanda were fortunate to have enough self-confidence not to settle for jobs for which they were ill suited. Once Amanda recognized the true nature of her problem, she asked for a transfer to a different type of work that would more fully use her talents. She's now working happily as the administrative assistant in a busy department where she gets to interact with many different types of people and use her fine administrative skills. And as for the artist—she's now living in Taos, New Mexico, a perfect setting for artists and watercolor painting.

Just because you aren't detail or big-picture oriented in one situation, doesn't mean you can't be in another. The trick is to find work that allows you to use both skills and to know when to apply each. The more you like your work, the greater the likelihood that you'll be able to call on the full range of your capabilities instead of relying exclusively on just a few strengths. It is the balance that assures success and enables you to avoid derailment.

One last anecdote before providing you with some suggestions for how to find that balance. I received a call from a man whom I had met during a supervisory-skills training program. He said that he was going to do an employee's annual performance review and wanted to run by me what he was going to say to make sure he wasn't being too subjective. He faxed me the review, and as I was studying it I noticed that it pretty much revolved around the need to develop more follow-through and attention to detail. When I called him back to discuss it, I mentioned that it seemed as though the employee might not enjoy what he was doing. Generally, when people like their work, they quite naturally pay attention to the details of it and complete it in a timely fashion. In other words, we do well the things we like doing and put off doing things we don't enjoy. After a moment's pause, the man said that was indeed true. He had spoken on numerous occasions with the employee about the fact that he seemed mismatched for the job, but that there were no more suitable jobs available in the company at the time.

I don't envy the manager who has to coach someone who is doing work that he or she dislikes. When an employee tries to fit into the wrong job, his or her energy is diverted by trying to make the work fit, rather than doing the job efficiently and effectively. Your ultimate success depends on doing work that you love and for which you are well suited. You cannot expect to achieve peak performance when you are not interested in the fundamental nature of your work. Certainly, there are aspects of all jobs that we may not like but need to do nonetheless. We have to learn to do these tasks with enthusiasm and attention equal to that which we bring to the tasks that we enjoy. Satisfaction comes from the nature of the work and our enjoyment of it. Balancing details and the big picture is much easier when you are in the right job than it is when you're doing something simply because it pays well or because someone always expected you would do it.

Factors Contributing to a Narrow Focus

The tendency to focus on details to the exclusion of the bigger picture is characterized by the need to micromanage people and processes, overattendance to minutiae, and the inability to see the relationships between issues or factors. People with high detail orientation typically do well in jobs that require precision and meticulous singular concentration. It is a wonderful gift to be precise and focus on detail, but it can be a derailment factor if not balanced with the opposite—the ability to think strategically.

Although there is evidence that the inclinations toward either detail orientation or strategic thinking are something we are born with, both can become overdeveloped. For example, logical, linear thinking, or detail orientation, is valued in our educational system. Overdevelopment of this particular strength can also stem from the need to function effectively in a chaotic childhood home or from having parents who were not sufficiently attentive to the child's needs. The child, then, learns to compensate for this household deficit by becoming hypervigilant. Fearing that important things will be overlooked or neglected entirely, he or she assures nothing is missed by paying close attention to the details of daily life. Paradoxically, however, things *are* overlooked because he or she is not able to view the entire situation.

In the workplace, acute attention to detail is displayed by people who follow instructions religiously and honor tried-and-true ways of doing things. They may be given an assignment with incorrect instructions and, instead of realizing that the instructions are wrong, they continue along the path until someone else points out the error of their ways. For example, when told to "hold all calls and take messages," a person may do as instructed, but fail to realize that when the company president calls it might be appropriate to put that particular call through (or at least check to see whether the boss wants to take the call). Or, someone may prepare reports with illogical conclusions because they fail to see that there has been a mistake in a formula or procedure used to reach those conclusions. This is why outstanding bookkeepers may not make particularly good financial analysts. The skills required to be accurate are not the same ones required to assess the broader financial picture. It is easy to see how someone with strong detail orientation adds only limited value to an organization.

In addition to the childhood factors contributing to detail orientation, there are a number of other reasons why people fail to think strategically. They include:

● **Fear.** A significant factor contributing to the inability to see the bigger picture is fear. In an effort to get it "right," some people miss the nuances in a message. They try too hard and wind up listening selectively. The fear may be generalized and apply to all situations or only to those that involve people in authority. I recall early in my career giving instructions to an assistant to cancel the arrangements previously made for a visit to a particular city. She asked me for all of the details about the date, flight, and airline and then canceled these, but neglected to cancel all concomitant plans such as car, hotel, etc. She was great when given specific instructions, but she could not take the next step to assure that all related aspects of a project were similarly attended to. The woman's fear of making a mistake caused her to miss the bigger picture in favor of focusing on a specific task. The value that she could add was limited by this fear.

● **Rigidity.** People who engage in ritualistic or other narrowly defined behavior frequently can't see new and different ways of doing things. They plod along the same path, every day, in the same way. They would never think of driving a different way to work, eating something different for breakfast, or solving a problem in an unorthodox way. Instead, they do things in prescribed and familiar ways. When asked why they didn't do something in a more effective way, they often reply that it never occurred to them. Rigidity impedes the ability to think broadly and strategically.

● **The inability to deal with ambiguity.** I've never forgotten a line from a college textbook that said something to the effect, "The sign of the mentally healthy person is the one who can deal best with ambiguity because that's all life is—ambiguous." Those people who must deal with the known, as opposed to the possible, have tremendous difficulty thinking broadly. By operating within a constant comfort zone of what is known, as opposed to what could be, such people never take the kinds of risks required to successfully balance detail orientation with strategic thinking.

● **High sense of urgency**. If there is a high sense of urgency, individuals may focus so hard on completing the task that they miss the how, why, and what of the project. In an effort to get the job done expediently, they fail to see how it may tie in to the bigger picture. Ironically, the opposite end of the spectrum being too involved in the big picture to the exclusion of attention to detail—can also result from a high sense of urgency for reasons that will be discussed later.

● **Low sense of urgency**. This factor affects people on both ends of the spectrum as well. People with an overdeveloped detail orientation and a low sense of urgency frequently underestimate the amount of time they actually have to complete a project and spend an inordinate amount of time on the technicalities involved. They spend their time making fail-safe plans, nitpicking, and reviewing the most mundane details as opposed to understanding that a project must be completed both accurately and in a timely fashion.

● **Narrowly defined roles**. One mistake made by many businesses is to define employee roles too narrowly. This was a trend in the 1970s and 1980s, and a generation of "specialists" emerged. People were asked to do one thing really well. They developed a depth of knowledge in their fields but lacked a breadth of experience that would later be useful to them. When the layoffs of the 1990s hit, they were ill equipped to take on broader responsibilities. Although job descriptions provide an in-depth understanding of a particular role, they can narrow the employee's perspective and expectations. In the past, organizations had plenty of people with each type of preference—detail and big-picture people—to meet their needs. As they have downsized, however, it is expected that the people remaining will be able to function comfortably in both arenas. It is now more critical than ever that people be able to both initiate and implement new ideas—a feat requiring both detail and strategic thinking skills.

Ways to Develop Strategic Thinking

The shift from detail orientation to strategic thinking is probably the toughest behavioral change suggested in this book. It requires not only specific behavioral changes, but also changes in how you look at the world. The factors contributing to the former are so strong that they completely eclipse the ability to engage in the latter. Even the term strategic thinking is ominous to some who perceive this function to be the exclusive domain of people in think tanks or strategic planning jobs. Instead, it is simply a way of describing the behaviors required to think more broadly.

The following suggestions can help you become a strategic thinker:

1. Avoid taking notes when someone is talking to you. The technique of active listening described under Reason #1 works well here. In order to comprehend the entire picture, you can't grasp only one aspect of it. I once coached a woman who tried to write down everything I said (can you guess what she had to work on?). Inevitably, she missed the point of what I was saying by attempting to capture the details. Surrender yourself to the speaker, ask questions, and paraphrase what you've just heard. This will allow you to hear and understand the subtleties of the message.

2. Ask yourself, "What is the bigger picture here?" Take time from the task to think momentarily about what it means, how it fits into other projects, and why you are being asked to do it. Avoid the tendency to jump into a project before you've thought it through completely. Learn to become comfortable with negligible delays— especially when those delays are for the purpose of up-front planning. Most assignments aren't as urgent as you might initially think. You may even be imposing your own sense of urgency where there is none.

3. Consciously seek ways to improve processes. Instead of doing the job in the same old way, think about how you might do it more efficiently or creatively. If necessary get input from others about how they might approach the same task. Make suggestions for improving processes in ways that might prove to be more cost-effective or in some other way add value to your department or company.

4. Read books and journal articles that expand your understanding of trends in your field of expertise. All too often we read only materials that address the technical aspects of how we do our jobs. This is important, but equally important are materials that ask you to think about where your field is headed, current challenges that it faces, and concepts that go beyond business as usual. See yourself as someone who anticipates and responds to the requirements of the future, not just reacts to it.

5. Broadly define your role. Whether you are a secretary, first-line supervisor, or division vice president, look for ways in which your role interfaces with those of coworkers, other departments and companies, or customers. Talk to these people about their needs and ways in which you can partner with them in an effort to add value, and envision yourself at the center of a complex network rather than as a lone performer. Consider the possibility that you can create the ideal job for yourself by expanding, not changing, your role.

6. Resist perfectionism. Perfectionists spend so much time attending to details that they often fail to see the large issues involved in a project. They wind up missing the clues to success that often lie in the periphery. Rather than spend time perfecting perfection, use that time to think broadly and strategically about critical points of interface, better ways to do the job, and anticipate tomorrow's trends.

7. Be creative. Betty Edwards's *Drawing on the Right Side of the Brain* and Julia Cameron's *The Artist's Way* are places to start. Both books provide exercises that stimulate right-brain thinking. You can also take classes in creative writing, drawing, or acting that will help you express your innate, creative talents. Most important, don't worry about being good at it or doing it right; do it for fun.

How Overutilization of Strategic Thinking Can Cause Derailment

Any strength taken to the extreme becomes your greatest liability. Even if you work in the most creative of environments where possibilities abound, such as a movie studio, fashion design house, or genetics engineering laboratory, you are still expected to produce well-thought-out and practical results. People who are gifted with the ability to think broadly, creatively, or strategically often suffer from analysis paralysis. They become so caught up in the idea that they overlook the need to turn the idea into reality.

I once worked with a man who was brilliant at conceptualization. He could come up with ideas for any major project on which our company was working. If you wanted to brainstorm, he was the man to go to. The only problem was that he was short on implementation. He often provided solutions so complex that they couldn't possibly be carried out cost-effectively. He was unable to work within boundaries and was forever exceeding his budget without really producing results. When the company went through a downsizing, he was one of the first people tapped because his contribution to the organization was limited. He couldn't make his dreams a reality.

Another form of overutilization of strategic thinking comes with people who are manic. They are often off the scale of the creative continuum. You may know some of these folks. They are energetic, enthusiastic, and innovative—but so much so that they exceed the bounds of acceptable behavior. They tire us mortals out with their continual flow of ideas and concepts. They are frequently successful in entrepreneurial efforts, provided they don't overextend their resources, because they believe in their ability to overcome any obstacle and won't take "no" for an answer. They are less successful in the corporate arena because they typically can't function within the bounds of expected social and group behavior and are perceived as loose cannons by their management.

The factors contributing to overutilization of strategic thinking are not quite as clear-cut as those contributing to acute attention to detail. Certain types of personalities seem more inclined to be able to think broadly and creatively than others. Certainly being raised in a home or working in an environment where creativity is valued and encouraged is a plus, but there must also be a degree of imagination in the individual to begin with. Whereas innovativeness can be thwarted and not allowed to blossom fully, the opposite is not always true. It may be more difficult for people who have never developed a creative pursuit to develop an ability to innovate later in their lives, no matter how much they are encouraged to do so. Yet we can all stretch the boundaries of thinking that confine us by rejecting strict adherence to outdated norms, self-limiting paradigms, and early childhood messages that have outlived their usefulness.

For those of you who think too broadly and strategically and overlook the importance of producing results, the following suggestions should help you achieve balance with greater attention to detail.

● **Schedule time for both project development and project implementation.** When you are given an assignment, allocate a specific amount of time to be used for brainstorming, research, or development. Resist the tendency to use more time than you have allocated or to cut short the implementation period. On the front end, realistically assess how much time it will actually take to complete the project once it is designed and schedule adequate time to meet that requirement. To avoid being top-heavy with creative types, be certain to include people who complement your strengths on project teams.

● **Solicit input from (and listen to) your more practical colleagues.** Bounce your ideas off people you can trust who can see the realities of a situation. Ask them for their opinion of the practicality of your ideas, reasonableness of direction, and value to the company or customer. Rather than viewing these people as overly simplistic or obstacles to your brilliant ideas, consider the counterpoint that they offer as valuable insight into what the organization might expect or find feasible.

● **Consider your audience.** When making presentations, consider the fact that you will most likely have to influence an array of personality types, most of whom don't share your big-picture orientation. Couch your remarks within a framework that will stretch the imaginations of the most conservative people in the audience without making them roll their eyes in disbelief or think that you are from another planet. Remember to include well-thought-out suggestions for how your idea can be implemented practically and efficiently.

● **Find an outlet for external creative endeavors.** If you work in an organization that just doesn't appreciate your creativity or ability to think strategically, ensure that you have outlets in your personal life to exercise those talents. Join clubs, write books, paint pictures, or associate with like-minded people who will validate and encourage you. A very creative woman who worked down the hall from me had a boring, mundane job poring over tables, data runs, and figures all day long. But to her, her work wasn't her life. Her life started when she left at 5:00 P.M..

● **Consider the possibility that you are in the wrong job.** As with the artist who is now in Taos painting, it is an awful feeling to think that you have to sublimate your greatest gifts in order to fit into your organization. Once you've tried all of the things suggested above, and you still can't quite focus on detail and planning to the degree that your management wants you to, then you might do better switching to a job or career that will value and use your unique skill set. There is a caveat here, however: *Wherever you go, you bring you with you,* and that means that your developmental areas as well as your strengths follow you from job to job. Although a more creative environment may not expect such excessive attention to detail, they will most likely expect *some* attention to it. Changing jobs typically doesn't solve the problem entirely.

Although balance is required in all the suggestions for overcoming your strengths contained so far in this book, it is in the areas of detail orientation and strategic thinking that it is most critical. Good technical skills balance good people skills, but good technical skills don't balance excessive detail orientation or overutilized strategic thinking. They balance each other.

Developing Skill in Strategic Thinking

1. Take a stress-management class so that you don't succumb to the need to treat everything with the utmost urgency.

2. Develop the patience and foresight needed to think strategically by learning to play chess.

3. Take small risks by doing things differently from the way you usually do them.

4. Look for the relationships between things instead of focusing on one thing at a time.

5. Plan projects before beginning them so as to allot sufficient time for completion in a timely manner.

6. Subscribe to a magazine that addresses trends in your field of expertise.

7. Trust your ability to do things right the first time and then use the remaining time to plan for the future.

8. Think about your role and your contribution to your organization broadly instead of limiting yourself to a job description or job title.

9. Question and stretch the rules now, and then.

10. Spend time brainstorming a project with creative colleagues before diving into it.

11. Once a week take a different route to work.

12. Take a class in drawing, writing, or sculpture just for fun, to open your mind to the possibilities.

Developing Detail Orientation

13. Take a time-management class so that you can more effectively balance design and implementation time.

14. Consider the practicalities of implementation before suggesting solutions.

15. Strictly adhere to deadlines—missed deadlines should be the exception rather than the rule.

16. Meditate to help improve your focus.

17. Be certain that presentations include concern conceptual validity and practical implementation.

18. Carefully prepare your message in your mind before you give your opinion.

19. Before beginning a project draw a schematic, flowchart, or other visual to help you focus on the practicalities.

20. Ask detail-oriented colleagues for input into the logistics of a project.

21. Volunteer to chair meetings and use an agenda to keep the group on track.

22. If you are a manager, hire staff who complement your own natural ability with their attention to detail.

23. Avoid taking on unnecessary or low priority projects before you've completed more critical ones.

24. Balance your checkbook.

Indifference to Customer or Client Needs

Strategy: Develop a "Can-Do" Attitude

I recently was waiting in the lobby of a large and well-known non-profit agency when the receptionist answered the phone. Although I could only hear half the conversation, I got the gist of what must have been said on the other end based on her responses. It went something like this:

Caller: Can you tell me where you're located?

Receptionist: 6578 West Main.

Caller: What's the cross street?

Receptionist: Sixth Street.

Caller: What exit is that off of the freeway?

Receptionist: Belleview.

Caller: Are you east or west of the freeway?

Receptionist: West.

Caller: Are there any landmarks?

Receptionist: There's a hospital on the corner.

Caller: I'm familiar with that area, but I can't picture your building.

Receptionist: We're behind the hospital.

Caller: Thanks.

Receptionist: [No response, just hangs up.]

Listening to the conversation, I was struck by the fact that the receptionist did nothing to help this person, who was obviously trying to figure out how to get to the building, find his or her way there. Despite the fact that the building is situated behind the hospital that she mentioned, and therefore easy to miss for a first-time visitor (I had the problem myself), she simply answered the questions she was asked.

The situation provides a good example of indifference to customer or client needs and the unwillingness to do anything more than minimally required. I am certain that if the receptionist were asked why she wasn't more helpful, she would be indignant at the implication. After all, she answered the questions the caller posed to her. How much different an impression the caller (and I) would have had if the conversation went something like this instead:

Caller: Can you tell me where you're located?

Receptionist: Where are you coming from?

Caller: The north end of town.

Receptionist: You'll take the freeway south to the Belleview exit and turn left. Go about four stop lights to Sixth and turn right. When you reach Main, you'll see a hospital on the right corner. Go another half block and turn right into the first driveway. We're located directly behind the hospital.

Caller: Thanks.

Receptionist: My pleasure.

Doing your job is no longer enough to ensure your success. People who avoid career derailment go above and beyond the obvious job requirements or requests—they anticipate needs and meet them without being prodded. Many of the behaviors discussed in the previous chapters contribute to what is commonly called a can-do attitude. For example, people who have relationships in place that contribute to getting the job done, who see the bigger picture and not only the details involved in a project, and who manage up successfully are more likely to view new or potentially complex assignments as interesting challenges rather than as obstacles to getting their routine tasks out of the way. Such people have the tools required to react confidently to nearly any request that may come their way.

A can-do attitude is exemplified by the second scenario described above as opposed to the first. It is having the outlook that "I'm not sure *how* I'll do it, but it *will* get done," as opposed to something more ambivalent like "I'm not sure I can do that," or even worse, a response that shuts the door entirely, such as "That's just not possible." Another way of looking at a can-do attitude is having a customer-service orientation, recognizing that *all those people with whom you interact are, in fact, your customers.*

People with a can-do attitude tend to check off most of the items on this list:

_____ I look at barriers to goal achievement as challenges, not insurmountable obstacles.

_____ I tend to be overly optimistic about how much I can accomplish in a day.

_____ It is unusual for me to turn down uncommon or special requests.

_____ I view my colleagues, management, and clients as my customers.

_____ I gain a great deal of personal satisfaction from knowing that I went the extra mile for someone.

_____ Although my initial internal reaction to unrealistic requests may be "no way," I rarely voice that to the person making the request.

_____ I have no problem with putting a routine project or task on hold so that I can attend to something more urgent that comes up.

_____ I believe that providing service to others is an integral part of my job.

_____ I typically search for new or better ways of serving my customers.

_____ If it is within the realm of my capability, there is no task too inconsequential for me to perform if it will further the goals of my organization.

_____ I promptly answer my phone messages, regardless of who they are from.

_____ I frequently offer to help others with their work when I see that help is needed.

_____ I don't promise what I know I can't deliver and I try to deliver more than I promise.

A can-do attitude is typified by the willingness and desire to serve the customer, meet all reasonable requests, go above and beyond the call of duty, and find creative ways to solve seemingly insurmountable problems. It is the opposite of what psychologist and author Dr. Judith Bardwick calls an attitude of *entitlement*. In her book *Danger in the Comfort Zone*, Bardwick describes the phenomenon of entitlement as "an attitude, a way of looking at life. Those who have this attitude believe that they do not have to earn what they get. They come to believe that they get something because they are owed it, not because they are *entitled* to it. They get what they want because of *who* they are, not because of what they *do*." The receptionist described above suffers from a serious case of entitlement. Bardwick finds an attitude of entitlement especially prevalent among workers who never reach their full career potential. I find it prevalent among people who have derailed.

A person who has a can-do attitude is not to be confused with a yes-person. Whereas a yes-person acts to please others in an effort to ward off criticism or garner the favor of others, the person with a can-do attitude acts in ways that further the goals of the company or department. He or she knows that adding value is part of his or her job, not adjunct to it. It's easy to see how you can get caught up doing the basic requirements of your job, without realizing that this often is not enough to assure long-term success. People who avoid premature derailment do something more than their jobs. This is what distinguishes them from their colleagues. They are viewed by their management as adding value based on a contribution over and above what may be contained in their job descriptions, and they understand what it truly means to be of service.

To Be of Service

A common complaint heard today is that "so-and-so acted as though he were doing me a favor when all he did was his job." And it isn't an ill-founded complaint. Whether in a restaurant or schoolroom, at the post office, in a department store, or in your own office, you see people performing the job to which they are assigned act as though they were being put out by requests from the very people they are there to serve. This was certainly the case with our receptionist at the beginning of the chapter. We each perform a service that, presumably, is of value to the company or the customer or we wouldn't be paid to do it. Why, then, do so many people resist providing the best service that they possibly can? Perhaps the answer lies, at least partially, in our interpretation of the word *service* and the fact that it is closely aligned with the word *servant.*

Although none of us likes to think of himself or herself as a servant, Robert K. Greenleaf, a former AT&T executive and founder of the Indianapolis-based Center for Applied Ethics, illuminates another way to think about it. Greenleaf's book, *Servant Leadership: A Journey into the Nature of Legitimate Power and Greatness,* significantly changed my view of the role that I play in serving others. His use of the term *leadership* in the title should be looked at broadly in the context of service, as opposed to simply a reference to those in authority. Even with formal leaders in place in organizations, we each play the role of leader from time to time. the example that Greenleaf uses is the character Leo in Hermann Hesse's *Journey to the East.* Leo is the servant, in the traditional sense, to a group of men who are on a mythical journey. He performs menial tasks for them, but he also is an influential spirit within the group. Leo buoys the men through his powerful presence. When he disappears, the men find that they can't continue the journey without him. Greenleaf writes: "to me, this story clearly says that *the great leader is seen as servant first,* and that simple fact is key to his greatness. Leo was actually the leader all of the time, but he was servant first because that was what he was, *deep down inside.*"

Unfortunately, we have come to regard service as something done by anyone in a lesser position than ours. Even in organizations that claim to be nonhierarchical, a pecking order still exists. It begins with the company president and continues down throughout the organization to entry-level positions. The pecking order dictates who you can have lunch with, be social with, and offer assistance to. It is somewhat ridiculous when you think about it because within any organization everyone is there to serve the customer or client. We are all, then, servants in one way or another. Whether or not we have direct contact with customers, our work affects the final outcome. You frequently hear line people describe staff people as "overhead." Staff people (also call "back office" or "corporate") don't directly contribute to developing, producing, or selling a product or service, so they are not thought of as contributing to the bottom line. Staff people, however, provide valuable services to line people—services without which the product or service could not be produced as efficiently or effectively.

This point was beautifully illustrated at yet another leadership program held at the Ritz-Carlton in Pasadena, California. To make the point about the importance of a can-do attitude, I asked if two of the maintenance men responsible for setting up the room would answer some questions about why they provide such high-quality service. Participants asked these men questions to help them better understand the can-do attitude exhibited by all the staff's employees.

Q: Why do you think you provide service so superior to that of your counterparts at other hotels?

A: Because we're treated so well. We're trained that we are ladies and gentlemen serving ladies and gentlemen. When we pass another employee in the hall, it's expected that we will treat that person the same as we would an important guest.

Q: Do you think that how you set up this room has any effect on the profits of the hotel?

A: Yes. If we put a tablecloth on that is stained, and you lift your glass and find a stain, then you'll look at that all day and remember it when you're deciding whether or not to come back and stay with us.

Q: How is it that you deliver even the most obscure requests?

A: We're each given a budget so that if a guest asks for something that we don't have, we can go out and buy it. All we have to do is present the receipt to the boss and we're paid back by the hotel.

Q: You mean you can just leave the hotel, get in your car, and go down to Office Depot and buy what we need?

A: Yes. After we tell our supervisor that we're going.

If you examine this notion of serving as Greenleaf does, that "the work exists for the person as much as the person exists for the work—the business then becomes a serving institution—serving those who produce and those who use," then being a servant isn't such a bad thing after all. We each serve others in different, but invaluable, ways. People with a can-do attitude understand that their positions exist to serve the customer as well as their colleagues.

I once walked past the employee lounge in a department store and saw a posted sign that read: "People are not an interruption of our work—they *are* our work." It was a simple sign, but one that I never forgot. It acted as a reminder to employees that their role was to serve others. A can-do attitude is prevalent in those who understand this very basic premise. Can you imagine working in a company where the executives see themselves as servants? Or in a school where the principal sees himself or herself as there to serve the teachers and students? How might it change the environment? Would their constituents think any less of them? On the contrary— it would create an enhanced sense of teamwork and customer-driven behavior.

Here is a list of some of the most common complaints that I hear about the absence of a can-do attitude. You can decide which ones may apply to you.

- **Works to rule.** Does just enough work to get by—doesn't do anything extra or beyond the scope of his or her job description.

- **Not a self-starter.** Does the work to which he or she is specifically assigned, but doesn't seek additional responsibility or see what else needs to be done unless told, and even then requires an inordinate amount of supervision.

- **Resistant to new ideas.** Prefers doing things in routine ways and is unwilling to consider new methods for improving the quality or quantity of work.

- **Not a team player.** Does only his or her own work—doesn't help out others in a pinch.

- **Lacks enthusiasm.** Does the job, but without excitement or energy.

- **Uncooperative.** Fails to help implement or may sabotage new ideas that others generate for improving products or services.

- **Unmotivated.** Meets not even the basic job requirements and requires constant prodding or coaxing.

- **Bad attitude.** This is usually a catchall term for a generally negative, critical, or condescending approach to customer service or team efforts.

If you see yourself in one or more of these terms, then you must seriously consider why this is the case—and do something about it. Let's take a look at why people fail to exhibit a can-do attitude.

Why No-Can-Do?

By now, it should be no surprise to you that I do not believe that people are born with a lack of service orientation. They develop it—and for good reasons. Whether it is developed as a childhood defense mechanism in response to unreasonable demands or as a method for dealing with ineffective leadership, it will quickly derail the best of employees before they realize it. An understanding of why and how it develops can help you to overcome a no-can-do attitude.

1. Poor management. Although managers are often quick to point the finger at employees who lack a can-do attitude, they fail to realize that they themselves may be the cause of it. The most common ways in which managers curb enthusiasm and motivation are to be too controlling or overly critical. If you are a manager, remember to delegate the project not the process. When managers control how someone does something, they eventually succeed in having everything done their way, but their way may not always be the best way. It only serves to thwart creativity and innovation. Similarly, overly critical managers make staff members afraid to show initiative for fear of being unjustly criticized for their efforts. In either case, employees eventually wait to be told what to do, how to do it, and brace themselves for anticipated disapproval.

2. Poor job match. Countless people are in jobs for which they are ill suited because they were steered into them by well-meaning parents or teachers, or because they can't see the options available to them. High salaries, family expectations, prestige, and other perks and benefits keep people in jobs they hate going to each day. These reasons become what are known as "golden handcuffs." People dislike the work, but remain tied to it because of social or financial reasons. As a result, they suffer from lackluster performance and low motivation. It is pretty difficult to enthusiastically perform a job you just don't like.

3. Powerless/powerful parenting. Either end of the power spectrum can impede a child from developing a healthy sense of initiative. On the one hand, when parents present themselves as all-powerful, it is tough for the child to think he or she knows the right thing to do; instead, he looks to authority for the answers. The old maxims "father knows best" and "children are to be seen and not heard" summarize what is at the root of these behaviors. Employees who won't make a move without being given permission or direction may have had parents who expected them to be compliant and submissive. On the other hand, parents who see themselves as lacking control over their own lives often instill the same in their children. Patents who allow themselves to be controlled by the desires of others may unwittingly impart the message to their children that their lot in life is to follow the instructions given to them and not make waves with their own ideas or methods for doing things. As adults, people who had either powerless or powerful parenting may lack the necessary confidence to take the kind of risks required to extend themselves beyond what is asked.

4. High detail orientation. What strategic thinkers call resistance to new ideas may in actuality be a manifestation of high detail orientation. Such people often see only the complexities of an idea and retort with the many reasons why it can't possibly work, instead of seeking solutions to those barriers that are less obvious to the big-picture person. They become overwhelmed by the morass of details required to make a new idea a reality and are unable to break it into smaller, manageable pieces.

5. Monopoly of products or services. The absence of competition can lead to a "take-it-or-leave-it" mentality. Whether it's the only grocery store in a small town or the only provider of air transportation out of a particular city, a monopoly can serve to diminish the attention paid to and value placed on customer service. People working in a monopolistic organization tend to forget that they are there to serve others and instead take advantage of their position in the market.

6. Depression. The incidence of depression in the U.S. population is far greater than most people realize. Statistics suggest that women have a 20 to 26 percent lifetime risk for depression and men an 8 to 12 percent lifetime risk. Symptoms of depression include, among others, the loss of interest in activities one normally finds enjoyable and feelings of general fatigue or lethargy. Depression is a significant factor that can contribute to one's lack of enthusiasm or motivation to perform the job in anything more than a perfunctory manner. In order to address the appropriate cause, it is important to understand that the work can contribute to the depression as well as the depression contribute to failure to perform the work.

No matter how difficult it may be for you to do so, exhibiting a positive, upbeat, can-do attitude is yet another factor critical to avoiding premature career derailment. It doesn't mean that you have to do everything that is asked of you, regardless of the reasonableness of the request; it simply means that you take a positive approach to work, serving the customer, and meeting unforeseen challenges. With the exception of an abrasive personality, the absence of a can-do attitude is easier to spot than any of the other derailment factors described heretofore. This is what makes it such a critical ingredient in your repertoire of skills.

Ways to Exhibit a Can-Do Attitude

Certain companies provide outstanding examples of the presence of a can-do attitude. One such company is the Four Seasons hotel chain. A number of years ago, I was caught in a snowstorm in Boston that began on a Friday morning. I was staying at the Four Seasons and was hesitant to check out for fear of not getting another room in the city if the storm persisted. The desk clerk assured me that there would be no problem. Knowing that "no problem" can mean anything from just that to "really big problem," I remained worried and skeptical throughout the day. By four o'clock that afternoon, Logan Airport had been closed, and I trudged through the snow back to the hotel. While I waited in line behind irate would-be guests demanding rooms that just weren't available, I noticed that the same woman who had earlier promised that there would be no problem was still there. I dreaded what I was sure I was about to hear. When my turn came and I stepped up to the desk, she smiled and said, "Welcome back, Dr. Frankel. When I heard the airport was closed I went ahead and checked you in. Here's your key."

I was more than just a little impressed by the woman's service orientation. She delivered exactly what she said she would—and a bit more. She could have made me feel fortunate to even have a room, given the fact that she could have sold it several times over, but she didn't. She made me feel like a welcome guest. In our respective fields, we are all capable of providing this kind of service, but most of us don't, despite the fact that it's what builds successful companies and contributes to successful careers. Instead, we rely on our technical competence and assume that it will get us over the rough spots. Then, we scratch our heads with wonder when we are passed over for promotions or developmental opportunities.

A second example of a can-do attitude is that of a company that redefined service in the retail clothes marketing arena: Nordstrom. Despite the fact that the company is a high-end concern, it flourished financially even in down markets in no small part because of the customer service attitude exhibited by its sales associates. When you shop at Nordstrom, you are usually met by friendly, knowledgeable, and helpful staff. Without being particularly pushy or aggressive, they make certain that you find what you are looking for. Long before Nordstrom's competitors were doing it, the company had a full return policy—no questions asked, your money was refunded. Countless times I've heard people say that even though Nordstrom costs a bit more they continue shopping there because of the service they receive. I wonder how many people can say that *their* customers exhibit the same loyalty for the products or services they offer.

Then there are the companies that, rightly or wrongly, are notorious for the absence of a service mentality. The only way that they stay in business is by offering a specialized product or service. The U.S. Postal Service is a case in point. With over a half-million employees nationwide, the Postal Service is the largest employer in the country and, until recently, offered products and services that no one else did. Giving credit where credit is due, postal employees perform the herculean task of moving massive amounts of mail around the country, in a timely fashion, at a reasonable cost, and with a very low percentage of letters or packages becoming lost. Now that they are given the choice, however, consumers have flocked to alternative sources for express mail service—despite the fact that the Postal Service offers the same service and at a more reasonable price. Why? In part because of the attitudes of some postal employees.

The topic of discussion at a recent neighborhood party was just this problem. There are four post offices within a three-mile radius of our neighborhood. As it turned out, most of us said that when we had the time, we went to the one farthest away because it had the friendliest staff. At the same time, everyone could name the surliest people at the other locations. The Postal Service provides an outstanding example of how poor management and, in many cases, a poor job match combine to create a no-can-do attitude that is noticeable to all who frequent an establishment. In this case, the fact that no one else manufactures or sells postage stamps or delivers routine letters surely affects customer service. Now, if a group of neighbors spend time talking about something as mundane as where they buy their stamps, what might they be saying about the product or service offered by your company based on your attitude?

There are seven specific things that you can do to assure that you are perceived as someone with a can-do attitude. I preface them by saying that logic and common sense must prevail when responding to any request. There are people who constantly demand unreasonable things of you, and to always have a can-do attitude with these people may be unrealistic or even inappropriate. The customer is *not* always right. You are not expected to be a doormat. On the other hand, you should consider the effect your attitude has on customers, clients, and colleagues and how you can be a better ambassador for the product or services that you provide.

QUESTION/REQUEST	NO-CAN-DO RESPONSE	CAN-DO RESPONSE
Do you think that you'll be able to meet the client's deadline?	I'm not sure. There are an awful lot of obstacles that make it look unlikely.	I have a few concerns, but nothing that can't be overcome if we put our heads together.
Can I exchange this pair of pants for a sweater?	There are no returns or exchanges on sale items.	It is not within the scope of my authority to approve the request, but let me see if I can find someone who can.
Because Todd is on vacation I'd like you to prepare the monthly status report for the president.	Well . . . I've never done it before. I'm not sure I know how.	Sure, I've never done it before but I'm sure I can fiture it out. If I have any questions, I'll ask.
Would you take a look at these recommendations for changes to our product delivery system and give me your input?	I don't know what's wrong with our old system. Besides, it will take at least six months to get it up and running and we've got a new product line coming out around the same time.	I'd be happy to. If we're going to make any changes, this is a good time, since it will take six months to get it up and running and we've got a new product line coming out just after that.
Would you mind processing this expense report for me today because I'm leaving town again tomorrow?	We only process expense reports on Fridays. You'll have to wait until you get back to get your money. Besides, this isn't filled in correctly. You'll have to go back and change it.	We normally process those checks on Fridays, but I don't think that there will be a problem making an exception for you. I did notice that it's missing some necessary information. Why don't I show you what's needed.
We need someone to train the new person on Windows. Would you mind doing it?	I'm not a trainer, you know. I'll need an outline of the goals and objectives before I start and someone else to relieve me of my duties for the six hours that it's going to take.	I've never trained anyone on it before, but I'm willing to give it a try if she'll be patient with me.

QUESTION/REQUEST	NO-CAN-DO RESPONSE	CAN-DO RESPONSE
I've never used your services before. I was wondering whether you could help me to understand what's available?	What is it that you need to know?	I'd be happy to. Which services in particular were you interested in, or would you like me to go over all of them?
I need some information for tomorrow's presentation by 4:00 P.M. today.	You've got to be kidding. Why is everything around here an emergency?	I don't think I'll be of much help because I'm already on a high-priority project. Let's find another way to get it done on time.

1. Develop self-confidence. Each of the following suggestions is predicated on the presence of a healthy degree of self-confidence. A can-do attitude stems from a belief in yourself and your abilities. It isn't a false sense of confidence, but rather one that comes from the knowledge that even when you're unsure of yourself, you know from past successes and accomplishments that you can do this too—and if you can't, you will find someone who can help. By exhibiting self-confidence, we often find that we can do more than we originally thought or learn something that will be useful in the future. In essence, we stretch ourselves to the limits of our abilities.

It appears to me that men tend to have more of an edge than women when it comes to exhibiting self-confidence in new or challenging situations. For example, when a job or assignment comes open for which a woman has no direct experience, she will often decline it, or fail to apply for it, because she thinks she can't do it. In the same situation, men tend to jump in wholeheartedly with the confidence that they'll figure it out as they go along.

Regardless of their sex, people who approach assignments and challenges with confidence instill in others a sense of confidence in them. They are perceived as performers who can handle any task, creatively solve problems, and add value to a department or company.

2. Create win-win situations. Success in creating win-win situations has a lot to do with managing the impressions that others have of you. You want to convey the message that you are ready, willing, and able to help—even when on the inside you're not sure how you're going to do it. When it's clear that you can't do something that you've been asked to do, you turn it into a win-win by helping to find an alternative solution. Consider how changing one's response in each of the situations given in the chart could make a significant difference in the perception of a can-do versus a no-can-do attitude.

3. Deliver what you promise—and more. It never ceases to amaze me how many people fail to deliver what they say they will. Although there are myriad reasons why people don't come through with what they've promised, not many of them are good ones. You may know people who have a can-do attitude but who don't produce what they've committed to. The natural corollary to meeting or beating deadlines is assuring that you don't promise *more than* you can deliver. Building contractors are notorious for having a can-do attitude, then not delivering. No matter how specifically you explain your requirements and closely supervise them, it seems that they finish the job late and over budget. They either underestimate the time required or the complexity of the task, and then they wind up falling short on delivering what they promise. Once this happens, their credibility is seriously damaged. As a result, you see contractors going out of business at a fairly high rate.

Going the extra mile to meet, or even beat, a deadline pays huge dividends in the long run. If it means that you have to work late, come in early, or skip lunch, then so be it. This is not to say that you should miss some important event such as your child's recital, your spouse's birthday, or a parent's anniversary in order to deliver what you promise. Rather, you must anticipate these events vis-a-vis your commitments and make certain that they are *all* met. It means that you must *realistically* plan your work and work your plan.

A common complaint heard from managers is that employees seem to lack the commitment to get the job done within predetermined deadlines. One client called bemoaning the fact that one of her best staff members comes in late and takes extended lunch hours, despite the fact that a particular project is already past due and her client is awaiting the results. Regardless of the employee's technical competence, his failure to deliver on his promises is derailing him more than he realizes. The person with a can-do attitude does whatever it takes to get the job done on time and under budget.

Delivering more than you promise serves to add chips to your account. For example, if you say you'll prepare an outline for an upcoming project, why not include more specifics than typically required, such as costs, a detailed methodology, and ways to overcome anticipated obstacles. If you are known as someone who does not only what you promise but more, then those occasional times when something prevents you from meeting an obligation are overlooked or tolerated (the key word being occasional). You have built credibility that fares well for you in the long term.

4. Anticipate requirements. It is often difficult for people who are detail oriented to foresee ancillary requirements or peripheral issues that will affect the completion of a project. They may be great at checking things off their written or mental lists, but if it's not on the list it doesn't get done. It is a bit like the situation mentioned in the previous chapter in which someone is instructed to cancel plane reservations but neglects to cancel related hotel and car arrangements. The person with a can-do attitude goes above and beyond what is specifically requested by considering all related factors and responding to them in advance.

I once appeared for an all-day training session in a client's office to find the office manager stewing over the fact that the person responsible for scheduling the training room had neglected to order the food for the meeting. When I asked whether she had specifically told the person that she wanted food ordered, she said, "I shouldn't have to. Every time we have an all-day meeting we have food. She should have known to do it." Although it could be argued that the manager shouldn't expect the person to read her mind, her expectation that this staff member will anticipate her needs, especially in light of the fact that a certain protocol is typically followed, isn't unreasonable.

Unfortunately, the old adage "If I knew better, I'd do better" holds true here. If someone isn't particularly good at anticipating requirements, it makes it difficult for him or her to do it. Many of the coaching hints suggested under Reason #6 for developing a better sense of the bigger picture hold true here. In particular, before beginning or completing a project or response to a request, take the time to think about it in its entirety. If you're not sure of what may be required in addition to the obvious, ask questions—particularly of people who are better than you at seeing the big picture.

5. Offer help freely—don't wait to be asked. Failure to offer to help does not always stem from a withholding or stingy personality, although it certainly can. People who are reticent to offer help often are afraid to be intrusive or overstep their boundaries. It reminds me of the person who watches as someone struggles to get through a door with an armload of packages, whereas someone else hurries to help open the door. It goes back to the need for a generosity of spirit.

A can-do attitude doesn't only mean that you can do your own job, it means that you have the best interest of the organization in mind and work to achieve its goals as well as yours. You may have worked with people who leave the office when their work is completed, even when they see others in their group or department working late to meet a deadline. It may not occur to them to offer help, or they may think that it isn't their job. Keep in mind that the job is to best serve the customer. This means that your work isn't limited by your specific job description.

6. Always offer a solution, or request assistance in finding a solution, to identified problems. Managers frequently express frustration with people whom they perceive as malcontents or troublemakers. They describe such people as those who complain about their workload, coworkers, or the injustice of a system that overworks and underpays, but who make no effort to do anything about it. Their whining and complaints bring down the morale of the entire office or department.

People with a can-do attitude, on the other hand, assume responsibility for making things better by pairing any complaint that they may have with suggested solutions or requests for assistance with finding a solution. They don't complain for the sake of complaining, but rather openly discuss problems with the parties concerned in an effort to make things better. If they can't find a solution to the problem themselves, they ask for help in finding one. They know that if things are going to get better, it will be because of their willingness to meet problems head-on.

This guideline is particularly pertinent for team building. People will grumble to one another in small groups about problems in the department, but seldom do they see improving the situation as their responsibility. Once it is made a norm for everyone on the team to assume responsibility, rather than only the manager or team leader, then entire departments move forward with a surge of new ideas and solutions to old problems. It won't work, however, if the team leader fails to empower team members and still expects them to resolve team problems. Success, in this regard, is contingent on the collective wisdom and energy that springs from groups of people who work collaboratively toward a common goal.

---

7. Do what you love—not only what you're good at. Doing what you love can contribute not only to the ability to think more broadly, but also to a can-do attitude. When you do what you love, you quite naturally want to be of service and share your enthusiasm with others. There's no problem that becomes insurmountable when you approach your work with passion.

If you're lucky, what you love and what you're good at are one and the same, but this is not always true. I know a surgeon who is brilliant in his field. He has a full practice and is trusted by his patients and admired by his colleagues for his skill. He once confided in me that he hates his work and, unfortunately, this is reflected in his attitude toward his patients. It is not uncommon to hear them complain about his curtness and dour attitude. Given a choice, many patients say that they would prefer another physician. He's a good example of someone who avoids derailment primarily because his skill is so specialized that he has no local competition.

A man with whom I used to work left the company at about the same time that I did to start his own business. Nearly two years after we were each on our own, we were talking about how quickly the days and weeks fly by now that we're doing what we love. His comment "My worst day on my own is better than my best day working for someone else" frequently resonates in my mind because it's true. Whether you work for someone else or for yourself, you know when you're doing what you love because the challenges are easier to meet and the positive attitude with which you approach your work is obvious to all those with whom you interact.

Some readers may now be thinking, "Doing what you love is easier said than done." From the surgeon who stays in practice for the money to the engineer who needs the health insurance that the job provides to his family, people become stuck in careers for which they no longer have enthusiasm. Social, family, and financial pressures keep people in unsatisfying jobs long after they have stopped enjoying their work and being productive. Feeling stuck contributes to lackluster performance and can also be one cause of depression and physical ailments. The belief that you have no options and are instead constricted by considerations outside of your control is frequently a factor in depression.

You may never have thought of yourself as depressed, but think about these questions:

- Have you given up after-work activities in which you were once interested because you lack energy to engage in them?
- Do you find yourself coming alive on Friday afternoon and becoming more morose on Sunday afternoon with the thought of the next day being a workday?
- Do you pace yourself, in terms of expenditure of energy, so that you can get through the week?
- Do you find yourself frequently daydreaming at work or unable to concentrate on the task at hand?
- Are vacations the highlight of your life?
- Do you catch colds easily and find yourself complaining about a host of aches and pains (either real or imagined)?
- Do you exceed your allowable sick days at work?

- Do you use alcohol or other substances to camouflage your feelings about work?

If you answer yes to any of these questions, it may be that you are in the wrong job and that your situation is making you more depressed than you realize. It is important that you objectively assess your situation and determine ways in which you can balance your obligations with a fulfilling career or outside interests. Talk to friends and family members about your dreams and aspirations and ask for their input. Speak with a career counselor. Interview other people who have successfully moved from an unrewarding job to one they now love. Once you do, you may find that you're not as stuck as you thought you were and that you have more support than you thought for making a career move.

About a year ago, a man named Brett asked me to coach him. At our first meeting, he described what seemed to be a wonderful job that he had as the chief financial officer at a midsize company. He reported that there were no problems with his supervisor that he couldn't handle, and announced that his pay and benefits exceeded his expectations. What then, I asked, could I possibly do for him? As it turned out, Brett was bored with his job and didn't feel that he was using the skills he valued most—working with his hands in the building trades. After exploring possible opportunities within his company, it quickly became clear that there were no jobs inside the company that would be any more appealing to him than the one he had. When it appeared that he would have to begin a job search outside the company, he said that this wasn't possible. His wife was in a low-paying job, and he bore the burden of supporting the family, his in-laws, and two residences. Brett felt like he was stuck.

Our work together focused on getting Brett to talk to his wife about his dreams, to a financial planner about how much the family *needed* to live on, as opposed to what they were living on, and to begin investigating the possibilities in the field where he would be most happy. He wasn't expected to make any moves right away, just plant seeds that might grow to fruition over time. It turned out that his wife was incredibly supportive—more so than he had anticipated. The financial planner gave him good ideas for how he could save money and areas in the country where he might be able to live more economically than where he currently resided. As a result of his legwork, Brett came up with a two-year plan for leaving the company and moving toward a career that would be more rewarding for him and enable him to spend more time with his family. He has another year to go before he actually leaves, but the past months have been a breeze for him at work because he knows he has a plan in place that will soon free him from the golden handcuffs.

The preceding example is intended to illustrate that you may not be as constricted as you think. Existential philosophers say that two of our greatest burdens in life are freedom and responsibility. Even in the most dire circumstances, we have the freedom to choose how we will handle the situation—and the responsibility to deal consciously with that choice. Staying in a job that you no longer like or that positively depresses you is a choice. Before you settle for that choice be certain that you have explored creative alternatives for living your life differently. Not only is your well-being at stake, but the well-being of your family as well.

The importance of having a can-do attitude should by now be abundantly clear. People with a can-do attitude attract similar people and positive experiences. The world works in synchronicity with the person who has a positive, upbeat attitude. Managers report that when interviewing job candidates, a can-do attitude is often weighted more heavily than technical competence. They know that they can teach the basics of a job to someone, but they can't teach someone to have a positive attitude.

Ways to Develop a Can-Do Attitude

1. Always deliver *more* than you promise.
2. Never miss a deadline—and when possible to do so without sacrificing quality, beat it.
3. Replace initial skepticism with creative problem solving.
4. Always accompany a complaint with a proposed solution or a request for assistance with finding a solution.
5. Leave your bad moods outside the office.
6. Actively search for ways to better serve the customer or client.
7. Regardless of your job title, view yourself as both a servant and as a leader.
8. Make certain that you're doing work that you love—even if it means carving a niche within the scope of less enjoyable work.
9. Volunteer for unusual or nonroutine assignments.
10. Use free time to develop systems that add value to the customer or company.
11. When appropriate—lighten up. Smile. Make it fun for others to work with you.
12. Seek help for depression.
13. Return all phone calls, regardless of whom they are from, in a timely manner.
14. Respond to requests with a time frame for completion—don't leave people guessing about what you're going to do and when you plan to do it.
15. Help others overcome their barriers to success.
16. Realistically assess what you can or can't do and don't promise more than you can deliver.
17. Turn lose-lose situations into win-win ones by looking for opportunities to negotiate.

18. Make saying that something can't be done the exception rather than the rule.

19. Carefully listen to the needs of your customers and make certain that what you deliver matches what they need.

20. Go the extra mile by broadly defining your responsibilities rather than performing within the bounds of a narrow job description.

21. If you can't figure out how something can be done, get someone who can to help you.

22. When your work is done, and sometimes even when it isn't, offer to help others with theirs.

23. Use positive self-talk to tape over messages that diminish your self-confidence.

24. Learn as much as you can about how your work contributes to your company's bottom-line profits or services.

Working in Isolation

Strategy: Network for Success

The training manager at a large firm requested that a networking program be developed as an in-house course. The manager thought that it was important for employees to understand the significance of networking for on-the-job success and how to network more effectively. After the program was advertised in the firm's internal newsletter, only eight people signed up to take it—all women. Despite the class size, it was decided that the two-day program would proceed as planned. At the end of the first day, the women commented on how helpful the information was and that they were learning a lot about the subject. The women were asked their opinions as to why, if the information was so beneficial, more people didn't sign up for the program. One woman said that she tried to talk a male coworker into taking the class with her, but that he laughed and said, "Networking? That's just a bunch of women standing around in high heels sipping white wine."

The impression that networking is only for women or members of a specific group, or that it is in some way manipulative, ignores what men have always practiced. Long before it was called networking, men gathered together to exchange war stories and undoubtedly other information pertinent to how to succeed in business by really trying. That was referred to as *the old boys' club*. Vestiges of the old boys' club remain in some cities where private facilities still exist that enable male executives to assemble for meals, meetings, or a drink after work. The men who belong to these facilities are, in effect, networking.

With the proliferation of information technology, and the increasingly popular movement toward team-based efforts, individuals are no longer expected to perform their job responsibilities in isolation. The Internet is testimony to this fact. Whereas in the past people worked independently on projects and were by and large rewarded for their individual contributions, today's worker is expected to function interdependently with a large base of information accessible through his or her relationships with others. Harvard professor John Kotter has conducted extensive research into the factors that contribute to success as a general manager. One of his findings, that a strong network is an essential ingredient of managerial effectiveness, holds true not only for managers, but for people at *all* levels in an organization. Kotter describes a network as the *sum total of the people, both inside and outside your organization, on whom you depend to get your job done.* As was already emphasized under Reason #1, building relationships is critical to creating an effective network. The people who prematurely derail are often the same ones who fail to understand, build, and nurture their professional networks.

Assess your networking acumen with the following checklist.

_____ I belong to professional groups related to my field and am actively involved in them.

_____ I can specifically name the people in my network.

_____ I know what I have to offer others in my network.

_____ I don't view networking as a waste of time, but rather as an invaluable tool for assuring ongoing success.

_____ I spend some portion of each week engaged in at least one networking activity.

_____ I freely share expertise, information, or another commodity with those in my network.

_____ I feel comfortable calling on others in my network and asking for help when I need it.

_____ I can honestly say that my work is made easier because of my network relationships.

_____ I have network relationships at all levels of my organization as well as outside of it.

_____ At times, I use informal gatherings as an opportunity to network.

_____ I'm known as someone who helps others to "connect" professionally.

From Organization Charts to Networks

In the old scheme of things, we used to refer to organization charts to determine where we fell in the pecking order. Hierarchical by design, they typically looked something like the chart presented on page.... Organizational charts provided order to the workforce but did so in a manner that preserved the ranking system, created vertical fiefdoms, and discouraged interdepartmental dependencies.

Today it is more helpful, and appropriate, to think of yourself at the center of a complex web of people, both inside and outside of your organization, with whom you interact in an effort to get the job done effectively. Although some facets of the hierarchy remain, the boundaries between organizational levels have become less clear and crossing them (intentionally and otherwise) is more acceptable while trying to accomplish interrelated tasks. The diagram on page...exemplifies how you might now look at your network. It takes Kotter's concept of the manager's network, described in his work *The General Managers* (The Free Press, 1982), and expands it to include any position within an organization. As you can see, in this new configuration, you are central to the interconnecting web of relationships required to successfully meet the organization's goals. With so many relationships to manage, you can also see why building and maintaining relationships is a factor critical to avoiding career derailment.

Networking is nothing more than simple cognizance of the fact that every person with whom you come into contact is potentially helpful, or harmful, to your success. The moment you enter into a discussion with a colleague about a mutual project, you are networking. When you meet someone at a party whose company uses the same products or services that your company provides, you are networking. The caveat is, you can't build a network for only selfish purposes. People will see through it if you do. You must approach your network relationships in the same manner as you do other relationships—with a generosity of spirit and genuine desire to help, and be helped by, others. At the moment you build a relationship, you are never certain whether you will help it or be helped by it. Remember, *when you need a relationship, it is too late to build it.*

Who Needs to Network?

Even people who are willing to change their behaviors in significant ways in order to avoid career derailment seem to resist networking and come up with a plethora of excuses for avoiding it. These concerns are addressed below.

Excuse #1: **I'm not a good networker.**

Response: Not one of us emerged from the womb a good networker. Although some people are better at it than others, most of us have to make a concerted effort to build relationships. As with other relationships, networking requires certain social skills and comfort with being with others. One tactic that makes networking easier is to use the active listening techniques described under Reason #1. Most people love it when others ask them questions and really listen to their responses. If necessary, take the Dale Carnegie course in how to make friends and influence people. The fact of the matter is, the more you network the easier it becomes.

Excuse #2: **It's a waste of my company's time and money.**

Response: Not true. The knowledge, goodwill, or potential business that you gain from networking is highly beneficial to your

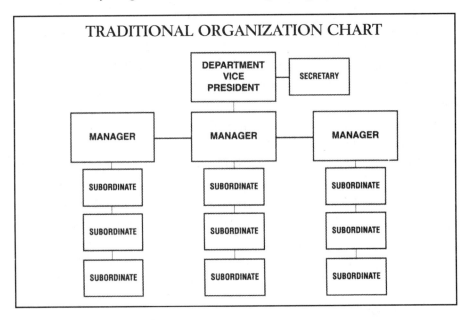

TRADITIONAL ORGANIZATION CHART

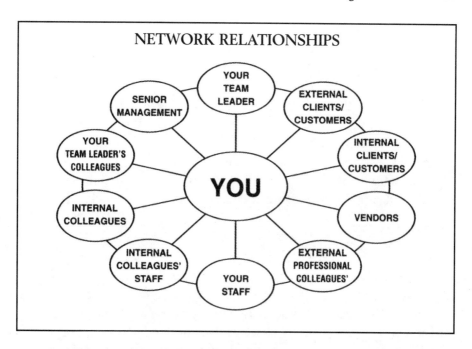

NETWORK RELATIONSHIPS

company. Through networking relationships you increase the pool of resources you may need in the future. Similarly, by acting as a resource for others outside of your firm, you indirectly call attention to your company's products or service. Even internal networking pays dividends in terms of the productivity, brainstorming, and cost savings that results from increased cooperation between teams and individuals over time.

Excuse #3: My workload doesn't permit it.

Response: Your workload may not permit it because you *don't* network. If your schedule is so heavy that you don't have time to network, it may just be that you aren't effectively pooling resources and building bridges of collaboration with internal and external colleagues. Instead, you wind up reinventing the wheel. You must view networking not as an option, but as a *responsibility*. It is your responsibility to have in place any relationships that can further the attainment of your company's, and your own, goals.

Excuse #4: I already have plenty of contacts.

Response: Except in cases where one's work suffers because of spending too much time networking, in which case you wouldn't be using this excuse, you can never have too many contacts. Go back to the networking chart on page and fill in the names of actual people in each category with whom you actively build positive working relationships. If any of the categories have few or no names, then these may be the areas that require your attention. Some people are great at internal networking but neglect their outside contacts. This situation works until a downsizing occurs. Others, especially people in sales and marketing, focus their efforts on external networking. The numbers look great, but often at the cost of a painful effort at getting the internal work achieved.

Excuse #5: Networking is manipulative.

Response: It is only as manipulative as you make it. If you network only for what you can get out of it personally, then it probably is manipulative. On the other hand, if you remember the quid pro quo of relationships—something in exchange for something else—then you are more likely to see and acknowledge opportunities for helping others when they arise. Whether you care to admit it, you are networking every time you meet someone. I'm only putting a name to what happens when people enter into mutually beneficial or rewarding relationships. There is no doubt that you gain personally and professionally from networking. It typically isn't an act of altruism, but it also isn't such a bad thing. Everyone walks away a winner when networking is done properly.

How Networking Works

Every interaction is a networking opportunity. The benefit or quid pro quo may not at first be clear, and it may *never* materialize; nevertheless, networking is important in building positive workplace relationships. Networking can be the difference between making and losing a career. A case in point is the brouhaha caused early in Clinton's presidency by naming his wife, Hillary, as chair of the White House task force on health care issues. The commotion can, at least in part, be ascribed to the fact that prior to the appointment Hillary had few allies in Washington. The Clintons were relative outsiders. There is no doubt that the First Lady could capably handle the assignment, but she had no network in place to support the unprecedented decision.

On the other hand, Lee Iacocca's success at turning around Chrysler was due, in part, to two key factors: bringing in a new management team and securing government funds to bail out the carmaker. Iacocca was able to do both not only because of his track record at Ford, but also because of the relationships that he already had in place when he arrived at Chrysler. He once said that building relationships did not come naturally to him early in his career. It initially made him feel uncomfortable and awkward, but he knew it was important and persevered at it in the same way he did each of his other goals.

People who fail to network, or see it as superfluous to their primary tasks, miss out on untold opportunities. Networking provides you access to inside information about upcoming trends in your business, client leads, information essential to accomplishing your work, assistance with special projects, and myriad other benefits. Often, the networking process isn't obvious and the benefits may not be realized until long after a relationship is established.

Here is an example. A woman I will call Rachael worked with me in the same corporation for a number of years. When I left the company to start my own business, she remained. Although we initially had intermittent contact, communication dwindled until there was no contact. After several years with no contact, Rachael called me. She had decided to start her own consulting business and she wanted to meet with me to discuss the ups and downs of entrepreneurship. We did meet on several occasions and spoke on the phone as Rachael got her business started.

After approximately one year in business for herself, Rachael decided she wasn't cut out for it. She missed the collegiality of working in a large firm as well as the steady income and benefits afforded by it. She took a job with a growing company. As the company grew, opportunities for a consultant with my skills began to emerge. Although she couldn't promise anything, Rachael arranged for me to meet with the people requiring services such as mine. Based on her recommendation, the company began to use my company for certain programs and services. I now have a wonderful relationship with not only Rachael but many of her colleagues as well, and I feel fortunate, professionally and personally, to call this company a client.

Even if you never plan on having your own business, you never know when you might be in the position of looking for a better job, trying to gain access to difficult-to-find information, or requiring assistance with a project. In the end, it always pays to offer help when needed and to build positive professional relationships.

Here are a few other networking success stories.

- Larry decided to take a voluntary separation package from his company. He knew that with the money he received he would have six months to find other, more satisfying work. Within six weeks colleagues from professional associations he belonged to called to let him know about opportunities in their respective companies. He is now considering several offers—all of which came through Larry's network contacts.

- Armando was working on a salary study for his department that entailed getting information from competitors about their salary structures. The project was made easier because of his membership in a professional organization of compensation specialists. In exchange for the information others provided, Armando offered to share his findings and final report with his network colleagues.

- Melissa works for a large corporation and was unhappy in her job but didn't want to leave the company entirely. She spoke with several people with whom she had kept in contact from other divisions and asked them to let her know whether any jobs became available that might provide new challenges for her. She was contacted by the vice president of one division and asked to apply for a job for which he thought she was qualified. Her network relationships enabled her to move into an assignment that is more rewarding—both financially and personally.

- Jacob had an idea that could substantially benefit his manufacturing firm. He explained his idea to his boss, but the boss didn't seem interested. He casually mentioned the idea to one of the company president's direct reports while they were flying home from an out-of-town conference. She thought it warranted attention and arranged for him to make a presentation to her boss. Jacob received a bonus, and public recognition, for his contribution to the company—a contribution made possible through a network relationship.

- Shirley was the administrator for a large commercial property management firm. As such, she had significant contact with building contractors, plumbers, electricians, and so forth and always took care to treat these people with the respect they deserved—something that many of her colleagues neglected. When she left the company to start her own property management firm, her clients were impressed with her ability to get vendors to respond to her requests promptly. Although Shirley's own company is nowhere near the size of her former employer, she is given the same service afforded a large company. She is successful where many of her competitors fail because of the network she built during her career.

Clearly, these and other similar experiences validate the importance and benefit of networking. You don't build network relationships with the intention of benefiting from them, but networking clearly pays dividends.

Characteristics of Effective Networkers

Certain characteristics form the basis for effective networking. People who network well typically possess a combination of the following:

1. Genuine interest in others. Having a genuine interest in others is at the core of every good relationship networking or otherwise. A genuine interest in others is manifested by asking people about themselves (and listening to the response), exhibiting a desire to be of help to them, seeing what they need without them necessarily telling you, and the willingness to go out of your way to help meet those needs. You can't fake genuine interest in others. If you try to fake it, others will perceive you as manipulative or exploitative.

2. Ability to put others at ease. If you are uncomfortable in networking situations you can overcome your discomfort by focusing attention on making others comfortable. It gives you a role to play that provides something valuable while assuaging your own anxiety in new or unfamiliar situations. One way you can put others at ease is to show genuine interest in them. Another is to introduce them to others whom you may know in the group. When you are the one who is new to a group, you might consider finding someone who may be sitting or standing alone and beginning a conversation with him or her.

3. Commitment to a cause greater than themselves. Kiwanis and Lions Clubs and chambers of commerce are good examples of groups committed to causes greater than simply promoting the well-being of the members. The boards of directors and operating committees of nonprofit organizations are often committed to the cause to which they volunteer their time. Networking through volunteer activities is a wonderful way to meet new people and contribute something to your community at the same time. Such causes bring people together in a positive and meaningful way without focusing exclusively on the benefits of membership.

4. Willingness to give more than they anticipate receiving in return. You don't network because of what you expect to get from it. You network because you believe in the need to work collaboratively and cooperatively with others. This often means that you find yourself giving more to others in your network than you yourself may be receiving at any given time. As described under Reason #1, you want to have an inexhaustible supply of chips in your account, earned by extending yourself to others without concern for what you might get in return. One of the best networkers I know is a Cleveland woman who is well respected in the community for her commitment to various charitable causes. Despite her busy schedule, she spends considerable time sharing her resources with others who ask for advice and information. She gives generously of her time and freely shares with others the knowledge gained through her networking activities.

5. Ability to ask for what they need. I've coached people who generously help others but who never ask for anything in return—

even when they need it. This ultimately establishes a scenario where others feel uncomfortable because they view themselves as indebted to the person. Eventually, the relationship suffers because of its lopsided nature. Obviously, you are not going to ask for help when you don't need it, but you have to be willing to let others assist you when it is required. You not only gain from their efforts, but you allow them to feel good about being able to reciprocate.

6. Ability to act as a conduit between others. Good networkers help others connect with the resources that they require. They don't simply build relationships for their own personal use; they also help others to succeed by acting as a referral source. For example, when you run into the woman from Cleveland mentioned earlier, she never fails to introduce you to the many people she knows. When she introduces you, she comments on something flattering about you both; for example, "Lynn Smith, let me introduce you to Steve Wilson. Steve single-handedly prevented my computer system from crashing last April right at tax time. Steve, Lynn knows more about investment strategies than anyone I know." This kind of generosity of spirit displays not only the ability to connect people, but the desire to showcase their talents at the same time.

7. Ability to remember people, information, and events. It does no good to network unless you remember the people that you meet and their unique circumstances or story. It is one thing to listen to someone as he or she tells you that it had been a particularly difficult year because his or her child was diagnosed with cancer. It requires something entirely different to remember this piece of information and ask how the person and the child are doing the next time you meet (or call that person). Remembering what people tell you is the sign of a good listener and of someone who networks not only for personal gain but because of a genuine interest in people as well.

Networking Opportunities

Even though nearly every interaction is a networking opportunity, it is also important to seek experiences that promote networking. Finding organizations or opportunities that blend with your own particular interests makes networking more natural and less burdensome. Ideally, you want to be able to spend time with people you enjoy and engage in activities that are of value to you—not only with people or causes who need you (or vice versa). Once you give it some thought, you will be able to come up with your own outlets for networking, but for now here are some ideas that may be of help.

● **Professional associations.** Nearly every profession has an association of members devoted to furthering knowledge in the field, developing expertise in its membership, and providing a forum for members to exchange ideas and information. Typically, if the association is large enough, it has local chapters in addition to a national body and provides members with benefits such as newsletters, magazines, and bulletin boards.

Everyone should belong to at least one professional association and actively participate in its events by attending meetings, volunteering for committees, and taking part in its conferences and special events. The Encyclopedia of Associations (see Resources) contains listings for thousands of organizations, briefly describing each organization, why it was founded, the size of its membership, and its publications. It is well worth a trip to the library to take a look at it. Here are just a few of the associations (some of them obscure) included in it:

- American Association of Handwriting Analysts
- Society for Commercial Archeology
- Society of Wood Science and Technology
- National Association of Women in Construction
- Institute of Food Technologists
- Independent Bankers Association of America
- Automotive Service Industry Association
- Black Data Processing Associates
- National Cosmetology Association
- American Electronics Association

If you're the kind of person who would have a hard time joining a professional association alone, do one of two things. First, check around your office to find out if anyone else belongs to the kind of organization you are seeking to join. If not, ask whether anyone else is interested in joining you in attending an association meeting. This may provide you and your colleagues with the opportunity for catching up outside the office while engaging in a mutual interest.

● **Nonprofit organization boards or committees**. Nonprofit organizations are frequently in search of committed people to join their boards of directors or to serve as members of functional committees. They typically look for businesspeople who have skill in one or more specific areas such as fundraising, finance, human resources, or a related technical field. By becoming involved with a nonprofit organization, you can make a valuable contribution to your community while gaining access to influential people in the community, learning more about the community itself, and developing skills in networking.

There are a number of ways to find out where opportunities for nonprofit involvement lie. Depending on your interests, try making these contacts for starters:

- Your company's foundation or human resources department
- The YWCA or YMCA
- Your church's pastor or synagogue's rabbi
- The Red Cross
- The board of education or schools in your community
- Friends who are involved with nonprofit organizations
- Political campaign offices
- The police department
- The chamber of commerce
- Hospices
- The Heart Association
- The human interest section of the newspaper
- Big Brothers or Big Sisters of America

● **Special interest clubs.** Networking doesn't have to be all work and no play. There are numerous clubs that cater to nearly every interest imaginable. Whether you like computers, chess, ballroom dancing, hiking, tennis, stamp collecting, or antique cars—there's a club out there waiting for you to join. Choose one that relates to something in which you have an avid interest, and network for fun.

● **Discussion groups.** Many cities have informal groups that gather to discuss recent books, movies, or topics of community interest. They provide a unique opportunity to network while discussing a subject of interest to you. If you can't find one in your town, why not consider starting one? This allows you to play a role instead of just mingling, and is especially helpful for those who are uncomfortable meeting strangers.

● **Informal gatherings.** Have you gotten into a rut where you only go to work and come home, rarely socializing anymore with friends? Why nor invite a group of people with whom you share similar interests to join you for a Sunday brunch or dinner? Or, organize a trip to a local museum. Networking can be casual and informal as well as professional and organized. The group may decide to have regular monthly events (hopefully not always at your house) or other weekend activities.

● **Doorway conversations**. Don't forget something as simple and obvious as making a point of dropping by people's offices for a few minutes of casual conversation. If you're uncomfortable with not having a specific purpose or issue to discuss, bring by an article that you think may be of interest to a person, or ask for advice in an area in which the individual has particular expertise. Again, it doesn't have to be work related. You can ask for a referral to a good pediatrician from someone who has children, or for a recommendation for a Friday-night movie.

● **Spiritual or religious groups.** Aside from recommending volunteer work, your church, synagogue, or other spiritual meeting place might have groups that you can join. Frequently, these organizations have groups tailored for various segments of the community—for single parents, singles in search of friendship, and the like—and typically welcome all prospective members.

For some people, it may be helpful to view networking the way you view physical exercise: it may be difficult (and sometimes painful), but you know it's good for you. Just as you wouldn't begin a running regimen with a twenty-six-mile marathon, don't choose the hardest opportunity you can think of as your first networking activity. It will only turn you off and make you reluctant to do it over the long term. How you network, or what groups you choose to join, isn't nearly as important as just getting out there, meeting people, and having a good time at it.

Strategies for Internal Networking

1. Organize group outings (but take care not to be viewed as a "camp counselor").

2. Join a task force.

3. Introduce people to one another.

4. Remember names and personal information.

5. Circulate articles to others who have similar interests or needs.

6. Reach out for help when you need it.

7. Mentor newcomers to your field.

8. Invite colleagues and their families to your home for a barbecue or potluck.

9. Keep a list of people with special talents to whom you can refer others.

10. Bring together people with similar interests over lunch or dinner.

Strategies for External Networking

11. Volunteer for a nonprofit board or committee.

12. Be an active member.

13. Stay in touch at the holidays with people you may not see throughout the year.

14. Take up a sport that requires at least one other person.

15. Join a service or community organization (e.g., Rotary, Kiwanis, Lions, chamber of commerce).

16. Be active in your college or university's alumni association.

17. Join a motivational group, such as LEADS or The Breakfast Club.

18. Be a docent at your local museum.

19. Do volunteer work for a political party.

20. Join a "fun" club (e.g., Sierra Club, a book club, a restaurant club).

21. Conduct pro bono workshops in your area of expertise for nonprofit organizations.

22. Attend public meetings on community issues.

23. Carry plenty of business cards.

24. Write articles for professional journals.

Resources

Now that you understand why successful people derail, and ways in which you may be teetering on the brink of it yourself, it is time to make a commitment to do something to prevent it. The following quotation from Johann Wolfgang von Goethe, one of the greatest and most versatile European writers and thinkers of modern times, sums up the need to take affirmative action on behalf of your career success:

Until one is committed, there is hesitancy, the chance to draw back, always ineffectiveness. Concerning all acts of initiative (and creation), there is one elementary truth, the ignorance of which kills countless ideas and splendid plans: that the moment one definitely commits oneself then providence moves too.

All sorts of things occur to help one that would never otherwise have occurred. A whole stream of events issues from the decision, raising in one's favor all manner of unforeseen incidents and meetings and material assistance, which no one could have dreamed would have come their way.

Whatever you do; or dream you can, begin it.

Boldness has genius, power and magic in it.

Begin it now.

In addition to the suggestions provided at the end of each chapter (including, hopefully, a few of your own), I've also made references to classes, programs, and reading materials throughout the book that might assist you with developing a plan for overcoming your strengths. Herein you will find a comprehensive listing of resources that you can call on to help you develop skills in a particular area. They are divided by the type of resource (books, consultants, training programs, etc.) and include phone numbers, addresses, and other references.

Do not misconstrue this list as one of products or services that I endorse without qualification. Don't assume that other resources not included are without value. Although I have taken care to include only consultants, companies, and products of which I have firsthand knowledge, your selection of any person or item included in this chapter should be made only after your own careful research and consideration. Consult with your personnel or human resources department for help with identifying alternative resources in your area.

Professional and Executive Coaches

The philosophies, styles, and fees of coaches vary greatly. Because after the initial face-to-face coaching session much of the remaining work is done over the telephone, the geographic location of a coach is not always the best determinant for selection. The most important considerations in selecting any coach are:

1. Assuring that there is a match between your personality and the coach's personality;

2. Assessing the coach's expertise in the area in which you require assistance (e.g., presentation skills, interpersonal skills, career development); and

3. Locating a coach whose fee fits within your budget. (Many companies today will pay for employee coaching in much the same way as they pay for other training programs. Check with your human resources department.)

When it comes to selecting a coach, be a smart consumer. Especially if your company is paying for it, you may get only one chance to be coached, so don't settle for someone with whom you have never spoken. So much of successful coaching depends on the coach-client relationship. Ask to speak with the coach in advance, either by phone or in a personal meeting, and ask questions such as:

- What is your coaching philosophy?
- What companies have sent clients to you for coaching?
- Are there any kinds of clients you don't like working with?
- How much time will be spent in face-to-face contact versus phone contact?
- What kind of information will you share with my employer?
- How long will the coaching process last?
- What kind of follow-up with you can I expect?
- Will you provide me with a written action plan?
- Do you make referrals to other professionals when needed?

Whether the coach you select is across the street from your office or across the country, you can anticipate that the coaching process will more or less follow these steps:

Phase 1. There will be a discussion that allows you and the coach to become acquainted and determine logistics. If you live at a significant distance from the coach's office, this initial discussion may take place by phone.

Phase 2. The coach will solicit feedback about your performance from colleagues, management, and, when applicable, staff reporting to you. This will be done through either interviews, the use of a feedback instrument, or both. Again, depending on distance, interviews may be conducted in person or by phone.

Phase 3. What follows is one or more days of in-depth, face-to-face discussions with the coach (you may go to the coach's office, or he or she to yours). If your offices are near one another, these sessions may be more frequent but of shorter duration.

Phase 4. Ongoing telephone consultation and follow-up sessions can be expected for anywhere from three months to a year.

Business has seen a proliferation of coaches over the past several years, each with their own unique niches. Here are the names of several whom I know to be professional and reputable:

Corporate Coaching International
540 El Dorado Street, Suite 102
Pasadena, CA 91101
626.405.7310
www.corporatecoachingintl.com

> The philosophy of Corporate Coaching International (CCI) is that in order for coaching to be effective it must take into consideration the career, interpersonal, and psychosocial aspects of individual development. CCI's staff includes experts in all three areas and, depending on the issues being addressed, you may be coached by one or more of the firm's associates. CCI offers different levels of coaching services for professionals, managers, and executives, each designed to fit the client's time and financial considerations.

Christine Belz
Belz & Associates, Inc.
55 Public Square, Suite 1715
Cleveland, OH 44113
216.664.1877
Belz@ex100.com

> Christine Belz is a seasoned coach with experience working both inside corporations and as an external consultant. She takes a team approach to coaching where not only the client, but also his or her boss and peers participate in a process where the developmental process is integrated into the business.

Christine Cowan-Gascoigne
The Leadership Company
21308 Halburton Road
Beachwood, OH 44122
216.991.9517
christinecg@hqcom.com

> Christine founded the Leadership Company in 1990 to foster responsible leadership. Her driving belief is that quality leadership, not quality strategy, determines organizational and individual success. She coaches in a wide variety of areas including influence skills, power sources and uses, visioning, and time management.

Essential Communications
www.essentialcomm.com

> Essential Communications is a company dedicated to helping business people increase their success through effective interpersonal communication. They help executives and aspiring executives to achieve the look and sound of leadership through one-to-one coaching and small group in-house workshops. Their driving belief is that direct, open communication between people creates unexpected opportunities.

International Coach Federation
www.coachfederation.org

> In addition to general information about the coaching process, this web site of this professional association of coaches allows you to sort potential matches using a variety of factors, such as discipline, location, price, etc. Once you've logged onto their site, go to the Coach Referral Service link.

Susan Picascia, MSW
11712 Moorpark, Suite 207
Studio City, CA 91604
818.752.1787

> Susan Picascia, MSW, combines her experience in the fields of mental health and human resources to help maximize individual growth directed toward achievement of corporate goals. Assessing job-person fit; the emotional, psychological, and spiritual aspects of personal development; and corporate culture are key to her coaching philosophy. She integrates management and employee coaching techniques to assure a balanced approach to conflict resolution.

Companies Offering Public Workshops or Training Programs

There are numerous companies that offer public (as opposed to customized in-house) workshops on a variety of topics. Programs are typically held several times throughout the year in various cities across the country. Included here are several companies that cover a wide range of developmental areas. I recommend that you write or phone each company to request a course catalog that lists all of their programs along with the content, location, and cost for each program.

American Management Association
www.amanet.org
800.262.9699

> The American Management Association (AMA) offers more than two hundred seminars for employees at all levels within an organization. Their programs typically provide participants with hands-on techniques for increasing effectiveness in areas such as communication skills, strategic management, assertiveness, management skills, and accounting. Here is a sampling of their course titles:
>
> Fundamentals of Finance and Accounting for Nonfinancial Executives
>
> Management Skills and Techniques for New Supervisors
>
> Business Principles for the Executive Assistant
>
> Strategy Implementation
>
> Listen Up! A Strategic Approach to Better Listening
>
> Negotiating to Win
>
> AMA also has a self-study catalog that can be requested by phoning 800-225-3215.

The Center for Creative Leadership
www.ccl.org
919.288.7210

> The Center for Creative Leadership (CCL) is a nonprofit educational institute with branches throughout the country and in Europe. It works to adapt the theories and ideas of the behavioral sciences to the practical concerns of managers and leaders throughout society. Through research, training, and publication CCL addresses the challenges facing leaders of today and tomorrow. They offer outstanding programs for executives and senior managers as well as an array of publications related to leadership.

Dale Carnegie
www.dalecarnegietraining.com
516.248.5100

> Many of us remember Dale Carnegie's former slogan: "how to win friends and influence people." The Dale Carnegie Course, offered at various

locations around the world, is designed to provide you with the skills and confidence needed to communicate effectively, deal with problem solving, and inspire coworkers. Course objectives include developing more self-confidence, controlling your fear of an audience, improving your memory, developing a more effective personality, and widening your personal horizons. Additionally, they offer both college credit and continuing education credits (CEUs) to anyone participating in their programs.

NTL Institute
www.ntl.org
800.777.5227

NTL, founded in 1947, offers an array of workshops for those who want to develop their interpersonal skills. Their workshops are experientially oriented and provide participants with the opportunity to explore their own values, attitudes, and actions as well as how others perceive them. They create a positive and supportive environment in which participants are free to explore behavior changes. A sampling of NTL's workshops include:

The Human Interaction Laboratory asks participants to assess their behaviors and interpersonal styles in relation to others and learn how to give and receive feedback effectively, project a more positive presence, and gain insight into their true potential.

Power: How to Create It, Keep It, and Use It Effectively is for anyone who wants to discover and develop sources of personal power and learn how to influence others effectively; investigate ways to focus intellectual, emotional, and physical power; and identify self-imposed limits to power and explore ways to overcome them.

Leadership Excellence is an advanced workshop for middle and upper-middle managers who want to improve their skills in leading and working with others. It focuses on building and maintaining high-performing organizations.

I have attended a number of NTL workshops and recommend them highly. A client who attended one of their programs described it as "a life-changing experience." Be aware that because they are experientially oriented, they can be quite intense and require more than simply passive participation.

Outward Bound
www.outwardbound.com
800.243.8520

> Outward Bound courses are designed to help people develop self-confidence, compassion, and an appreciation for selfless service to others. They are not a survival school. Their challenging curriculum enables participants to learn by doing, and personal growth is central to the Outward Bound experience. Their programs enable you to realize individual success and encourage you to develop a team spirit that results in the camaraderie and interdependence necessary for your team to achieve its goals. In addition to their public programs, they also customize events for individual company retreats or team buildings. I highly recommend an Outward Bound program for anyone who wants to learn to take more risks, develop confidence, and understand the value of teamwork.

Toastmaster's International
www.toastmasters.org
800.993.7732

> Toastmaster's is not really a workshop, but rather a group of businesspeople who meet regularly to discuss and practice issues related to presentation skills. There are chapters located throughout the world, most typically in downtown business districts. You can use the toll-free number above to find out where groups meet in your area. People who belong to Toastmaster's report a significant increase in their comfort level and skill in speaking before groups. Even if you don't have occasion to do a lot of public speaking, participation can help you to improve your verbal communication.

Classes

You'll need to do some legwork to find classes, degree programs, and groups that will address your specific developmental needs. These kinds of learning experiences can be more beneficial than a workshop because they provide the opportunity to explore a topic in greater depth and, typically, provide time to practice or apply the skill. Most major cities have universities and community colleges that offer programs through extension schools that are targeted for the working person. Some public television stations even offer classes.

These are a few classes that I recommend that you consider:

Acting. People are often surprised when I recommend an acting class as part of their developmental plans. Acting classes can help you to overcome discomfort in front of groups, allow your emotions to emerge, and hone your presentation style. They require that you pay more attention to the fact that we are all actors on a corporate stage.

Art. Art classes are great for bringing out your creative talents—something you can later apply to strategic thinking. Even if you don't consider yourself an artist, take a drawing, sculpting, or painting class and allow yourself to use the side of your brain that may not normally be put to use.

Assertiveness. I prefer that assertiveness be learned through a class rather than at a one-day workshop, because this skill requires practice over time. A class allows you to practice the techniques taught one week, and return the next week to fine-tune them.

Creative writing. In addition to the fact that a writing class can stimulate creative thinking, it can help you to hone your business writing skills.

Drawing. A beginning course in drawing can help to develop and expand your observational abilities.

Inner child. They may be called by different names, but inner-child programs are designed to enable participants to work through childhood issues that continue to influence present life functioning.

Journal writing. Especially when used in conjunction with coaching, psychotherapy, or other workshops, keeping a journal can be a valuable tool to help you clarify your thoughts, feelings, goals, and objectives.

Photography. A photography class can help you to look at the world differently and, when combined with learning to use the darkroom, can assist you with paying closer attention to detail.

Self-defense. As well as providing skill in the obvious, self-defense classes can also be particularly useful in developing assertiveness and increased self-esteem.

Time management. A time-management class is especially appropriate for anyone who finds himself or herself saying that there is no time to develop skill in the areas included in this book! It can help you to take back control of your work environment so that you have more time to focus on matters pertaining to your own career development.

Yoga. Taking a yoga class may seem a bit far out to many businesspeople, but in reality it can have a number of beneficial effects. Through meditation and exercise it can help to diminish stress, increase focus, and enhance clarity of thought. Some of what you learn in a yoga class can even be practiced in the privacy of your office.

Inventories and Self-Assessment Tools

No inventory or test can tell you more about yourself than you already know. They can, however, help you to understand your own behaviors and ways in which to maximize your natural talents. When it comes to using a 360 feedback instrument, a tool through which colleagues give you feedback as to how they perceive you, results can be surprising and difficult to comprehend. Therefore, use such tools carefully and, whenever possible, in conjunction with professional guidance. Such guidance can come in the form of a coach, mentor, human resources professional, or psychologist.

Consulting Psychologists Press, Inc.
www.cpp.com
800.624.1765

> Consulting Psychologists Press (CPP) is the publisher of the Myers Briggs Type Indicator and other self-assessment tools. CPP's business catalog includes assessment instruments and reference materials useful in organization, career, leadership, and management development. Not all of their psychological instruments are available to the general public, so ask your human resources department for assistance when specialized skills or education are required.

Pfeiffer & Company
www.pfeiffer.com

> Known primarily as a resource for trainers and consultants, Pfeiffer offers a comprehensive array of tools, instruments, and reference materials for developing individuals and teams. Although many of the offerings contained in the company's catalog will be of interest to only human resources professionals, the layperson will find items such as the Leadership Development Inventory, The Team Handbook, Group Power: The Manager's Guide to Using Task Force Meetings, and Career Anchors, to name a few, useful in personal development.

teleometrics international
www.teleometrics.com
800.527.0406

> Teleometrics produces videos and publishes self-assessment tools on topics such as empowerment, motivation, interpersonal relations, organizational culture, and conflict and change. Not only are the company's instruments validated, reliable, and research based, but they also include clear and understandable instructions for interpretation.

Books

Books about how to succeed in business by really trying (or not really trying) are abundant. All you need to do to find them is to visit your local bookstore and peruse the career, self-help, business, or management aisles. In an effort to help you select ones that might be most useful, a reference is included for each of the books mentioned throughout the previous chapters and a few additional ones that are worth taking a look at.

The Artist's Way: A Spiritual Path to Higher Creativity. Julia Cameron with Mark Bryan, G. P. Putnam's Sons, 1992

Be a Kickass Assistant: How to Get from a Grunt Job to a Great Career. Heather Beckel, Warner Books, 2002

Beware the Naked Man Who Offers You His Shirt: Do What You Love, Love What You Do, and Deliver More Than You Promise. Harvey MacKay, Ballantine Books, 1990

Certain Trumpets: The Call of Leaders. Garry Wills, Simon & Schuster, 1994

Coping with an Intolerable Boss. Michael M. Lombardo and Morgan W. McCall Jr., Center for Creative Leadership, 1984 (You'll have to call CCL at the number listed above to obtain a copy of this monograph.)

Danger in the Comfort Zone. Judith M. Bardwick, AMACOM, 1991

Difficult Conversations: How to Discuss What Matters Most. Douglas Stone, Bruce Patton, Sheila Heen & Roger Fisher, Penguin, 2000

Drawing on the Right Side of the Brain: A Course in Enhancing Creativity and Artistic Confidence. Betty Edwards, J. P. Tarcher, 1979

Emotional Intelligence. Daniel Goleman, Bantam Books, 1995

Finding Your Perfect Work: The New Career Guide to Making a Living, Creating a Life. Paul and Sarah Edwards, Putnam, 1996

Feel the Fear and Beyond: Mastering the Techniques for Doing It Anyway. Susan Jeffers, Random House, 1998

Gifts Differing. Isabel Briggs Myers with Peter B. Myers, Consulting Psychologists Press, Inc., 1980

Hardball for Women: Winning at the Game of Business. Pat Heim, Ph.D., with Susan K. Golant, Plume, 1993

How to Think Like Leonardo DaVinci. Michael Gelb, Dell, 2000

If My Career's on the Fast Track, Where Do I Get a Road Map? Anne B. Fisher, William Morrow & Company, 2001

Influencing with Integrity: Management Skills for Communication and Negotiation. Genie Z. Laborde, Syntony Publishing, 1987 (Don't be thrown by the title. It's not only for managers—everyone can learn influence skills from this one.)

Letitia Baldrige's New Complete Guide to Executive Manners. Letitia Baldrige, Rawson Associates, 1993

The Magic of Conflict. Thomas F. Crum, Touchstone/Simon & Schuster, 1987

Mining Group Gold; How to Cash In on the Collaborative Power of a Group. Thomas A. Kayser, Serif Publishing, 1990

The Organized Executive: A Program for Productivity. Stephanie Winston, Warner Books, 2001

Organized to Be your Best! Simplify and Improve How You Work. Susan Silver, Adams Hall Publishers, 2000

Paradigms: The Business of Discovering the Future. Joel Arthur Barker, HarperBusiness, 1992

People Skills: How to Assert Yourself, Listen to Others, and Resolve Conflicts. Robert Bolton, Ph.D., Simon & Schuster, 1979

The Plateauing Trap. Juditb Bardwick, Ph.D., Bantam Books, 1986

Please Understand Me: Character & Temperament Types. David Kiersey and Marilyn Bates, Gnosology Books, 1984 (If you aren't qualified to purchase the Myers Briggs Type Indicator, this book contains a variation of it with a complete explanation of your score and type preferences.)

Preventing Derailment: What to Do Before It's Too Late. Michael M. Lombardo and Robert W. Eichinger, Center for Creative Leadership, 1987 (You'll have to call CCL at the number listed above to obtain a copy of this monograph.)

Sacred Hoops: Spiritual Lessons of a Hardwood Warrior. Phil Jackson and Hugh Delehanty, Hyperion, 1995

Same Game, Different Rules: How to Get Ahead Without Being a Bully Broad, Ice Queen or "Ms. Understood." Jean Hollands, McGraw-Hill, 2001

Servant Leadership: A Journey into the Nature of Legitimate Power and Greatness. Robert K. Greenleaf, Paulist Press, 1977

Talking from 9 to 5: How Women's and Men's Conversational Styles Affect Who Gets Heard, Who Gets Credit, and What Gets Done at Work. Deborah Tannen, Ph.D., William Morrow and Company, 1994

Taming Your Gremlin: A Guide to Enjoying Yourself. Richard D. Carson, HarperPerennial, 1983

The Tao of Leadership: Leadership strategies for a New Age. John Heider, Bantam New Age Books, 1988

Team Players and Teamwork. Glenn M. Parker, Jossey-Bass, 1996

Type Talk at Work: How the 16 Personality Types Determine Your Success on the Job. Otto Kroeger with Janet M. Thuesen, Tilden Press, 1992

Warming the Stone Child: Myths & Stories About Abandonment and the Unmothered Child. Clarissa Pinkola Estes, Ph.D., Sounds True, 1997

The Way of the Wizard: 20 Lessons for Living a Magical Life. Deepak Chopra, Crown Publishers, 1995

What Color Is Your Parachute: A Practical Manual for Job Hunters & Career Changers. Richard N. Bolles, Ten Speed Press, 1995

When Money Is Not Enough: Fulfillment in Work. Eileen R. Hannegan, M.S., Beyond Words Publishing, 1995

The Wisdom of Teams: Creating the High Performance Organization. Jon R. Katzenbach and Douglas K. Smith, Harvard Business School Press, 1993

Women, Anger, and Depression: Strategies for Self-Empowerment. Lois P. Frankel, Ph.D., Health Communications, 1991

Working with Emotional Intelligence. Daniel Goleman, Bantam Doubleday Dell, 2000

You Are the Message: Getting What You Want By Being Who You Are. Roger Ailes, Currency Doubleday, 1989

You Just Don't Understand: Women and Men in Conversation. Deborah Tannen, Ph.D., Ballantine Books, 1990

Zen and the Art of Making a Living: A Practical Guide to Creative Career Design. Lawrence G. Boldt, Penguin, 1993

Magazines and Newspapers

In addition to subscribing to and reading technical journals related to your field, it is also important that you have a breadth, if not depth, of knowledge of current affairs, business events, and issues relating to the workplace. For this reason, I am including a wide variety of magazines that will help to keep you abreast of all three—and stretch you to explore issues that you might not normally. For example, if you have a difficult time making small talk in conversation, try reading *Sports Illustrated* or *People* magazine so that you have an idea of what's going on in the world of sports or entertainment and can refer to something interesting that you've read. My suggestion is that you subscribe to and make time to read at least three of the following on a regular basis:

Time	Condé Nast Traveler
Harper's	The New Yorker
Sports Illustrated	Science
Harvard	Your Local Newspaper
People	Omni
New York Business Review	Reader's Digest
Newsweek	Worth
Times Review	Ms.
Working Woman	Fortune
Wall Street Journal	

Mental Health Contacts

If you think that the help that you require goes beyond the scope of a workshop, coach, or book, you might want to consider entering into counseling with a licensed mental health practitioner. Most business coaches report that about 75 percent of the people they coach are referred for some kind of longer-term counseling in conjunction with or following the coaching. Counseling isn't for people who are "sick," but rather for people who want to lead fuller, more productive lives. Good counseling can help you to understand what part your past plays in the present and how to avoid allowing it to control your life.

Most people will do well with a licensed psychologist or psychotherapist. Psychiatrists are physicians (M.D.s) who typically use a medical model for the treatment of psychological problems. Psychiatrists can prescribe drugs whereas the other two classifications cannot. I recommend beginning with a psychologist or psychotherapist and, if needed, a referral can then be made to a psychiatrist.

There are many people who call themselves counselors or psychotherapists, and licensing varies from state to state. When seeking psychological assistance you want to evaluate a number of things: the person's professional credentials and licenses, his or her experience dealing with the problems you want to address, the match between you and the therapist, and the cost. Don't be afraid to ask questions. Remember, you are the consumer.

Depending on the part of the country in which you live, the average cost of therapy can range anywhere from $75 per hour to $150 per hour or more. When you are ready to find a therapist, there are a number of ways to locate someone reputable.

1. Referral from a trusted friend or relative. This is probably the best way to find a therapist. Be aware, however, that just because your best friend loves his or her therapist, it doesn't mean you will too. Give yourself at least three or four sessions before you decide a particular therapist isn't for you.

2. Your family physician. Your own physician can be a good source for a referral. Make certain that you let him or her know what you are looking for in a therapist so that an appropriate referral can be made.

3. Local mental health agencies. If you look in the yellow pages under "mental health" there are agencies listed that provide psychological services. These are often nonprofit community agencies where treatment is reasonably priced.

4. Your company's Employee Assistance Program (EAP). Many companies today have EAPs that are designed to help employees in distress. Some even offer a limited number of confidential therapy sessions paid for by the company. Ask your personnel or human resources manager for more information.

5. The American Psychological Association (APA). APA consists of members who are licensed psychologists and psychotherapists. Each state has a chapter of the APA and can refer you to a licensed member in your area. When calling information ask for the name of your state's Psychological Association (e.g., Illinois Psychological Association).

You can avoid derailment by following the suggestions given herein and taking advantage of one or more of these resources. Remember, your career lies not in the hands of your boss or management, but in the choices you make next. You have no control over the past, but you can take charge of your future. Begin today to overcome your strengths.

About the Author

Dr. Lois P. Frankel, President of Corporate Coaching International, is an author and internationally recognized expert in the field of workplace behavior. She travels throughout the world to consult with organizations of all sizes to help them meet their business objectives by maximizing the development of individuals and teams. Her clients include major corporations such as BP, Amgen, Miller Brewing Company, and ARCO Indonesia, to name a few. With over twenty years experience in the field of human resources, Dr. Frankel's particular expertise lies in coaching people to avoid career derailment and develop the skills required to successfully compete for leadership positions.

A frequent guest on talk radio and television programs, at association conferences, and at corporate workshops and retreats, Dr. Frankel's views about workplace issues are sought after by writer's for magazines and newspapers such as the Wall Street Journal, Fortune Magazine, the Los Angeles Times, and Fast Company Magazine. She is the author of numerous books and journal articles. Her last book, *Overcoming Your Strengths: 8 Reasons Why Successful People Derail and How to Get Back on Track*, was named "the best unsung business book" of the year by Fast Company magazine. Her next book, *Quit Bein' a Girl: 101 Dumb Things Smart Women Do to Sabotage Their Careers*, is scheduled for publication by Warner Books in Fall, 2003.

She is a member of the National Speakers Association, American Psychological Association, and Society for Human Resources Management and is a licensed psychotherapist with a doctorate in Counseling Psychology from the University of Southern California. Although she is originally from the Northeast, she currently enjoys residing in Southern California where she can hike and play tennis year-round. You may reach Dr. Frankel through her website: www.corporatecoachingintl.com.

Give the Gift of

Overcoming
Your
Strengths

to Your Friends and Colleagues

CHECK YOUR LEADING BOOKSTORE OR ORDER HERE

❑ **YES**, I want ____ copies of *Overcoming Your Strengths* at $25.00 each, plus $4.95 shipping per book (California residents please add $2.06 sales tax per book). Canadian orders must be accompanied by a postal money order in U.S. funds. Allow 15 days for delivery.

❑ **YES**, I am interested in having Lois P. Frankel, Ph.D., speak or give a seminar to my company, association, school, or organization. Please send information.

My check or money order for $_____ is enclosed.

Please charge my ❑ Visa   ❑ MasterCard

Name _____

Organization _____

Address _____

City/State/Zip _____

Phone_____ E-mail _____

Card # _____

Exp. Date_____ Signature _____

Please make your check payable and return to:
Corporate Coaching International Publications
540 El Dorado Street, Suite 102 • Pasadena, CA 91101
Call your credit card order to: 877-452-2654
Fax: 626-405-7312

Acknowledgements

Many individuals and organisations have been most helpful in providing material, advice, free education and comments on early versions of all or parts of the manuscript. Some of these are anonymous, such as people who have asked me a question or made some comment after talks that I have given; the originators of several anecdotes that I have accumulated are unknown to me; and my many discussions with speakers at the British Association for the Advancement of Science, at Rutherford Appleton Laboratory and at the European Centre for Nuclear Research in Geneva (CERN) are too numerous to mention other than collectively.

I would also like to express some personal thanks. Professor V. Levin from the USSR took time out from a conference in Hungary to tell me of his experiences in the Tunguska region of Siberia and provided much of the colour for that part of the story. The library staff at Rutherford Appleton Laboratory and at CERN have helped me trace obscure literature on many occasions. I would like to thank Nick Brealey, Gill Close, Paul Davies, Ali Graham, Mike Green, Beverly Halstead, Iain Nicholson, Liz Paton, Roger Phillips, Martin Rees and Sheila Watson for their reading of parts or all of various versions and Ted Barnes, John Barrow, Victor Clube, Brian Combridge, Nigel Henbest, Duncan Ollson-Steel, Subir Sarkar and Peter Worsley for their help in clarifying some specific questions. I think that I adopted around 90 per cent of your suggestions: I hope that this final version meets with your approval. Thanks to you all.

Frank Close
Oxford
September 1987

APOCALYPSE WHEN?

Cosmic Catastrophe and
the Fate of the Universe

FRANK CLOSE

William Morrow and Company, Inc.
New York

Our thanks to:

Elizabeth A. Close
for the photograph of the author
(back jacket flap)

Dr Jean Macqueen
for preparing the index

Copyright © 1988 by Frank Close

Originally published in Great Britain by Simon & Schuster International.

Library of Congress Cataloging-in-Publication Data

Close, F.E.
Apocalypse when? : cosmic catastrophe and the fate of the universe
/Frank Close.
p. cm.
Bibliography: p.
Includes index.
ISBN 0-688-08413-3
1. Cosmology. 2. Disasters. 3. Meteoritic hypothesis.
4. Universe, Destruction of. I. Title.
QB981.C634 1989
523.1—dc19   88-37298
CIP

Printed in the United States of America

First U.S. Edition

1 2 3 4 5 6 7 8 9 10

Contents

1

Apocalypse - When?

Beyond Xanadu, in the Temple of Brahmin, priests are counting the days to the end of time.

According to legend, the temple contains three divine pyramids of stones representing Brahma, the Creator, Vishnu, the Preserver, and Shiva, the Destroyer. On the first day Brahma created The World and built a single pyramid of 42 stones, the largest at the bottom.

Each day at sunset the priests move one stone from Brahma to Vishnu, Vishnu to Shiva or perhaps directly from Brahma to Shiva. The only rule is that they must never put a large stone on top of a smaller one. Eventually all stones but one will be moved from Creator through Preserver to the pile belonging to the Destroyer. As the Sun sinks and the final stone is moved, the priests' work will be completed. Brahma created and now Vishnu destroys. The Sun will never rise again.

If the legend were true, how long will the Universe last – how many moves must they make?

It is easy to see that, if there had been only two stones, a total of three moves would have done the job. With three stones, the number more than doubles to seven moves. The solution is shown in Figure 1.1. You may care to discover the sequence for four stones – it takes 15 moves. Each extra stone more than doubles the number of moves required. For 42 stones the priests must make one move less than two times two, 42 times ($2^{42} - 1$). At one move per sunset this will take them a little more than 10 billion years, which is how old the Universe is – NOW!

1

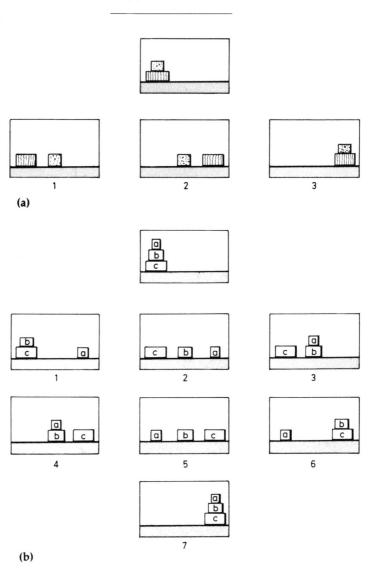

1.1   The end of the Universe puzzle

The Universe may indeed be this old but the Sun and Earth are much younger; slightly less than 5 billion years old in fact. The priests are only half way through their task, so the Sun and we still have 5 billion years to go – and modern science agrees with this estimate of the Sun's future.

One day 5 billion years hence the Sun will be gone and we shall be too. However, worlds end in many ways, and the more that science progresses, so the more contenders emerge for the Apocalypse.

Though astronomers are familiar with constellations and even remote galaxies, we know relatively little about our immediate neighbourhood, yet it is that which poses the greatest threats in the short term. Periodically, lumps of rock, even pieces of minor planets (asteroids) and comets, drop in from the sky – the scars remain as evidence. There have been suggestions that the extinction of the dinosaurs and the ends of geological epochs may be witness to catastrophic collisions in the past. How long before another maverick rock drops in, or one big enough to destroy a vast area including nuclear power plants? The Chernobyl disaster in 1986 gave a hint of what that additional hazard could do to the environment.

If we are not destroyed by extraterrestrial invaders, or by ourselves, our continued existence will require the Sun to go on steady and unchanging, much as it appears now. In reality the Sun is not as constant as many people think. We are now learning a lot about the way the Sun works, and can even peer inside and examine its thermonuclear core; some strange things appear to be going on that we do not yet understand. In the second part of the story, I will concentrate on our relationship with the Sun, describe how well we understand it and how we are trying to resolve the puzzles that have recently been discovered.

The Sun is the nearest star to us but it is only one of a billion in our galaxy, and our galaxy in turn is but one of countless such islands in space. In the third part of the story I will describe how those more distant stars can affect us.

As we swing round the Sun, so is the Sun dragging us on a grand tour of the Milky Way. Not everywhere is as bland as the part we are currently in. We will meet clouds of dust that can affect the climatic balance; we might encroach too near other stars, which could disturb our orbit, moving us out of the narrow zone that makes life comfortable or even flipping us out of the solar system entirely.

Not all stars are as stable as our Sun. Stars can explode – known as 'supernova'. In 1987 one lit up as bright as a whole galaxy in the southern skies. The cataclysm took place nearly 170,000 years ago but so far away that news has only just arrived. It was too distant to cause us harm, but the blast from a nearby supernova could rip off our atmosphere.

In Part IV we will look at the Universe as a whole and evaluate its future. By re-creating the sort of conditions present in the first moments of the Big Bang, we are learning about the start of the Universe and gaining clues as to how it may all end. Will it expand and cool or instead collapse and fry us?

We will also look into the make-up of matter – the stuff that everything in the known universe appears to be made of. Imagine the ultimate erosion where everything in sight, including the atoms of your body, instantly collapsed or changed into some new form. Bizarre though this may sound, recent discoveries in particle physics suggest that it might be possible. We are also getting hints that there may be 'strange matter', more stable than us, which could destroy us, the Earth, and everything if it came here in enough concentration. There are even serious suggestions that the structure of space itself may be unstable, and that the entire universe could slip downhill' if some trigger unfortunately occurred somewhere.

These ideas are very new; we could not have imagined them seriously even ten years ago. At the very least they are making us re-examine our place in the universe and question our assumptions that it will always be as it is now.

We are living at a critical period in history. Once primitive peoples feared storms, the night, and lived by superstitions. Then science rationalised things, created order and brought us to the point where we can create theories of Genesis and test them in the laboratory. We began to feel omnipotent. We were aware that there are man-made threats – nuclear weapons, stocks of deadly germs – which could wipe us from the face of the Earth. But the Universe – that would go on for ever.

Now we are not so sure. We are becoming increasingly aware of our vulnerability and so far have done very little about it. With planning we could one day escape the Earth and colonise space –

after all, transatlantic flight is commonplace today but would have been regarded as dreaming in Columbus' time

Some scientists believe in the anthropic principle – mankind's arrival is so improbable that it is as if Nature conspired to bring it about. They see hints that the Universe created life to be its agents for immortality. As far as we know we are the carriers of that task. If we can avoid extinction in the short term, be it self-inflicted or from external causes, then we may propagate throughout space into the indefinite future. We may bear little resemblance to the human flesh and bone of today: in a mere billion years primitive molecules have evolved into us who can contemplate the Universe within which we live; what will another billion billion bring?

You and I have no right to life; we inherited it by chance. Now that we are here we have the duty to do our bit in the great human relay race. If the Universe is to avoid ultimate extinction, then life – and that may mean us here on Earth – has to keep going. If we can learn how to live with the possibility of nuclear destruction we then have to deal with the threat of natural extinctions. I conclude with some ideas that are emerging on how we might deal with them and on what the long-term future of life might be.

To advertise that this isn't idle musing, I will begin with an example of a near catastrophe that happened this century.

Part 1

Our Own Backyard

2

Cosmic Close Encounters

Beyond the Ural Mountains, 1,000 miles East of Moscow, lies a vast unspoiled region of swamps, rivers and forests. Stretching from the Arctic Sea in the north to Mongolia in the south, and from the Urals to Manchuria, it is a sparsely inhabited area larger than the whole of Western Europe, known to only a handful of outsiders. There are few roads, fewer towns and for much of the year everything is covered by a blanket of snow. Strange things have happened here and many years passed before the rest of the World learned of them.

In the remote heart of this lonely continent is the hidden valley of the Tunguska river. Here for a few weeks during the summer the snows recede and reindeer graze among the endless pine trees. Into this peaceful scene, one morning in June 1908, a comet burst from outer space. In an instant the reindeer and the trees were annihilated for 30 miles around. A 10 million tonne gravel-filled snowball, with a diameter longer than a football field, exploded in the atmosphere with the force of several hydrogen bombs and sent shock waves around the whole World. It threw so much dust into the stratosphere that sunlight was scattered from the bright side of the globe right around into the Earth's shadow. A quarter of the way round the World in London, 6,000 miles away, the midnight sky was as light as early evening. Everyone realised that something odd had happened, but what and where?

Even today, 80 years after the event, very few outsiders have visited the devastated site. To see the scars you have to make a major expedition. You must choose your starting time carefully so as to reach the site, and get back again, during the summer. Set out from Moscow at the end of April on an internal flight eastwards. As the plane rises shakily into the sky you look down with a comet's eye view of the Earth. Only occasional houses are scattered around and soon even these give way to continuous forest. The ribbon of the Trans-Siberian railway is the only clue that people live on this planet.

We reach central Asia and must leave the relative comfort of Aeroflot and transfer to a small plane for the journey over the mountains. The going is tough. Your pilot may have to wait for up to two weeks for the weather to clear enough to fly at all. Even then the nearest airstrip is still many miles from the site and you must continue on foot. Arrange with your pilot for food to be dropped by parachute at places on the route. White water rushes through gorges and canyons; trees cling to the sheer rock faces. Crossing the terrain will take three weeks if the summer is dry, but, if the spring has been wet, the rivers will run high and your inward journey (let alone your return) may take as long as two months. Even the flat areas aren't easy. There are extensive swamps and persistent mosquitoes. At last you come to a tree-filled valley – the valley of the Tunguska river. The Tunguska is named after the Tungus people, a small ethnic group who survive by hunting bears and deer in the forests. It was they who saw and later recounted the fateful day in 1908.

The first scientist to reach here was the Czechoslovakian Leonid Kulik in 1927. At the point immediately below the explosion he saw a vast mud plain as if a thousand bulldozers had cleared the forest to prepare the foundations for a city the size of London. Surrounding this bleak scene was a ring of charred tree stumps. Beyond this the trees lay scattered like matchsticks, felled by a tumultuous hurricane, the blastwave from the exploding comet. Life had been totally destroyed, and remained so for over a quarter of a century.

The lonely desolation of the site matches the awful privations suffered in reaching it. It is this very remoteness that has hidden it from the World, leaving us cosily ignorant of the forces of cosmic assault. This was not the first time that the Earth was blitzed from outer space, nor is it likely to be the last. It is merely the most recent.

Pictures from spacecraft show the blue jewel of planet Earth brilliant against a black velvet of seemingly empty space. This image of a solid Earth rushing through an empty void is deceptive. On our journey round the Sun – a journey of half a billion miles in 30 million seconds – we are accompanied by over half a dozen other planets, various moons, asteroids, comets, volcanic dust, gas, nuclear radiation, neutrinos, the solar wind and other bizarre bits and pieces; all of them hell bent on their own journeys, their paths interweaving and criss-crossing. Every second we rush through 20 miles of space and if anything is there already waiting for us, or is heading towards the same spot as us, then we hit it.

The Earth is constantly under fire. About 1,000 tonnes of extraterrestrial debris hit the upper atmosphere each day. Most of the pieces are so small that the atmosphere burns them to cinders, leaving the familiar trails known as shooting stars. But on time-scales of millions of years much larger objects can hit us, and will continue to do so once in a while.

Things are on the move all around us and the signs are there to see. Go outdoors on a fine night and look up at the sky. A man-made satellite comes into view: the rays of the sun catch it and make it visible, shining for a few minutes as it orbits around the globe. A shooting star suddenly streaks leaving a trail across the sky; no sooner have you realised that it is there than it is gone. Both of these sights are quite likely if you look at the sky for an hour on a clear night away from city lights. Occasionally a comet may appear, like Halley's comet in 1986, and be visible to the naked eye for weeks on end. If you live in the far north, you may be fortunate enough to see a display of cosmic rain – such as the aurora borealis or northern lights.

Man-made Hazards

There are several thousand man-made satellites on record, and many unlisted military ones, all orbiting in the sky. In addition there is a lot of junk – extinct rocket motors, astronauts' spanners and pieces that have fallen off satellites. The thin atmosphere gradually brakes them and eventually they fall, usually burning up in the process. Occasionally something goes wrong and a satellite makes an unexpected premature return. On such occasions the world's news media have a good story for a day or two as scientists continually update the projected landing site and public relations spokesmen blithely assure us that the satellite's nuclear power source poses no real threat. Eventually the thing plunges into some remote place. The laws of chance make it very unlikely that something dropping from the sky at random will end up landing on a city. As the journey to the remote Tungusku reminds us, overpopulated though the World may appear, the uninhabited *area* vastly exceeds the populated.

These man-made hazards are occasional annoyances and embarrassments, but rarely more than that. They are vastly outnumbered by the natural junk that is continuously hitting the Earth.

Natural Junk

Smallest of all are pieces of atoms that rain down on the upper atmosphere above our heads.

These are produced by violent processes deep in space, such as when stars explode. Powerful forces eject them into space where some, approaching too near to the Earth, are entrapped by our planet's magnetic poles, and pulled in.

Scientists sent balloons into the upper atmosphere to meet these cosmic rays and recorded images of them. They gave some of the first hints of the power within the nucleus, and much of modern nuclear science has grown from those early discoveries. Their power is immense – a single atomic particle in the cosmic beam may have enough energy to raise a human 3 cm off the ground.

When these rays hit the upper atmosphere their energy dissipates as they disrupt atoms in the air and produce a shower of less powerful subatomic particles. These finally reach ground as a gentle rain – interesting for scientists but no real hazard for humans, although long-term exposure at high altitudes or in high-flying aircraft rapidly increases the chance of skin cancers developing from this radiation.

The auroras are seen only by people in extreme northern or southern latitudes, near to the Earth's magnetic poles. Even if you have not seen this spectacle, at some time or other you will probably have seen the results of rather larger extraterrestrials crashing into the upper atmosphere.

Meteors are pieces of dust from dead comets out in space. Each time a comet swings in towards the Sun it loses some of its ice. Gradually the cement holding the gravel all melts away and a shrapnel of stones and boulders fly independently around the solar system like the rings of Saturn on a larger scale. The small stones spread out all around the orbit and form a long sausage of debris. When the Earth passes through one of these we experience a meteor shower. We rush towards the individual stones at 20 miles a second, and gravity pulls them Earthwards, wind friction burning them to white heat. It is this that causes the bright trail – the 'shooting star'.

You can see one or two on any clear night as we hit random pieces in space. We pass through one of the Sun's 'rings' at the same point on our annual orbit and on those nights you may see dozens of meteors each hour. For example, every August we pass through one of these tubes of debris and the result is a meteor shower called the Perseids. There are other rings of debris circling the Sun and when we meet them, regularly each year, our atmosphere burns some up and produces a meteor shower.

Occasionally, however, some quite sizeable pieces survive and make landfall. We call these meteorites.

Meteorites: Pennies from Heaven

Stones falling from the heavens have been recorded in the literature for millennia. Whereas comets usually stay up in the sky, visible to all, 'stars' falling from the heavens are seen by only a few people but can be quite terrifying. They are the ultimate in *son et lumière*.

First a fiery mass appears in the sky – what we see is the

compressed air in front that heats up by the friction of the rock's motion and can be far bigger than the rock itself. The surface of the rock melts, sparks fly off the tail and smoke trails remain long after landfall. Then it may disintegrate and unseen dark pieces fall to ground at 200 metres per second – the speed of a jet in a nose dive. There is a shock wave that rumbles and echoes 'like the sound of guns thundering in battle'.

One morning in 1972, a meteorite shot through the skies in the Rocky Mountains, bright enough to show up in broad daylight. The scenery in those parts is exquisitely beautiful and provides an ideal background to Nature's display of awesome power, reminding us of the primaeval forces that fashioned the planet. Keep on the lookout – these fireballs are rare but not so rare as you might think. On the average one or two fireballs like this occur somewhere on Earth each week. Between 10 and 20 less brilliant ones also arrive each day.

Meteorites may be either stone or lumps of iron. In general they have a different chemical and mineral content to Earthly rocks; as a result it is easy to recognise one on the ground even if no one saw it actually fall. Laboratory tests have shown common features suggesting that some meteorites may be fragments of a single large body, possibly the size of Earth, that has broken up, its remnants orbiting the Sun in perpetuity. One theory is that they, and some of the asteroids, came as a result of a planet disintegrating after a collision with some other large body. If this is true then it hardly lessens our concern that some day the Earth could be similarly devastated.

Iron meteorites can withstand the shock of hitting the atmosphere whereas stone meteorites tend to break up. If the explosion takes place high up, then the shower can be huge. 100,000 stones fell in one shower during 1868 in Poland. 10,000 fell in Holbrook, Arizona, in 1912, and many thousands in a shower in the Soviet Union during 1947. In a large shower most pieces are smaller than grape shot. Lots of dust lands and can show up as dark powder if it falls on a snow-covered landscape. The largest known stone meteorites fell in a shower of 100 over Kansas in 1948, and include one monster of 1 tonne. There are other large ones on record including one of over half a tonne in Long Island, New York, one third of a tonne in Finland and similar weight in Czechoslovakia.

These must be the large fragments of even bigger rocks that hit the outer shield of air, tens of miles above our heads. Indeed they are puny compared to the largest pieces of iron that have fallen. The biggest of all that is still visible on the surface weighs 60 tonnes, the weight of a dozen juggernauts, and lies where it fell on a farm in South-West Africa. From debris around the area it is estimated that this is the largest fragment of an iron core that weighed 100 tonnes. These pieces are the largest on the ground but there is no record of their arrival in the distant past. In the Soviet shower of 1948 a single piece weighing 2 tonnes was seen actually falling to Earth with astonishing fury.

Meteorites hit the upper atmosphere at speeds of up to 50 miles per second and then air resistance slows them down. The damage that they do depends upon the amount of kinetic or motional energy that they have. Two objects moving at the same speed as each other have energies in proportion to their masses: if one is twice as massive then it has twice as much energy as the other. So if a small stone is travelling at the same speed as a car, the stone will have only a millionth as much energy as the car and will do correspondingly less damage in a collision.

The damage also depends on how fast they are travelling. If you double the speed then you quadruple the energy; treble the speed and the energy increases ninefold. So a fast-moving stone can have as much energy as a slow-moving car. In fact, a piece of dust weighing only 1/10 gram and moving at 50 miles in a second has as much energy as a 1 tonne car travelling at 50 miles an hour! A small stone weighing 1 gram hits the atmosphere with a punch similar to that impacted by a fast-moving truck. The ultimate monsters enter at Mach 50. These are the ones that disappear far into the ground and leave a deep extensive crater as a scar on the landscape.

Down at sea level we are protected by the Earth's atmosphere, but out in space even small bits of gravel could be lethal. The energy released if one hit a spacecraft could be a thousand times that of an equal weight of TNT. A pinhead particle could make an airleak in the hull; a pebble the size of a fingertip could destroy the spaceship entirely. There have even been suggestions that the occasional and tragic break-up of airliners at altitude might be due to meteorite impact shattering a tailfin or other crucial equipment.

The awesome sights and sounds announcing the arrival of a meteorite from the heavens convinced primitive peoples that the gods had sent them. As a result meteorites became treasures and were venerated in temples as literally 'gifts from the gods'. In the Acts of the Apostles, chapter 19, v 35, we read of the Ephesians who worshipped the goddess Diana and 'the symbol of her which fell from heaven'. King Maximilian I of Germany went off to the crusades encouraged by a stone falling near Ensisheim in the Alsace during 1492. The stone still resides in the village church.

When you see 'relics of the cross' you are rightly sceptical. Similar scepticism attended claims to possess 'stones that fell from heaven' in the eighteenth century. The emerging acceptance of science, led by the French Academy of Sciences, decreed that such irregular phenomena were impossible. Claims to have examples of meteorites became discredited as relics of a superstitious bygone age and many European museums threw them out from their exhibits.

Pennyweights from heaven started to become respectable after an iron meteorite fell in Austria in 1751. Several hundreds of people heard the thunder and saw the ball of fire in the sky. Stories about the fearsome vision of the night spread far and wide and pieces of iron were found scattered around. With speculation rife about this supernatural experience, the church quickly became interested and priests set out to interview witnesses. Clerics collected sworn testimonies and sent them to the Austrian emperor. In turn this stimulated E. F. Chladni, a German physicist, to defend the reality of the phenomenon and scientists began to take an interest. Meteorites became 'official' when a shower of stones fell near Paris in 1803. Even the French Academy of Sceptics could not ignore a shower in their own backyard and at last the whole scientific community agreed that meteorites really do fall from the sky.

The idea of cosmic catastrophes is very popular in science fiction and disaster movies. However, unlike some of the bizarre offerings in that genre, rocks dropping from the sky and destroying whole cities are not impossible. There is plenty of evidence for gargantuan invaders. Remote sensing satellites send back images of the ground showing that the Earth is pitted with the evidence of impacts.

Known impact craters that exceed 1 kilometre in size fairly pepper the globe, as we can see on the map (Figure 2.1). There are more than a hundred of them and these are only a small percentage of the total. The vast regions of central Asia, Africa and Brazil, where few craters are listed, have been explored less than other areas. Where meteorites have fallen in the jungles, or in geologically active regions, all traces will have been overgrown or otherwise obliterated by the living Earth. Oceans cover most of the surface and anything landing here will leave no trace (though one suggestion is that the Caribbean Sea is the result of a huge impact several millions of years ago). Only in dry undisturbed areas like the Arizona desert or the cratered arid regions of central Australia do the marks survive in pristine form.

In the south-western corner of the United States lie thousands of square miles of beautiful desert wilderness. The air is so still and the sun so bright that you can see a grey windswept plain stretching for miles against the backdrop of a turquoise sky. In the middle of this open country is a grotesque scar, a huge hole left one day 30,000 years ago when a lump of rock the size of an oil-tanker dropped from the sky and hit the ground while travelling thirty times faster than Concorde. The heat of the impact vaporised the soil and threw up a huge cloud high into the stratosphere. Boulders bigger than houses rained down from the cloud, adding to the devastation.

The crater remains, uneroded, much as it did once the dust had settled all those years ago. It is so huge – over 1 mile wide and 3 miles in circumference – that it is easily visible from outer space, like a piece of the Man in the Moon. Photos taken from satellites 900 miles high show the Colorado river, the extensive desert and a single pockmark where the boulder landed.

The crater may appear insignificant from the spy satellite, but come down to Earth and see it in close-up (p.1 of photos). The City

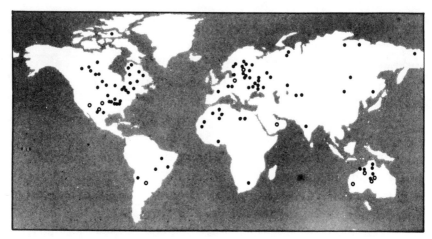

2.1 Terrestrial crater sites Open circles denote craters less than 1 km across with meteorite fragments and shock features. Dots denote larger older structures (from R. Grieve, 1983).

of London could be placed inside it and very few of the buildings would even reach the rim.

Hordes of tourists come and marvel at this awesome hole in the desert. Many of them think that it is unique. The Tungusku event already shows us that it is not. We are not alone in space and unwelcome visitors drop in from time to time: woe betide anyone who is around when the next one calls.

You might wonder what is the largest impact that the Earth has survived, or might be likely to suffer. Although the ravages of time have covered over most of the traces of impacts on Earth, the dead worlds elsewhere in the solar system preserve a record of collisions. These give us clues of what Nature has on offer. The Moon is our nearest neighbour and its scarred face shows what the Earth would be like if there were no atmosphere to protect us. We can see huge craters on the Moon from 250,000 miles away. Imagine them at ground level and how they were fashioned.

The Moon's craters vary in size, many being smaller than a coin while half a dozen exceed 100 miles diameter, as big as Sicily or the length of Long Island. Many of these were caused when the Moon was very young and the planets were still being formed. The cooling pieces of small 'protoplanets' hit the Moon and left their marks for ever. However, these are not really relevant for estimating the likelihood of collisions on Earth *today*. What we need is evidence that major collisions have occurred in recent times and are still going on.

When the Apollo astronauts visited the Moon they left behind four seismometers to measure Moonquakes. When these relayed signals back to Earth, the listening scientists were surprised by the sounds of large meteorites hitting the Moon, some as big as 10 metres across.

The flux of hits of the Moon varied through the year, peaking with the known meteor showers. The biggest one is at the end of June when we pass through the Taurid meteor stream. We on Earth didn't notice much thanks to the blanket of air surrounding us, but the airless Moon carries the scars. The stones hitting the moon sandblasted the old craters, creating the moondust that the astronauts kicked up as they walked the surface.

The Moon is a good detector and is teaching us a lot about what is going on 'out there'. From the distribution of hits – their size and frequency – we can estimate the number in the swarm (we only sample a small fraction), and it comes out close to 1 million. We can also calculate the distribution of sizes and so estimate the size of the biggest. If there are 10,000 of 1 metre and 1,000 of 10 metres diameter, then we can be fairly sure that there will be many of 100 metres and a few of 1 kilometre and maybe one of tens of kilometres. Now 'one' could be zero or it could be two or three – the statistics are risky at the end of the distribution. But there is little doubt about the rest: there will be several whose girths are larger than a football field. We know what such impacts can do: Arizona's crater and the Tunguska event are examples.

There are many pieces in the annual Taurid meteor shower that we would be aware of if we ran into them. In the last few years we have found objects in this stream that are 10 miles across. Such impacts would threaten life on Earth but fortunately are exceedingly rare. There is a greater chance of encountering a swarm of Tunguska-sized objects.

With modern technology we ought to be able to contemplate doing something about these. But how long do we have to prepare, and how big an invader can we expect? Surprisingly little work has been done – we are adept at looking deep into the Universe but the timetable of debris in our own backyard is not very well known.

For the moment we take refuge in the game of chance. The Moon's craters provide a record over the aeons, which suggests that a major impact, leading to a crater exceeding 1 mile, should occur once every 10,000 years on average; the larger they are, the rarer.

Think of what lies within a mile of your home and imagine it all extinguished. Even half a mile is not trifling and impacts of that size should happen much more often. The chance that one will happen in a populated area is small, as the Earth's area is dominantly uninhabited. The Tunguska event is a good example; people around the world noticed its occurrence like the Krakatoa eruption, but it didn't affect many people directly. Had the invader been bigger it could have disrupted much of the atmosphere. The extinction of the dinosaurs 60 million years ago may have been an example of such an extremis.

The Universe is a hostile place and there is nowhere to hide from its effects. Arizona yesterday, Siberia today; where next?

3

The Neighbourhood

Mercury, Venus, Earth, Mars, Jupiter, Saturn, Uranus, Neptune and Pluto. Nine planets are orbiting the Sun in regular processions. In addition, billions of tonnes of cosmic debris are swarming around. Some have rained down on the innermost planets scarring them for life. Debris is still pouring in. Comets zoom in from deep space; rocks drop out of the sky and burn up as meteors; some asteroids have orbits that cross our own.

The Sun outweighs all the planets put together and its gravity holds the planets, comets and asteroids in continuous orbits on their recurring journeys.

The innermost planets are like the Earth – small, with surfaces of solid rock enclosing cores of molten iron. Then come four giants consisting of hydrogen, helium, ammonia and methane all frozen solid in cold depths of space. Jupiter weighs more than the rest put together, its gravity so strong that it has a miniature orbiting system of its own with over a dozen known moons. Saturn and Uranus also have entrapped many moons and rings of smaller rocks. Neptune awaits the Voyager probe in 1989 and we expect to find a complex system of satellites there too. Beyond the big four lies tiny Pluto, whose satellite, Charon, is almost as big as it is.

Although Jupiter outweighs the rest, it is still 1,000 times lighter than the Sun; it is the *Sun*'s huge gravity that dominates the solar system.

Isaac Newton proposed his law of gravitation in 1687. He showed not only that apples drop on to people's heads but that the planets are held in orbits around the Sun too. We know we're safe

21

3.1 Conic sections A horizontal section gives a circle, an inclined cut gives an ellipse. If the Sun is at the focus of an ellipse (either of the dots) planets will orbit along elliptical paths. Cut the cone parallel to one side and you get a parabola. If the Sun is at the focus, the path is the line that goes off to the left for ever – such as a trapped comet that makes a single pass but that is always ensnared by the Sun's gravity. Cut the cone vertically and you have a hyperbola. This is the path that a body follows if it is not trapped by the Sun but is merely deflected by the solar gravity in its passage.

from them because Newton showed what sort of paths solar orbiters can follow. Newton's law implies that if a body is attracted to a massive object (such as the Sun) with a force that weakens in proportion to the square of the distance, then the body will move along one or other of a set of characteristic paths. These are the 'conic sections', the shapes that you get when you cut ice-cream cones (see Figure 3.1).

The Earth and the major planets all follow orbits that are nearly circular and keep well away from one another. Even Neptune and Pluto, whose orbits *do* cross, are never at the crossover at the same time. Some of the asteroids follow pronounced ellipses that cross our orbit twice.

The Sun is at the focus of the ellipse (see Figure 3.2), quite unlike the portrayal on the British pound note which showed it at the centre. It is amusing to recall that Newton was once in charge of Britain's Royal Mint. His successor in the 1970s, responsible for the

22

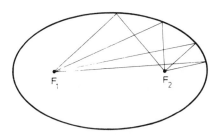

3.2 Ellipses   The sun is at the focus of the ellipse. There are two foci, F_1 and F_2. The distance from F_1 to F_2 via the edge is always the same. To make an ellipse choose a piece of string pinned to the paper at two points near enough that the string is slack. Now stretch it tight with a pencil and, keeping it tight, draw a curve. The pins will be at the foci and the curve will be an ellipse.

design, was obviously not educated in Newton's theory of gravity and the orbits of planets around the Sun.

Periodic comets, such as Halley's, follow very elongated elliptical orbits. From its period of 76 years, and Newton's law of gravity, we can calculate the orbit and find that its remotest point is further from the Sun than is Neptune. It hurls in, as in 1985/6, crossing our orbit once on the way in as in November 1985, once on the way out as in April 1986, missing us both times to return again another day.

It is 300 years since people realised that comets could be travelling around the sun in very elongated ellipses or making a single pass on a hyperbola. In the former case they would be part of the solar system, much as the planets are, but coming in from far far away and being visible only for the short time that they are near the sun. In the latter they would be cosmic wanderers that happen by chance to be deflected by the sun's gravity en route from the distant past to a lonely future. Of the 700 or so known comets some 600 have periodic orbits of the elliptical kind, the remainder being once-only voyagers.

We will look at these mavericks that cross our orbit and put us at risk in Chapter 4. Here we will concentrate on the nearly circular orbiters. They pose no threat but are interesting in that they provide fossil relics of past collisions showing what has happened in the past and could happen again.

Measuring the Solar System

Our nearest neighbour in space is the Moon. Astronauts can get there in a week. We can measure the distance by bouncing radar or laser beams off it and seeing how long it takes for the signal to return – it takes the time of three heartbeats to get there and back, a round trip of nearly half a million miles. We know the speed of light, or radar beams, so accurately that we can measure the distance of the Moon to a precision better than the thickness of this book. We can even tell that it is receding from us at a rate of about 3 cm each year – 3 metres in a century.

So not only are things on the move around one another, but their orbits are changing. The Moon raises tides in the seas and strains the rocks of Earth; as a result of these tidal forces it is receding and has become locked in to us so that it always presents the same face. The Earth too in its journeying round the Sun is gradually slowing its spin; in some distant future it will present the same face continuously to the Sun. Atomic clocks can record this slowing – a fraction of a second each year – and every so often we have to adjust our time clocks by adding a second on to a year: 'time stands still' for that moment. Conversely, in the past the Earth spun faster and so there were more days per year. Prehistoric geological records show that there were 400 days per annum several hundred million years ago. So over the epochs everything is readjusting – a theme that will pervade our story.

The radar beam that measured the distance from Earth to the Moon can also reach to Venus. Our nearest planetary neighbour is some 30 million miles away at its closest approach.

The next benchmark in scaling the Universe is the distance to the Sun. We can't bounce radar beams back from the Sun so we have to start with the information on the distance to Venus and use that to set the scale. Newton's theory of gravity implies that the time taken to orbit the Sun depends on the distance you are away from it, not on your mass. (As we can predict the occurrence of eclipses to within seconds we have no doubt that the theory is reliable.) The further away you are, so the slower you move (or else you would fly out of the solar system like a car trying to take a corner too fast), and as you have further to travel in a circuit it takes you longer. If you are four times further away than another body it will take you eight times as long (in general, the time taken is in proportion to the distance multiplied by the square root of the distance, hence four times two equals eight in our example).

Now the Venusian year is 224 of our days, which means that on average the distance from us to Venus at closest approach is about one-third of the distance from us to the Sun. The radar blip showed us how far away Venus is from us and so we can work out how far away the Sun is. We travel around the Sun in an elliptical path so the distance isn't the same throughout the year but the mean distance is 93 million miles. If you could fly to the Sun on Concorde it would take about a dozen years. A ray of light makes it in just over 8 minutes.

Bode's Law

The nearly circular paths of the planets have sizes that fit with a simple numerical rule. We're going to compare the distances from the Sun to the planets with that from Sun to the Earth. For simplicity we will define the Earth to be 10 units distance from the Sun. Then Mercury, Venus, Mars, Jupiter and Saturn are very nearly 4, 7, 15, 52 and 95 units distance respectively.

These were the only planets known in 1766 when Johann Titius first noticed that these numbers fit into a series. If you subtract 4 from each then the data are very similar to a series where each successive number is double the previous one: 0, 3, 6, 12, 24, 48, 96, 192 and so on. On adding four in again you have 4, 7, 10, 16, 28, 52, 100, 196. These are very good comparisons with the orbits out to Mars. The member at 28 is missing but at 52 Jupiter occurs on cue and Saturn is only 5 per cent out.

Johann Bode succeeded Titius at the Berlin Observatory, published Titius's rule and got the credit. This numerology is often referred to as Bode's law.

No one paid much attention to it until 1781 when Caroline and William Herschel discovered Uranus. Its distance from the Sun is 192 in these same units. This is quite remarkable since the Titius–Bode rule predicts 196. The agreement was sensational enough

the Caloris Basin, a crater that is nearly 1,000 miles across. Whereas the Arizona meteor crater is a spot in the desert, the Caloris Basin would fill Arizona along with much of the six states covering America's south-western corner; almost a quarter of the whole sub-continent! The shock waves were so strong that they travelled right through the planet, leaving gorges and hills on the far side.

In 1977, the United States launched two further probes, the Voyager spacecraft, which have given us close-up views of the outer planets and their environs. So far they have visited Jupiter (1979), Saturn (1980) and Uranus (1986). We already knew that Saturn has beautiful rings and Voyager showed that Jupiter and Uranus have too. These three giant planets have many moons and the Voyager pictures reveal that these moons contain a record of aeons of impacts. The messages imprinted on the surfaces of these moons are making some scientists on Earth ponder. These lonely worlds bear testimony to the power of Nature. They have gathered it and kept it for millennia, unknown until the day that the first space probe arrived.

Voyager's pictures of Callisto, one of Jupiter's many moons, showed the results of violent impacts in unexpected detail. Callisto is more than 3,000 miles across, nearly half the diameter of the Earth, and its entire surface is utterly cratered, not a single square metre has escaped. Indeed, you could not create a new crater without destroying one that is already there. Rocks and huge boulders must have been crashing into Callisto for millions of years.

Callisto's surface is a mixture of ice and rock, a global Antarctica. Glaciers flow into the meteor craters. The biggest impact sites were originally marked out by huge holes and high cliffs, but have now levelled out so that only the surrounding walls remain. The smaller craters survive in their pristine form; the ice can support the wall of a small crater permanently but the larger craters collapse.

Among this awful desolation is a spectacular and beautiful bull's-eye of multiple rings. A stupendous collision, singular even among Callisto's continual bombardment, made a crater 400 miles across. This melted the ice beneath the surface and huge blast waves of water spread outwards. The temperature is 180 degrees below zero. In this biting cold the waves froze into mountainous rings 2,000 miles around. We know that this happened rather recently because there are no craters on its floor; this bulls-eye has splattered the earlier craters and in time will be peppered again by further ones.

This is an apt illustration of the raw power of Nature and reminds us of our puny insignificance. Who could have imagined the reality of frozen mountains the extent of the USA, centred on a crater larger than the state of Kansas? While this gives us pause, hopefully it is not a good guide to what we are likely to feel on the Earth. Callisto is near to Jupiter, whose huge gravity pulls debris into its stratosphere. So its moons are peppered with flying rocks much more often than they would be were they near to the Earth. Callisto inhabits the solar freeway whereas Earth is off the main road.

After visiting Jupiter's environs Voyager set off deeper into space reaching Saturn in 1980 and giving our first views of its cratered moons.

One of Saturn's moons, Mimas, is only 250 miles in diameter but contains a crater that is 7 miles deep and a full 60 miles across. A crater that is one-quarter the size of a moon represents a collision in extremis; a slightly larger impact would probably have shattered Mimas. Indeed, it appears that Mimas may be flawed right through, as there are cracks on the far side opposite the crater.

This is reminiscent of Mercury's cleavage and shows that that is not unique. Nor is this the limit of Nature's potential devastation; even more violent collisions have happened to the Saturnian moons – one of which *has* been broken in two. The two halves are still circling and are the moons with the unromantic names 'S_{10}' and 'S_{11}'.

These twins orbit Saturn at a distance of 100,000 miles yet their paths lie within 30 miles of each other, little more than the width of the English Channel, closer than the northern and southern extremities of New York City. S_{10} is 150 miles across while S_{11} is an odd shape, a fragment that is 50 miles high and 20 miles across; twice as long in one direction as the other. The only way that Nature could have fashioned such irregular shapes is by breaking up a larger object.

These co-orbiting moons are not on *exactly* the same paths and so they take slightly different times to orbit Saturn. Consequently they must pass each other periodically. It is a mystery how they manage to do this since their sizes are bigger than the separation of their orbits. But now astronomers believe that, instead of rotating periodically, some objects in the solar system behave chaotically. Jack Wisdon of the Massachusetts Institute of Technology showed in 1987 that Hyperion, one of Saturn's moons, is now tumbling chaotically. Orbital chaos was once thought to be a dynamical impossibility but astronomers now think it answers a variety of questions about the solar system. Chaotic orbits may explain how asteroids reach Earth in the form of meteors. They add a new and utterly unpredictable ingredient in the risk stakes.

Voyager spent the next five years, from 1980 to 1985, travelling onwards from Saturn to Uranus. At last, on 24 January 1986, it sped past Uranus and found again evidence of craters and even shattered satellites. It is possible that Uranus itself has been flipped over by some ancient collision. Whereas the Earth's magnetic poles are near to its rotation axis, the magnetic poles of Uranus are nearly on its equator; unique in the solar system.

Voyager also found more evidence of chaos. Miranda, one of Uranus' moons, 300 miles in diameter, has a peculiar geology, with rifts and oval gorges, which appear to be the result of it having been tumbling and lurching erratically for millions of years in chaotic motion instead of rotating at predictable intervals.

At the farthest outposts of the planetary solar system, where Voyager will reach some day, lie Pluto and Neptune. (Voyager will meet Neptune, but Pluto is currently on the far side of the Sun and so won't be encountered this time.) We tend to think that Pluto is the farthest away from the Sun, but in fact these two planets criss-cross in their orbits, and currently Neptune is the farther away. (This will continue to be the case until March 1999 when Pluto will cross over and return to the outside.) There is no danger of these two colliding, however. Their orbits take 165 and 248 years, neatly in the ratio of 2 to 3. Pluto goes round the Sun twice while Neptune goes round three times. When Neptune is at the crossover point, Pluto is somewhere else. When Pluto arrives at the crossover, Neptune has moved on to another place. So it continues, round and round. These two planets are safe from one another.

Percy Lowell, the great American astronomer, initiated a search for a planet beyond Uranus and Neptune. He died in 1916 and it was not until 1930 that Pluto was found. The discovery was announced on Lowell's birthday and the symbol for the planet is ℞, a monogram of his initials and the first two letters of the planet's name.

Pluto is smaller even than our own moon. Furthermore it is only three times heavier than its own moon, Charon (discovered by James Christy in 1978). It is hard in the circumstances to think of Pluto as a planet, rather it and Charon form a pair of planets orbiting one another as they move collectively around the Sun.

Pluto is an overgrown snowball and may even be a satellite that escaped from a parent planet, probably Neptune. There are several pieces of circumstantial evidence supporting the idea that at some time in the past a maverick body passed near to Neptune and disrupted its moons. Pluto may be one of them, ejected outwards and now looping in and out of Neptune's path as if trying to orbit that planet as they both slowly circle the distant central Sun. This is unique in the whole solar system – all the other planets have orbits far removed from one another.

Another of Neptune's moons, Triton, behaves strangely. All other close-in moons orbit their parent planets in the same direction as our moon orbits the Earth; Triton orbits Neptune the opposite way. Our moon is also typical in following the equatorial regions, pursuing the Sun through the heavens; Triton's path is inclined at 20 degrees to Neptune's equator – it is as if our moon looped up over our heads and dipped below the horizon as we faced the sun.

Finally there is Neptune's other moon – Nereid. This moves so fast that Neptune can barely hold on to it. And it doesn't keep its distance, it comes in close and then moves off far away on a tight ellipse. Imagine our moon sometimes filling the sky close in and then heading off to a remote small disc and then hurtling back in again. That is how Nereid would appear to a Neptunian.

In 1979 R. Harrington and T. van Fladern wrote an article in the astronomy journal *Icarus* explaining how all these orbits might have arisen. We can even test their theory because it predicts that a tenth planet exists far beyond Pluto.

Suppose that Neptune originally had four moons in near circular orbits, much like Jupiter's largest moons. All that is required is that a planet, three times the bulk of Earth, plunges through the satellite system. The cannibal planet captures the innermost moon and carries it off into deep space. The second nearest moon also escapes and ends up in a remote orbit: Pluto. The third moon has its orbit flipped and is Triton, while the fourth just manages to survive in orbit around Neptune and is Nereid.

This is not contrived. If you start off with four reasonable circular orbits and study the effects of a bulky object passing through, then these weird orbits emerge naturally. And that is indeed what Pluto, Triton and Nereid look like today. The search is now on for the lost planet, the tenth planet – Planet X. Perhaps in the outer reaches of the solar system we have the most extreme examples of what can happen when encounters get too close. Had such near misses involved the Earth, they would have been terminal for mankind.

Jupiter: King of the Planets

Astrologers are much enthused by planetary alignments. Although most people do not take astrology very seriously there are still many who think that there might be a physical basis for its predictions, especially when all the planets are in the same part of the sky. For example, in 1982 many people believed that the gravitational forces engendered by a 'grand alignment' of the planets would act in concert and could provide a physical mechanism for triggering earthquakes or other disasters. Indeed, one mystic even predicted World's End.

Although at first sight this may appear very reasonable, in fact the sums simply do not add up. Gravity is the only force that measurably affects the motion of planets and their moons. The force of gravity acting between two bodies is in proportion to their masses and varies inversely as the square of the distance between them. In other words, it is bigger the more massive the bodies and feebler the further apart they are. We are trapped by the Sun because it is the most massive thing around here, outweighing the rest of the solar system 500 times over. The Moon, by contrast, is lightweight but it is very near by: it is its nearness that makes it play an important role. Everything else is insubstantial and remote; for example Jupiter, the biggest planet, has less than 0.5 per cent of the Sun's mass and is at least five times further from us.

The Moon's motion around the Earth raises tides as it orbits. Gravity's strength weakens with distance, so the tug on the Pacific Ocean is greater when the Moon is directly over Hawaii than when it is away round the corner above the Atlantic.

Similarly the revolution of the planets raise tides in the Sun, causing small bulges in their wake. The outer planets orbit slowly while the inner ones fairly rush round. Once in a while the planets will all be on the same side of the Sun and all tug in concert. Devotees of the so-called 'Jupiter effect' noticed that between 1977 and 1982 the planets would be grouped on the same side of the Sun. They believed that the collective gravitational tug would stretch out the Sun, causing great disturbances on its surface.

Now it is indeed the case that we on Earth are much more affected by inconstant behaviour in the Sun than perhaps we realise. The Sun may appear to be a shining ball far away from us, but its thin non-luminous outer atmosphere extends far beyond the Earth. We are literally journeying *inside* the Sun! Storms in the glowing Sun can reach its outer regions and directly disturb our own atmosphere, interfering with radio communications and affecting the weather. According to the advocates of the 'Jupiter effect', if the Sun is really disturbed, then it would severely disrupt our upper atmosphere and perturb our rotation. The jolt would strain the Earth's crust, causing disastrous earthquakes as weak spots gave way.

These dramatic catastrophes sound plausible because of the imagery in the emotive phrase – 'stretching out the Sun'. However, the planets do no such thing; their effect is nugatory. The Sun is oscillating up and down by several miles all the time without us being particularly aware of it (the glowing Sun is nearly 1 *million* miles across so these oscillations are comparable in relative scale to the tides on the Earth). The additional effect due to the planets aligning amounts to less than the thickness of this book. So the planetary tides in the Sun are over a million times less effective than the lunar-induced tides on Earth.

Changes in the Sun, like all random motions, are the result of forces acting – which means gravity in the present context. A common misconception is that the motion of the planets around their common fulcrum is important. Proponents argue that when the giant outer planets are all lined up, the centre of the Sun will be furthest away from the centre of the solar system and so the Sun will 'pull in the opposite direction to balance the added effect of the planets'.

However, the fulcrum plays no role in determining the size of the forces acting on the Sun or anywhere else. It is important to remember this before getting too carried away with predictions of disasters stemming from *distant* planets. The outer reaches of the solar system are incredibly remote. The distances from the Sun roughly double with each successive planet (recall the Bode numbers on page 25); thus a journey from the sun to Jupiter, passing Mercury, Venus, Earth, Mars and the asteroid belt, brings you only half way to Saturn. When you reach Saturn you are still only half way to Uranus, and Uranus is only the midpoint in a trip to Neptune (see Figure 3.4).

As if this isn't enough to make the outer planets impotent, the tidal forces result from the gravitational force *difference* across the body that is of interest and die away in proportion to the distance *cubed*: double the distance and the effects die eightfold. The result is that little close-in Mercury raises tides in the Sun almost as effectively as distant mighty Jupiter does and Venus is comparable to Jupiter. Jupiter is less important than Mercury, Venus and the Earth combined.

None the less, Jupiter could cause us problems *indirectly*. As comets swing in from the cold depths of space, they may pass near the huge outer planets and be ensnared by their pull. Comets that would otherwise have looped in around the Sun and off again to

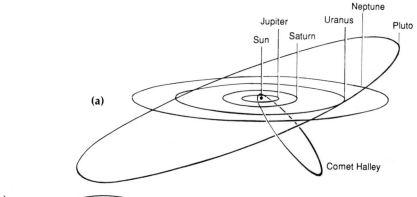

(a)

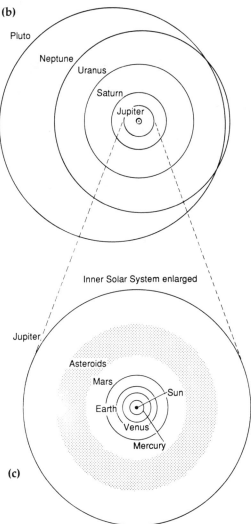

(b)

3.4 The solar system

(a) All of the known planets, with the exception of Pluto, orbit the Sun in the same plane. Pluto's orbit, and that of Comet Halley, are very different from this. This is one reason for suspecting that Pluto's orbit has been drastically disturbed in the past.

(b) Projected onto a plane we see that Pluto's orbit crosses Neptune's. The relative distances to the outer planets are so vast that the inner solar system has to be shown on an enlarged scale (Fig. 3.4c).

Inner Solar System enlarged

(c)

distant space can be whipped like slingshot on a new path. Most of them are trapped in orbits around the Sun, whirling in tight elliptical paths, like Comet Halley. Some end up in paths that cross those of the planets.

Almost inevitably some day one will be heading towards the same point in space as us, as in June 1908 when the Earth ran into 10 million tonnes of rock and ice which fell out of the sky into the Siberian wilderness.

If you were placing bets on the most likely natural global disaster, collision with an asteroid or a large piece of a dead comet are leading contenders.

4

Chicken on the Roundabout

Comets

On 30 August 1979 a satellite orbiting the earth recorded a cata-strophic event – the death of a heavenly body. The Sun's gravity had ensnared Comet 'Howard-Koomen-Michels 1979XI', which fell headlong into the stellar furnace. Within a matter of seconds the comet, larger than the Earth, was destroyed. The immense power of the Sun vaporised the comet as an elephant destroys an ant. The debris scattered for millions of miles in the Sun's atmosphere.

Comets date back to the start of the solar system and are probably its most primitive members. They are balls of gravel and ice, most of them spending much of their time far beyond Pluto in deep space where we're unaware of them until one zooms into view on a looping path towards the Sun, whipping behind it and setting off back into deep space.

The comet's head is deep frozen when far from the Sun where the ambient temperature is −270 degrees Centigrade. The ice contains deep-frozen ammonia, methane and amino acids, the stuff of life. There are suggestions that cometary impacts may have contributed to Earth's early terrestrial atmosphere and brought the primitive organic molecules for prebiotic evolution.

As comets approach the Sun, its warmth vaporises the ice. The ejected gas and dust reflect sunlight and appear from the Earth as a bright head, or coma. The comet's nucleus consists of one or two lumps of rock of about a mile diameter. The coma is usually bigger than the Earth and may be as much as 100,000 miles across. The solar wind (high-speed particles coming from the Sun) and the radiation drive very fine dust particles and ionised gas from the coma, forming a lengthy tail which always points away from the Sun. This can extend for enormous distances, even as long as the distance from the Earth to the Sun. This elongated shape in the heavens is the characteristic signature of a comet, recorded in the Bayeux tapestry, paintings and literature.

The melting ice releases the stony pieces with the result that the comet eventually becomes a mile-sized ball of gravel weighing over a million billion tonnes. Large though this sounds, it is trifling on the scale of the Earth and other heavenly bodies. As far as we know, comets have never perturbed the motions of the planets or even their moons. In 1770 and again in 1886 comets passed between the moons of Jupiter without noticeably affecting the moons' motions even though the comets' trajectories were significantly deflected. So a near miss will not affect the course of the Earth; it will take more than a comet to send us headlong into the Sun or flip us out into deep space.

A direct hit is a more serious matter. Comets are moving at several miles per second, as is the Earth, and a direct hit from a mile-sized lump of rock can't be ignored. The Arizona and Tunguska impacts involved objects 'only' 100 metres across.

Some of the comets pass near the major planets, Jupiter and Saturn, and are dragged in. Small pieces break away leaving a trail behind the main mass. The beautiful rings around Saturn are probably pieces of dead comets, as are the rings around Jupiter, unknown before the Voyager spacecraft arrived there. And in January 1986 Voyager arrived at Uranus showing us rings there too. Cometary fragments are everywhere.

There are huge rings around the Sun. When the Earth passes through one of these we experience a meteor shower as the dust burns up in our atmosphere. Some of the larger pieces reach ground as meteorites. The largest pieces may orbit on long after the rest have dispersed or been burned up in collisions. These extinct comet heads form some of the asteroids.

The largest asteroids are as big as countries. Ceres spans France and Belgium. Pallas and Vesta are as big as Southern Scandinavia and Juno is the size of Ireland (see Figure 4.1). None of these comes anywhere near our orbit to threaten us, but many much smaller asteroids actually cross the Earth's orbit. These mavericks are called 'Apollo Objects' after the half-mile diameter asteroid Apollo, which was discovered when it approached near to the Earth in 1932.

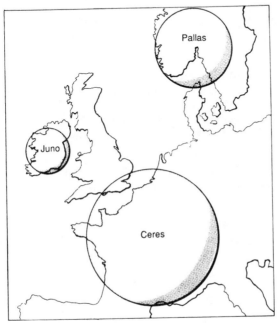

4.1 Asteroids Asteroid sizes compared with European countries. Ceres, the largest, obliterates France; Pallas covers southern Norway and Sweden; Juno compares to Ireland.

Apollo Objects

Recent searches for Earth-crossing asteroids suggest that they could be numerous. None of them is larger than a few miles in diameter but a collision would wreak havoc for hundreds of miles and the disturbance of the atmosphere would cause great storms at least.

The first hints of such an awful possibility emerged in 1898 with the discovery of Eros, an asteroid that comes within Mars's orbit.

For the first time astronomers realised that asteroids are not restricted to the space between Jupiter and Mars. Eros takes only a few months longer to orbit the Sun than we do. In doing so it encroaches nearer to us than we ever get to Venus, our nearest neighbour among the planets.

Soon other examples of wandering asteroids turned up. In 1911 a small one cosily named Albert was found, and lost. Where it is now is anyone's guess. This illustrates a worry – there are Earth-crossing asteroids whose schedules we do not know accurately or at all.

Gradually as more examples turned up, the perils became sharper. In 1932 Apollo came within 7 million miles of us. Now that might sound a long way off, nearly 30 times more distant than the Moon. However, unlike the Moon, which stays at a regular distance from us, Apollo whirls far away and rushes in, crossing our path. Indeed, it had missed us by only six weeks. If the Earth's orbit had been only 100 miles nearer the Sun, we would have been moving fast enough to have arrived at the crossover six weeks earlier.

In 1936 Adonis appeared and missed us by less than 12 days. The insurance premiums are rising! In 1937 the closest encounter in modern times involved Hermes, an asteroid that is a mile in diameter, which crossed our orbit less than six hours before we arrived at the crucial spot. Six hours – less time than it takes to fly the Atlantic.

There's no sign that these occurrences are unusual. On 20 October 1976 we were missed by less than half a day. And if you feel confident that 'surely by now we must know the timetable and there can't be any new shocks to come', I offer you the night of 28 February 1982 when two 'Earth-grazers' were discovered.

H. Schuster at an observatory in Chile discovered an asteroid that comes near to our orbit but never crosses us. Later that night E. Helin at the Palomar Observatory in California caught sight of an asteroid that was alarmingly close. Tracking its path from night to night soon showed that it was flying away from us and had already crossed our orbit twice! On its way in towards the Sun it had crossed our path three months earlier and had done so again on its way out just three weeks before Ms Helin sighted it. No one had detected it while it was heading towards our orbit. This highlights one of the major problems: these Apollo objects are large enough to damage us severely but they are too small to detect easily.

In 1987 the asteroid Icarus passed within 4 million miles of us – a mere 16 times more remote than the Moon. Icarus is sometimes the nearest major object to the Sun. At its nearest approach it flies within Mercury's orbit and then hurtles outwards, passing Venus, the Earth and Mars before turning round again near Jupiter. Its orbit is regular and it will be a long time before it comes as near as in 1987. However, close encounters with one or other of the various objects that it passes during its adventures may perturb its orbit such that it will be a hazard one day in the far distant future.

The last time that Icarus approached us, scientists at the Massachusetts Institute of Technology asked themselves what action we could take if some day we discovered that an asteroid was headed directly at us. Hollywood picked up this idea.

The film makers didn't go at it half-heartedly either. They weren't satisfied with a disaster from a single hit. Their story concerned a collision of a comet and an asteroid out in the belt beyond Mars. The collision broke up these bodies into several fragments, some of which headed towards Earth. Scientists first detected the large comet head out in space, and realised that it was coming right at us. The USA and USSR combined to send out all of their nuclear weapons on rockets aimed at the invader with the intention of breaking it up and deflecting it, or at least reducing the effects of its impact.

Building up the tension, the story had some of the small fragments heading towards Earth in advance of the main rock. These small fragments crashed on New York and other major cities (quite remarkable aiming as the odds are that they would land in the sea or in the vast wastes as we remarked in Chapter 2). Finally the central core bore down in the disaster movie to beat them all.

Currently the largest known Apollo object is Hephaistos, which is 6 miles across. In Chapter 5 we will see that an asteroid might have extinguished the dinosaurs 65 million years ago. The suspect was 5–12 miles across. So there is the chance of a life-threatening collision, although the known Apollo objects do not make this very likely; but for one thing – we now have nuclear installations on the planet. If one of those was destroyed the consequences could be very worrying.

In this century we have on several occasions come within days or even hours of hitting an asteroid. The future is not likely to be any different. Every few years one or other of the Earth-crossing Apollo objects will come within hours of hitting us. In time it is certain that we and one of them will score a bull's-eye, but the odds are against it happening in our lifetime.

Meteors

The Apollo objects are outnumbered by the debris of smaller comets which cause the annual meteor showers. We pass through the debris and then voyage around the Sun for a whole year until we come back to the same relative position and pass through the ring again. Although the ring as a whole appears stationary, it is in fact in permanent motion. It consists of pieces of gravel and dust that are themselves orbiting the Sun. One piece of stone rushes past, pursued by another, and another, so that there is a continuous stream of pieces all the time.

Most of the individual pieces of dust in the stream of meteors weigh only a few grams, but the head of a comet might be lurking, several miles across – an Apollo asteroid in the making. Very likely there are many large lumps of rock that could hit and leave a big mark. If so, each year the Earth is crossing a lethal freeway whose traffic travels at 30 miles per second, most of which are gnats but one or two could be boulders the size of mountains.

This is like playing chicken on the roundabout. The Earth is going round and round, missing the big head this time, last time, until eventually the odds run out and we collide.

If a comet has been utterly destroyed then its debris may be distributed uniformly around its entire orbit. We see a meteor display on the same nights each year as we pass through; the intensity is the same from one year to the next. However, if the comet is still around, or only partially decomposed, the density of the debris may vary considerably, being large in the vicinity of the head and negligible far away. In this case the meteor showers will have dramatic peaks in certain years when we pass near to the head while being disappointing in intervening years.

There are a few major meteor streams each year. These include the Leonids (12 November), the Perseids (mid-August), the Beta Taurids (peaking on 29 June) and the Geminids (14 December). Let's look at them in turn.

On average there are about ten meteors per hour when the **Leonid** shower occurs each November. There is a wood-cut in the American Museum of Natural History showing hundreds of trails in a Leonid shower. Even allowing for artistic licence this is excessive, but there must have been a spectacular shower to impress the artist.

It was the great meteor shower of 12 November 1833 that really started serious study of meteors. Hundreds of thousands were seen all over the eastern coast of North America. All of them seemed to radiate from a point in the constellation Leo – hence 'Leonid'. It didn't matter where you were, in New York or the south, the radiant effect was the same point in the sky for all. This showed that the meteors came from outside the atmosphere and their apparent divergence from a single point was simply the effect of perspective: the meteors are really moving in parallel paths.

Records of the Leonid shower have been traced back as far as AD 902. The Norman Conquest was indeed portentious – accompanied by Halley's Comet and followed by a peak Leonid display. The ring of debris has a high-density region that orbits the Sun every 33 years. This is clearly the remnant of the comet head where the final pieces broke up. The nearer we are to the densest bit as we cross the road, the more spectacular the display turns out. In 1833 and 1866 it was very bright but in 1899 and 1932 it was rather poor by comparison, though still brighter than in intervening years. The Leonids were again spectacular in 1966, shooting up to 10,000 per hour at one stage. What does 1999 portend?

In some interpretations of the prophecies of Nostradamus the Apocalypse will occur in that very year. Moreover, a comet will herald it, appearing around 21 June. So the year looks promising, but the date is more akin to the Beta Taurids than Leonids. In addition, the prophecy implies that the comet will come from Ursa Minor rather than Leo, if that gives you comfort.

Whether or not Nostradamus has been correctly interpreted, even assuming he is right, the Leonids are unlikely to be the source of a cometary collision. When tens of thousands of meteors rain in an hour, we are clearly passing through the head of a comet *that has already broken up*. There is unlikely to be any huge core left to strike us.

So much for the Leonids. The **Perseids** in August are more tantalising. These meteors were once known as the 'tears of St Laurence'. They are a steady annual show at the rate of about one a minute at their 12 August peak and extending, less spectacularly, for two weeks on either side of this date. Or at least they were until 1980 and 1981 when the stream suddenly brightened. This may be worrying in 2102 for the following reason – astronomers have lost track of a comet.

The Swift Tuttle comet orbits the sun with a period of 121 years. It was last seen in 1860 and should have returned in 1981 but failed to turn up.

Now a comet can't go off at a tangent any more than the Earth can. It is a part of the solar system and orbits the Sun under the same gravitational forces that hold the Earth and the planets in their courses. If it fails to turn up then it must have died, broken up.

This fits in with the sudden brightening of the Perseids in that very year – the Perseids are its garbage. The big unknown is: is there a big unknown? Is there a huge piece of rock whirling around? In 2102, or 121,242,363 years later, our descendants may find out.

Now you may think that I am trying to impress you with unlikely eventualities. To remove any lingering complacency let's look at the case of the **Beta Taurids** and one of the most devastating natural phenomena this century.

This meteor shower maximises on 29 June. And it was on the morning of 30 June 1908 that a giant fireball streaked across the sky and levelled 7,000 square miles of forest in the Tunguska valley. From reports of the flash and the size of the destruction scientists have estimated that the power of the explosion was like that from a large hydrogen bomb. Various sensational explanations have been proposed: aliens visited in a nuclear-powered spacecraft which crashed; antimatter hit the earth; a mini black hole struck. These all ignore important facts. There is no radioactivity at the site so nuclear explosions by aliens are out. Antimatter would have caused gamma ray bursts and residual radioactive traces. Mini black holes, if they even exist, would have emerged from the other side of the Earth (as they have not eaten up the Earth in the meantime), but there are no records of amazing phenomena in the Atlantic Ocean that day. You can choose the bizarre if you wish to, but there is a natural explanation that fits all the facts.

The consensus among scientists is that a large part of a comet head hit the Earth that day. A comet's nucleus is fragile, being a snowball full of gravel, and as it broke up it left no impact crater even though it caused great damage at the site and disturbed the atmosphere. On this occasion we played chicken once too often and a large piece hit us. This probably implies that the comet associated with the Beta Taurids is now finally broken up and we don't need to worry about it any more.

Finally there are the **Geminids**, which hit us every 13 December. In 1983 a satellite carrying sensitive infra-red detectors (the IRAS – infra-red astronomical satellite) discovered a comet. This was given the codename 1983TB and its orbit was seen to coincide with the Geminid meteor stream.

The satellite discovered it in October 1983 and after watching it for two days plotted its course. It appeared to be heading directly for Earth with impact estimated to be due on 13 December! As more days passed and the comet approached the scientists watched its flight ever more carefully and began to discern that it wasn't exactly in line with the Earth. From far away an object may appear to be heading for you whereas when it is nearer your perspective is better and you see that it will make a near miss. That is how it turned out with 1983TB (obviously, or you would have been aware of it!). It passed between the Earth and the Sun, which is close on an astronomical scale, close enough that maybe you saw it with your own eyes for a few nights.

It wasn't particularly bright and may be nearing the end of its life. Its orbit was calculated and it will periodically return within one-tenth of the distance from the Earth to the Sun, that is within 10 million miles. Jupiter, the most massive planet, will perturb the comet's orbit and pull it away from us. After 2150 it will be totally outside the Earth's orbit and so we have nothing to fear from this one.

However, we can be sure that deep in space there are other comets heading towards us right now. Most of them miss us by 100 million miles or more; occasionally one crosses our orbit, as in 1983.

A 100 metre fragment devastated an unpopulated valley in Siberia in 1908. Where and when will the next one strike?

Nemesis and the Lost Planet

During the 1980s we have learned more about our place in the Universe than ever before. Yet at the same time we have highlighted a surprising area of ignorance about goings-on in our own backyard.

Modern telescopes peer deep into space revealing thousands of galaxies of stars. There are spirals, elliptical shapes, spherical ones and more besides. We can watch galaxies tugging at each other by their mutual gravity, distorting and distending. Within our own galaxy (the Milky Way) we have studied many stars in detail. We know how they are born, how they live and die. Close to home we are rapidly learning much about our solar system, aided by the space missions. Human footprints mark the Moon, robot craft have landed on Mars, we have sent space probes to photograph Jupiter and Uranus, soon to reach Neptune, and have flown through Halley's Comet. There are even plans to send a probe into the Sun. However, we have not yet landed on, or even made a flypast of, an asteroid. So we still have much to learn.

Between the inner solar system and the distant stars there is a real gap in our knowledge: we know almost nothing about the remote outer solar system. The distant planet Pluto was found only 50 years ago. Its sizeable moon, Charon, was unknown until 1978! This shows how little we know of dark objects even when they are fairly near to us.

Astronomers discover about six new comets each year. Occasionally one comes near enough to be visible to the naked eye. The most famous regular visitor is Comet Halley whose pass in 1986 was too remote to be dramatic. In the past it has come much closer; stretching across whole constellations it made an awesome sight. In the future it may come close again.

There must be a huge number of comets in and around the solar system as a whole if a new one is discovered every other month. Jan Oort, a distinguished Dutch astronomer, has estimated that there are 100 billion of them. The orbits of many comets show that they come from a common place deep in space, 50,000 times more remote than the Earth from the Sun, a quarter of the way to the nearest star.

Travel out beyond Neptune and Pluto, further than Voyager has yet reached. The Sun is now a distant dimness. Carry on into the darkness beyond the planets into interstellar space. The next star is still far off. You are travelling through blackness, perpetual nighttime. This is not an empty void; out here in the frozen depths of space comets are icebergs several miles across, invisible from Earth. They have no light of their own – like the rest of the solar system they merely reflect sunlight, and out in this darkness they are as difficult to see as the iceberg that sank the Titanic.

This reservoir of 100 billion icebergs is called the 'Oort cloud'. These cosmic hitchhikers, freeloaders to the solar system, are slowly orbiting the Sun far beyond the planets, so remote that they barely hang on. The slightest disturbance in space could tip millions of these icebergs in towards us.

The existence of craters and other features of the Earth's geological and fossil record suggest to some that we are bombarded by asteroids and comets every 28 million years or so. The last major happening was 11 million years ago, so we are in a quiet period at present. The question is: What is stirring up the distant comets periodically?

The most natural explanation is that the cycle is related to our motion around the galaxy. We orbit the Sun once a year; the Sun and the entire solar system is orbiting the centre of the galaxy every 200 million years (see Figure 4.2). Sometimes we pass near to other

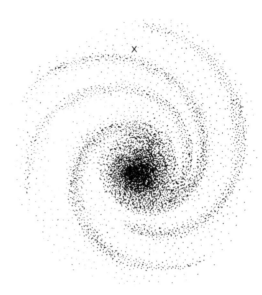

4.2 Milky Way External view of the Milky Way
galaxy. The position of the Sun is marked by the X.

stars and they disturb the comets in the outer reaches. Some will be
released into deep space, others will fall in towards the Sun.

Two other theories place the blame closer to home. One theory
is that in the dark regions beyond the known solar system there
may be a tenth planet – called Planet X of course! There is little
doubt that something is lurking beyond the outer planets. The
discoveries of Neptune and Pluto were stimulated by anomalies in
the motion of the planets. Already in the eighteenth century
astronomers had noticed that Uranus moved as if under the
influence of a distant body. The discovery of Neptune in 1846
explained the perturbation of Uranus but in turn exhibited anomalies of its own. The search began for a more distant massive planet.
Pluto was found in 1930 but it is very lightweight. The discovery of
its companion Charon in 1978 doesn't really solve the problem;
both Pluto and Charon are very small, too tiny to provide the
missing tug. Hence the suspicion that a tenth massive planet is still
to be found out in deep space. We don't know where or how far
away it is with any confidence but we suspect that it is larger than
the Earth, some two or three times more remote than Pluto and

orbiting the Sun once in 1,000 years. The only clues are that Uranus and Neptune were disturbed in the nineteenth century, whereas in recent decades these planets have been acting 'normally'. This suggests that Planet X was near the planets 100 years ago but is now far out of the plane of their orbits.

Searching for Planet X is a real enterprise. In August 1989 the Voyager 2 space probe will pass by Neptune and head out of the solar system. It will continue to send back signals to scientists at NASA's Deep Space Tracking Network on radio telescopes in California, Australia and Spain. If it, or its sister craft the Pioneers and Voyager 1, should come under the influence of Planet X their trajectories will deviate from those expected. It is very unlikely that in the vastness of space they will chance upon the planet, but it is a possibility none the less.

In 1987 NASA held a press conference at which they reported results from the Pioneer spacecraft, by then in the farthest reaches of the known solar system. Pioneer felt nothing untoward. Pioneer carries instruments that are very sensitive to disturbances. The nineteenth-century disturbances of Uranus and Neptune were big enough to see; the lack of any extra tug on those planets in the twentieth century and the very precise measurements by Pioneer constrain the possible orbits of the tenth planet. Put all this information together and NASA proposes that Planet X is in an orbit tilted relative to those of the known planets (see Figure 4.3). It could be travelling perpendicular to them and could even be the lost moon of Neptune.

Planet X may well exist, but it is unlikely to be responsible for the cometary bombardment. The inner edge of the Oort cloud is at least 20 times more remote and beyond the influence of Planet X in a normal orbit. Encounters with galactic material could disturb the planet's orbit every 28 million years and in turn it would affect the comets. If Planet X exists then it is possible that this sequence occurs. But it seems unnecessarily complicated to invent Planet X for this purpose alone. Why not assert that whatever disturbs Planet X, disturbs the comets directly. A more exciting theory is that the Sun has a small dark companion, a sister star with the romantic name Nemesis (the Greek goddess of doom), moving in a

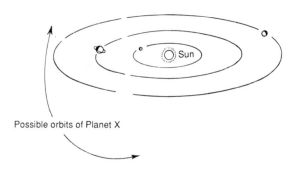

Possible orbits of Planet X

4.3   Planet X – a tenth planet? Possible orbits of
Planet X according to NASA in 1987.

long tight ellipse about it. This star is never nearer than 250 times
Pluto's distance and reaches as much as 4,500 times as far. With
such an orbit it would sweep through the Oort cloud every 30
million years. At present it could be three-quarters of the way to
the nearest bright star, Proxima Centauri.

Estimates are that Nemesis is only 1 per cent as massive as the
Sun, some 10 times as bulky as Jupiter. This would be a typical
example of a dark star, containing too little mass to set the nuclear
firers burning. It would give out heat, but not light, like a fire before
it glows. So it will not show up in an optical telescope. However, it
may already have been detected by IRAS, the 'infra-red astronomical satellite'. If so, information about it is lurking on the data
tapes awaiting discovery. It will be 10 years or so before all the data
are analysed.

There seems good evidence that something is 'out there' disturbing the comets periodically. As such this is a reminder that even in our own backyard there may be unseen dark objects. There could be a whole plethora of such debris pervading the galaxy and even the entire cosmos, an invisible shadow universe accompanying our own. Such an idea would have been science fiction a few years ago but there are accumulating clues that things may be this way (see Chapter 12). Whether this ghostly matter is responsible for the cometary bombardment is still moot.

When a comet enters the inner regions of the solar system, the gravitational pull of the large planets might destroy it by impact or break-up, might sling it away for ever, or might capture it in a tight path around the Sun.

Some comets are pulled into such tight orbits that they not only cross our path but also graze the Sun. If their orbit is in the same plane as ours they lie in the line of sight of the Sun. This makes it very hard to see them. Only members bright enough to show up in twilit skies are seen. Several examples have been discovered during total eclipses; indeed, enough to make one suspect that there are many more sungrazers yet to be found.

The comet Howard-Koomen-Michels 1979XI was one of these. The cameras on the US Air Force Satellite recorded the comet closing on the Sun at over 150 miles per second. The comet entered just above the plane of the planets, missing us but hitting the Sun. The tail extends further than Venus, over 60 million miles, but on the far side of the Sun and over our heads. After impact the debris scattered over the inner solar system.

So one comet at least has hit the Sun. The Earth is a small target – there's less than 1 in a billion chance that we and a comet will be in the same place at the same moment. But if there are 100 billion comets in the Oort cloud, and if as few as 1 in 100 is disturbed by a passing star, then 1 billion comets have entered the solar system. This makes it almost certain that a comet will hit us some day.

A Halley-sized comet could hit us from the rear or head on. This means that it closes in at anywhere between 10 and 50 miles per second. Taking 30 miles per second as an average one finds that the impact releases as much energy in a second as the Sun brings the entire globe in four months. It is as if all the world's nuclear arsenals were exploded simultaneously in the same place; it corresponds to half a million earthquakes of magnitude 9 on the Richter scale – the largest magnitude ever recorded – all happening at once.

This is enough energy to remove the entire atmosphere of the Earth. This is a dramatic but alarmist way to think of it, since the energy will most probably be dissipated. So we should estimate its effects using other comparisons.

If this energy dissipates as heat throughout the atmosphere it would heat the air up by 190 degrees Celsius. A rise in temperature of the atmosphere would destroy life. High humidity in hot air would condense inside cool bodies as animals breathed it in. Sea animals might fare best if located away from the shock; the oceans overall would warm up by a few degrees only but an enclosed sea like the Mediterranean could boil. The intense heat would vaporise rocks and they would fall back to ground as glassy marbles similar in form to 'tektites' (see Chapter 5). The presence of tektites around the globe may be the smoking gun from catastrophic collisions in prehistory.

A shroud containing billions of tonnes of dust could be thrown in a circle around the Earth, cutting off sunlight. Your bare skin can sense the shadow of a cloud crossing the sun on a summer's day; a dust cloud lasting years could destroy plants and disrupt the food chain. So even though it is alarmist to present it as 'removing the atmosphere', this is hardly more comforting.

This may be what killed the dinosaurs. There has been a lot of detective work trying to identify the culprit. Some scientists now believe that they know the answer.

5

Death of the Dinosaurs

The arrival of mankind and the development of nuclear weapons have created the possibility of self-inflicted Armageddon. It is far more likely that Doomsday will come this way than by a natural catastrophe. With this exception nothing has changed significantly in the natural risk stakes. The chances that we are eliminated tomorrow are pretty much the same as that we were bombarded yesterday. If there is a strong likelihood that we will be struck by a comet or asteroid in the next millions of years, then it is likely that we have been hit in the past.

And we know that we have. The Tunguska event in 1908 and the historic Arizona meteor crater are examples of 'small' impacts. I say 'small' here because a repeat could threaten a city but hardly a country let alone the whole world. What I am more concerned about is the possibility of an entire comet or an asteroid wiping out life as we know it. If that is a real threat in the next 10 million years, say, then major impacts must have happened several times in the past and left their mark in the geological and fossil record.

There are abundant fossil records covering 570 million years, one-quarter of the Earth's existence. During this period there have been five great biological crises when many varieties of organisms disappeared. The most dramatic was the end of the Permian period 250 million years ago, when 96 per cent of all species died out. Towards the end of the Triassic, 215–225 million years past, whole varieties of early amphibians and reptiles disappeared and the dinosaurs first came on the scene in abundance. The most recent of these great extinctions happened 65 million years ago. About one-half of the genera living at that time perished, including marine and flying reptiles, microscopic floating animals and plants, and the most celebrated extinction of all – the death of the dinosaurs. This discontinuity defines the boundary between the Cretaceous and Tertiary epochs.

Within the Tertiary epoch there is sufficient detail in the fossil record that we can recognise subdivisions and it is these that stimulated the first serious suggestions that the Earth suffers bombardment. The death of the dinosaurs is but a recent entrant in the story; it is over 30 years since the initial suggestion that extraterrestrial bombardment has left recent imprints.

Extinctions need have nothing to do with extraterrestrial collisions; alterations in climate, such as occurred in the ice ages, or periods of extreme vulcanism may be sufficient. Indeed the onset of the dinosaurs' dominance is widely thought to be the result of them winning out in a competition with the prevailing species as they adapted better to a changing environment. Rather than a sudden abrupt change, the evidence here points to a relay of competitive replacements of old forms by new ones over a span of 10–25 million years.

Their demise, 65 million years ago, seems rather different however. Very few now believe that mammals competed, stealing the dinosaurs' eggs and thereby eliminating them. Nor did these 100 tonne, 30 metre long beasts become incapable of procreating. Dinosaurs made love delicately and successfully for 150 million years; and participants at the British Association for Advancement of Science annual meeting in 1987 were given a demonstration of how.

Dr Helen Haste bent over a stool and extended her left leg in the air pretending that this was the female dinosaur's giant tail. Beverly Halstead, playing the role of the male dinosaur, then hooked his left leg over hers while keeping his right foot on the floor. The left legs of both were then intertwined. The purpose of the demonstration, apart from being great entertainment and one of the high spots of the entire meeting, was to show how the male dinosaur must keep one leg on the ground to avoid crushing his partner. The juxtaposition was relatively straightforward, and there is no reason to believe that they suddenly became incapable.

Their extinction seems to have been a relatively abrupt chance event and there has been much debate over what caused this.

One of the best publicised is extraterrestrial interference. There are many clues in the geological record that an asteroid or comet the size of Manhattan rammed the Earth, darkening the skies with the dust that it kicked up, blocking out sunlight and killing off plants and animals. This idea, which was originally regarded with some scepticism, leapt to people's attention recently when some physicists concluded that there is evidence that the dinosaurs were killed by the intervention of an extraterrestrial. The attendant publicity has made this explanation something of a 'factoid'. Geologists, palaeontologists, physicists and geochemists now discuss this topic together at conferences. As we shall see, it is still an open question, but as my theme concerns extraterrestrial threats to the planet I shall present their case.

The first clues came from a phenomenon that appears, at first sight, to have nothing at all to do with dinosaurs and extraterrestrials. The story begins with the mystery of the tektites.

The Tektite Mystery

The soil and rocks beneath our feet conceal the history of the Earth. 'The present is the key to the past', wrote the geologist James Hutton in the eighteenth century, and as more and more geologists studied rocks in the field it became clear that the Earth's surface took millions of years to form. Volcanic eruptions, the advance and retreat of the seas as the land rose and fell, the uplifting and eroding of mountains, left layers of rocks that are today far underground but were once at the surface. In mountainous regions, in cliffs and gorges, the ages are revealed. The fossil remains in these rocks tell us about the plant and animal life of past epochs.

The Earth is made of rocks, which are in turn made of minerals – inorganic chemicals (inorganic meaning that it is not like an animal or plant). Familiar examples include gypsum, quartz, topaz and diamonds. Rocks are classified according to their origin. Igneous rocks are the result of molten lava that has cooled. Sedimentary rocks result from sediments, such as sand and pebbles, being compressed into solid bulk such as sandstone, clay and chalk. Metamorphic rocks are rocks that have been changed in some way from their original state, for example being worn down like soil.

Many rocks and minerals have been fashioned into tools, such as stone, flint and iron in early societies, or treasured for their beauty, such as gold and diamond. Among these have been curiosities, such as tektites.

Tektites are dark natural glass marbles (the word 'tektite' comes from the Greek 'tektos' meaning melted). The first examples turned up in Moldavia, Czechoslovakia, in the eighteenth century. They were a deep bottle-green colour and could well have been from a long-forgotten bottle works except that they covered too wide an area. 10,000 pieces, most weighing 10–20 grams, were strewn around.

Since about 1860 several sites have been discovered around the world, with the same lack of explanation. They are named according to their location, thus Moldavites in Bohemia, Darwin glass in Tasmania and Libyan Desert Glass for example. They arrived at widely different times: for example, North American tektites are some 35 million years old; European tektites are 14 million years old; while the Australian and Ivory Coast tektites are more recent, between 700,000 and 1 million years old.

The tektites are all natural glass, weighing as little as 1 gram or as much as 8 kilograms. Most are black, some are green, a few are yellow. They are lustrous with a delicate sheen, and have ridges and furrows which follow a contorted inner structure. They come in many shapes – spheres, dumbbells and discs. Their allure has caused them to be cherished as charms in some parts of the world.

Their chemical make-up is similar to sedimentary rocks, but no known Earthly process can account for the transformation of those sediments into glassy balls. At first people thought that tektites came from volcanic eruptions. However, they turned out to have a different chemical composition than the familiar glassy materials from such eruptions. Moreover, there were no obvious volcanic sites near to the tektite fields. Most of them are small and round, suggesting that they fell through the atmosphere, but no one has ever seen a tektite fall, nor are they found in meteorites.

Suggestions for their origin have included lightning in a dusty atmosphere, the heating of stony meteorites, the collision of a meteorite with a natural Earth satellite (unspecified as to what this was), and the fall of antimatter. The operative word is 'fall'; these ideas fell if ever they were regarded very seriously.

Tektites have always been a major puzzle to people who 'pick up rocks and think'. By 1982 there were two major contenders, both involving extraterrestrials. One was that they are volcanic products from the Moon, the other that they are due to the impact of comets or asteroids hitting the Earth.

The Apollo Moon craft brought back lunar samples. As a result of the analysis of the lunar rocks it seems increasingly unlikely that lunar volcanoes are the explanation of Earthly tektites. Supporters of lunar origin theory are in retreat and the impact theory is gaining ground.

Harold Urey's Theory of Cometary Bombardment

In 1939 L. J. Spencer had suggested that tektites are the result of meteorite falls. As there were no obvious craters associated with them it was supposed that the meteorites broke up before impact.

Years later Harold Urey (best known for his 1934 Nobel Prize for the discovery of deuterium – 'heavy hydrogen') started to think about the problem from a physicist's perspective and decided that tektites don't come from outer space. First, he realised that they could not be due to the break-up of a large mass. Such an occurrence could rain down marbles over a few miles but couldn't explain the presence of tektites all over southern Australia. Nor could they have arrived in a ready-made diffuse swarm; the gravity of the Sun would have broken up the swarm and spread tektites all over the Earth. The meteorite break-up didn't give us enough; this other extreme gives too much.

A dense swarm could avoid the global spreading at the expense of giving much too dense a distribution of tektites on the ground. Tektites are spread diffusely over a large area; they do not cover the globe uniformly nor are they piled up to 100 grams per square centimetre. Urey was foxed. As a 'last resort' he thought that there might have been a collision between the Earth and a minor planet (asteroid) and that some unknown mechanism had covered over the crater, as the tektite sites seemed to imply landfall.

This isn't a very satisfactory explanation. Urey remained puzzled. Then the approach of the comet Arend-Roland set him thinking: what would happen if a comet hit the Earth? Apparently no one had worked out the consequences of this in any detail, so Urey set about the task. Suddenly everything began to fall into place.

Urey made his calculations years before the Giotto mission to Comet Halley showed us what the inside of a comet is really like. Giotto's results imply that Urey could well be right.

The comet's head is a loose structure that is being buffeted by high-speed particles coming from the Sun (the solar wind). The effect is as if the material in the comet's head is slow-burning high-explosive chemicals. Urey calculated how much explosive power there is inside the comet. If its head is 7 miles across, and it is moving at 25 miles per second (typical velocity of impact meteors or any body moving under the influence of the Sun's gravity at Earth orbit), then it contains the energy of 50 million atomic bombs. This energy is released when it hits the atmosphere. At such a speed the impact between the comet and the atmosphere is like hitting a solid barrier. Compression and heating make the comet explode. Most of its mass is disrupted into a high-speed hot gas which continues to Earth, heating the surface to melting point.

It is easy to describe such extremes as 'like so many hydrogen bombs', but this isn't quite accurate. The disruption of a comet begins 40–60 miles up and has some similarities to a high airburst of a nuclear bomb. However, it has rather different effects because of the compressed air and relatively low temperatures distributed through its mass. A nuclear explosion is compact, millions of degrees and emits lethal radiation. Disruption of a comet is much cooler than this, with temperatures similar to the surface of the Sun (still hot in our parlance but trifling on the nuclear scale). The effects are more like a propellant than a detonating type of explosion.

The mass hits the surface and is stopped within a second. The maximum pressure can be 40,000 times greater than atmospheric. A broad area is involved, with the result that no deep penetration results. The qualitative features of the Tunguska event are akin to a feeble version of this.

The surface temperature at the impact is a world where rocks vaporise. The blast ejects this maelstrom up into the atmosphere where it cools into glassy pellets. It is these little marbles that we find on the ground and call tektites. So tektites are like the smoking gun. They come from the Earth's surface: rock that melted and cooled again. The theory explains why tektites have a varying composition – they result from the local rocks. The impact provides a natural high temperature for melting and the markings on many tektites are like those expected from cooling solidifying liquids. The occurrence of tektites over a wide area is also explained.

Not only does this explanation fit with the qualitative features but it also agrees well with the quantities of tektites and the expectations based on our knowledge of comets. This is important. Many pseudo-science 'explanations' fail when one confronts them *quantitatively*; apparently nice ideas sometimes just do not fit the scale of the phenomenon.

If the tektites are really strewn about as the result of an impact, then we can deduce the size of the invader from the extent and amount of tektites it spawned. The North American tektites are found in an area covering millions of square miles. The sums imply that the invader must have weighed at least 50 billion tonnes, its girth being several miles. This is an underestimate because the size of the fallout region could be greater; there could be tektites undiscovered in the oceans for example. This mass is quite reasonable for a comet; Comet Halley, for example, is some 20 times this size.

If the tektites are caused by collisions, then their ages suggest that four major collisions have occurred over some 35 million years. This fits with random chance and is easy to calculate.

Many comets come within the Earth's orbit each year. We have to estimate the chance that one of them, and us, are in the same place at the same time. Comets come from all directions, below or above the plane of our orbit, so the chance of collision is much less

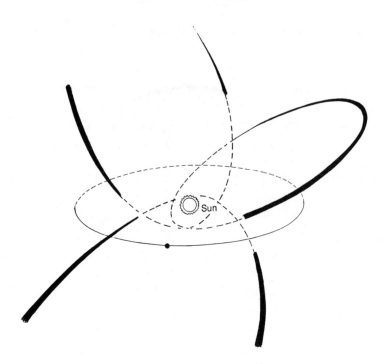

5.1   Earth – crossing trajectories   The Earth is represented by the black dot travelling around the Sun on the near-circular path, radius about 100 million miles. I have shown a sphere of this radius. Any comet or other heavenly body that comes from remote space to approach closer to the Sun than we do must cross this sphere.

than if they and we were travelling on the same flat plate. Instead of thinking of the circle that the Earth orbits around, we should imagine a sphere whose radius is the same as the Earth's orbit. We are interested in comets that come from without and enter the sphere.

At the moment a comet crosses the sphere, the Earth is somewhere on the surface. Imagine it as the little black disc in Figure 5.1. The chance that the comet hits the Earth is in the ratio of the area of the disc to the area of the sphere's surface, namely 1:2,000,000,000. In fact, the chance is twice as big as this because if the comet misses on the way in it still has a chance to hit us on the way back. The earth's gravity reaches out into space and can ensnare comets that might otherwise have missed. This is not a dramatic effect; the Earth isn't like Jupiter for instance, but it does increase the odds by

2 to 5 (depending whose estimates you believe). The result is a chance of 1 in 200–500 million per comet.

Each year about a dozen comets are known to encroach like this. This brings us to the original estimates that a cometary impact occurs on average once in 20–50 million years. However, it is generally agreed that this is an underestimate. It only includes comets that we detect; estimates are that there as many as eight undetected for every one that is. So 1 in 10 million years is being suggested by some scientists.

Anyone who gambles knows that sometimes you have runs of good luck, other times you have to wait a while. The odds against four collisions occurring during the last 35 million years are 1 in 4 – the same as the chance that you will correctly guess the suit of an unseen playing card. If you are successful, you are hardly likely to be accused of cheating – one in four is reasonable odds. So it is plausible that the tektites and cometary collisions go together.

These arguments have assumed that comets irradiate the inner solar system at random. However this may well not be the case since we are journeying around not just the Sun but also the whole galaxy. Conditions change and the chance of tipping comets is bigger at some periods than others.

The events that we have been concerned with are on the scale of global catastrophes. They involve collisions with pristine comets. Comets break up as they journey repeatedly around the Sun – Halley's comet is getting smaller each time as material trails off in its tail. A comet that has broken up has a much greater extent and greater chance of hitting us, but the consequences are correspondingly less severe. The Tunguska event is an example. At the extreme we meet the debris from dead comets every year in the annual meteor showers.

So when we ask 'What is the chance of hitting a comet', we are trading off the size versus the chance. We hit small pieces every year. Whole comets every 10 million years or so. Once in 100 million years we may hit a real monster. Then the consequences could be truly catastrophic. Urey's calculations imply that the dissipation of the impact energy could vaporise the oceans and seriously affect the climatic conditions across the entire globe.

EPOCH		TEKTITE	
Pleistocene			
	1	Australites	0.7 ± 0.1
		Ivory Coast	1.2 ± 0.2
Pliocene			
	13	Moldavites	14.7 ± 0.7
Miocene			
	25	Libyan Desert Glasses	28.6 ± 2
Oligocene			
	36	Bediasites	34.7 ± 2
Eocene			
	58		
Palaeocene			
	63		
Cretaceous			

5.2 Ages of tektites compared with epochs (as of 1973)

Comets and Recent Geological Changes

The origin of tektites fits well with Urey's theory of cometary invasion. But is it correct? The impact of a comet can devastate rocks, so explaining tektites, but will disrupt a lot more besides. Surely the geological record must show evidence for these singular occurrences.

Urey first published his idea in *The Saturday Review of Literature* but later commented that 'no scientist but me, as far as I know, reads that magazine'. As a result he developed the idea in the leading scientific journal *Nature* in March 1973.

Urey proposed that tektites are just one result of cometary collisions. He went further and suggested that these impacts caused the major changes that we now identify as the end of the geological epochs. As far as I know this was the first *quantitatively* evaluated proposal of such dramas. Alvarez's later studies of the Cretaceous–Tertiary boundary and its connection with the demise of the dinosaurs stem in part from this. Indeed, Urey explicitly suggested such a connection with a cometary collision as the source of the dinosaurs' demise, based on the (apparent) success of his confrontation between his theory of tektites and the end of geological epochs. (I say 'apparent' because developments since the appearance of his theory call this part of it into question.)

In the comparison in Figure 5.2 the geological periods with the transition times in millions of years are listed in the left-hand column and the ages of the tektites are listed on the right. These are the data as they appeared in Urey's paper – the tektite dates originate with a 1971 paper by S. Durrani and the geological ages came from the standard 1961 work of J. Laurence Kulp.

There is indeed a tantalising correspondence between tektites and the ending of recent epochs. The Australites and Ivory Coast samples coincide with the most recent change. The Moldavites and Libyan Glasses almost coincide with the Miocene to Pliocene and the Oligocene to Miocene transitions respectively. The Bediasites are right on the end of the Eocene period.

That is how things stood in 1973. However, since then there have been some important revisions in the accepted dates of the geological epochs. The ages of rocks, and tektites, are fairly well agreed upon and have changed only very slightly if at all. However, as knowledge of rocks has improved so has the ability to subdivide them, and the agreed boundaries between epochs have changed in some cases. The boundary between Pleistocene and Pliocene has moved back to 1.6 million years, making the correlation with the Australite and Ivory Coast tektites less impressive. The boundary between Miocene and Pliocene has changed dramatically, moving up from 13 million to only 5½ million. The Moldavite tektites, at 15 million years, bear no correlation at all with the change in epochs. (See Figure 5.3.)

It is still possible to make a case for tektites being the smoking guns of collisions with extraterrestrials. However, it is quite another matter to go further and correlate them with other major geological events. The most celebrated attempt to do so involves the Cretaceous–Tertiary epochs and the death of the dinosaurs.

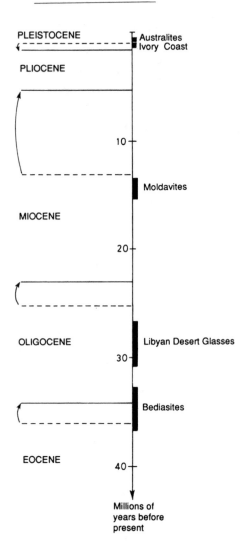

5.3 Comparison of tektites and epochs (as of 1987) Major tektite
fields are shown on the right according to their ages (in millions of years)
including uncertainties in those ages. On the left they are compared with
the transitions between epochs. The dashed lines show transition dates
from Kulp (1961); the solid lines are from Snelling (1987) and the arrows
show the changes. The correlation noted by Urey between Kulp's
transition dates (dashed lines) and the ages of the tektites (in solid black)
has vanished.

Extraterrestrial Footprints

Not all of the atomic elements are equally common on Earth. Carbon, oxygen and nitrogen are the familiar stuff of life; iron is the most stable heavy element in the universe and is the stuff of rust; the rarity of gold and platinum makes them valuable.

Platinum is one of a group of similar rare metals – platinum, iridium, osmium and rhodium. They are as rare as their names are unfamiliar. But they are quite common in average solar system material and meteorites. Indeed there is agreement among geophysicists that the low concentrations of the platinum group in soil and sediments around craters come from meteorites that have passed through the atmosphere. Even where craters have been long destroyed by erosion and vegetation, the concentration of the platinum group metals still reveals where meteorites have landed.

Luiz Alvarez decided to look for these metals in sediments at the boundary between the Cretaceous and Tertiary layers. If the rocks from the end of the Cretaceous era, where the dinosaurs roamed, and the new age (Tertiary) are separated by clays containing these rare metals, then it would bolster the prosecution's case for an impact. They decided to look for iridium as it is easy to detect even in low doses.

Being a nuclear physicist, Alvarez knew how to do this; he irradiated the material with neutrons. When you direct slow neutrons at large amounts of uranium they can release energy catastrophically – the atom bomb. Firing them at iridium, however, is harmless. The energy comes off in the form of gamma rays, a form of light more powerful than X-rays. The gamma rays from iridium are like an autograph, easy to identify.

This is such a sensitive technique that you can detect iridium even when it is present in only the minutest traces. You have to be very careful to ensure that there is no other iridium around that could contaminate the delicate search. As iridium is so rare you might think that this is a needless worry, but this is not so.

In 1981 Alvarez thought that he had evidence for iridium deposits in samples from the Cretaceous–Tertiary boundary in Montana. In fact the iridium didn't come from this at all but was in a wedding ring worn by one of the technicians who prepared samples for analysis. Platinum for jewellery contains about 10 per cent iridium as a hardening agent. If a platinum ring loses one-tenth of its mass in 30 years, which is fairly typical, then the average loss each minute is 100 times greater than the measurement sensitivity of Alvarez's experiment. Tests showed that the same is true for gold rings. It is very easy to contaminate the samples and Alvarez has taken great care about this. There have been disputes as to whether there is an effect or not, but it is now agreed that there almost certainly is. This is how Alvarez found the evidence.

In the Apennine mountains of northern Italy there are exposures of sedimentary rocks representing the period from Early Jurassic to Oligocene, from 185 to 25 million years ago. These contain the end of the Cretaceous and beginning of the Tertiary epochs in the form of pink limestone interleaved with clay. The abrupt change in the nature of life is clearly visible when samples from the boundary layer are put under a microscope. In the Cretaceous layer for instance there are foraminifers that are about 1 millimetre in size. These disappear abruptly across the boundary and are replaced by a different genus, of less than one-tenth of a millimetre.

In well-exposed sections the limestone beds from the two epochs are separated by a band of clay about 1 cm thick. There are no fossils in the clay so you cannot 'watch' the extinction occur. Instead it is a case of 'now you see it, now you don't'.

Alvarez took samples from the boundary layer in the Bottaccione Gorge near Gubbio in Umbria, Northern Italy. The gorge reveals rocks through a span of nearly 400 metres covering the passage of the ages. He chose various samples from the Cretaceous rocks, some from the Tertiary rocks and the crucial samples from the boundary layer. The main question was whether or not the chemicals in the boundary layer were markedly different from those in the other rocks, and in particular whether the tell-tale signs of iridium were there.

He concentrated on 28 elements that showed up clearly in the samples. The relative amounts of 27 of them were very similar throughout the whole range of rocks, representing 155 million years of time. It was the 28th that stood out anomalously: this was iridium. There were only faint traces in the rocks below and above the divide, but as you crossed the boundary the iridium count shot up by a staggering factor of 30. None of the other elements as much as doubled in the boundary layer. There was no doubt – a lot of iridium was deposited at the time of the disaster.

This is as expected if the extinction was caused by extraterrestrial invasion. However, you can't immediately infer that here you have absolute proof. There was the possibility that fate had played a cruel trick and that some anomalous conditions in the vicinity had caused the iridium to deposit in those crucial centimetres of the gorge that happened to coincide with the boundary layer.

Fortunately the Bottaccione Gorge is not the only place where the Cretaceous–Tertiary boundary layer shows through. To test whether the iridium anomaly was just a fluke, Alvarez analysed sediments of a similar age from other sites.

One of the best-known places where the boundary layer shows up in Northern Europe is the sea-cliff of Stevns Klint, some 30 miles south of Copenhagen. Here the Cretaceous layer consists of white chalk and the boundary layer is marked by a 35 cm thick deposit of clay. At the Danish site they were able to study 48 different elements, more than half the number that occur in totality on Earth. As in the Italian sample, the iridium increased dramatically in the boundary layer. Indeed, in the Danish sample the iridium increased more than a hundredfold.

Similar results have been found in New Zealand, where iridium in the boundary layer at Woodside Creek is 20 times as intense as in the remaining rocks. There is no doubt that the effect is real and worldwide.

Some geologists argue that certain volcanic eruptions spew out magma whose elemental abundances are like this. (There is a good and detailed survey of this in the 1987 *Nature* article by C. B. Officer and co-workers.) Part of the debate centres on whether the iridium was laid down over an extended period, as in the volcanic theory, or suddenly, as in an impact.

One of the features of the boundary layers in both the Italian and Danish sites is the existence of a layer of clay about 1 cm thick. Alvarez has suggested that it is made of material that fell out of the stratosphere following the disturbance of the impact. Geologists counter by saying that this is naïve; geology is no less complicated a science than physics – the physicists have their physics right but that doesn't make them experts in geology. It is possible that the clays have quite 'ordinary' origins.

So we are left with two questions, each of which is still being hotly debated: were the dinosaurs killed by this catastrophe; and was the catastrophe caused by an extraterrestrial blast?

If one concentrates on the demise of the dinosaurs to the exclusion of all others then you might happily believe that the broad features of the extinction fit in with the idea that there was extended darkness at noon owing to dust in the atmosphere, whether from impact or eruptions. However, the globe contained much more than dinosaurs at that time and this gives many worries about the details. For example, tropical plants managed to survive though you might have expected that they would suffer from lack of light more than most. One palaeontologist tells me that he has fossil reptiles weighing several tens of kilos that survived the catastrophe. How? Why were the extinctions so selective?

Critics of the impact theory point out that there are hints that the extinctions weren't sudden but were spread over some thousands of years – though at a remote 60 million years a few thousand might simply be due to sampling errors.

However, if there was not an impact, Nature certainly conspired to make it look as if there was one. First, if the iridium in the boundary layer came from an asteroid, then you can estimate its weight. It comes out at 1 billion tonnes or, in a more visualisable form, the lump of rock would have been some 5 miles in diameter. Second, if the clay is the result of the dust thrown up by the impact, you get a similar estimate of the rock's size that caused this mess. Third, other noble metals in the Danish clay, such as gold, nickel and cobalt, appear far in excess of their usual terrestrial abundances, suggesting a rock size as much as 8 miles across. All these figures come out the same; and there is no doubt that if we were hit by a blast like that it would certainly disrupt the environment in a catastrophic manner.

The evidence may be only circumstantial, but after 60 million years it is something to have any evidence at all. I know a respected physicist who believes that the case is established, and a well-known palaeontologist who asserts that the verdict is not guilty. My own verdict is 'not proven'. One thing that we would all agree on is that research into this question should continue; it fascinates and stimulates youngsters to become scientists and may be a sobering reminder of what can happen to us when the Earth's environment is drastically altered, be it from extraterrestrial causes or self-inflicted. The dinosaurs died out after 150 million years, the dominant creatures of their time; we have lorded over the Earth for a mere 1 million years – there is nothing to guarantee that we are here for ever.

human race. Even if we don't inflict darkness on ourselves, Nature could switch out the light.

I remember as a child seeing a spot on the sun one misty day and being astounded at my discovery. All the children in the playground were looking at it and rushed out from their class-rooms at lunchtime to see if it was still there. It was, and in my imagination seemed bigger than before. I was certain that this dark spot was growing and would blot out the Sun. The thought that the Sun might disappear instilled panic of the kind that primitive societies must feel when they see the Sun being eaten up at total eclipse. Like them, I needn't have worried. Sunspots appear regularly, peaking every 11 years or so.

Sunspots have been blamed for many things. There are claims that they affect the weather and even the results of political elections. Changes in the Sun can leave a mark on the Earth – literally. These marks enable us to see how the Sun has behaved over 700 million years.

The Sun is the nearest star to Earth. It is close enough that we can watch it in detail and learn how stars work. Our whole existence depends on it, so the better we understand its workings the better placed we are to contemplate our immediate future. The problem is that our best theories don't fit everything perfectly; there are some disturbing hints that the Sun, or something, is misbehaving. How much do we know?

Measuring the Sun

We know how far away the Sun is. In Chapter 3 we learned how that measurement is made; it involved bouncing radar from Venus to see how far away that planet is and then comparing the time that Venus takes to orbit the Sun as compared to our own year. Put those two pieces of information together and the distance to the Sun comes out to be nearly 100 million miles.

The Sun is about as big as a thumbnail viewed at arm's length. The Sun is 100 billion times further away than that, so we can 'measure' its diameter as 100 billion thumbnails – that is about 900,000 miles, or about 120 times the diameter of the Earth.

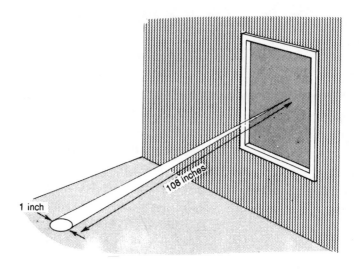

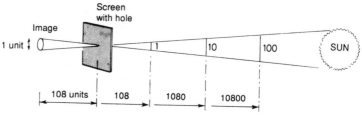

6.1   The size of the Sun   (a) Measuring the size of the Sun through a pinhole in a blind.

(b) The Sun's diameter is 1/108 of its distance from the Earth. This scale of 1 to 108 is seen in its pinhole image whose size is always 1/108 of its distance from the pinhole. Simple geometry shows this is true of the actual Sun relative to its distance from us.

A simple experiment will give you a more accurate measure of the Sun's size (see Figure 6.1). On a sunny day cover a south-facing window with a blind and make a pinhole in it. On the floor you will see an image of the Sun. Measure its size accurately and also measure the distance to the pinhole. You will find that this distance is 108 times greater than the diameter of the image. It doesn't matter how big your room is: in a small room the Sun casts a small image while in a big room the image is correspondingly bigger. If your room was nearly 100 million miles big, the size of the image would be the same as the real size of the Sun. Simple geometry shows that the image and the distance will always scale like this. So

76

the Sun's diameter is 1/108 as big as its distance from us, hence some 900,000 miles (so the thumbnail sketch was pretty good).

So we know how much space it occupies. How much does it weigh?

Apples and hailstones fall to the Earth. The Earth and we on it are falling into the Sun at a rate of about 3 millimetres each second. We are also moving forwards at several miles each second, with the net result that we travel around the Sun in a huge near-circle completed in a year.

When an apple drops from a high branch it will fall 16 feet in the first second, which is 1,500 times as far as we fall into the Sun in a second. This is because the centre of the Earth is only 4,000 miles away from the apple whereas the Sun's gravity has extended over 100 million miles. Gravity declines in proportion to the square of the distance, so the Sun's gravity is enfeebled more than 500 million times relative to that of the Earth. That it is only 1,500 times less in reality is because the Sun is so massive – it is a much more powerful source of gravitational attraction than is the Earth. Indeed, divide the 500 million by 1,500 and you can work out how much more massive the Sun is than the Earth. Doing the sums carefully you find that the Sun's mass is 330,000 times that of the Earth.

The volume of the Sun is about 1 million times that of the Earth and so we deduce at once that its mean density is about one-third of ours, or two to three times that of water. But don't get the impression that the Sun is like this right through. It is a ball of hydrogen gas which is very tenuous on the periphery and conversely very dense indeed at the centre. To maintain such a situation the centre of the Sun must be incredibly hot, over 10 million degrees. We can infer that the temperature of the outer surface is only 6,000 degrees. So already we have deduced quite a bit about the Sun from a range of 100 million miles.

Our current theories give the following picture of the Sun's inside. A quarter of its radius contains an active core in which thermonuclear reactions produce solar energy: protons (the nuclei of hydrogen atoms) fuse together to build up heavier elements and produce ghostly particles called neutrinos as byproducts, which stream out into space (see Chapter 7). Above this core (up to 70 per cent of the Sun's radius) extends a zone where heat radiates upwards. The outer 30 per cent is called the convective zone where the heat is transported by turbulent motion of the gases.

In this heat atoms are unable to hold themselves together and are disrupted into their component parts – negatively charged electrons and positively charged nuclei. The swirling motion of these electrically charged particles creates intense magnetic fields whose structure alternates on a 22-year cycle. It is like north magnetic pole flipped to south and back again, with the result that if you measure only the strength of the field but not its direction you will perceive two 11-year cycles of intensity. The strength of the magnetic fields can vary tenfold during a cycle, being least in years when the Sun appears quiet; in active years the magnetic field breaks through the surface and gives rise to sunspots and solar flares.

Sunspots

There is a deep-seated psychological belief that the Sun is change-less and perfect. The Sun's regular rising and setting have been watched, even worshipped, for millennia. The remnants of that worship are still with us today. Druids visit Stonehenge, almost certainly an ancient computer for measuring the seasons – survival depended upon sowing and reaping at the right time. Even the date of Christmas Day, 25 December, is a reminder of an ancient festival, namely the rebirth of the Sun following midwinter.

The Aztecs worshipped the Sun. Visit the beaches of the Mediterranean or southern California and you will see modern adherents to the cult, lying full length beneath its rays.

The circle of gold in the blue sky symbolised perfection, God's creation – the Church persecuted Galileo when he first reported seeing spots on the Sun. The desire for perfection and constancy may have led us to see such where it is not warranted. Nor is the Sun constant – it wobbles and currently is fading at a rate that could produce a mini ice age in another 50 years. This is not as bizarre as you might think; the Sun's variability has caused climatic changes lasting decades in recent times.

We may complain about the weather but however bad the winters they are nothing like 300 years ago. A mini ice age hit northern Europe. Glaciers that usually end high in the mountains encroached on villages in the alpine valleys. The River Thames froze and there are many paintings from the seventeenth-century Dutch school showing ice skaters on the dykes of Holland. During this period something unusual was taking place on the Sun's surface, noticed by Europeans, Oriental and mid-Eastern astrologers.

A meeting of the US Geophysical Union early in 1986 brought together a number of independent scientific studies which all agreed that the Sun has steadily declined since 1979. Satellites in earth orbit, rockets, balloons and measurements at ground level all showed that the Sun is fading. This appears to be a continuing trend on top of which is a short-period cycle which may be related to the sunspot cycle, but there is no definitive knowledge yet whether these are related or not.

Sunspots come and go, small spots lasting for only a few hours while some large ones as big as the Earth can survive for months. In peak years as many as 200 may occur. In between the activity dies and only half a dozen spots might occur in the minimum of the cycle.

The amount of heat output – the Sun's brilliance – drops in proportion to the amount of the surface that has been masked by the spots. In terms of the *total* radiation arriving at the Earth, this is a small effect and the balance is restored later. However, there is still a lot that we don't know about the dynamics behind this. Is there more X-ray and less infra-red, or more ultra-violet and less radio emission? It is as if a great orchestra dimmed a chord – did all the strings diminish or did the double basses quit while the violins increased a little? We need to know more about this because the different parts of the electromagnetic spectrum affect the chemicals in our upper atmosphere in different ways.

There has been a lot of debate as to whether or not sunspots correlate with our weather. If you want to pursue that debate read the articles cited in the Suggestions for Further Reading. These correlations are often controversial though the prolonged cold snap in northern Europe coincided with the 'Maunder Minimum' between 1640 and 1720 (named after E. W. Maunder, superintendent of the solar department of the Greenwich Observatory). During that period the Sun seemed spotless. Some people claim that no one was looking, but that seems facile; the astronomers of the day were as good as any and the minimum of solar activity seems real.

It may seem fanciful that distant spots can have any effect on us here. However, although the Sun's shining face is very remote, its atmosphere extends far beyond the Earth; we are orbiting *inside* the Sun!

Magnetic fields within the Sun are being twisted in knotty contortions. They suck in the bright surface region and cool it, leaving it relatively dark. These magnetic forces can also lift up electrically charged particles from the Sun in huge prominences or flares which can be spectacularly visible, especially at total eclipse. A good-sized prominence weighs as much as a mountain and yet the Sun's magnetic fields are powerful enough to eject this mass upwards at several hundred miles per second. The Sun's magnetic field is being stretched and suddenly released like elastic, whipping a solar flare up into space, escaping the Sun's gravity.

Any flares that shoot towards the Earth make their presence felt. Beautiful auroras are a particularly noticeable sign. The auroras are caused by pieces of atoms – negatively charged electrons and positive protons – which have been ejected by the Sun and then interact with the Earth's magnetic field. This accelerates them; they collide with atoms in our atmosphere and disrupt them with resulting flashes of light.

To see auroras you need clear weather and must live far from the equator, preferably near to the poles. Auroral displays occur most nights in northern Siberia, Lapland, Greenland and Alaska, none of which was overflowing with natural scientists in the seventeenth century. South of this zone are populous regions such as Sweden, Norway and northern Scotland where auroras occur between one per fortnight to as much as three per week on average. Even in London there is one every other month, or 500 in 70 years. During the Maunder Minimum one might have expected

300–1,000 nights of auroral displays in those parts of Europe where astronomers were living. From 1645 to 1715 only 77 were seen. When Edmund Halley saw one on 15 March 1716, it was the first that he had seen – and he was by then 60 years old and had been an avid skywatcher for decades.

If you make a list of the numbers of auroras seen from year to year you will find another interesting message. There is a turn-on in numbers starting in the sixteenth century, with a pronounced pause during the Maunder Minimum before a surge upwards after 1716. Some sensationalists have claimed that this switch-on of the northern lights shows that the Sun has been changing drastically during the last 400 years. However, there is an alternative explanation. The Renaissance in southern Europe during the sixteenth century gave rise to interest in learning and science in particular. But it took time to reach northern Europe, so the growth in auroral observations could mirror the late arrival of the Renaissance in auroral latitudes.

There is no doubt that the Sun does affect us directly, as the auroras show, and this in turn relates to sunspots. Sunspots wax and wane over 11-year cycles. They leave a mark on Earth, the ephemeral auroras, but also make a more permanent record. And by tracing back this record we can tell how the Sun behaved as much as 700 million years ago!

Carbon 14 and the History of the Sun

We are being bombarded continuously by extraterrestrial radiation – cosmic rays. Nuclei of elements produced in distant stars whirl through the magnetic fields of the galaxy, are trapped by the Earth's magnetic arms and hit the upper atmosphere. But first they get blown by the solar wind.

When the Sun is very active, as in sunspot years, it emits flares and the solar wind is strong. This gale shields us from the cosmic rays. Conversely, when the wind is quiet the cosmic rays arrive in hordes. They hit the atmosphere, converting nitrogen into a special form of carbon, called carbon-14. The nuclei of all carbon atoms contain six positively charged protons. Most have six neutrons as well, making a total of 12 constituents in all and called carbon-12. The unstable form, made by cosmic rays in the atmosphere, has six protons as before but *eight* neutrons – a total of fourteen and hence 'carbon-14'. This floats in the atmosphere, mainly in carbon dioxide.

Plant life and trees absorb this carbon dioxide and the carbon decays at a known rate, ending up as the stable form carbon-12. So if you have a piece of wood of known age, you can chemically measure the carbon-14 present now, and work back to infer how much was laid down originally. Tree rings are an ideal source. Each ring represents a year's growth and so the rings in old trees can provide a record of climate, and of the Sun's activity, over several centuries. The proportion of carbon-14 depends on the known age of the ring and the intensity of the cosmic rays that year. There is a pronounced increase in carbon-14 during the reign of the French King Louis XIV, peaking around 1690 – right in the middle of the Maunder Minimum of the sunspot cycle. It is well known in carbon dating circles as the 'De Vries fluctuation'. John Eddy, an astronomer at the Center for Atmospheric Research in Boulder, Colorado, has noticed that the carbon-14 abundance does indeed seem to be related to solar activity. Again this shows up minima and maxima, suggesting that there is a grand cycle of hundreds of years, though it is hard to detect a cycle of a decade because the carbon dioxide settles from the atmosphere over a number of years and its delayed entry into matter smears out the short-term fluctuations.

We can study the carbon-14 content over very long time-scales, back to about 6000 BC. This shows fluctuations superimposed on a grand wave. The carbon-14 was low in the time of the Pharaohs, increasing to a peak in the first 1,000 years AD. It then fell steadily until the early years of the twentieth century, since when there has been a sudden increase. This does not imply that the Sun is to blame; rather that modern society is burning up fossil fuels rapidly and introducing carbon dioxide into the atmosphere, the carbon-12 and carbon-14 content of which contains various mixes over the ages.

The long-term trend – the up and down on a time-scale of

thousands of years – is due to changes in the Earth's magnetic field. The shorter-term fluctuations are most likely due to changes in solar activity which cause changes in the Earth–Sun system and hence changes in the cosmic ray absorption. So there is indeed an 11-year oscillation, which may or may not affect the weather, and longer-term effects, like the Maunder Minimum, which almost certainly do.

An important question is: What is going on inside the Sun that causes these effects? All the solar physicists agree that the solar activity is caused by magnetic forces within it. There are two main theories that build on this.

One theory supposes that the Sun's present magnetic field is what is left over from the time of its formation. In this case the magnetism will be slowly running down and the solar activity with it. If so, the character of its effects on Earth will be changing over long time-scales: even 1,000 years will be too short to reveal this.

The other major contender supposes that there is a dynamo inside the Sun. 'Dynamo' is the general term for a device where mechanical energy is transformed into energy of the magnetic field. The swirling motions of the charged particles sustain the magnetic field over long periods of time. The solar cycle will survive with little change over billions of years. To test time-scales as long as these requires knowledge of geological epochs and some signal of annual activity. Recently George Williams, an Australian geologist, has found out how the Sun was behaving 700 million years ago in Pre-cambrian times.

Near Adelaide in South Australia are the Flinders Mountain Ranges. In a creek bed, lined with eucalyptus trees, are red siltstone and fine sandstone rocks known as the Elatina formation. They are nothing exceptional to look at, but they are important because they carry a coded message about the weather before any life existed. At the end of the ice ages, the amount of the annual floodwater in ancient lakes was greater or lesser depending on the mean temperature. These floods laid down sediments, called varves, which form layers as distinct as tree rings. The Elatina formation is an example.

R. N. Bracewell of Stanford University in California has made a detailed analysis of the varves, which cover a period of 1,337 years. They show clear evidence of 11- and 22-year rhythms modulated by cycles of 314 and 350 years. These tell us about the heat arrival at Earth, and are only indirectly related to the question of the sunspot cycle, but the 11- and 22-year cycles are suggestive.

Now comes the interesting discovery. Sunspots cycle at 11 years on the average but the variation can be as short as 8 or up to 15 years. The internal clock of the Sun seems to put things back on course every 22 years, so that a short span is followed by a long one. Bracewell has found that the cycles in the varve thicknesses also show this sort of behaviour. And it comes about because of the 350-year modulation and its interplay with the 11-year cycle. In the scientific journal *Nature* in 1986 he also showed that the 314-year cycle provides an envelope which determines the strength of the peak activity in the 11-year cycles.

His theory of the four cycles fits the ups and downs of the sunspots remarkably well. He predicts that there will be a steady rise in solar activity until 1991 and that there will be a peak sunspot number of around 100 that year. If he is shown to be right it will prove that the ancient varves are telling us how the Sun is behaving today.

If the Sun's cycle today is much the same as all those years ago then the 'dynamo' theory must be the right one. I await the outcome of Bracewell's prediction for 1991 sunspots with interest. If all goes according to the theory then we can be assured that the Sun is all right; nothing much is changing – at least on the surface. But there *are* hints that something untoward is going on deep in its interior.

7

Is the Sun Still Shining?

Stargazing has always been fascinating. The Sun is the nearest star to us and as such provides a unique opportunity for us to learn in detail how stars shine. This isn't just an academic point, for we rely on the Sun – if it goes out then so do we.

We know how big the Sun is and that it is made of the same sort of stuff as you and me. Pieces ejected during violent flares have blown into our own atmosphere, so although we have yet to visit the Sun, bits of it have visited us. We know its chemical make-up by the dark lines permeating its spectrum; we can see the conditions on its surface, such as its temperature of 6,000 degrees; we know how much heat arrives here and hence how much the Sun puts out. Here on Earth we are desperately trying to satisfy our energy needs while the Sun, each second, is outpouring into space enough energy to keep us going for 1 million years. It has been doing this for 4½ billion years. What is its secret supply?

A burning coal fire releases the energy stored in molecular bonds: chemical energy. The chemical energy emitted by a gram of almost anything is about the same. When you metabolise food your body liberates energy as heat; a chemical explosion gets it over and done with much faster but the net output is about the same.

In the nineteenth century scientists thought that the stars burned much like a conventional fire, different elements combining to form new compounds, giving off heat in the process. This is what happens in a fire: carbon atoms in the coal or wood and oxygen in the air combine and convert into carbon dioxide (smoke) and carbon monoxide (a poisonous gas). This chemical reaction gives off heat.

Gravity is an efficient way of liberating energy. On Earth waterfalls have turned wheels and ground corn for centuries. Today the tumbling cascades of dammed water can generate hydro-electric power enough to light a city. The strong gravitational pull of the Earth's mass is the key and as things weigh 30 times more on the surface of the Sun than they would on the Earth, so is the Sun's gravity more effective as an energy source. It could generate a lot of heat by collapsing under its own weight. A nice analogy that I once heard is that if you dropped a gallon of gasoline into the Sun it would produce 2,000 times as much energy as you would get by burning the fuel.

Stars form when clouds of gas in space fall together under the influence of their mutual gravity. This produces the initial warmth in protostars – fine early on, but stars wouldn't last long if this was the whole story. To generate its heat this way the Sun would have to be using up its fuel at a phenomenal rate to keep us warm at a range of 100 million miles. It would be shrinking by a few tens of metres each year, the distance that a sprinter covers in a few seconds. This is too gradual for us to detect, but go back in time and the Sun would have been much bigger than it is now: 500 million years ago it would have filled the sky. The geological record shows that that cannot be; photosynthesis seems to have been occurring 700 million years ago much as it is now, implying that the sunshine hasn't changed much on that time-scale. Whatever fuels the Sun it is able to do so without significantly altering the Sun's size or its fuel content over hundreds of millions of years.

This puzzle taxed the nineteenth-century scientists. Some anti-evolutionists argued that the solution was obvious: the 'paradox' proved that the Earth was only a few thousand years old, as in Bishop Usher's literal interpretation of the Bible. (In the seventeenth century Bishop Usher had added up the ages of the patriarchs and dated the Earth's creation as precisely 6 p.m. on 22 October 4004 BC.)

Lord Kelvin, one of the leading scientific figures of the time, had addressed the problem too. He also found another conundrum, which concerned the Earth but, as we shall see, bears on the Sun's fuel source as well.

Kelvin had thought about the warm Earth – 300 degrees above absolute zero, isolated in space which is colder than a deep freeze. During the day it absorbs some heat from the Sun but reflects much of the sunlight back into space. By night it is giving up heat rapidly into the coldness of space. Year after year the Earth must have been losing heat: Kelvin calculated that it would have taken no more than 20–40 million years to have cooled from an initial glowing gas ball to its present ambient temperature. Geologists meanwhile were insisting that rocks on Earth were more than 100 million years old. So how come the Earth was still habitable; that it was not already colder than a Siberian winter?

The first clues that there is more going on in the Universe than the Victorians knew came with the rapid series of discoveries on the nature of the atom around the turn of the century. The discovery of X-rays, with their threat to reveal what you had on underneath your clothing, astonished Victorian society. Then in 1896 Henri Becquerel in Paris discovered radioactivity – spontaneous radiation by salts containing the element uranium. Soon Marie Curie and her husband Pierre had isolated an element, radium, whose spontaneous radioactivity is so great that it feels warm and glows in the dark. Here was the evidence for a source of energy that was totally new, something that is beyond mere chemistry. If one could convert the energy to power with 100 per cent efficiency the energy contained within 1 gram of radium would be sufficient to drive a 50 horsepower ship all the way round the world at 30 miles per hour.

Ernest Rutherford and his collaborators in Cambridge and Manchester in England and McGill University in Canada realised that in radioactivity the atoms are exploding; atoms are changing from one variety to another rather than mixing together as in the case of coal or wood burning.

Atoms consist of lightweight electrons surrounding a more massive and compact centre, the atomic nucleus. The atomic nucleus in turn has an inner structure made from bulky particles called protons and neutrons. Chemical reactions involve the peripheral electrons; radioactivity involves the rearrangement of the protons and neutrons in the nucleus.

Here was the promise of unprecedented utopia: atoms of a useless element might be transmuted into those of a more useful one and vast quantities of energy given out in the process. It hasn't quite turned out that way, but there is no doubt that the energy latent in an atomic nucleus is millions of times more than that given up in chemical processes. In a single gram there are so many atoms that they pour out this energy effectively unabated over the ages. Rutherford realised that this was the key to Kelvin's conundrum: radium and other radioactive elements in the Earth's crust provide an extra source of heat that warms up the globe. This extra warmth slows the cooling, with the result that the planet has taken several hundred million years to fall to its present temperature.

This less rapid cooling meant that the planet could live longer into the future as well as being older now. When Rutherford announced this at the Royal Institution in May 1904 the press heralded it as 'Doomsday Postponed'.

Lord Kelvin, proponent of the original idea, was in the audience, which made Rutherford rather uncomfortable. However, soon after Rutherford began speaking, Kelvin fell asleep. Rutherford was worried about the part of the speech where his ideas conflicted with Kelvin's. At last he came to the crucial bit, at which point Kelvin opened one eye and looked at him.

Inspiration arrived on cue, saving Rutherford. He announced that Lord Kelvin had limited the age of the Earth *provided* that no other source of energy was *discovered*. He then attributed to Kelvin that this had been a prophetic remark in that 'tonight we see that radioactivity is the new energy source'. By report Lord Kelvin smiled.

Electrical forces hold the electrons in their remote orbits; much more powerful forces operate within the nucleus and release huge energies when its constituents – the protons and neutrons – are disturbed. We are all too aware of this in the awesome power released in nuclear weapons; it is nuclear reactions that are the cause of the blast.

The atoms of different elements differ in the number of protons in their nucleus. Hydrogen is the simplest and contains but a single proton. Helium, the next simplest, contains two; carbon and oxygen have six and eight respectively. Iron is the most stable configuration of all and contains 28 while the eruptive uranium nucleus contains 92.

Nuclei with more protons than iron's 28 prefer to break up, or 'fission', and release energy. This is the sort of process that occurs in atomic bombs. At the other extreme of light nuclei, such as hydrogen, two or more may join together, building up the nuclei of heavier elements and again releasing energy. This process is called 'fusion'. It is the principle behind the hydrogen bomb and is the source of the Sun's power. So two paradoxes have been solved by the discovery of nuclear energy: the breaking up of heavy elements helps to keep the Earth warm in the refrigerator of space; the fusing together of light elements provides the heat output of the stars.

Atomic Elements

Atoms consist of negatively charged electrons surrounding a central positively charged nucleus; the electrical attractions of opposite charges is what helps to hold an atom together. The simplest atom consists of a single electron and a nucleus with one unit of positive charge. This is an atom of hydrogen. A nucleus with charge +2 attracts two electrons, forming the helium atom. The number of electrons identifies the element.

The number of electrons in the lightest elements and some common heavy ones are listed below:

1 Hydrogen 2 Helium 3 Lithium 4 Beryllium 5 Boron 6 Carbon 7 Nitrogen 8 Oxygen 9 Fluorine 10 Neon 11 Sodium 12 Magnesium 13 Aluminium 14 Silicon 26 Iron 47 Silver 79 Gold 80 Mercury 82 Lead 92 Uranium

The source of power in these nuclear processes is the conversion of matter into energy. Nuclear power stations split the nuclei

Gamma ray

7.1   Hydrogen conversion to helium in the Sun   Protons (p, denoted ●) collide and change to neutrons (n, O) by the process $(p) + p \rightarrow (p) + n + e^+ + v$, where e^+ is a positron and v a neutrino which are radiated away. In stage I (top left or top right)

$$p + p \rightarrow p + n + e^+ + v$$
$$p + n \rightarrow {}^2H,$$

the proton and neutron having gripped one another tightly to make the nucleus of 'heavy hydrogen' (also called a deuteron), labelled ^{2}H. In stage II (mid-left or mid-right) the deuteron captures a proton and forms a nucleus of helium consisting of two protons and one neutron. Having a total of 3 constituents this is labelled ^{3}He. The process is written

$$p + {}^2H \rightarrow {}^3He + \gamma$$

where γ is energy radiated as light.

Stage III (centre). The two ^{3}He nuclei collide, which brings a total of 4 protons and 2 neutrons together. This combination is unstable and fragments instantly into the stable nucleus of helium ^{4}He ($2p$ and $2n$), the remaining two protons being released to initiate the whole cycle again:

$$^3He + {}^3He \rightarrow {}^4He + p + p.$$

The total chain began with 6 protons and ended up with ^{4}He ($2p$ and $2n$), 2 protons and energy liberated as neutrinos and light. The net change is that 4 hydrogen nuclei (protons) have produced one helium nucleus and radiated energy.

of heavy uranium atoms into lighter nuclei whose combined masses are less than that of the original uranium. The difference in mass appears as energy – the most famous equation in physics,

$E=mc^2$, is at work. If a mass of m grams were totally converted into energy, then an amount E in ergs is produced, where c is the velocity of light (3×10^{10} cm per second). Thus the energy equivalent of 1 gram of anything is 9×10^{20} ergs – some 25 million kilowatt hours. The Sun is producing energy over a million million times faster than this; in each second it loses 5 million tonnes. The Sun could have been radiating energy throughout its life and converted less than 1/5,000 of its total mass into energy.

The process used in atomic power plants cannot operate in the Sun: the Sun consists almost entirely of hydrogen, not of heavy elements such as uranium – 92 per cent of the Sun consists of hydrogen nuclei, 7 per cent is helium and the rest consists of the nuclei of heavier elements, the waste products of the reactor.

The most common occurrence is that after a series of collisions four protons will have fused and produced a single nucleus of the helium atom. This is lighter than the four protons and the spare mass is liberated as energy, ultimately felt as warmth here on Earth.

Protons fuse when they touch, but getting them to do so is like forcing the north poles of two magnets together with a precision of less than a billionth part of a thousandth of a millimetre. To overcome the electrical repulsion the protons must collide at high speed, or equivalently at high temperature. On Earth we can speed protons up in huge accelerators, such as that at the European Centre for Nuclear Research (CERN) in Geneva. The results of such experiments, where protons are fired at one another or at the nuclei of other elements, and other experiments where the energy released in nuclear reactions is measured, are all combined and enable us to deduce the effects of the nuclear reactions that are going on inside stars like the Sun. They imply that, for proton fusion to fuel the Sun, the temperature at its heart must be over 10 million degrees. This thermal agitation throws the protons together; the energy liberated maintains the heat and the conditions for the reactor to continue working.

These are the conclusions from nuclear experiments in laboratories on Earth: 'if the Sun works this way it has to be that hot'. The miracle is that in fact the Sun *is* indeed this hot, and we know this because we know how heavy it is. Its weight causes intense pressure at the centre, some 200 billion times our own atmospheric pressure. The Sun survives collapse because the gas at the centre presses back. Gas under pressure in a fixed volume heats up. From the mass and size of the Sun we can compute the temperature required to prevent collapse. It is 15 million degrees, hot enough to hurl the protons together and fuse them. The various things that we have deduced about the Sun – its mass, the pressure on its inside and the consequent heat, the self-sustaining nuclear fusion under these conditions – all fit neatly together.

So there can be no doubt that this is the source of the Sun's output. Our existence is thus the result of a delicate balance. The fusion happens fast enough that the Sun keeps burning, yet slow enough that it survived long enough for intelligent life to develop on one of its planets.

The conversion of hydrogen into helium is most, but not all, of what cooks inside the Sun. Occasionally three helium nuclei collide and fuse to make a single nucleus of carbon. Now the chance of this would be very small indeed but for the fact that the carbon nucleus happens to vibrate a little with a characteristic or 'resonance' energy. The energy of such a vibrating carbon nucleus is almost identical to the energy that three helium nuclei have and this turns out to make it much easier for the helium nuclei to form the carbon. Were this not so, we would not be here. Indeed, the universe would have very little of anything heavier than helium!

Once formed, the bulky carbon is an easy target for the ubiquitous protons. It absorbs one and turns into nitrogen. Two more hits by protons and a dash of radioactivity produces oxygen, gamma rays and 'hot' ghostly particles called neutrinos which pour out from the Sun into space and can be detected here on Earth. One more hit by a proton and the oxygen splits up into a single nucleus of helium and one of carbon. So we have gone through a cycle: carbon back to carbon with energy radiated in the process. This carbon is like an egg awaiting fertilisation by one of the many protons still in the Sun's centre, ready to go through the cycle again.

The result of all this is that carbon is a catalyst, eating up protons from the Sun's core, changing their spots several times before ending up as carbon and helium and liberating energy. Protons are being used up at the rate of 5 million tonnes every second, each day, year and century through the ages. Slowly the Sun is being changed from a hydrogen bomb into a helium ball. In the meantime, for another 5 billion years or so, there is enough to keep us warm. Unless . . .

Suppose the thermonuclear processes in the heart of the Sun have run down. It could be a long time before news of the changed circumstances in the Sun's core reach Earth's surface. Thus we could be somewhere in this period, waiting for the surface light to be turned off. But the fusions in the Sun's heart have a byproduct – the neutrinos – and their number is like a thermometer: detect them on Earth and you can measure the Sun's internal temperature. A low neutrino flux could be our advance warning of a real energy crisis.

And here we meet the problem: too few neutrinos are arriving compared to the numbers expected if the Sun is behaving as we believe it should. What is wrong? Several people are trying to find out and there is no certain explanation yet but there are several possibilities. Some of these have their own bizarre consequences not just for the Sun but for the future of the entire universe.

First I will describe what these neutrinos are and how we detect their arrival on Earth. Then I will review the ideas that are the current favourites for explaining their shortfall.

The Neutrino Mystery

The neutrino is one of the most pervasive forms of matter in the universe, and also one of the most elusive. Its mass is less than a millionth that of a proton. Indeed, it may weigh nothing at all – no one has yet been able to measure such a trifling amount. It is electrically neutral and can travel through the Earth as easily as a bullet through a bank of fog. As you read this sentence billions of neutrinos are hurtling through your eyeballs as fast as light but unseen. Theorists estimate that there are 100–1,000 neutrinos in every cubic centimetre of space.

An intense but unfelt 'wind' of neutrinos emanating from the nuclear processes in the Sun plays continuously on the Earth. In addition there are lesser breezes of neutrinos from collapsing stars and other catastrophic processes in our galaxy. The Sun is shining in neutrinos with nearly as much power as it shines in visible light and its neutrinos swamp those from other stars as the daytime Sun blinds the other stars.

If our eyes saw neutrinos we would be able to see in the dark. Indeed, there would be perpetual daytime, for the Earth is transparent to the solar neutrinos; there is no neutrino shadow. Neutrinos shine down on our heads by day and up through our beds at night undimmed!

Even the Sun is transparent to these weird particles. Whereas the light produced in the nuclear reactions at the Sun's heart takes 1 million years to fight its way to the surface, the neutrinos stream out in under 2 seconds. When we see the Sun we are seeing the end-product of processes that took place in its centre when *Homo sapiens* first walked the Earth. If we could see neutrinos we could look into the heart of the Sun and see it as it is NOW.

The catch is that you must capture the neutrinos. The difficulty is obvious: if they can escape through the whole maelstrom of the Sun, why should they give themselves up for our convenience? The trick is that, although any one neutrino is extremely unlikely to interact, given a lot of them and enough material waiting for them, occasionally one will be caught. The scale of the problem is illustrated by the fact that a full half-century passed after the Austrian physicist Wolfgang Pauli predicted that neutrinos exist, before anyone captured them and proved the idea to be correct.

Two physicists working at the Los Alamos laboratory in New Mexico in the 1950s were inspired by the idea of 'doing the hardest physics experiment possible'. Clyde Cowan and Fred Reines argued that if neutrinos really existed there ought to be some way of proving it. Neutrinos must do *something*, however rarely, if they have any physical reality. They decided that brute force should do the job: put lots of target in the way of an intense stream of neutrinos.

At first they thought that atomic explosions could provide a suitably intense supply of neutrinos. This is probably true, if rather risky to do as an experiment. Eventually they realised that a nuclear reactor produces neutrinos sufficiently intensely and under controlled conditions. The neutrinos coming from a reactor should occasionally hit atomic nuclei in the target and reveal themselves by changing their spots and changing into more easily detected forms of matter, such as electrons.

Their enormous detection apparatus consisted of 1,000 pounds of water directly in the stream of the neutrinos from the US Atomic Energy Commission's reactor at Savannah River. They named it Project Poltergeist because of their quarry's apparent undetectability. They estimated that the flow of neutrinos from the reactor is about 30 times that expected from the Sun. They succeeded in detecting one or two collisions of neutrinos with the hydrogen nuclei in the water every hour. This was a very feeble signal, but enough to show that the neutrino really exists.

The science of neutrino astronomy arrived in 1964 when Raymond Davis's team from the Brookhaven National Laboratory in New York built a huge detector deep underground. They had to do this in order to hide from all the other debris that continuously hits the upper atmosphere – the ubiquitous cosmic rays. These are mostly atomic nuclei, produced in violent processes deep in space and captured by the Earth's magnetic field. The atmosphere shields us from these as effectively as from other larger invaders – no more than a gentle drizzle of atomic particles reaches ground level, and very few get through a few *metres* of earth. Go down a deep mine and neutrinos are the only survivors.

So not only are neutrinos hard to capture but you have to go to extreme lengths – or rather depths – to eliminate the competition.

Davis's team went down a full mile in the Homestake Mine at romantically named Deadwood Gulch, South Dakota. The mine was too small for the gargantuan device they had in mind. They first had to remove 7,000 tonnes of rock, then the tank had to be built on the surface and lowered bit by bit to the mine. Once they had it all assembled deep underground they filled it with over 100 tonnes of perchlorethylene – dry cleaning fluid!

They chose this common liquid as it contains a lot of chlorine atoms. When a neutrino from the Sun penetrates into the chamber and hits a chlorine atom it has a good chance of changing the chlorine into argon. Periodically Davis flushed the argon from the tank and measured how much there was. Knowing how much argon is being formed tells you how many neutrinos have hit.

They started the experiment in 1970 and have repeated it some 60 times. They are seeing the Sun shining in neutrinos, but it is dimmer than expected. On the average only one-third as many neutrinos arrive in their detector as ought to if our understanding of the Sun is correct. In addition there are small fluctuations in the neutrino flux, which some people claim follow the pattern of the sunspot cycle.

In a talk about the neutrino experiment at an American Institute of Physics conference in 1984, Ray Davis's group described how the neutrino flux varied year by year from 1970 onwards. Each year they have a datum that is uncertain by some amount owing to the many complexities of the experiment and trying to draw conclusions from a small sample of neutrino hits. If you ignore these uncertainties, there appears to be an up and down that correlates with the sunspot cycle; if you take the uncertainties into account, however, the correlation is much less impressive.

J. Bahcall of Princeton, one of the leading theoreticians, has made a detailed study with G. Field and W. Press of Harvard to see if there is a real correlation or not. He finds that the data are 'suggestive but not statistically significant'. The suggestive correlation stems almost entirely from a low neutrino flux near the start of 1980 during a sunspot maximum. The correlation may be insignificant but interest has been aroused and so we await the next sunspot maximum to see if the neutrino flux drops again.

Something untoward is happening and we don't yet know what it is. New experiments are under way trying to solve the puzzle. To appreciate what new insights they will offer we need to review what burns inside the Sun according to present wisdom.

Inside the Sun

The simplest stable particles, the electrons and protons, were formed in the heat of the Big Bang. Radioactivity can transmute protons and their electrically uncharged counterparts, neutrons, back and forth one into the other and help build up the nuclei of heavy elements. Great heat is required to bring the various ingredients together and cook them like this. Gravity provides the fuel in that it tugs the ubiquitous protons (nuclei of hydrogen) together, heating them up into conglomerates that we call stars. It is by means of the stars that Nature can cook the elements that are necessary for the complexities of life.

I described on p. 92 how the Sun does this. Let's look at this again but concentrate this time on the 'waste' products – the radiant energy.

The path to you and me began with the meeting of two protons in the centre of the Sun billions of years ago. They fused, one of them turning into a neutron, and in combination they formed a stable system, a nucleus of 'heavy hydrogen'. A single proton and a single neutron can bind tightly and survive; their combined masses are less than those of the two protons and the spare energy is radiated, in part by neutrinos. These neutrinos can carry off anything up to 420,000 electronvolts of energy (a 1 volt battery could give a single electron an energy of 1 electron-volt, or ev for short). This is the most important neutrino producer in the Sun – over 99 per cent of solar neutrinos are produced this way.

Another possibility in the hot dense conditions of the Sun's centre is that three particles meet. Two protons and an electron can fuse to make the same nucleus of heavy hydrogen as before but this time releasing more energy – 1.4 MILLION eV – again carried away by a neutrino. These nuclei of heavy hydrogen soon are hit by further protons, building up nuclei of the next simplest element, helium. Again, energy is liberated as the protons cluster into ever more stable configurations, but in the building of helium the energy comes out as gamma rays, a high-energy form of light. Collisions among the helium nuclei produce small quantities of the next lightest elements: lithium, beryllium and boron. In this latter stage a few neutrinos are produced with energies as high as 14 million eV (14 MeV for short), but this is 10,000 times as rare as the lower-energy neutrinos produced in the initiating reactions above.

The basic concentrate of reactions in the Sun is producing neutrinos whose individual energies are low but in such vast quantities that they are the main energy carriers in total. The experiment on Earth which has a detector of cleaning fluid sees *none* of these; it is able to capture only neutrinos whose energies are *more* than 1 million eV, and the vast majority of the solar neutrinos have energies that are far below this threshold – recall that over 99 per cent of the neutrinos have energies less than 420,000 eV.

The neutrinos that we are detecting at present are produced by a relatively insignificant process where the elements boron and beryllium are being transmuted in the Sun. The important neutrinos from the proton thermonuclear fusion are out of the reach of present detectors. It is as if the detector's ear is sensitive to notes in the treble clef whereas the Sun is sounding primarily in the double bass. To 'hear' these, the largest part of the orchestra, new types of detector must be built.

You can detect these low-energy neutrinos if you use a target consisting of the element gallium instead of chlorine (cleaning fluid). Gallium responds to impacts from neutrinos having as little as a quarter of the minimum energy needed to affect the cleaning fluid. This will enable us to 'listen' to the Sun's main theme tune. The problem is that to do so we need many tonnes of gallium, which is larger than the annual world production. However, even a modest effort here would be better than nothing and two groups are developing such an experiment. One is in the USSR and the other is an international collaboration that will hide underground in the Gran Sasso tunnel beneath the Alps.

A group from Oxford and a European collaboration are each attempting to develop detectors comprising the rare element indium, which will be sensitive to neutrinos as low as 150,000 eV – a 50 per cent improvement even on the gallium detector – and which, if it works, will pick up the neutrinos from the Sun's most important thermonuclear reaction.

So it is possible that experiments so far, which captured fewer neutrinos than had been expected, are merely picking up the whisper of the Sun's higher register, which is a bit quieter than we expected, while the deep bass is playing fortissimo but unheard as yet.

In a few years when the new experiments begin we may know if this is the answer to the puzzle. Many astrophysicists doubt that the solution is that easy; they believe that we will find a shortfall in those neutrinos too. If they are right, then there is a genuine problem. So we must look at two suspects. Is it the Sun's centre that is cool, or does something happen to the neutrinos en route?

Suspect Number 1: A Cooler Sun

The reaction of some theorists who believe strongly that they understand the workings of the Sun is to declare that the experiment must be wrong. Experiments like these are complicated and sophisticated. Dry cleaning fluid sounds like a kitchen sink enterprise, but don't be fooled, this readily available commodity is surrounded by highly detailed technology. Somewhere in the chain of electronics and computer logistics something might be going wrong, misleading us into thinking that fewer neutrinos arrive than in fact do.

The experimentalists respond that they have checked their apparatus in detail. They have performed a series of tests of the large-scale chemistry, verifying their efficiency at extracting the crucial argon from the chlorine target. Anomalous results when the neutrinos come from the Sun do seem to imply that something is happening in the Sun, or to the neutrinos en route, and not that there is a fault in the apparatus.

So perhaps the standard model of the Sun is wrong.

The neutrinos picked up in the Dakota mine are the end-product of a series of fusion reactions that are driven by heat. It is this heat that throws the protons together; the hotter or colder the Sun is, so the faster or slower the fusion occurs. The rate of neutrino production depends very sensitively on the temperature, varying in proportion to the temperature multiplied by itself 10 times. This makes me nervous: if the temperature is only 10 per cent less than your theory expects (and that doesn't seem un-reasonable) the neutrino flux will be cut back by more than a factor of two. Even so, some theorists say that they are confident in their temperature predictions to this level of precision and that this 'easy' way out is not the right one.

However, these calculations implicitly assume that the heart of the Sun consists of protons and neutrons – constituents of the forms of matter familiar to us – and that there are no hitherto unknown particles in there. Which brings us to the modern theories of matter, which some theorists believe could radically alter our picture of the solar furnace.

These new theories suggest that there may be very massive stable particles around, produced at the Big Bang and very rare today. They interact with matter very weakly and are known as WIMPS – Weakly Interacting Massive Particles. Experiments are in progress around the world looking for such things, but there is no direct evidence for them yet. One idea is that, being massive, any on the Earth will sink into the centre under the influence of gravity. In turn, any in the solar system will tend to gravitate into the Sun, and accumulate in its heart.

The standard theory of the Sun implies that its temperature rises rapidly as you near the centre. WIMPS can smooth out this temperature rise, effectively cooling the Sun's heat. To do this the WIMPS have to be between 5 and 20 times as massive as the ubiquitous protons that are the fuel. Lighter than this and they evaporate out from the centre; heavier and they sink there for good. But in the middle mass range they sink in, circulate and carry heat away from the centre as they depart, returning inwards again in perpetual orbit. With this lower central temperature, the fuel cycle is slowed down and the flux of neutrinos reduces in line with observation.

Or at least the neutrinos that the cleaning fluid detects will be reduced. Although the WIMPS are sluggish they could bump into one another occasionally and mutually destroy themselves. A byproduct of this cataclysm will be neutrinos whose individual energies are thousands of times greater than those from proton fusion – the main fuel supply. If the energies of the neutrinos in

100

solar fusion are compared to the sounding of the double bass, then WIMPS give neutrinos a high pitch like a dog whistle. Taking this analogy further: present solar neutrino experiments are sensitive only to a limited range in the treble clef. A search for such a high-pitched (or high-energy) signal is now underway but it will be some time before the results are known.

Suspect Number 2: Neutrinos Are Fooling Us

The smart money lays the blame for the solar neutrino problem on the neutrinos themselves. If neutrinos are massive they can change their character en route from the Sun in such a way that one only detects about one-third of those that set out. Then everyone could be happy: the flux of neutrinos setting out from the Sun would be exactly as theorists predict; the Sun would be shining to order – and the universe will eventually collapse under the weight of these neutrinos!

First things first!

Three varieties of neutrino are known. The processes in the Sun produce one of these (known as the 'electron-neutrino'). If this variety of neutrino is massless it will stream across space to the waiting detector in pristine condition. The flux recorded in Dakota will be a direct measure of that put out by the Sun. However, if the neutrino has a mass, it can change into one of the other two varieties en route. As the detector only records the arrival of the electron-neutrino variety, it will record fewer than set out.

But do neutrinos have masses or not? There is no known principle that says that they must be massless. There is even an experiment performed in Moscow that claims to have measured a small mass, but as this has not yet been independently reproduced current scientific opinion is that the question is still open.

Everyone agrees that if neutrinos have masses, they are very small. The best experiments in laboratories on Earth imply that the electron-neutrino can weigh in at no more than one-thirtieth of a millionth the mass of a proton. People are looking at the flux of neutrinos coming from reactors and accelerators on Earth to see if the flux dies off with distance as the electron-neutrinos change their form. Some groups claim an effect; others dispute this. This is an active area of research at present. The whole nature of neutrinos is one of the great mysteries of matter that the particle physicists are trying to unravel. The problem of the Sun highlighted the conundrum.

It is possible that the neutrinos are changing their identities in flight across space, but recently several theorists have looked back nearer to the start of the neutrinos' journey. Produced in the solar core, the neutrinos have first to shoot through half a million miles of solar material. Could it be that the solar environment is affecting them before they emerge into the light of day?

In 1986 Hans Bethe, famed for unravelling the cycle that produces heavy elements in the stars, extended and popularised an idea of the Soviet physicists Mikhaev and Smirnov. They had pointed out that the propagation of neutrinos through matter, as in the Sun, could have remarkable effects and explain the solar neutrino problem.

As light can become distorted as it propagates through materials with differing refractive indices, so can a beam of massive neutrinos perform funny tricks when it passes through matter of varying density. The Sun is a perfect example of such an environment. The Sun puts all its energy into one type of neutrino (the electron-neutrino) but a resonance phenomenon as this variety of neutrino passes through the Sun's gases can cause the energy suddenly to drain into another variety. To describe how this works would be of little help, but there is a simple analogue that you can build and is a fun party trick.

With a long piece of string and two weights make two swings suspended from a bar. Tether one end of the string and attach the other end to a handle so that you can vary the length of one swing. Start off with the swings having different length and set ONE swinging.

All the energy is in one swing; this is like the neutrino put out by the Sun – all the energy is in this one.

Now change the length of the swing *very gradually* so that the lengths of the two swings get more and more similar. You will find that as the lengths coincide, suddenly one swing will cease and the other will take up the motion. Without touching them, all the energy will have gone across from the initial swing into the other one. The changing length of the swings is the analogue of changing density in the Sun. At a critical condition (in the case of swings it is the equal lengths) one neutrino gives up the ghost and the other takes over.

If this is the explanation of the solar neutrino problem it works because the Sun has a certain density profile AND because the neutrinos are emitted in a certain critical energy range. Consequently the experiments now beginning, which will be sensitive to the lower-energy neutrinos, will see very different effects from those done so far. The science of neutrino astronomy is now beginning in earnest and promises to be fascinating. I suspect that our understanding of stars will prove to be still primitive.

A Link with Sunspots?

Finally, there is the tantalising suggestion that the rate of neutrino detection by Ray Davis's experiment varies with the sunspot cycle.

The Sun responds only slowly to changes, so the neutrino production at the core should be constant for periods in the range 10,000 to 1 million years. It would be a surprise, then, if variations in neutrino flux on a period of the sunspot cycle – a mere handful of years – were due to changes in the core. However, as Lev Okun and a group of Soviet theoreticians have pointed out, if neutrinos interact with magnetic fields then a correlation with the solar cycle should happen.

Neutrinos spin as they fly. The earthbound detector can only detect neutrinos spinning in one particular direction – which is fine if they're not magnetic but disastrous if they are. If they are magnetic, the magnetic field in space will perturb them in flight and change their orientation, with the result that not all will be detected on Earth. The flux will appear to have dimmed. Moreover, the neutrino flux would also be affected by the Sun's magnetic cycle. The sunspots are the outward sign of magnetic activity in the Sun, which varies over an 11-year cycle. If the neutrino is magnetic, then the flux of neutrinos arriving at Earth should vary in phase with the sunspot cycle.

The Sun is spinning, so it has a north and south hemisphere as we do on Earth, and the direction of its magnetic field is opposite in the two – like the north and south poles of a magnet. The Sun's equator is tilted relative to our orbit, so in one half of the year we look more at the Sun's south pole and six months later we're peering in from the north.

If neutrinos are affected by magnetic fields, those streaming out of the northern hemisphere will have been affected differently from those emerging from the southern hemisphere. There is a slit in the Sun's magnetic field along its equator (which is why no spots are seen in this region) and so neutrinos coming out in equatorial regions won't be affected at all by magnetic forces.

The Earth's orbit crosses the solar equator in June and December, so neutrinos that hit us in mid-summer and winter aren't affected by magnetism. However, in spring and autumn of years when the Sun is active the neutrino flux should be affected if these ideas are right. So there may be a six-month variation in the neutrino flux as well as a larger-scale 11–22-year cycle.

There may be signs of this in the data but it is not significant statistically. (If a coin lands heads four times in a row that is chance; 40 times and someone must have loaded the coin – the solar data so far are like the former.) Whether the effect is there or not all hangs on 1980 when solar activity peaked and the solar flux dipped. Ignore that one year and there is no effect visible over several years. But the question has been raised: will it happen again when solar activity peaks (as we expect) in the early 1990s? If it does it will teach us about the neutrinos – they feel magnetism – and the variation will be real. However, this is up and down on top of an overall depletion. The cause of the average depletion may still remain an open question.

In the next few years studies of solar neutrinos promise to teach us a lot about neutrinos, about the Sun and maybe even about the fate of the universe. If any of these explanations is the reason for the anomalies then it is likely that neutrinos have a mass. If Bethe,

Mikhaev and Smirnov are right, then neutrinos are affected inside the Sun not outside, and it is unlikely that we will be able to measure their mass on Earth. But we will be able to test the idea when the new detectors of the low-energy neutrinos, those produced in the core, come into operation. According to Bethe these neutrinos will be affected very differently from the ones we've seen so far. In a few years we may know if this is the answer. If so, the neutrino mass is very small and will have only a marginal effect on the gravity of the Universe.

However, if the neutrino's behaviour in flight is the reason, then neutrino masses could be large enough that they will significantly control the future evolution of the universe. There are so many of them around that they could provide more mass than all of the stars that we have ever seen through the most powerful telescopes. The gravity of these neutrinos could make the universe collapse in a big crunch.

If this is the future, the collapse is still many billions of years away but it would be an incredible achievement of the human intellect if a careful study of our Sun and the solar neutrino problem led us to foretell the eventual fate of the entire Universe.

Arizona meteor crater with San Francisco Mountains in the distance.
Photos © Meteor Crater Enterprises
Close up of the crater with tourists setting the scale.

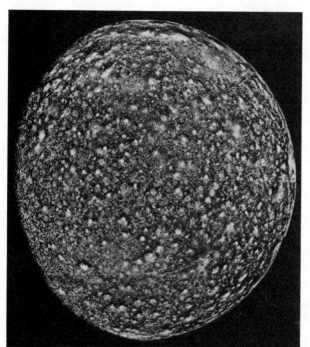

Craters on Callisto
Meteorite impacts have cratered the entire surface of Callisto, one of Jupiter's satellites. A close up view of the region at top right (*shown below*) reveals a huge impact basin over 350 miles diameter. The concentric rings are the result of the icy crest responding to shock waves produced by the large impact. They extend over 600 miles.
Photos © NASA/Science Photo Library

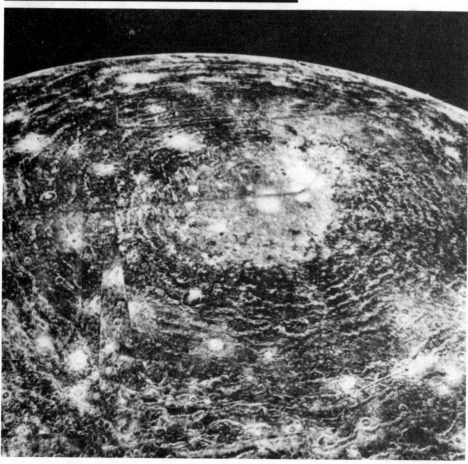

Epimetheus (*top*).   Saturn's eleventh
satellite is shaped like a tooth 80 miles by 40
miles, and is probably the fragment of a
violent collision. Similarly Saturn's satellite
Hyperion (*bottom*) whose shape has been
compared to a peanut 200 × 100 miles across.

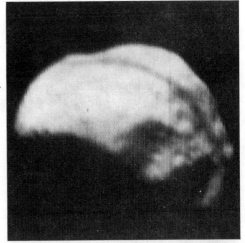

Mimas (*centre*).   The Herschel crater on
Mimas, one of Saturn's satellites, is 80 miles
diameter, 7 miles deep with a central peak
that is 4 miles high; it was probably caused by
impact with a body about 8 miles wide. It fills
about 1/3 of Mimas' size. An impact with a
body only slightly larger would have
smashed Mimas into several pieces.

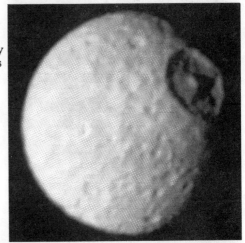

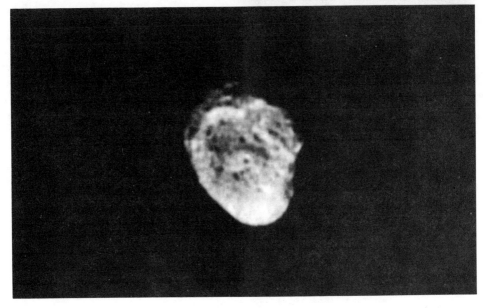

(*Above*) **A southern hemisphere view into the heart of the galaxy.** The trail is due to a meteorite which may have landed in the Australian bush.
© *Fitzharries Astronomical Society*

(*Left*) **Comet West**, photographed in 1976, the year of its discovery. This bright comet will not return for thousands of years.
© *Betty Milor/Science Photo Library*

(*Top of opposite page*). **Our Galaxy In Space.** This shows how we would appear to observers in remote galaxies. The Milky Way is half way up on the extreme right. The faint galaxies near to us are our satellites, The Large and Small Magellanic Clouds. Below us are two major galaxies, Andromeda and M33. This cluster of galaxies forms the "Local Group" which in turn form part of the Local Supercluster of galaxies centred on the Virgo Cluster (extreme left).

Milky Way in Space (*see caption opposite*) © *David Parker/Science Photo Library*

Cannibal galaxies; NGC 7752/3. Gravity is pulling stars from the small galaxy into its large neighbour. © *Royal Greenwich Observatory/Science Photo Library*

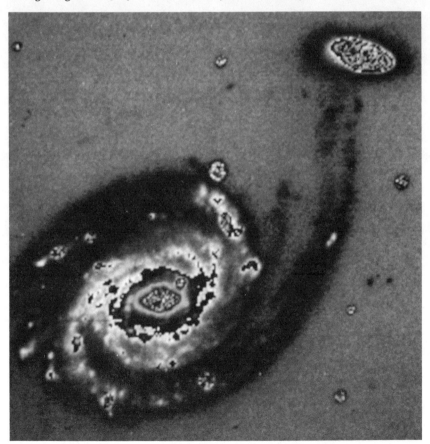

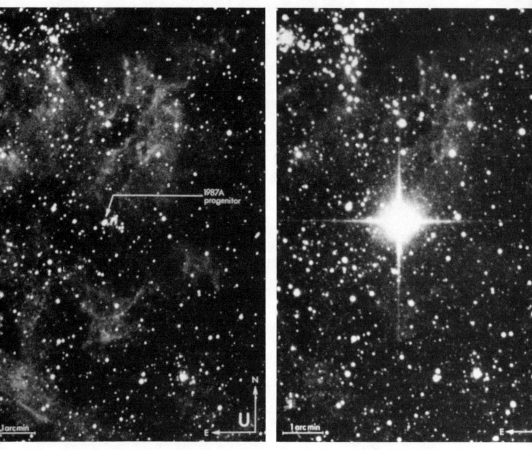

Supernova in the Large Magellanic Cloud   The Large Magellanic Cloud became famous in 1987 as the home of the first naked eye supernova for four centuries. These two images show the supernova and the surrounding stars photographed with the ESO Schmidt telescope on Feb 26, 1987 (The cross is an optical effect in the telescope). The surrounding stars can be identified in the left hand picture which shows the scene before the central star exploded; the picture on the right shows the same star field after the supernova explosion.
Photos © European Southern Observatory

(*Opposite page; top*) **The Crab Nebula** is the ejected remains of the supernova of AD 1054. They are moving away from the centre at 1000 miles per second, so fast that the shape changes in a human lifetime. A pulsar, neutron star, has been detected at the centre of the Crab Nebula.

(*Opposite page, bottom*) **The Ring Nebula in Lyra**, M57, is a shell of gas thrown off by the explosion of a dying star 5500 years ago. The ring is expanding at 12 miles per second and comes from the star at its centre which is probably a white dwarf.

Crab Nebula (*see caption opposite*)
© *Hale Observatories/Science Photo Library*

Ring Nebula in Lyra (*see caption opposite*)
© *Lick Observatory/Science Photo Library*

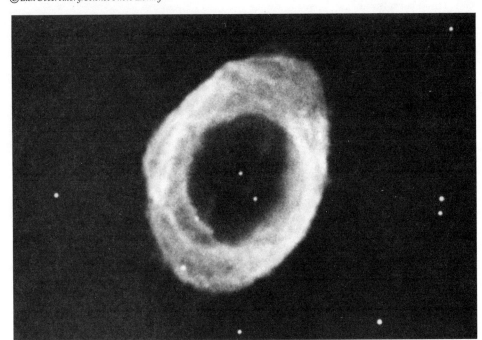

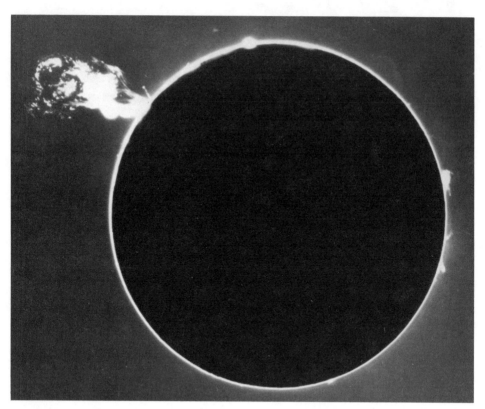

A massive solar flare photographed in 1974 by Robert Fisher of the Halekala Observatory on Maui, Hawaii

Giant solar prominence
Photos © High Altitude Observatory of National Center for Atmospheric Research, Colorado/SPL

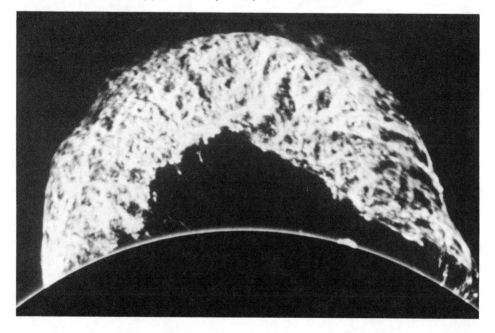

Part III

A Galaxy
of Stars

8

A Journey around the Milky Way

The Scale of Things

Two policemen were driving across the desert in California one night 30 years ago when they saw a flying saucer. Or at least, that is what they reported.

Hovering over the road, directly in front of them, was a bright light. In their report of the event they described it as 'blinding'. At first they thought that it was the landing light of a plane from a nearby airforce base, but it hovered, absolutely still, and then suddenly shot away into the distance at 'incredible speed'. As UFOs were then the rage, they decided that the light must be from another world.

They were right! The light indeed came from another world – the planet Venus. On some nights if the conditions are clear and Venus is low in the sky it can appear as bright as a car headlight. Once you mistakenly interpret the light as being nearby, the dimming by a passing wisp of cloud gives the impression of sudden departure. Many reports of UFOs turn out to be sightings of Venus.

Not only Venus but Mars and Jupiter also can shine brighter than any star. Yet none of the three, nor indeed any of the planets, shines of their own accord. Unlike the stars which emit their own light, much like the Sun, the planets are mirrors. We see sunlight reflecting from their atmospheres or surfaces.

These planets reflect only a minute portion of our Sun's light. Yet they outshine other stars completely. Ponder this fact for a few moments and you will begin to get a feeling for how remote those twinkling stars really must be. The distances involved are so vast that it isn't helpful to express them in miles. Do you have a feeling for the difference between a billion billion billion billion and a million billion billion billion billion? They are both huge, beyond comprehension. So astronomers use another measure – the time that light takes to get from 'there' to 'here'. Even these can be confusing unless you relate them to more familiar time-spans.

Light is the fastest mover in the universe. It travels 300 metres in only one-millionth of a second. Human reaction times are a few thousandths of a second. On the freeway your car will have travelled a few metres before you react to an emergency. Light will travel 1,000 miles in this time. People in the north of England receive their radio time-signal from London delayed by one-thousandth of a second. The message in a long-distance telephone call between Glasgow and London takes a similar time. We don't notice such brief delays; they are 'instantaneous' for us. When you make a transatlantic call the signal may be routed up to a satellite far above the Earth, and back down again to the other party. The delay of up to ½ second can be quite disconcerting. You are beginning to be affected by the finite speed of light and radio signals.

We see the Moon as it was 1.5 seconds ago – the time of two heartbeats. The Sun is more remote. You can cycle 1 mile in less time than it takes sunlight to reach us. The Sun is '8 light minutes' distant.

Now that we are sending space probes to the outer reaches of the solar system, we are beginning to feel the 'light lag' directly. Good athletes complete a marathon in the time that light travels out to Uranus. This created real problems for scientists when the Voyager probe arrived there in 1986. Voyager passed through the rings and moons of Uranus, preprogrammed to take pictures and transmit them back to Earth. For 3 hours the signal rushed across space towards the waiting scientists.

At last the first exciting pictures emerged. It was no use anyone asking 'Can you tell the probe to point its camera back so that we can have a closer look at that new moon?' The moment anything new turned up, it was already too late. It would take 3 hours for a message to reach Voyager, by which time it would have left Uranus far behind.

It takes half a day for light to depart the solar system. The nearest stars, Proxima Centauri and Alpha Centauri, are nearly 4 years distant. These are visible in southern skies. Northern viewers can see bright Sirius shining as it was 8 years ago.

When we look at the stars we are looking back in time. We see Betelgeuse, the red star in Orion, as it was at the Norman Conquest, the bright nebula of new stars in Orion's sword in the early Christian era, and the Crab Nebula in the time of the Egyptian pharaohs.

Our galaxy consists of 1 billion suns, most of which are in a thin disc with a bulge at the centre. When you see the Milky Way arching overhead you are looking through the plane of the disc. If you live in the southern hemisphere you can follow the Milky Way to Sagittarius where you will be looking right into the central bulge – the heart of the galaxy. There are so many stars there, so far off, that individual stars cannot be distinguished; the galaxy's centre appears as a pool of light. That light has been travelling 33,000 years to reach us.

All the stars in the constellations are in our galaxy but appear thinly spaced because we are looking out of the plane where most of the stars lie. On a clear night you will also be able to make out some nebulous objects that look like thin misty clouds reflecting moonlight. Some of these are not in our galaxy. In southern skies there are the Magellanic Clouds, visible to the naked eye and named after the exploring seafarer Magellan. These are two galaxies, smaller than ours, satellites of the Milky Way. Trapped by our galaxy's huge gravity, they orbit around us continuously. They are nearly 200,000 light years distant; we see them as they were when Neolithic man occupied the Earth.

In northern skies you can look at the constellation Andromeda and see a faint wisp near its second brightest members. Through a telescope this is a marvellous sight. It is a huge galaxy much like our own, where the stars appear in spirals (Figure 4.2). It is 2 million light years away; its light has been travelling as long as mankind has existed. If we could see the Milky Way from outside it would look much like the Andromeda Nebula does from here. Viewed from a planet orbiting a star in the Magellanic Clouds, our entire Milky Way would be a brilliant vision in the heavens.

Here we begin to be aware of the clumpy nature of the Universe. The Sun is our nearest star and the entire solar system surrounding it occupies distances that light can travel in a single morning. The next star is 3,000 times more remote than this, a light voyage of 4 years. Stars occur on average some 4 or 5 light years apart throughout the galaxy, extending 100,000 light years from edge to edge. Then vast darkness again until we find our nearest galactic neighbours, the Magellanic Clouds 200,000 light years away. Then there is nothing but the vastness of space, dark gases until the next major galaxy of stars, Andromeda, 2 million light years away, ten times more remote than our satellite galaxies. The nearest quasars (quasi stellar objects) are 10,000 million years distant. This is over half way to the start of time, for the Universe was born at the moment of the Big Bang, some 20,000 million years ago.

Viewed from the Earth our Sun is very bright because it is so near to us, but place it in a constellation and it wouldn't be visible; it is an unremarkable boring star. Viewed from the Magellanic Cloud, looking into our galaxy from outside, a creature wouldn't notice the Sun either. Suppose that we were looking at the Milky Way galaxy from outside; whereabouts would the Sun be?

The most noticeable feature of the galaxy is the bright central bulge. But we don't live there. Radiating out from the centre are dense spiral arms (see Figure 4.2, page 48). We don't live there either but you're getting warm. Once upon a time it was thought that the Earth was at the centre of the solar system. Now we know that is not so and that the Sun isn't even at the centre of the galaxy. Our galaxy isn't anything very special either: encircled by two minor galaxies – the Magellanic Clouds – and replicated throughout the cosmos, Andromeda being distinguished merely by its proximity.

There are two ways to hide and the most effective is anonymity – lost in the crowd. The stars in the galaxy are as numerous as grains of sand on a beach. We are one of millions of unremarkable points out in the suburbs. That's us – the X in Figure 4.2. No one living in the Andromeda galaxy would give our sun a second glance, even supposing that they had seen it! How many existences are out there orbiting a star that we haven't even noticed?

It is impossible to stay at rest when you are being tugged by the gravity of all these stars and galaxies. All stars in one galaxy collectively tug on those of a neighbouring galaxy. Whole galaxies are on the move. Over the aeons galaxies will disrupt one another, which will affect the long-term future of the Universe. Of more immediate concern is the behaviour of the stars within our own galaxy, and the ones near us right now.

Just as the galaxies are in motion so are the stars within. As the Sun and Moon make tides within the Earth, so do nearby galaxies make tides within our own galaxy. The stars are tugged this way and that over the aeons. Our galaxy is rotating like a huge Catherine wheel. This fluid of stars is turbulent; within the general flow there is chaotic motion. Since you started reading this sentence the Earth has travelled 100 miles around the Sun; the Sun has moved 1,000 miles in its circuit of the galaxy; and the Orion Nebula has distanced itself another 100,000 miles from us. The Universe is restless. Everything everywhere is on the move. But not everything within the galaxy is moving away from us. Not only do asteroids cross our path locally, but on a grander scale the constellation Hercules is currently moving towards us, getting 15 miles nearer each second.

The galaxy is not a uniform mix of stars, each neatly away from its nearest neighbours. Around our neighbourhood things are rather quiet. Within 17 light years of the Sun only 45 stars are known and there is no likelihood of one of them disturbing us in the immediate future. But not far away things are different. There are clusters, such as the Hyades and the Pleiades, both visible to the naked eye, in which up to 100 stars are in close association. These two clusters are a little over 100 light years away.

Although the stars near us appear to be randomly distributed, at larger distances there are many clusters like these. The positions of these clusters are *not* random. They all lie in the Milky Way, the flat plate of our galaxy. This flat plate is called the galactic plane and forms the central line of the Milky Way, which we see as a bright arc across the night. This plane is indeed very flat. It is 500 times thinner than its diameter; it is 15 times more narrowly confined than are the planets in our solar system. The members of the clusters are very young, most having shone for less time than humans have been around. They are so loosely bound to each other that one escapes every 100,000 years. At this rate of evaporation the clusters cannot survive more than 100 million years. So clusters of stars must be forming and evaporating continuously.

As well as these young clusters of 100 stars, there are also sparse clusters of up to 1 million stars. These spherical groups are called globular clusters. They are very old and close packed. Whereas the small clusters are over 300 light years apart and spread throughout the Milky Way plane, the globular clusters are concentrated in a sphere around the centre of the galaxy. And at the heart of the whole maelstrom is a black hole, a region where gravity is so strong that even light cannot escape its pull.

If we could look at the galaxy from outside we would see a spiral structure much like the familiar shape of the Andromeda Nebula. The dense catherine wheel type spirals are called the 'spiral arms'. These are regions of compression where the fast-moving stars come to a traffic jam, entering at the rear and eventually passing out through the front. Careful measurements of the positions of many stars and clusters show us that our galaxy is like this. Moreover, we can look at distant galaxies through our telescopes and find many others that have this appearance.

There is no doubt that over half the stars form a flat disc that we call the Milky Way, and that they are rotating about the galactic centre much as the planets orbit the Sun. But not exactly like the planets. There is an important difference that is not yet fully understood and which could have implications for the future Earth.

The planets orbit around a central Sun – the bulk of the solar system is in the centre; there is nothing competing on the periphery. One result of this is that you move slower the further out you are. Thus Mercury moves very fast, Earth moderately so, but distant Uranus moves at a much more leisurely pace. If the stars in a galaxy were orbiting a central mass they too would obey the same rule (close-in move fastest, far-out slowest). But this is not what happens in practice. The stars on the edge are moving almost as fast as those nearer the centre. In the periphery where the central gravity is feeble, a fast mover should escape, flying off the spinning wheel. Yet somehow they manage to remain attached. The galaxies appear to be almost rigid bodies, as if space is filled with unseen massive agents all contributing to the general tugging, speeding up the outer regions at the expense of the centre and gripping them permanently in the system.

What is this dark matter? You may well ask. This is currently one of the forefront questions in astronomy and in high energy particle physics. One possibility is that there is a whole new species of matter pervading the Universe that we have so far been unaware of. This will be described in Chapter 11. A more down to earth possibility, if that is the right metaphor, is that there are a lot of objects made of ordinary matter, but cold and dark, not hot enough to shine. These could form balls of gas like Jupiter, but much larger.

If there are such stars, then how many are there around here? Some astrophysicists suspect that the Sun has a dark companion, Nemesis. This could well be the nearest star to us, less than 100 light days away. In cosmic terms that is in our own backyard.

The solar system and Nemesis, if it exists, travel around the galaxy together. If they encroach on other stars, their motions will be disturbed. In turn Nemesis could disturb the Oort cloud of comets and tip millions into the solar system.

So in the long term we need to know what the orbit around the galaxy is like, what hazards we can meet along the way. The annual orbit of the Earth around the Sun in one year takes us through rings of small debris which give rise to meteor showers. The journey around the centre of the galaxy takes 200 million years and much more exotic possibilities arise. Recorded history spans 10,000 years, a mere one ten-thousandth of an orbit. So life has witnessed but a few hours on a summer's day and we have no experience of the depths of winter.

During this voyage we pass through empty regions and also

several densely packed regions. We encounter one of the 'spiral arms' every 60 million years or so, and the chances of a collision are greater at these times.

At present we are in a quiet region where the risks are very small. What does the future hold? What clues do we have as to the galactic December? Clues come from the past. The Earth is 20 galactic years old and so has passed through the spiral arms on many occasions. Although humans were not here to record it, fossils provide clues of what things were like.

Dust to Dust

Every scientist, or indeed anyone fascinated with Nature, can recall the magic moment in their childhood when their wonder began. Jean Heidmann, astronomer at the Paris Observatory, recalls how one evening, just after sunset, red Mars and Venus brilliant white were close together in the twilight. His father said, 'Three months ago we were up there, between Venus and Mars'. It was an astonishing revelation to the youngster that he had travelled so far in such a short life. Spaceship Earth had transported him, along with the rest of us, through three-dimensional space and now he could look back on where we had been.

There is a vast amount of 'space' and the planets, stars and galaxies are an insignificant fraction of the total volume. The space between these three is referred to as 'interplanetary', 'interstellar' and 'intergalactic' respectively. But none of it is empty. We have already met the solar wind of subatomic particles that permeates the solar system and forms most of the interplanetary medium. The interstellar medium consists of gases, mainly hydrogen and helium and minute dust motes.

Although space is not empty, the density of gas is in most places exceedingly thin, much rarer than can be produced in the best vacuums on Earth. If you shone a light beam out across the galaxy it would encounter more gas on its way out of the Earth's atmosphere than in the rest of its journey across the galaxy and out to the vastness of the Universe.

The volume of the galaxy is so huge that although the gases are very thin on the average there are vast amounts in total. Add it all together and it amounts to more than 10 billion Suns in mass, about 10 per cent of the total mass of the entire galaxy. Most of it is in the spiral arms of the galaxy, in a layer no more than about 100 light years across. Some clouds of gas are so opaque that they prevent light from distant stars getting through – the 'coal sack' in the Southern Cross is an example. They contain the same sorts of gases as bright clouds, or 'nebulae', but these latter have stars nearby that illuminate them.

As the Sun and its attendant planets voyage around the galaxy they periodically encounter dust clouds and pass through them. We are doing so at the moment, though it is only a thin cloud and hasn't noticeably affected us. Indeed, it is providing a unique opportunity to learn about the way that the Earth and Sun would be affected when we pass through a dense cloud, such as one of the galaxy's spiral arms.

The cloud that we are currently passing through is nothing like that. There is no more than one atom of hydrogen or helium in every 10cc volume. We are travelling through at 12 miles per second about 50,000 mph, which is about two-thirds of the speed that we are orbiting the Sun. The cloud is blowing from the direction of the constellation Centaurus, heading towards Cassiopaeia. It is as a result of this discovery that we have, in only the last 15 years, begun to understand the interaction between the Sun and the interstellar medium.

If a star that is five times hotter than the Sun is encompassed by such a cloud, its heat radiation can strip the hydrogen atoms of the cloud, leaving a gas of free negatively charged electrons and positively charged protons known as 'plasma'. This zone of plasma is known as the Stromgren sphere and can reach out 100 light years, encompassing several stars. The Orion Nebula is an example where hot young stars and the interstellar medium coexist. The resulting light show makes the Orion Nebula one of the splendid sights of the January sky, and is a favourite pin-up in posters and astronomical picture books.

Rockets have taken sensitive detectors high above our atmosphere and recorded the effect of the dust cloud on sunlight. Its behaviour is nothing like the Orion glow. Instead the instruments recorded an intense diffuse ultra-violet light with a wavelength characteristic of excitation of neutral unionised hydrogen. This showed that neutral hydrogen exists in considerable amounts in interplanetary space.

At first this was a surprise because scientists had believed that any hydrogen in the vicinity should be ionised by the Sun. Then Hans Fahr and Peter Blum at Bonn University came up with the solution. Interstellar gas engulfs the solar system, but we are rushing through it so fast that the gale blows far into the solar system before being ionised by the Sun's rays.

Whereas a meeting with a tenuous cloud is hardly noticed, an encounter with a dense cloud, as in the spiral arms of the galaxy, can lead to global change.

Imagine that you are sunbathing on the sort of summer day that is familiar in Britain. The temperature is about 20 degrees Centigrade and then a cloud crosses the Sun. The temperature falls, just a little but you are already calculating the speed of the clouds – 'should I lie here and sweat it out' (wrong metaphor) or 'do I get up and put a shirt on?'

Well, that is what just happened to me and, as I write, the cloud has passed and it's sunny again. There are more clouds still to come and I wonder what it would be like if clouds were around permanently.

Sometimes in Britain or Northern Europe it feels as if that is how things are all the time! But one can always go to southern France, California or the equatorial regions and get the warmth. Suppose that there were clouds between the whole Earth and the Sun continuously. There would be a global cooling of a few degrees. You are sensitive to a cooling of just a couple of degrees. This is the subtle difference between the swimming pool being tolerable and numbing; between sunbathing and going inside; between comfort or putting the heating on indoors.

The clouds above my head are a few hundred metres high at most. The golden sun is 100 million miles away, hundreds of millions of times more remote. If that intervening space were filled with dust clouds then we would be in for a significant cold snap.

That is what happens every 100 million years or so when we encounter the dense spiral arms of the galaxy.

A spiral arm is a region where short-lived bright stars are illuminating large clouds of interstellar dust and gas. Stars and gas must be moving through the dense spirals because otherwise the spirals would become tightly coiled from the differential rotation rate of the galaxy as one moves further from the centre. The fact that the spirals survive implies that they are some wave pattern moving through the disc of stars and gas, like a traffic jam on a freeway. Traffic arrives at the rear of the jam while the vehicles at the front escape. Viewed from above over a period of time you see the traffic jam move backwards until the once-captured car finds itself at the front and escapes to freedom. The traffic jam, and the spiral arms, are patterns through which the objects move.

From observation of the spiral structures astronomers have found that objects enter an arm at its inner or concave edge where there is a dust build-up. This is a shock wave effect whereby the clouds are compressed for a short while as they cross this dust lane. The compressed clouds are almost certainly the sites of new star formation. The brightest of these stars illuminate the arm as they move along their way, but burn out before emerging into the region between arms.

The material orbiting around the galaxy may pass through these compression waves many times before being squeezed enough to collapse into a star. At each passage through an arm only a small percentage of the diffuse material forms stars or else the arms would disappear.

Our Sun and the planets were formed in a compressed cloud about 5 billion years ago. Since that time we have all circled the galaxy 20 times and encountered spiral arms on some 50 occasions, that is roughly once every 100 million years. It takes 10 million years to cross the main part of an arm and for 1 million of those we are in the compression lane.

Several people have drawn a connection between the great ice ages and encounters with the dust clouds in the spiral arms.

The ice epochs occur roughly every 250 million years and last for a few million years. They contain several glaciations of about

100,000–200,000 years each. The most recent glaciation ended some 11,000 years ago.

These facts all fit in with an encounter with a dust cloud at a spiral arm. We are currently at the inner edge of the Orion arm, having entered a compression lane 1 million years ago and recently exited. And we have only recently emerged from a period of glaciation. The time it takes to pass through the clouds also fits in with what we know about glaciations. The sun is moving at about 12 miles per second relative to the nearest stars and so at 3–15 miles per second relative to individual dust clouds. There are lots of tenuous clouds (such as the one that we are passing through at the moment) which do not affect us, but a dense cloud, typically 1 light year in size, is another matter and, at a speed of 12 miles per second, it takes us 50,000 years to get through.

Fred Hoyle and R. Lyttleton argued as long ago as 1939 that there was a connection between the ice ages and such galactic encounters. William McCrae has recently developed and extended these ideas and argues that there is a strong case for believing that ice ages and encounters with interstellar dust clouds are connected. The way in which the Sun's radiation triggers the ice age is still conjectural; the meteorology is still poorly understood. But there are compulsive features. Very dense clouds DO exist and the Sun must go through them. When it does, its radiation must be affected. The periodicity and extent of the glaciations fit in with these encounters too.

If the great ice ages are explained this way then we don't have to appeal to more sensational ideas such as that the Sun is intrinsically variable. We need not anticipate a major glaciation for a long time yet.

Encounters with the spiral arms may also be the cause of comets raining into the solar system. We are in a quiescent epoch at present, but when we encounter a dense cloud next, we may expect an increase in the risk of collisions.

There is some evidence that extinctions of flora and fauna have occurred at roughly 150 million year intervals since the Palaeozoic era 600 million years ago. Lunar rock samples suggest that meteor collisions with the Moon peak on a similar time-scale. The buffetings from the last such passage occurred some 60–70 million years ago when animal life had just emerged. At this epoch the dinosaurs disappeared. If this is all true then we are midway between such transits. The million years since humans have lived here has been a quiet period. We have tended to generalise and assume that this is the natural order of things. It will not always be so peaceful.

Lifestyles of the Stars

Nature operates on a whole range of time-scales. Stars live for billions of years, humans for decades, insects for only a few hours. But living on one scale need not prevent you being aware of the evolution of others. Let's come down to Earth and imagine a cosy peaceful scene.

It is a warm summer's day. A family is picnicking at the side of a river. Baby sleeps in the afternoon sunshine. Older children are playing with their parents. Grandparents are dozing. Hovering above the lilies, dragonflies enjoy their brief moment of existence. Their lifespan is but a millionth part of a human life. An average human life is but a millionth part of a geological epoch, which is in turn 1 per cent of the age of the Universe. So as the dragonflies are to the humans on the riverbank, so are the humans to the stars.

Suppose that dragonflies were highly intelligent. In their moments of existence they would be aware of the seven ages of man at the picnic party. Although their own life is very short by comparison, they would see the evidence of much longer time-spans. They will see the development that individual humans have already experienced, or have yet to go through.

We human insects in our turn perceive the grander epochs of time. Our three-score years and ten are like a dragonfly's afternoon. When we look at the stars we see the past and future of our Sun. There are misty nebulae, stars in gestation; middle-aged ones like the Sun today; old ones, the future dying Sun.

For all stars are not alike – you can see this with your own eyes. Orion is one of the best-known constellations. If you live in the northern hemisphere, then on a clear winter's night you will be able to find bright red Betelgeuse at the top left corner of the shoulder. Nearby is Sirius, a bright blue-white colour. Vega in Lyra can be seen blue in the summer sky. In the southern hemisphere you can see the Southern Cross. This contains three bluish-white stars and one red star.

With binoculars you can see millions of stars in a host of colours. The colours tell you about the temperature at the surface of the star. Just as an electric fire glows red-orange, then yellow as it warms, so the hotter the stars, the further across the spectrum the colouring is. Blue Vega shines at 30,000 degrees, our yellow sun is some 6,000 degrees, while red Betelgeuse shines at 3,000 degrees.

You can feel the warmth of a fire before it begins to glow. The same is true of the stars. Stars that are too cool to emit visible light none the less emit heat rays, infra-red radiation. In 1984, IRAS surveyed the skies and sent back vast quantities of data about fledgling stars of the future. The astronomers are still processing this wealth of new information through their computers but already they have learned a lot of things about star formation.

How are stars formed?

No one has yet given a complete detailed and totally accepted answer to this question. However, from watching the behaviour of many different types of star in the distant parts of the cosmos, and putting together the various clues and experiences gained from decades of observation, we have a pretty good idea of the general scheme of things.

Nature's cycle is of life leading to death, which in turn seeds new life. The seasons on Earth are a rapid and small-scale cycle compared to the grander and slower scale in the Universe at large. The deaths of some stars give birth to the next generation. Catastrophic supernova explosions (see Chapter 9) can destroy nearby planets and life (if there are any elsewhere), just as a conventional bomb blast can destroy solid matter in its vicinity. These cosmic blasts also send out shock waves through the interstellar gases, compressing them. In some regions the gas becomes concentrated enough that clumps form. The patchy mist thickens here and there.

Gravity begins to exert its influence, tugging these clumps feebly but insistently towards one another. Gradually, over thousands and millions of years the gas collapses into a huge ball. Its own weight continues to crunch it smaller and smaller. This would go on until no room is left except that something happens to prevent it. The random jostlings of the atoms generate heat and light – the gas begins to shine. The heat within resists gravity's inward pull.

The temperature of the gas in its quiescent state was 3 degrees above absolute zero; a chilly −270 degrees Centigrade. As the atoms begin to bang together, the temperature rises, eventually reaching temperatures familiar on Earth. These are still far too low to glow visibly, but already gas is emitting low-level heat radiation, infra-red radiation.

Very light clouds of hydrogen gas don't have enough weight to collapse under gravity's pull and so they never get hot enough in the middle for thermonuclear fusion to begin. These failed stars are clouds of cold gas like Jupiter. There could be a lot of these 'dark suns' around, such as Nemesis, a suspected dark companion of our Sun. These dark stars have been invisible in the past; science is only now beginning to be able to detect them by their infra-red heat.

Special heat sensitive cameras can 'photograph' objects by the heat they give out. They can image the human body by its heat. Infra-red cameras have been sent up on satellites and sent back images of gases beginning to warm up in this way. At this stage we say that it is a 'protostar'. Finally the gas is warm enough that the infra-red radiation gives way to a dimly glowing visible red.

But gravity still beats the feeble glowworm, squeezing the star until nuclear reactions begin. Now at last a fully fledged 'main sequence' star erupts. Nuclear reactions take over. Hydrogen nuclei fuse to make helium. The temperature rises to a staggering 10 million degrees or more. These are bright spots that we call stars.

So stars are in a state of internal conflict: gravity pulls them in while thermonuclear fusion keeps them alive. The outcome depends on the amount of gravitational pull (the size) and the status of the nuclear reactor (how much useful fuel is left and of what type).

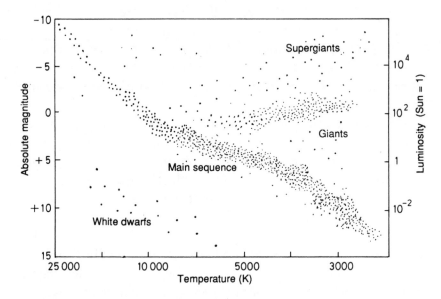

8.1 Hertzsprung–Russell diagram of star types The absolute magnitude or brightness of the star is plotted along the vertical axis and its temperature along the horizontal. Brightest are at the bottom and hottest to the left. Cool stars on the right shine red; hotter ones to the centre are yellow; and very hot at the left are blue. Stars are not randomly distributed. Many are grouped in a narrow band on the diagonal called the main sequence. Another group, known as the giant branch, extends horizontally above this. The dim cool stars are very big and are called giants and supergiants ('red' giants because of their colour). The very bright hot small stars are the (blue and white) dwarfs. Our Sun is presently near the middle of the main sequence.

It has taken only a few million years for the interstellar cloud to condense and start to shine as a star. I say 'only' because it is short in cosmic time. For example, this is the sort of time that humans have existed on Earth. Interstellar clouds that condensed when Neanderthal man walked the planet are now shining in the heavens.

Hans Bethe, a German-born theorist at Cornell University in the USA, worked out the sequence of nuclear reactions that drive the stars. This explains the varied stars that we see. It has made us realise that the stars in the sky are not permanent, but are continuously changing. In particular, it enables us to work out the future of our Sun.

To place our Sun's present position in the stellar evolution needs a scheme for classifying the stars we see. The Danish astronomer Ejnar Hertzsprung and the American Henry Russell independently (in 1911 and 1913 respectively) came up with the idea of classifying stars by brightness and surface temperature. These two characteristics are sufficient to identify a star's status and eventual fate. The Hertzsprung–Russell diagram is a chart of the stars (see Figure 8.1). The scale from left to right measures the temperature; from top to bottom measures the true brightness (the brightness of the star were we to view it at the same distance as we view the Sun – this takes into account the fact that some stars appear dim because they are far away, whereas they may be much brighter than the Sun when viewed close to). Thus stars at the right side are red hot; in the middle they are yellow and white hot; to the left they are blue. Very bright stars are at the top; dim ones are at the bottom.

The Sun's brightness puts it about halfway up the chart, and its heat puts it about halfway along the chart. You do the same for each and every star and you find them scattered all over the plot.

Well, not quite all over. What you immediately notice is that the stars don't occur at random. The majority lie on a line, known as the main sequence, which includes the Sun. A handful of dim white stars, the white dwarfs, is at bottom left. Rather more red giants are at the top right corner.

The amount of time a star spends in the various regions depends on how big it is. A massive star will be sucked tighter under its own gravity than a small one. Its collapse is prevented by the heat generated from burning its nuclear fuel. As it burns, it gets hotter to remain stable. The hottest brightest main sequence stars are the heaviest (top left-hand corner). They are burning fuel so quickly in generating the heat that their lives are the shortest. Their deaths can be dramatic and the sequel bizarre, as we shall see in Chapter 9.

Less bulky stars burn their fuel more sparingly: their gravity is less crushing, less heat is required to hold them up, and they live longer. Our Sun is such a star.

A star like the Sun can shine like this and be quite stable for 10

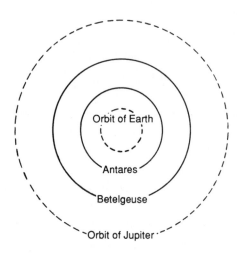

8.2 Sizes of stars   There is an immense variation in the sizes of stars. Those with diameters of about half a million miles, like our own Sun, are quite common. The largest stars are red giants and supergiants. Antares has a diameter 300 times that of the Sun and if placed at the centre of the solar system it would swallow the orbits of Mercury, Venus and the Earth. Betelgeuse in Orion is even bigger. At the other extreme, white dwarfs are about the size of the Earth, while neutron stars are only a few miles across.

billion years. It converts 600 million tonnes of hydrogen fuel into helium every second, radiating energy in the process. There is enough hydrogen for this to continue for another 5 billion years. The solar system is about 4½ billion years old, so the Sun is about halfway through its hydrogen stock.

When it has used up all of the hydrogen in its central core, the thermonuclear reactions will spread outwards. In the process, the Sun will expand rapidly a hundredfold and become a bright red giant. The inner planets wil be engulfed; vaporised. The Earth will cease to exist.

In the red giant phase it will be unsteady for some thousands of years. It may become a 'variable' star, expanding and contracting every few hours. The pressure of the gas within the star pushes it outwards beyond its average size until gravity pulls it back. It keeps overshooting and falling back like a swinging pendulum. There are many examples of such stars in the sky. Betelgeuse, the bright red star in Orion, varies gradually in size from 300 to 400 times the diameter of the Sun. (To gain some feeling for what this means, it is as if the Sun consumed the Earth, extending beyond the orbit of Mars.)

Finally all nuclear burning in the core will end. No fuel remains to resist the gravitational force. The star collapses under its own weight. It becomes a white dwarf. There is no source of energy within to generate new heat and light, but even so it cools so slowly that it shines for another billion years.

So there will come a day, in some 4 billion years, when the Sun will rise for the last time over the eastern horizon. When an audience in Washington learned that the Sun had 4 billion years left, one member asked, in a slight panic, 'Did you say 4 billion or 4 million?' On being assured that it was 4 billion they sat down, at ease.

This shows how difficult it is to gain a feel for large numbers, so let's describe the Sun's lifestyle on the more familiar time-scale of a human span: a century.

Its gestation, the protostar phase, lasts a mere two days. It spends 80 years on the main sequence, consuming its hydrogen fuel. When this is through it becomes an unsteady variable red giant for a fortnight and then spends eight years in retirement, living off its reserves until its ultimate death. On this time-scale the Sun is now about 40 years old – halfway through its present 'active' phase, at which time intelligence arrived on Earth: life begins at 40!

The Sun is typical of many stars; that is why we can make such confident assertions about its future life cycle. It gives us ease to realise that the Sun has a healthy long-term future, and that the Earth will not suddenly turn into a stellar furnace of its own accord (another Hollywood myth thankfully disproved).

However, some stars in the sky will change form catastrophically. If this happens to a star in our vicinity the consequences could be very grave. Although our Sun will form a red giant and then collapse into a white dwarf, it will do so only slowly. If the Sun had been 50 per cent heavier, it would have gone through these stages much faster. Indeed it might already have died, its collapse having run out of control and a nuclear blast shot out across space. The end result of such a catastrophe is a neutron star – an atomic nucleus the size of a city. If the starting star was even heavier, then it may end up as a black hole in space.

So let's learn more about the neutron star and the supernova blast that spawns it.

9

Exploding Stars

In 1967 Jocelyn Bell was a student of astronomy at Cambridge where she was working under the guidance of Antony Hewish, one of the leading radio astronomers of the day. Rather than observing stars by optical means, they were looking at the sources of radio waves coming from the cosmos.

Day by day the radio telescope peered at different parts of the sky, into the depths of space. It was fairly routine stuff. Their idea was to measure the size of the sources, 'quasars', by seeing how much they twinkled. You are familiar with the fact that stars twinkle as their light passes through the atmosphere, whereas the nearby planets, with their larger angular size, do not twinkle. By analogy, the radio waves from relatively small sources will twinkle as they pass through the solar wind whereas those from larger sources will be less disturbed.

Bell recorded lots of twinkling radio signals until one day she noticed one that looked odd. It seemed 'scruffy', for that is how she described it to Antony Hewish as she discussed with him what to do about it. He suggested that she set the apparatus up to be able to record the twinkling at a faster rate – to resolve the radio signal as it flickered back and forth. When she did so she discovered that the 'scruff' resolved into a series of pulses, regularly once a second or so.

They thought that they had picked up the signal from some radio beacon but after detailed enquiries it became clear that this was caused by no terrestrial source. What could be going on?

Members of their department jokingly suggested that they

were signals from LGM – little green men – which the media seized upon and propagated. Hewish said that if the signal was real then it was most unlikely that they had stumbled across the only one in the entire Universe and suggested that she search for more. Soon a couple more examples turned up and the 'pulsars' became official.

They had discovered a special type of star which beams out its signal like a lighthouse, whirling the light round and round. You see a flash only when the beam points at you. It circles around, away from you, and you see nothing until it points at you again.

Bell's original sightings were of stars that emit radio waves, and so had been picked up by the radio telescope. Today we know of pulsars that emit visible light and flash on and off, up to 30 times a second as the beam whips round and round. The culprits are a special kind of star that consists entirely of subatomic particles called neutrons. Their existence had been suspected for 30 years but no one had anticipated the pulsing lighthouse signal. Hence the initial confusion when Jocelyn Bell discovered the first one.

Neutron stars are the dense cinders of heavier suns, the end-products of a catastrophic explosion which destroyed a huge star. The outer mantle of the star erupts into space, covering an incredible 30,000 miles in the first seconds. The remaining core is a dense pack of neutrons – the mass of the sun compressed into a ball no bigger than New York.

Neutron stars are fascinating objects. The blast that spawns them can light up the sky: the brilliant sight is called a 'supernova'. (The Latin for new is 'nova'. The flash from the white dwarf is superbly bright; hence the name 'supernova'.) It is like witnessing a gargantuan nuclear blast across space. If one happened in our vicinity it would mean the end of life on Earth. If the nuclear radiation didn't finish us immediately, the shock wave and debris following on behind would disrupt the atmosphere.

On 23 February 1987 a supernova burst out in the Large Magellanic Cloud, a nearby satellite galaxy to our own. This is 200,000 light years away; far enough to be no harm while near enough to excite astronomers and physicists. In the southern hemisphere it was visible to the naked eye – the first such since the invention of the telescope. This highlights how important it was;

everyone has been watching it closely. More about the sighting and what we have learned later; first – what do we know so far?

Route to the Neutron Star

Have you ever been at the bottom of a pile of people, underneath a collapsed rugby scrum for example? As more and more weight piles on top, the pressure becomes unbearable. Think what it must be like at the base of a mountain. The pressure of the overlying rocks, piled miles high, can be literally crushing.

The summit of Mount Everest is 5½ miles above sea level. The island of Hawaii is the tallest mountain from its undersea base to the top, some 6 miles. On Earth no mountain could survive more than 12 miles high. The material at the base would flow like liquid owing to the pressure of the rocks on top.

Gravity is an inexorable crusher. Thermonuclear reactions in stars resist its force but even so the centre of the Sun is 100 times denser than water. When the nuclear fuel is exhausted, stars can no longer support themselves against gravity. In extreme cases, such as neutron stars, a thimbleful of matter can weigh millions of tonnes.

Matter at extreme densities takes on forms that are unfamiliar on Earth.

There are many different elements that go into building up the world around us. But they all have one thing in common. The matter that we are made of is remarkably empty. You can compress mud into small balls with the strength of your hands. Even metal can be compressed under the pressure of pile drivers. The rocks under mountains may be liquefied by the pressure. At the atomic level there is more empty space than matter! Less than a billionth part of the atomic volume contains matter – electrons encircling a nucleus of protons and neutrons.

To get an idea of how empty the atom is, imagine the diameter of a hydrogen atom (one electron orbiting a single proton) scaled up to the size of a 500 metre long hole at a golf course. This is the longest fairway that you will find and a top-class golfer will take three or four good shots to reach the green from the tee. The goal is a tiny hole, some 2 or 3 cm at most, known as the pin. The size of the pin relative to the length of the huge fairway is as the size of the nucleus relative to the extent of that atom. All of the distance from the tee to the green and to the pin is as empty space in the atom. (If you are a football fan, you can imagine a pea at the centre spot of a pitch.)

An atom is about one-hundreth of a millionth of a centimetre across. This is unimaginably small. Yet its nucleus is 100,000 times smaller. Whereas electric and magnetic forces bind the electrons loosely in atoms, the nucleus is gripped by powerful forces extending only one millionth of a millionth of a millimetre. At these short distances the nuclear forces dominate over everything else – gravity and electromagnetic forces are trifling by comparison.

An atom's size is determined by the lightweight cloud of electrons whirling in the peripheral regions. These govern the chemical behaviour and physical properties of matter on Earth. In our daily experience we are aware of electromagnetic forces and the electrons, carriers of electricity, but the nuclear forces do not directly affect us (though the waste products of radioactivity cause immense political problems). The protons carry positive electricity, which balances the negatively charged electrons in neutral atoms. We can think of the protons as ensuring the neutrality of atoms, and the neutral neutrons being needed to stabilise the nucleus. Together they provide 99.95 per cent of the mass of bulk matter, such as you and me.

So we are made of atoms and our mass is concentrated in less than a billionth part of their volume. Put another way, the density of nuclear matter is a billion times more than the matter that we are familiar with on Earth.

We can squeeze atoms nearer to each other but cannot compress individual atoms. Their sizes are fixed by Nature and depend on unchangeable constants such as the strength of the electromagnetic forces and the mass of the electron.

But gravity is the ultimate compressor. As we add more and more material, the pressure of its weight becomes so intense that the atoms fragment. Their electrons no longer remain in their orbits but are displaced. Instead of matter containing atoms built of nuclei and orbiting planetary electrons, we have nuclei sitting in the midst of a dense homogeneous gas of ubiquitous swarming electrons. This form of matter, plasma, is the most common form of matter in the Universe. It is we on Earth, with the beauty of diamonds and crystals, with chemistry, biology and life, who are the exception. Plasma rules.

This gas of free electrons is what would occur if we kept on adding weight to the Earth. The atomic electrons would not be able to sustain the ordered structures. The solid Earth would give way to a dense homogeneous gas of electrons and nuclei.

As we learned in Chapter 2, debris from space is continually falling to Earth, adding to the Earth's mass. However, this is such a trifling amount that we needn't worry. We would need to exceed the mass of Jupiter by a lot before the solid Earth changed its state.

Once the atoms have been disrupted they can no longer resist the crush. If more and more matter were added the result would be a white dwarf. This is a star as massive as the Sun but as small as the Earth. There are no free protons available in the gas of electrons and atomic nuclei to fuse and sustain thermonuclear reactions. One tonne is crammed into each cubic centimetre (less than a teaspoonful).

What happens if we go further? The atomic volume, once disrupted, can be compressed 100 billion times. The pressure that gravity brings to bear is 1 million billion times greater than anything ever achieved in an Earthbound laboratory, so we need not fear a self-induced Armageddon by some mad scientist crushing matter and changing the nature of the Earth. We cannot yet change the stars nor planets.

We cannot, but Nature can and does.

In white dwarfs the density is 1 million times that of water. At first no one understood how these extreme densities could be maintained without the star collapsing. Then, with the discovery of atomic structure and the rules governing the stability of atoms, the stability of white dwarfs was in turn explained.

The electrons are moving relatively slowly in this gas. As the density increases, the electrons speed up. Soon they are moving near to the speed of light and the mathematics no longer applies. Instead of using the laws of low speeds we have to go over to high speeds, the province of relativity. This requires a few changes in the mathematics and, in 1930, Subrahmanyan Chandrasekhar worked out the consequences.

He did this in an unusual set of circumstances.

Chandrasekhar, still only 19 years old, was on a boat en route from Madras to England where he was going to study. To pass the time he calculated what would be the effect of increasing the density in a white dwarf. He found an astonishing result: white dwarfs cannot exist if their mass exceeds that of the Sun by more than 40 per cent. The effect of relativity is to enfeeble the electrons' resistance to the inward pull of gravity. If the mass gets big enough, bigger than the 'Chandrasekhar limit', gravity wins out and the star collapses; the white dwarf can no longer exist.

Chandrasekhar checked his calculations and couldn't find any mistakes. Next he began to wonder what would happen to a would-be white dwarf that had too much mass, too much inward pull to survive. He thought that it would collapse and become a black hole, a dense star where the force of gravity is so powerful that it drags back even light before it can escape.

As the boat docked, Chandrasekhar possessed a secret of the Universe that no other living soul knew. He told Arthur Eddington, one of the leading physicists of the time. Eddington disbelieved it. So did other senior scientists. Who was this 19 year old calculating on a boat trip and announcing the death of stars? It was all a bit rich.

But Chandrasekhar was right, as people gradually recognised. It is all very well with hindsight to criticise Eddington and others, but the claim was quite outside current thinking, star shattering indeed. Many years later, Chandrasekhar's genius was recognised; for this work he won a share of the Nobel Prize in 1983.

Chandrasekhar was wrong on only one thing – his belief that the overweight white dwarf would collapse into a black hole. This wasn't a mistake; at the time it was the logical conclusion, and may in part have been the psychological barrier that prevented scientists immediately accepting his theory. No force was then known that could prevent the electrons and protons in the star collapsing inwards under gravity's pull. In 1931 electrons and protons were the only known atomic particles. No one yet knew that a neutron, an electrically neutral version of the proton, exists in atomic nuclei. The neutron was discovered only in 1932 and its existence provided the crucial missing ingredient in the story of the stars.

Soon after Ernest Rutherford identified the existence of the atomic nucleus in 1911 and of positively charged protons, he had suggested that there could exist a neutral particle formed by a negatively charged electron being absorbed in a proton. Several people then speculated that there are two varieties of nuclear particles – the positively charged proton and a neutral counterpart, the neutron. Marie Curie's daughter, Irene, had almost discovered it early in 1932 but had misinterpreted her results. Rutherford, at that time a professor in Cambridge, had stimulated his colleagues into being on the look out for such clues and his deputy, James Chadwick, immediately realised that Irene Curie probably had been producing neutrons. He set to work at once and almost overnight produced, identified and proved the existence of neutrons.

Telegrams announcing the discovery went to the leading scientific establishments around the world. In Copenhagen Lev Landau, a leading Soviet theoretician who was visiting at the time, immediately started to consider the implications of the discovery. That same day he gave a seminar and announced that neutron stars should exist.

Here was the missing link in Chandrasekhar's theory. When the overweight white dwarf undergoes a catastrophic collapse, its electrons and protons encroach on one another to the point that they fuse into neutrons, and the collapse stops. The remnant of the 'supernova' explosion is the tiny neutron star.

So a white dwarf that is slightly heavier than Chandrasekhar's limit (40 per cent heavier than the Sun) will collapse and end up as a neutron star, no more than a few kilometres across. If the white dwarf is less bulky than this, say the same sort of mass as the Sun, then it may remain a white dwarf or end up as a neutron star (which of the two depends on what other disturbances it experiences). Typically the size of a solar-mass neutron star will be 12 miles diameter – the mass of the Sun contained in a sphere whose size is like Amsterdam or New York. If the mass exceeds 3.4 solar masses, then even the neutrons cannot prevent the collapse and, barring new unknowns, the neutron star *will* fall into a black hole.

If you were on the surface of a neutron star, the force of gravity would be 100 billion times greater than you experience on the Earth. Whereas on the moon the gravity is less and you can jump higher (anyone could break the 'world' high jump record on the moon!), on a neutron star the gravity is so intense that your head would weigh as much as 100 ocean liners. Indeed, mountains could not resist the downwards pull: even a Mount Everest would be under 1 metre high. Its head would stick up through the atmosphere, which would be all of 5 cm thick. Mountaineering would be an exhausting enterprise as it would take the energy expenditure of a lifetime to climb 1 centimetre.

This is what the astrophysicists claim, but how sure can we be that they are right?

In the 1930s, neutron stars were no more than an idea. No one had seen one and most people doubted that anyone ever would, even supposing that they existed! For 33 years nothing happened, until the day when Jocelyn Bell noticed a regular bleep coming from a distant star as if something, or someone, was sending a signal.

Neutron stars exist. The remains of supernovae, the evidence of past cataclysms, are out there. From their numbers and the age of the galaxy we deduce that a supernova occurs somewhere on average once every 20 years. What are the chances that one will occur near enough to be a hazard?

Supernova

What were you doing at 07.30 GMT on 23 February 1987? I was having breakfast as, unknown to me, a burst of neutrinos passed through my cornflakes. All the time we are bathing in a breeze of neutrinos coming from the Sun; but the sudden burst that February morning was quite different. It was a blast from a dying star, 170,000 light years away in the Large Magellanic Cloud galaxy.

For over 25 years astrophysicists have believed that the gravitational collapse thought to be associated with supernovae and neutron star or black hole formation is a copious source of neutrinos. In fact they argued that the brilliant flash of light – the traditional manifestation of a supernova – is only a minor part of the drama, perhaps less than 1 per cent of the whole energy output. The bulk of the energy radiated by the collapse comes off in invisible form – the neutrinos.

'Invisible' in the past, but not now that we have built neutrino telescopes. The exciting news is that in this case, for the first time, we have detected neutrinos emanating from outside our galaxy (previously we had only seen those from the Sun) and have proved that the theory is right: when stars collapse they throw off their energy as neutrinos.

The theorists are still poring over the data, learning more about supernovae and the death of stars than ever before. This is the culmination of a long story that began with the idea that supernovae are the birthpangs of neutron stars.

The first hints came with a suggestion from W. Baade and F. Zwicky, German and Swiss astronomers working at the Mount Wilson Observatory in the United States in 1934. They realised that the process of collapsing into a neutron star will emit vast amounts of energy. This radiation appears as a sudden flash visible in the sky like a new star.

Occasionally such flashes do appear; In AD 1006 'a new star of unusual size', which 'dazzled the eyes, glittering and causing great alarm,' shone for three months according to reports from central Europe. This is the only example reported outside the Far East before the Renaissance, so it must have been bright. The Chinese and Arabs saw it on 30 April 1006. Could this be an example of a 'supernova'? To answer this we first need to know how much energy is emitted in a supernova.

You start off with a white dwarf – the mass of the Sun in the volume of the Earth, a radius of some thousands of miles. After the collapse the mass is concentrated within a sphere no more than about 7 miles across. The whole mass of a star has fallen through a distance of about 1,000 miles. Falling objects have a lot of energy (drop a brick on your foot if you want a demonstration!). A glass falling from a table can shatter with a crash; the energy in its motion (kinetic energy) is changed into the energy of sound waves. A meteor falling in towards Earth can burn as bright as the Moon for several seconds as energy is transformed into light. Now imagine a whole star falling inwards through hundreds of miles under the pull of gravity.

The energy emitted is enormous. We are used to hearing of megatonne (millions of tonnes) hydrogen bombs. A megatonne bomb is 70 times as powerful as that dropped on Hiroshima. The heat is 5,000 degrees, hotter than the surface of the Sun. This is a world where fire bricks melt, where steel balls vaporise. That is the result of 1 million tonnes. The masses in stellar collapse are in a different league entirely – 1 megatonne for every cubic metre in a volume as big as the whole Earth. The energy released is the same as our Sun emits in 1,000 billion years. The Sun is only about 5 billion years old at present, so the energy emitted in a supernova burst is over 100 times greater than the Sun has put out *since before the Earth began*. And the supernova does this all in a few days!

Astronomers watch the skies continuously. Suddenly, in the space of a few days they see a star become tens of billions of times brighter. For a brief period this single star can outshine an entire galaxy of stars. When a supernova occurs in a distant galaxy you first identify which galaxy it is shining from; this tells you how far away it is, as the remoteness of most galaxies is known to within a factor of two. You then compare its brightness to that of a galaxy and hence deduce the total energy that it is giving out.

We can easily illustrate that the energy output agrees with our estimates. The crucial feature is that the supernova can outshine an entire galaxy for a few weeks. A typical galaxy contains 100–1,000 billion suns. Our own Sun has been burning for about 1,000 billion days. Its lifetime output is akin to the daily quota for an entire galaxy. So if a supernova outshines a whole galaxy it is competing with the Sun in all history.

Perhaps the most famous remnant of a supernova is the Crab Nebula, which has been called the Rosetta Stone of the life and death of the stars. This erupted in 4000 BC. The blast threw off intense radiation and ejected the outer shell of the star into space. The radiation, containing lethal X-rays and gamma rays as well as visible light, set out across space. 5,000 light years away planet Earth awaited, unaware of the approaching lightwave.

Early in the morning of 4 July 1054 Chinese astronomers (actually we would call them astrologers today) saw a bright new star rising in the east just before the Sun. They called it a 'guest star'. During the next few days it brightened further until it outshone all the other stars in the sky. For nearly a month it was so bright that it shone by day as well as by night. This was the light from the supernova. After 5,000 years, travelling, the rays were too sparse to cause trouble, but the sight was awesome none the less. Gradually it faded and within 18 months was no longer visible.

Not only do we have the Chinese records of its visible light, but the Earth has preserved the record of the gamma radiation.

Go to places that are changeless and you may find ancient records remaining. The Antarctic continent is a unique example where, by digging deep down into the snowpack, scientists can examine the snowfall each year over a millennium.

Rain and snow bring dust from the upper atmosphere. The rain washes away; the snow preserves the dust. When gamma rays hit the atmosphere, they fuse the indigenous nitrogen and oxygen into nitrous oxide. The Antarctic snowpack of hundreds of years past shows an increased presence of nitrates in years that supernovae have been seen. This fits with the sudden pulse of gamma rays hitting the upper atmosphere.

The rest of the debris of the star, its outer shell, is following more slowly. The bright light is the herald of shocks to come. With modern telescopes we can today identify the wreckage from the Crab supernova. It travelled 30,000 miles in the first few seconds. It is still approaching us 900 years later, at the rate of a few miles each second, and is bigger now than the images in photographs taken in 1899. But it is still over 6,000 light years away and at this rate of progress it will not reach us for another billion years. Our descendants need not worry, as by then its force will be utterly spent. Most likely the dust will be trapped by the gravity of other stars en route or will form new stars as the shock wave perturbs the gas in interstellar space.

The dim nebulous mist was first seen in 1731 by the English astronomer John Bevis. It is in the constellation Taurus and if you have a telescope you may be able to see it for yourself. This constellation is in the same part of the sky where the Chinese saw their 1054 guest star. In the nineteenth century the English amateur astronomer, the Third Earl of Rosse, was the first to resolve crablike filaments protruding from its southern extremity. This allusion to the legs and pincers of a crab gave the nebula its popular name.

Although it is now fairly dim in visible light, it still shines brightly in ultra-violet, infra-red, X-rays and radio emissions. Indeed, it ranks with the most brilliant of all celestial objects. All in all it still shines as bright as 30,000 suns.

It is now an egg shape, 15 light years long by 10 light years across. We know that it is expanding at a few miles each second and is slowing under the tug of its own gravity. If we turn the clock back, then in the past it must have been much smaller and hotter than it is now. Calculations imply that it was a single point around AD 1000, so indeed it appears to be the remnant of the 1054 supernova.

Further proof that the theory of stellar evolution looks right came with the discovery of a neutron star at the heart of the Crab Nebula. This shows up optically, blinking on and off 30 times each second. There can be no doubt that neutron stars are the remnants of supernovae. The Crab has all of the ingredients: visual sighting of the light in 1054, the gamma ray record frozen in the snows, the debris still approaching us, and even a neutron star remnant.

After the Crab supernova in 1054 another big one occurred on 7 August 1181. The next two were very close: 1572 and 1604. Astronomy and telescopes were flourishing by then and so these outbursts were opportune and well recorded. The 1572 supernova shone as bright as Venus (brighter than anything apart from the Moon). The 1604 one was somewhat dimmer, shining as bright as Jupiter – still a fine sight. Since then we had had nothing for nearly 400 years until February 1987 when a supernova visible to the naked eye burst into prominence.

Actually the violence really took place 170,000 years ago in the Large Magellanic Cloud, a satellite galaxy of ours that is visible in the southern hemisphere. A flash of light, brighter than 1 billion suns, and a blast wave of neutrinos flew out from the debris. Travelling 10 million miles each minute they raced out from the site, left the galaxy and headed out across intergalactic space, their 1987 rendezvous still far in the future.

Ahead of them lay the large Milky Way, within which one insignificant star, the Sun, was orbited by a lump of rock on which molecules had organised into life. The most advanced of these life forms were humans who had progressed to the Stone Age.

The shell of radiation travelled onward, while on Earth humans procreated and discovered science. In the 1930s they came to realize that radioactive processes spawn neutrinos, but scientists doubted that anyone would ever be able to catch one, so feeble are the interactions between neutrinos and matter.

Meanwhile the wave from the collapsed star came inexorably on and was approaching the Earth through the southern heavens. Slightly more than 30 light years ahead of it two American scientists cleverly managed for the first time to prove that neutrinos exist by capturing a few that had been emitted by a nuclear pile. That was in 1956, since when the study of neutrinos has become routine, yet even now we don't know if they weigh anything or not.

The blast wave was some 15 light years away when Ray Davis started operating his solar neutrino detector in the Dakota mine. Although ideal for catching the breeze of solar neutrinos it is almost blind to the neutrinos coming from the supernova.

A few years ago, however, some physicists began building apparatus underground that had nothing to do with supernovae or neutrinos but which has turned out to be eminently useful as a neutrino telescope. Their hope was to find evidence of decaying protons – the whisper of a dying universe (more about this in chapter 11). To capture such a rare event it is necessary to hide far below ground where the earth above one's head acts as a blanket against the incessant bombardment of cosmic rays. Very little can penetrate to the bottom of the deep mines in which the apparatus is contained; neutrinos can though.

In these caverns scientists have constructed vast swimming pools filled with thousands of tonnes of water. If a large number of neutrinos pass through there is the chance that one or two might interact with atoms in the water and give their presence away. On 23 February 1987 the neutrinos from the exploded star, having travelled for 170,000 years, passed through the Earth onwards into space. As they did, a handful were captured in the water tanks.

The supernova has been seen shining as bright as the entire Magellanic Cloud, and is the first major supernova since the invention of the optical telescope. And for the first time in history humans have detected the explosion of a star in neutrinos. This proves that the astrophysicists were right all along about the way stars collapse, and adds to our confidence that we understand a great detail about what is going on 'out there'.

Go to the hot desert at high noon in summer and you will feel the scorching furnace of the Sun – 100 million miles away. After a few hours you will suffer from severe sunburn – the first stage of radiation damage from exposure to a distant nuclear blast. Now imagine all that power accumulating for aeons and then suddenly shot at you in an instant. If something like this occurred near the Earth, we would be utterly annihilated. The supernova was close enough to be invaluable for science, but remote enough to be no danger to us, though we will never know what other civilisations may have been destroyed within its immediate vicinity 170,000 years past.

We can survive the billion-sun supernova if the outburst is more than 50 light years away. The nearest star to the Sun is 4 light years away, though stars are on average 1 light year apart. Thankfully there are not that many stars around in the danger zone. At most one or two are likely 'future' supernovae.

Present theory implies that supernovae occur for stars that are much bulkier than the Sun. Such stars are bright; you can't miss them. You can see an example on most clear nights wherever you live. On the left shoulder of the constellation Orion is bright red Betelgeuse. This shines like a ruby and promises to be a wonderful sight should it explode; it is 650 light years away and will cause us no problem.

142

We do not know what other civilisations may have been destroyed, or are currently threatened by supernovae. We appear to be safe, so long as our understanding of stellar workings is correct.

Countdown

The blast on 23 February 1987 was preordained, an unstoppable sequence of events programmed millions of years before. Hydrogen burned to helium, like in our own Sun, but with ten times the mass of the Sun the core heated up to 150 million degrees, at which point helium nuclei combined to build carbon, neon and silicon. Our Sun can burn for 5 billion years more but the onset of heavy elements in the more massive star means that by this stage its death is less than a year away.

The temperature of the core is a staggering 2 billion degrees as the silicon squeezes together building up iron until the heat is like 1,000 of our suns condensed in a single star.

Iron is the most tightly bound of all atomic nuclei. It can't fuse spontaneously into heavier elements as that would consume energy instead of liberating it, and so the fusion fire goes out in the iron core. The star has less than three days left. If we could have looked inside the distant star in 1987 we would have seen the beginning of the iron core on 20 February. The silicon fusion rapidly uses up the reserves until the iron is about 50 per cent more massive again than our Sun. The star is configured like an onion skin with a dense central iron core surrounded by burning layers of silicon, oxygen, neon then carbon and finally helium and hydrogen. It no longer makes enough energy to support its enormous weight and it starts to collapse under gravity. It has less than $1/5$ second to live.

A lot happens in that brief moment as the implosion begins.

The core collapses at up to one-quarter the speed of light and shrinks from a diameter of about half the Earth to only 6 miles. Its matter is shattered into its basic constituents – protons, neutrons and electrons – and is three to five times denser than an ordinary atomic nucleus. This is very unstable and the inner core bounces back, doubling or tripling in size, sending a shock wave at over 10,000 miles per second into the outer layers which are still rushing inwards. The shock wave has more energy than an entire galaxy puts out in a year.

The blast changes some of the nuclei in the outer reaches into heavy forms, leaping the iron barrier and producing elements as heavy as lead and uranium, and also some indium. It ejects them into deep space, polluting the universe with a mix of elements, perhaps the seeds of future life forms. The seeds of our atoms were formed in such blasts more than 5 billion years ago.

This has all taken place in less than 1 second. In the next 4 seconds the inner core emits a burst of neutrinos – as detected here on 23 February 1987 – as all its nuclear material turns into neutrons. It is in effect a huge atomic nucleus containing 10^{57} neutrons.

The shock wave, meanwhile, travels on outwards and exits the outer surface after about an hour. Previously hidden from view by the opaque outer surroundings, now the energy of the shock is unleashed as light. This is first ultra-violet and then the full flash of visible light that has historically been the famous sign of the supernova star.

This is now visible in southern skies and was the sight that Ian Shelton, a Canadian astronomer working at an observatory high in the Andes, first photographed and was thereby credited with the discovery. What is new this time is that we can see with other eyes: underground detectors captured some of the neutrinos produced from the collapse.

Although astrophysicists agree about the general scenario of the collapse, there is still much argument about the detailed mechanism for ejection of the outer regions of the star. These uncertainties limit the amount of information that we can deduce about neutrinos coming from the supernova. They poured through the detectors in a span of less than 10 seconds. At first many people argued that this implied a small but non-zero value for the neutrino mass: a spread of 10 seconds after 170,000 years' travelling limits their relative speed and hence mass *if* one assumes that they come out instantaneously. However, the theorists are now less certain about this. The 10-second spread might be due to the intrinsic duration of the neutrino emission, in which case they

144

all got here at the speed of light, which is only possible if they are massless. At the other extreme one can imagine possible, if unlikely, scenarios where slow neutrinos come out first and the fast ones later; the fast ones then gradually catch up with the slow ones during the 170,000 year journey.

More papers have been written than neutrinos have arrived! The major differences among them have been the assumptions about the details of the neutrino production in the supernova. The most general conclusion is that the (electron type) neutrino has a mass less than or comparable to the maximum currently allowed by laboratory experiments (which involve radioactive decay of tritium and the indirect study of the neutrino that implicitly emerges in this process).

So a major question being debated is: what are the details of the stellar collapse that produces the hordes of neutrinos?

When a star like this collapses some 10^{57} positively charged protons merge with negatively charged electrons, neutralising their electrical charges to form neutrons, which are massive and remain to form the neutron star, and neutrinos, which fly off. This happens in less than 1 millisecond (1/1000 second), effectively instantaneously. This is dramatic and sudden to be sure, but these neutrinos carry off less than 10 per cent of the energy. The remainder come from processes occurring in the hot conditions, such as electrons meeting and annihilating with antimatter counterparts, 'positrons' (identical to electrons in all respects but for positive electrical effects in place of negative). This annihilation emits neutrinos and antineutrinos (the antimatter counterparts of neutrinos). More than half of the neutrino and antineutrino emission occurs in the first second and the rest comes out over the next tens of seconds as the newborn neutron star cools down into the familiar cold neutron star or 'pulsar'.

The detectors on Earth are sensitive to the arrival of the *antineutrinos*, but are almost blind to the neutrinos. Now the millisecond burst produces only neutrinos and these aren't seen on Earth; we only capture the antineutrinos emerging during the next *tens* of seconds. Hence, in part, the difficulty in learning much about the (anti)neutrino masses from the span in their arrival times

– it could well tell us more about the relative times of their production than about their flight.

There have also been some puzzles, so far not totally resolved, in that a 'small' ('only' 90 tonnes) detector under Mont Blanc responded differently to the burst than did larger, 1,000 tonne, detectors in Japan and the USA. The Mont Blanc detector was designed to detect antineutrinos from collapses in our galaxy, not from more remote sources like the Large Magellanic Cloud. The huge detectors in Japan and USA were designed for quite different physics, namely the search for signs of decaying protons, and their suitability for extragalactic neutrino astronomy has turned out to be a serendipitous bonus.

The discovery proves that our theories of stars are right – stars can and do collapse and change into neutron stars. Previously this was a conjecture with circumstantial evidence, but capturing the neutrinos from the blast is like a smoking gun – we have caught Nature at it.

There is much excitement at the prospects for the future of neutrino astronomy. The supernova occurred in another galaxy, at least six times more remote than anything in our own. So when a supernova occurs in our galaxy we should in future detect the neutrino blast with ease.

Supernovae are not that rare. Astronomers detect them in distant galaxies regularly. In our own galaxy, a supernova occurs on average every 20 years or so. The galaxy is a huge place and we are forced to look across it, rather than in from the outside where the view would be clearer. The chances are that the supernova is hidden from view by dust and other stars, or too distant for the naked eye to see. Only occasionally does one occur in full view. It is as if we are in the middle of a cosmic minefield, with explosions going off all around but so far, thankfully, not too near us.

Figure 9.1 shows the sites of those seen in our galaxy in the last millennium; we are long overdue for another visible one. However, the galaxy is rather transparent to neutrinos, so neutrino bursts from 'local' supernovae should reach us even if the light doesn't. And now we will be able to see those neutrinos – the observation of neutrinos from the Large Magellanic Cloud proves that we can do

146

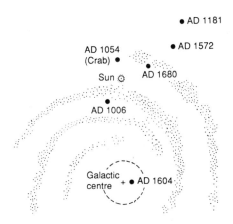

9.1 Supernovae in the Milky Way Location of supernovae in our galaxy relative to the Sun, spiral arms and galactic centre. There have probably been many more than these but obscured from view.

it. All we have to do is wait, and as the source of a signal in our galaxy is much nearer than the Large Magellanic Cloud so it should be much bigger. The message is that if a star collapses *anywhere* in our galaxy then, regardless of the luminous visibility of the supernova, we should observe it by its neutrinos.

Within a human lifespan we expect three or four such occurrences. With luck we will have the first by the end of the century and then we will learn in detail what happens when stars collapse. Meanwhile we watch the development of the new supernova with interest.

Moreover, now we can see if our theory of neutron stars is right. For as the shock wave rushes out into space it will thin and reveal the neutron star that we believe has been formed at the centre. Possibly, if enough mass is concentrated there, it will have collapsed further and become a black hole. We will know the answer in a few years; all we have to do is be patient.

Did a Supernova Kill the Dinosaurs?

According to current wisdom there do not appear to be any candidates for future supernova bursts in our immediate neighbourhood. Maybe this is because all suitable candidates have already erupted. There is some evidence that a supernova 5 billion years ago caused the formation of the solar system. Did a more recent blast kill the dinosaurs?

We know how elements are cooked in stars and so can calculate how much iridium should be ejected in an average supernova blast. In Chapter 5 we learned how Luiz Alvarez measured the amount of iridium in the Italian boundary layer between the Cretaceous and Tertiary geological strata. From this one can deduce how much was deposited worldwide. It is a vast amount, so much in fact that if it came from a distant supernova then that star must have been very near, at most 0.1 light years distant (the nearest known star of any sort currently is 4 light years away).

The chance that a supernova explosion occurred so near to us within even 100 million years is less than one in a billion. With such a low probability a nearby supernova is a one-off event. It either happened or it didn't. There are experimental tests that you can do and they prove that it didn't.

The trick is to use the fact that not all atoms of a given element are alike. Electrically neutral atoms contain electricity within them. Negatively charged electrons whirl around a positively charged compact nucleus containing positively charged protons. A single proton has as much positive charge as an electron has negative charge. So neutral atoms contain the same number of electrons as protons. It is this number that determines the chemical character, identifies which element it is. Thus hydrogen, the simplest, contains one electron and one proton. Helium, the next simplest, contains two electrons, while uranium contains 92.

A compact nucleus containing many positively charged protons would be highly unstable: 'like charges repel'. Nuclei survive because of a stabilising agent – electrically neutral particles called neutrons. Atomic nuclei contain protons and neutrons. Adding neutrons to a nucleus changes its mass but does not change the chemical identity. For example, U-235 and U-238 are two 'isotopes' of uranium; each contains 92 protons – the identifier of uranium – but they have different numbers of neutrons in their nuclei. U-235 contains 143 neutrons (making a total 235 of neutrons and protons), while U-238 contains 146 neutrons and so 238 neutrons and protons.

When elements are cooked in stars neutrons and protons are fusing together to form the nuclear seeds of atoms. A star will produce several different isotopes of any given element, the actual mix depending on the conditions within the star. Neutron stars, as their names suggest, provide copious neutrons and easily form heavy isotopes rich in neutrons. Highly evolved stars, on the other hand, tend to provide fewer neutrons and so the mix of isotopes is different. Astrophysicists can predict what abundance of elements and what mix of isotopes should result from various types of star, in particular a supernova.

A supernova explosion should send out iridium and also plutonium. There's plenty of iridium in the boundary clays, as Alvarez found, but no traces of plutonium at all. This was the first hint that a supernova was not the cause.

Iridium has two stable isotopes, iridium 191 and 193. Different supernovae will produce these two isotopes in different relative amounts. The solar system was formed from a primaeval gas cloud that was fuelled by the explosions of countless supernovae and the overall mix ended up with about twice as much of the 193 isotope as the 191.

Alvarez had discovered that the amount of iridium increased dramatically when he compared the boundary layer and the other rocks (page 66). Yet the ratio of the two isotopes is the same in both. A modern supernova would eject its own particular ratio of the iridium isotopes, which would be most unlikely to coincide with the particular value that the solar system contains. The two to one mix is the fingerprint of material from the solar system.

So although there are still arguments as to whether it was earthly or extraterrestrial, there are some things that we can be sure of. The disaster was not caused by a collision with some nearby star as we passed through the galaxy's spiral arms, nor was it due to a supernova.

10

A Universe of Galaxies

How Far Is It to Betelgeuse?

On a small lump of rock orbiting an insignificant star groupings of molecules have organised themselves in such a way that they have consciousness. They are aware of the awful gulf that separates them from the nearest star, the constellations and remote galaxies. Peering out from under a blanket of air they can measure how far away are those fellow partners in the ultimate joke. To be able to determine the make-up of those distant lights is one of the great accomplishments of human culture.

The ancient Greeks knew of the Milky Way but not what it consisted of. Not until the seventeenth century, when Galileo turned his telescope at it, did it reveal itself as millions of stars and misty patches or 'nebula'. Nebulae look similar to comets at first glance, so much so that many people thought they had seen Halley's comet in 1986 when in fact they had been gazing at nearby nebulae. Charles Messier in 1771 listed over 100 nebulae so that comet hunters wouldn't be confused by them. They are named after him, listed M (for Messier) in his catalogue – M1 (the Crab Nebula), M2, M3 and so on, like British motorways.

But what are nebulae?

Most people at that time thought that the nebulae were gas and dust in our neighbourhood. The philosopher Immanuel Kant, however, thought differently. He suggested that some of the nebulae are in the Milky Way but that others, like the beautiful spiral ones, are distant clusters of stars like our own. Nobody took

150

much notice, not least because there was no way of testing his idea at the time. The first key to unravelling the universe came with the invention of the spectroscope. This split light into colours, like a prism but so fine that the Sun's spectrum, for example, was seen to be interlaced with hundreds of black lines. In the laboratory scientists discovered that each chemical element, when heated, gave out a tell-tale light, which a spectroscope analysed like a detective reading a fingerprint. Comparing the laboratory spectrum with that from the Sun revealed that the Sun contained hydrogen, iron and sodium along with other elements. Suddenly the dream of the ages became reality: we could tell what stars are made of.

William Huggins – a wealthy London chemist and keen astronomer – analysed the light of many stars in the mid-nineteenth century and then started on the nebulae. He found two types. Some were gas but others had spectra like the Sun, suggesting that they consisted of stars.

Now the problem was whether the stellar nebulae are inside or without our galaxy. Astronomers in the nineteenth century had little idea of how far away the stars are.

We know how far away the Sun is (p. 24); a ray of light makes it in just over 8 minutes. This mean distance to the Sun is called an 'astronomical unit' and is the baseline for measuring the distance to nearby stars. In six months' time the Earth will be on the opposite side of the Sun. It will be *two* astronomical units of distance away from its present position.

The view you have of the stars today and in another six months will be slightly different. As your left and right eyes in combination give you binocular vision and a sense of distance, so does the six-month interval give you a 'left'- and 'right'-eyed view of the stars. Nearby stars will be displaced by parallax relative to the more distant ones. Knowing how far the baseline is between January and July we can determine how far away a star is by its slight movement against the background (see Figure 10.1).

Our nearest stellar neighbours are Proxima Centauri and its more brilliant neighbour Alpha Centauri, visible in the southern hemisphere. The amount of parallax shows that Alpha Centauri is

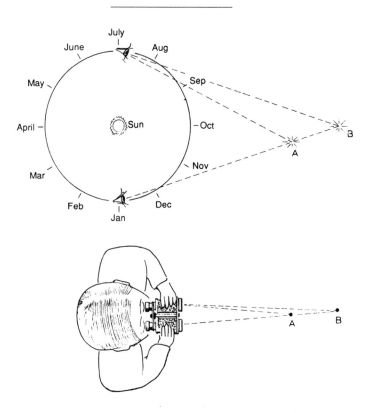

10.1   Binocular vision and parallax   The human's right eye sees object A and B aligned whereas the left eye sees them separated. This parallax enables us to deduce that B is more remote.

   The Earth orbits the Sun. In January, stars A and B are aligned ('right eye'); in July, we have the 'left eye' view and can tell that star B is more remote than star A.

275,000 times more remote than the Sun. A flight in Concorde would take 2 *million* years; light takes 4½ years. To express the distance in miles would be incomprehensible, so instead we say that it is 4½ light years distant.

   We want to know not only where stars are 'now' but where they are moving, for things will not always be as we find them today. A star's motion can be broken down into two components – the 'radial motion' along the line of sight and the 'proper motion' at right angles to the line of sight.

   The radial velocity is found by measuring the spectrum of light from the star, deducing what elements are giving the characteristic

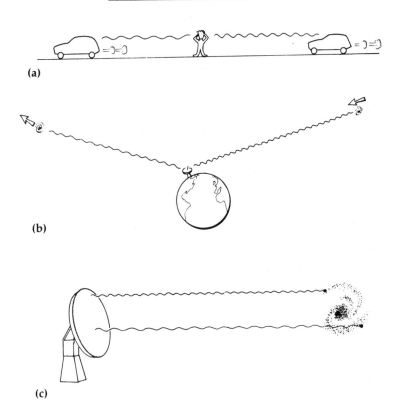

10.2 The Doppler shift (a) Car siren rushing towards or away from the listener appears to have higher or lower pitch respectively.

(b) Similarly a shift occurs in the colour of light. The galaxy on the right is approaching and its light waves are compressed – blue shifted. The one on the left is receding. Its light is stretched out to the red.

(c) A telescope can even detect the rotation of a galaxy from the different red or blue shifts of the spectrum of light coming from stars in different parts of the spiral.

colours and then comparing with the spectra that such elements give on Earth. The wavelength of the spectral light is Doppler shifted in a similar manner to the familiar shift in the pitch of sound as a car horn wails coming towards you, and dips as it departs: the spectrum of light is shifted to the red for a departing star and towards the blue as it approaches (see Figure 10.2). Radial velocities can be measured accurately for stars and entire galaxies out to the remotest reaches of the cosmos.

To measure the proper motion requires decades of careful

observation, comparing pictures of the star relative to the deep background. This is so subtle an effect that only the nearest stars show up a detectable proper motion. Stars more distant than 20 or 30 light years are too remote to show any motion against the background or any parallax as the Earth orbits the Sun; the third dimension is lost. A bright star or the Andromeda Nebula could be as far as 1 million light years and intrinsically blindingly radiant, or relatively faint and only 100 light years away.

So at the end of the nineteenth century astronomers spent their time collecting stars like stamps, recording spectra and colours. At Harvard, Henrietta Leavitt was collecting data on variable stars – ones that dim and brighten regularly. Some of these are very noticeable and go through their cycle in a few hours, days or weeks. The first one to be found was in the constellation Cepheus and so they have been collectively known as Cepheid variables even though they occur throughout the sky.

Leavitt discovered that the *brighter* the Cepheid, the *longer* it took to go through its cycle. She found this because by chance many of the Cepheids that she was looking at were in the Magellanic Clouds – the two satellite galaxies of our own Milky Way. The clouds are 150,000 light years away so all of their Cepheids are equally distant from us, give or take a few per cent. Confusing differences in brightness caused by varying distance (the plague of stars in our galaxy) were washed out. So Leavitt was able to show that the time that Cepheid took to go through its cycle tells its intrinsic brightness. Comparison with apparent brightness reveals its true distance.

Astronomers measured the Sun's drift among its fellow stars and managed to estimate the distance to nearby Cepheids. This gave an absolute distance scale and at last the third dimension had been added. At short distances parallax was the answer; further out the Cepheids provide the yardstick.

Now we come to the first decade of this century and meet Harlow Shapley at the Mount Wilson Observatory in California, housing what was then the world's largest telescope with a 60 inch diameter mirror. He was looking at Cepheid variables which are rather common in globular clusters – groups of as many as 100,000 stars of amazing beauty. Shapley collated data on the Cepheids in them and then began to map out a three-dimensional impression of the globular clusters in the galaxy.

Over 100 globular clusters are visible from the Earth. In a dozen of the closer ones he identified Cepheids and measured distances. In some of these nearby globulars he isolated bright red giants and supergiants and systematically compared their apparent brightness with that of the Cepheids. Soon he had gathered enough data to gain a feel for the intrinsic brightness or 'absolute magnitude' of these giant stars.

In distant globular clusters the bright giants are about all you can see; the Cepheids are too faint to study. But with these giants as 'standard candles', reference scales of brightness, Shapley began to chart the distances of globular clusters deeper into the galaxy.

By 1920 he had a three-dimensional map of the globular clusters. What it showed astonished him.

The globular clusters aren't spread out randomly around the Milky Way. They are concentrated in a vast sphere as if they are components of a 'super globular'. The centre of this sphere is 30,000 light years from us in the direction of the constellation Sagittarius. Shapley made an inspired guess: the centre of the globular sphere is the centre of our stellar system, the Milky Way. Ptolemy had put the Earth at the centre of the heavenly sphere; in 1543 Nicolaus Copernicus had overthrown this and proposed that the Earth orbits around a central Sun. Now Shapley suggested that the Sun isn't at the centre of the galaxy but is instead far out in the remote suburbs. Once it has been suggested it becomes almost obvious. Compare the Milky Way viewed from northern and southern skies. It is relatively faint when we look out in North America and Europe, but in South America and Australia you see rich brightness as you look through 90 per cent of the disc and into the heart towards Sagittarius.

One thing that Shapley overlooked was the dimming effect of interstellar dust. He thought that dimness was due to remoteness and estimated that the galaxy is 200,000 light years in extent. In reality it is smaller, nearer 100,000 light years; the dimness is due to the fog. It was probably because of this overestimate that he failed to discover that ours is but one in a family of galaxies. The Magellanic Clouds are satellite galaxies of the Milky Way 150,000 light years away – 50 per cent more than the extent of the parent galaxy. Shapley's overestimate of the Milky Way's size had the Magellanic Clouds inside rather than separate entities.

The discovery of a Universe of galaxies was made by Edwin Hubble working at the new 100 inch diameter telescope at Mount Wilson in the 1920s. With this he was able to resolve spiral nebulae, like Andromeda, into stars. The proof that they were galaxies came when he was able to photograph 50 Cepheid variable stars in a galaxy visible in southern skies and deduced that it was several hundred thousand light years away. This was so far away, several times more remote than a voyage across our entire galaxy, that Hubble was relieved to discover that deep in the cosmos the same physical laws were at work. This enabled him to carry on outward.

The two largest spiral nebulae visible from the Earth are Andromeda and M33. M33 is oriented face on to us and Hubble photographed it with the 100 inch telescope over two years. He resolved it into stars and identified 35 Cepheid variables. In February 1926 he wrote his report: M33 is 2.4 million light years away. This was far out compared to anything previously known. Without doubt it was a spiral galaxy separate from our own. And at Christmas in 1928 he published a paper on what he had discovered about Andromeda. The million light year barrier had been crossed. So for the first time, and within the memory of senior citizens still alive today, human culture had identified its place within the cosmos; the Universe is divided into galaxies separated by vast spaces void of stars.

It had taken a long time to get from the Earth as centre of the Universe, to us orbiting the Sun in a remote corner of the galaxy. And now it is no longer *the* galaxy but *a* galaxy; one of a billion stars in one of a billion galaxies.

Once Hubble had realised that the Universe is built of island galaxies in the vast sea of space he quickly discovered that the Universe is expanding, evolving in time, that the galaxies are rushing away from one another.

This is an insight of truly cosmic significance for it teaches us about the origins of the Universe. If the Universe is expanding then imagine stopping the clock and playing the film in reverse. In the past everything must have been much closer than it is now. About 10–20 billion years ago all of the material in the Universe must have been crammed into a volume smaller than a clenched fist. The explosion out from this dense ball is called the 'Big Bang'. Genesis occurred in an explosion 20 billion years ago and has been expanding ever since. None of this was known; then Hubble knew it and now it is part of human wisdom.

He came upon this by accident. Initially he had wanted to know how fast the Sun is moving around the galaxy. If you are on a roundabout you can tell how fast you're moving by looking fixedly at distant reference points. Use distant galaxies as the fixed references and see if the Sun is moving towards, away or across them, then work out the carousel.

A few nearby galaxies showed the random motion expected. More dramatic was a marked tendency for distant galaxies to be rushing away, and faster the more distant they are from us. Hubble worked out their speed by breaking down their light with a spectroscope and seeing how much it was shifted compared to the catalogue of colour-fingerprints that was by then well known.

Hubble charted clusters of galaxies deep into space and by 1934 improved photographic materials enabled him to take pictures of galaxies that were like dots, more numerous than the foreground stars. Hubble and his team found distant galaxies that are rushing away at one seventh the speed of light. The current record is held by galaxies so remote that their light has been travelling across space for 10 billion years until some of it chanced upon a telescope on an insignificant planet. When we look at such images we are looking back towards the start of the Universe.

The question that this raises is whether the Universe will continue to expand or whether it will eventually collapse under its own weight. That is a question currently taxing the cosmologists and also particle physicists who recreate the violent conditions of the early universe in earthbound laboratories.

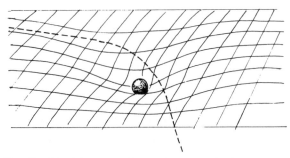

10.3 Gravity warping space–time A massive body warps space and time. The dashed line shows the path that a ball rolling across this imaginary space–time surface would follow. The deflection around the warp is interpreted as resulting from the force of gravity.

The End of the Universe as We Know It

Albert Einstein made a blunder when he wrote down his general theory of relativity – the theory of gravity that superseded Isaac Newton's great seventeenth-century work. Einstein got everything right but for one thing.

In Einstein's theory of gravity, space and time are subtly intertwined. He viewed space as warped by the presence of things; when we meet a twist it tips us off our straight path. The apparent shove is what we call the force of gravity. Step off a high bridge and it is the spacewarp caused by the Earth that pulls you down.

An old analogy may help. We live in three dimensions but suppose that it were two – that we were 'flatlanders'. Represent this by a taut two-dimensional rubber sheet. If you drop a pea on it, it will make a small depression; a heavy ball will make a deep warp in the elastic sheet. Roll a ball across the sheet and it will curve around the warp. A flatlander would say that a force – 'gravity' – attracted it. We, with our greater vision, say that it is the warped space that was responsible – the warping caused by the object's mass.

In the real universe, space appears three-dimensional and masses – the Earth, Sun and galaxies – warp space in a fourth dimension. This may be hard to visualise; in fact it is even harder! Einstein says space AND time are warped. The Sun bent space around it and we are circling in this warp.

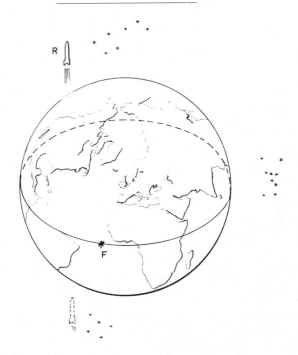

10.4 Round trips in higher dimensions Flatlander F can experience only two dimensions, circles the globe and finds itself back at the starting point!

The rocket ship R contains intelligence – we know of 3D. We set off north towards the northern stars, eventually to return via the Southern Cross having circumnavigated the universe – curved in the fourth dimension.

Massive objects warp space more – galaxies warp it more than you or I do. But how is space-time warped on the scale of the whole Universe? The long-term future of the Universe depends on the answer to this.

This is where Einstein made his blunder.

At the beginning of the century astronomical data were much more sparse than today and of poor quality. They appeared to suggest that the Universe is static, permanent and unchanging. Einstein's theory, however, implied that the Universe is evolving. This conflict worried him and so he introduced an extra piece (known as the 'cosmological constant') into his equation to fit with what Nature seemed to require. Present data show that it is not needed. The Universe *is* expanding and if Einstein hadn't tinkered

159

with his pristine theory he might have discovered this for himself. In fact it was not until 1922 that a Soviet mathematician named Alexander Friedman showed that the Universe is evolving and is either 'open' or 'closed'.

A 'closed' universe is like a huge self-contained black hole. There is so much mass within it that space is curved right back on itself. If this is hard to imagine, think of the two-dimensional analogue again: space is like a sphere, in which the flatlander will crawl off eastwards and circumnavigate the globe. In the real universe, head off from the North pole towards the pole star, circumnavigate the cosmos and return to Earth from the direction of the Southern Cross. In other words the Universe is finite; if there is an 'outside' or 'beyond', we cannot reach it. In the 'open' universe, by contrast, space curves away gently forever. The two-dimensional analogue is a saddle.

Which do we live in? We don't know. It depends on the average density of matter throughout space. If it is more than a critical amount, the universe is closed; less, and it is open. Einstein's theory allows no other possibility. Some theories of the Big Bang (the so-called 'inflationary universe') require that the density is exactly equal to the critical amount. If we could detect all the forms of matter in the heavens we could predict whether the universe will collapse or expand for ever. But there is a lot of stuff too dark to see and the big question today concerns the nature and abundance of this 'dark matter'. The modern 'superstring theory' (Chapter 12) suggests that there could be an entire dark universe operating in parallel with our own! We need to know if this dark stuff is there or not. How can we hope to see 'invisible' stars?

What Is Hiding in the Dark?

Go around a corner too fast and you will leave the road. Rush around the Sun or the galaxy too fast and you will spin off into deep space. Planets feel less gravitational pull the further away they are from the Sun, and their speed in perpetual orbit is correspondingly less. Each of us has settled at a speed such that we fall in and centrifuge out in balance.

When we look at spiral galaxies, however, the stars appear to rotate too fast to survive; the visible stars do not have enough mass to hold the systems together by gravity – yet survive they do.

Clusters of galaxies move around one another. Here again they move too fast and yet manage to continue in their cosmic dance. Something else must be holding them together – a ubiquitous ectoplasm too dark to see, permeating the galaxies, utterly invisible and with enormous mass. No one yet knows what this stuff is but astronomers are certain that it is there. The galactic dance shows what tune Nature is playing and there is more in the orchestra than we have detected so far.

Roughly 90 per cent of the mass of the Universe must be made up of this dark matter. The ordinary visible matter, shining in the heavens, picked up in X-rays, infra-red and radio telescopes, is a flotsam in a sea of invisible stuff. The dark matter is controlling the show.

There can't be much of it in our immediate neighbourhood because the planets orbit the Sun on schedule. However, it hasn't always been like this. The most famous successful prediction of dark matter was that of the planet Neptune. 150 years ago Uranus was the outermost known planet and its orbit didn't 'obey the rules'. In 1843 John Adams in England predicted that another unseen planet existed and told the astronomers where to look for it, but he was a young unknown and no one took much notice. Three years later Urbain Le Verrier in France independently had the same idea and a squabble ensued following Neptune's discovery that year as to who should get the credit.

The discovery of Neptune was a great success: the prediction of dark matter from its effects on the visible – like H. G. Wells' invisible man giving his presence away by jostling the crowd. Le Verrier tried to repeat his success in the case of the innermost planet Mercury. This too didn't obey the rules and Le Verrier suggested that there is another planet, which has been named Vulcan, near to the Sun. None has been found, and today we know that the cause of Mercury's anomaly is the failure of Newton's theory of gravity in strong gravitational fields like those near the Sun. In such circumstances Einstein's theory of general relativity applies instead and describes the orbit of Mercury perfectly.

Some physicists have tried to avoid dark matter altogether by suggesting that Newton's laws break down on the galactic scale, hence the 'anomalous' behaviour of the outer regions of galaxies. However, other physicists claim that this idea runs into problems with an empirical relation between the luminosity and velocity of galaxies. Current opinion tends not to favour this solution to the conundrum.

There may be a little dark matter about in the outer reaches of the solar system that is responsible for anomalies in Neptune's orbit. (As I remarked on page 48, tiny Pluto doesn't really fit the bill and Planet X, as yet unseen, is the favourite.) Incidentally, this is an amazing testimony to the precision of the measurement of Neptune's motion. Neptune orbits so slowly that since its discovery 150 years ago it has not yet completed an orbit!

The stars in distant galaxies behave as if the dark matter forms haloes on the periphery of the galaxies. Being immersed in our own dust-filled galaxy it is sometimes more difficult to learn about things in our own Milky Way than in remote galaxies where we can peer in from the outside, watching the whole scene. But we can get indirect hints by watching the dwarf galaxies, near neighbours of ours, and seeing how their stars behave – they are near enough to us to wallow in any dark halo that we may have.

These dwarf galaxies have as few as a few hundred thousand stars. They lie in a plane along with the Magellanic Clouds and our huge Milky Way, suggesting that we are all connected, the remnants of an original protogalaxy in the early Universe. These romantically named clumps – Sculptor, Draco, Carina and others – are so small that you would hardly notice them if you were looking in from Andromeda. So, in turn, if Andromeda has dwarf galaxies as small as these, we are unlikely ever to know much about them short of making a trip. This suggests that dwarf galaxies throughout the Universe could add up to a considerable amount of 'dark' matter.

Unfortunately, it is very difficult to see our own dwarf galaxies at all, let alone make precise measurements on their constituent stars. Some observers claim one thing, others another.

However, the great Milky Way and our giant neighbour Andromeda do seem to be misbehaving. We're rushing towards one another, closing at about 100 miles every second. Now we don't need to worry about this, as it will take several billion years for us to collide even if we are on collision course, but the fact we're doing this at all causes some concern.

It is possible that we are just like ships passing in the night; two great galaxies that are on independent journeys through the cosmos. But it seems rather a fluke if it is so. Given the immensity of space that either of us could have been in, these two galaxies seem to be connected, bound in mutual orbits around one another as are the planets around the Sun. If we have been inextricably linked since our formation in the post Big Bang, then we shouldn't be closing so fast. Lots of dark matter must be around to provide the extra tug; the dwarf galaxies alone are trifling.

The consensus is that dark matter abounds, but we are not sure about the details of how much of it there is and where. It is important to answer this question because the Universe is an expanding, ever-changing, living thing and it will be the dark matter that determines its eventual fate. If there is a lot of matter around, its gravitational pull will weigh the Universe down, slowing its outward flight to the point where it stops and collapses in a big crunch. If there is less than this critical amount then the Universe will expand forever, the stars and entire galaxies will exhaust their fuel, matter will erode away leaving only electrons and radiation. We cannot say with certainty which way things will turn out, because the Universe appears to be very close to the critical dividing line between collapse and continual expansion.

No one yet knows what this dark matter consists of. Astrophysicists have had to turn to particle physics for ideas. Neutrinos could be the answer. If the Universe began with a hot Big Bang, then theory predicts that there should be about 100 neutrinos in every cubic centimetre of space – 100 million times the density of protons, which provide most of the visible matter in the stars. The visible galaxies would be merely islands in a vast sea of neutrinos.

If neutrinos have a little mass they would have been moving at almost the speed of light during the first 10,000 years after the Big

Bang, rushing outwards with the expanding Universe. As the Universe cooled, the massive neutrinos would have started forming clusters under the influence of their mutual gravitational attraction. These conglomerations would have covered the entire Universe. Local instabilities within them would have formed the core of galactic clusters out of which individual galaxies condensed. In the jargon of astrophysics this scenario is called 'top down' because the small galaxies emerge from the large clusters. However, the galaxies in the real universe are more patchy than computer simulations of the top down mechanism would lead us to expect.

Modern theories of matter and the natural forces are remarkably successful in describing experiments performed with subatomic particles at particle accelerators. Indeed, many theorists have been encouraged to apply these ideas to phenomena at present out of reach of laboratory experiments but accessible elsewhere in the Universe. One example is that they make profound statements about the nature of the early universe in the hot Big Bang and the origins of matter in that epoch.

However, not everything is perfect. There are some technical mathematical problems that many theorists believe can be solved if massive particles, as yet undiscovered, exist. These have exotic names like axions, photinos, Higgs bosons and monopoles, and experiments are currently looking or being planned to search for them in the near future. Until we find proof that they exist these particles are just postulates – but if they are real then they will have been formed in the Big Bang along with the particles that eventually seeded our atoms. Although uncommon today they may have left fossil imprints in the way that the Universe developed.

Some of these particles are predicted to be much heavier than protons, thousands maybe billions of times so. Some may even be stable. In the first moments of the Big Bang when the Universe was unimaginably hot, much more so than in any star today, any massive particles would have flitted around like everything else. But the Universe cooled faster than a cup of coffee in Siberia; the massive particles froze still within seconds. As the other lighter particles clustered to build the galaxies, the stars and eventually the matter that we are familiar with today, their sluggish cousins would have gravitated together, forming conglomerates that may be in stars like our Sun or may be on their own. Indeed, one theory is that these bulky lumps were the seeds that ensnared the fast-moving lightweight electrons, neutrons and protons forming clusters on all scales, from clusters of stars to individual galaxies or groups of galaxies. The small ones would have developed first and then coalesced later into larger clusters. This is known as 'bottom up' and seems to be what the actual universe is like.

So the motion of stars within the galaxies suggests that there is unseen dark matter around. The distribution of the galaxies throughout the Universe seems to imply that this dark matter consists of massive particles not yet seen in experiments at the world's high-energy accelerator laboratories. The future not just of the Sun, but of the galaxies and the entire Universe depends on unknown forms of matter. The future of astrophysics and cosmology is coming to depend more and more on particle physics – the study of the basic constituents of matter.

Recent discoveries about the behaviour of these fundamental particles turn out to have surprising implications for the future of large-scale structures, including you and me.

Part IV

The Heart of the Matter

11

How Stable is Matter?

All the rivers, lakes and oceans froze with a 'great *vvarroomph*' as Kurt Vonnegut's mad scientist dropped some molecules of 'ice-nine' into a stream. Ice-nine was a (hypothetical) form of water, more stable than the familiar form, which froze at room temperature. In the story, ordinary water is metastable and changes into the stable form – ice-nine – when it encounters the minutest traces of it.

Put ice-nine in a whisky and soda and you would have instant scotch on the rocks; but don't drink it or the water in your body will immediately polymerise. If water were metastable then we would have a hazardous existence.

Thankfully that's science fiction. However, some theoretical physicists believe that the Universe might contain stuff similar to ice-nine, called 'strange matter', more stable than the stuff that we're made from. Atomic nuclei, the seeds of matter, are electrically charged and could attract strange matter like the north and south poles of two magnets grip one another. The stable strange matter would then devour conventional matter. Not just water but all atoms of everything would be vulnerable. Your world could literally collapse around you.

We are fairly confident about the Universe that we can see: we can reproduce details of it in the laboratory, watch it at work under controlled conditions, predict eclipses, build machines that can fly across space – all based on our understanding of the physical laws. We can look at the light coming from distant constellations and remote galaxies; the spectral fingerprints show that the same laws operate universally. We can even predict the death of stars, and when one does implode, as in the 1987 supernova, we can watch it and we find that it behaved as our theories implied it should. The message is that the visible Universe out there is made of the same varieties of particles as you and me, the ubiquitous electrons, protons and neutrons, but combined in different ways at different temperatures and pressures. This is a remarkable generalisation and must rank among the great achievements of the human intellect.

Having the basic ingredients available to us here on Earth, we can study them in the laboratory under conditions that they would encounter in the stars and see how they behave. We can even push them to temperatures prevalent in the first moments of the Universe's existence and learn about the origins of bulk matter. And when we do this we begin to see hints that the Universe that we know may be only a small part of the whole.

So far in this story we have been concentrating on the Universe in the large – the behaviour of bulk matter ranging from little stones in the meteor showers, through comets and asteroids, the life and death of stars and ultimately the collective motion of entire galaxies. As we have looked into these more closely we began to see hints that there are some gaps in our knowledge. What is going on deep inside the Sun? What is the dark matter that gives itself away by jostling the galaxies? Are these problems that are intellectually interesting but of no practical concern or might they pose hazards for us?

We met some suggestions as to what is going on. The particles called neutrinos coming from the Sun brought the message that something was untoward and the debate centres on whether it is the neutrinos that are themselves to blame or whether there are unknown massive particles, WIMPS, at the centre of the Sun. Maybe there are WIMPS throughout the cosmos and they are the dark matter. Whether this is the case or not remains to be seen but I'm recapitulating it here to bring out the change in direction that we are about to take in this tale. We are beginning to concentrate less on the bulk matter, more on the little particles that build it up. By watching neutrinos in the laboratory we hope to see if they behave anomalously or not, and hence whether they or something else is responsible for the solar neutrino problem. By smashing electrons or nuclear particles into each other, we can reproduce such concentrations of energy that it can congeal into new forms of matter, such as WIMPS if they exist. The basic particles of the Universe emerged from the intense heat of the Big Bang, and by recreating that heat in the laboratory we can see what Nature has on the menu.

Already there are tantalising and disturbing questions being raised as a result of this research. Are the basic particles stable or do protons decay, albeit very slowly, and thereby make the Universe erode inexorably? Space and time appear like a skeleton on which the living Universe evolves. Could space–time collapse? Could time stop and run backwards, jump about discontinuously, one region of space disconnect from another so that we became cut off, stranded on some huge cosmic analogue of a melting ice floe? We are all descendants from an initial Big Bang that erupted out of nothing, creating space and time with it; could this happen again within our present Universe? Why are there three spatial dimensions, or are there higher dimensions than those we are familiar with? Could they bubble up in your living room so that the familiar dimensions of up, forwards and sideways fragmented into some unimaginable foamy structure? Could there be other universes, unseen, operating in parallel with our own? Are there dark stars with their own planets in our immediate neighbourhood?

Many of these questions are currently being debated. A few years ago a list of questions like these would have been dismissed as no more than ideas for a science fiction novel. Today it is hard for the layman (and even many scientists) to tell which questions are clearly fictional and which are serious science. A paradoxical change is taking place at the moment. On the one hand we understand the Universe more deeply than ever in history, and have testable theories of how it emerged through to how it will die. Yet we are also becoming aware that the more we understand so the more bizarre are the possibilities for our ignorance. The Universe may indeed be stranger than we can ever know.

So we will now take a voyage into matter to see what it teaches about the fate of the Universe. Then we will look at the latest theories and learn of things that are stranger than science fiction.

The Core of the Cosmic Onion

The study of the Universe at large has been the province of astrophysicists, astronomers and cosmologists. They have concerned themselves with structures whose dimensions exceed light years in extent. At the other extreme we find the microscopic wonderland of crystals, molecules, atoms and subatomic particles. These so-called 'elementary particles' are the common building blocks of all known matter in the Universe. So to understand our origins and perhaps see clues to the ultimate fate of the Universe we need to study its smallest pieces.

Take a deep breath! You have just inhaled oxygen atoms that have already been breathed by every person who ever lived. At some time or other your body has contained atoms that were once part of Moses or Isaac Newton. The oxygen mixes with carbon atoms in your lungs and you exhale carbon dioxide molecules. Chemistry is at work. Plants will rearrange these atoms, converting carbon dioxide back to oxygen, and at some future date our descendants will breathe some in.

If atoms could speak, what a tale they would tell. Some of the carbon atoms in the ink on this page may have once been part of a dinosaur. Their atomic nuclei will have arrived in cosmic rays, having been fused from hydrogen and helium in distant, extinct, stars. But whatever their various histories, one thing is certain. Most of their basic constituents have existed since the primordial Big Bang at the start of time.

Atoms are the complex end-products of creation. Their basic constituents were created within the first seconds of the Big Bang. Several thousand years elapsed before these particles combined to make atoms. The cool conditions where atoms exist today are far removed from the intense heat of the Big Bang. So to learn about origins we have to see within the atoms, study the seeds of matter.

If you want to see what things are made from, you must look at them closely. You see things by shining radiation on them, such as light from the sun or a lamp bouncing off this page into your eyes. However closely you look you will not be able to see the carbon atoms in the ink of these letters. Magnify them as much as you like – it simply isn't possible.

The power of a microscope is not its ability to enlarge things; rather it is the ability to separate things that are very close together – its resolving power. To see atoms you must be able to separate one from the next. Visible light can't resolve distances smaller than about one-thousandth of a millimetre. There is a law of Nature which asserts that the smaller a thing is, the more energetic radiation you need to resolve it. I can't explain why it is this way – that is how Nature is. Visible light does not have enough energy to do the job.

This is where electron microscopes come in useful. By accelerating beams of electrons in a high voltage you can create a powerful enough radiation to resolve structures as small as atoms.

This is the world of high-energy particle accelerators, which reproduce the intense heat of stars in the laboratory and create feeble imitations of the Big Bang in small volumes of a few atomic dimensions. Huge machines, miles in length, accelerate pieces of atoms until these particles are moving near the speed of light. They then smash into atomic nuclei of material waiting at the end of the acclerator. These experiments show us the inner structure of the atomic nucleus in fine detail. We have identified the processes that fuel the stars as a result.

In 1967 at Stanford in California a 2 mile long accelerator of electrons began operation. Over 20 *billion* volts speed the electrons along an evacuated pipe. Starting their journey near the San Andreas fault, they dive under a freeway before emerging 2 miles distant into a huge hangar where concrete protects humans from the intense radiation. In the electrons' path sits a target of material whose inner details are about to be revealed.

The deep structure of matter is layered like an onion. Atoms consist of negatively charged electrons encircling a positively charged compact nucleus. The nucleus consists of positively charged protons and neutral neutrons.

The electron beam at Stanford is so powerful that it can reveal the fine details not just of atoms or of the atomic nucleus but of the

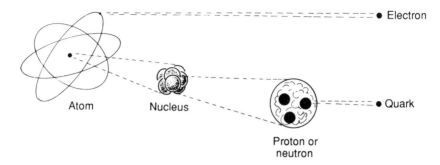

11.1 Structure of matter smaller than atoms Atoms consist of negatively charged electrons surrounding a positively charged compact nucleus. The nucleus is built from positively charged protons and electrically neutral neutrons which help to stabilise it. The protons and neutrons in turn are clusters of quarks. Present experiments have not found anything smaller than electrons and quarks and these are the currently accepted elementary particles of matter. The motion of electrons in the atomic periphery or the vibration of protons and neutrons in the nucleus can liberate energy in the form of light (photons) or electrically neutral neutrinos.

protons and neutrons that build up the nucleus. Here for the first time we could peer inside protons! And we found that these little particles have a detailed inner structure of their own. They are made of smaller pieces called 'quarks' (see Figure 11.1). (You can read the story of this voyage into matter and see pictures of the particles in *The Particle Explosion* listed in the Suggestions for Further Reading.)

To the best experimental accuracy yet available these quarks, along with electrons, appear to be the basic building stones of matter and were fashioned within one-billionth of a second of the Big Bang. They are the fossil relics of creation.

The discovery of the quark layer of reality may one day be perceived to be the crucial key in unlocking an entire new concept of the natural laws. It has changed the outlook in high-energy particle physics and made us realise that it teaches us not simply about the stuff of present matter, but also about its origins, *our* origins, in the Big Bang. It is making us aware of the possibility of new forms of matter that could pervade and disturb the Universe and suggests that the Universe could be a much more fragile thing than we had thought.

The Universe erupted from nowhere in the so-called Big Bang some 10–20 billion years ago. The matter that now fills the heavens, out beyond the limits where even the most powerful telescopes have yet peered, was in those first moments contained in so small a ball that you could imagine it all compressed within the dot at the end of this sentence.

Under these conditions everything would have been unimaginably hot. Heat has many forms, one of which is that the bits and pieces are all crashing into each other very violently. This is the sort of thing that the particle physicists are doing in the laboratory. By accelerating the basic particles of matter to high speeds, and then smashing them together, they are re-creating in the laboratory, in a small region of space, the sort of conditions that were present in the Universe in the moments following the Big Bang.

Ironically they are finding that it is relatively simple to describe the laws operating under these initial and extreme conditions. In the cool environment of the Earth a wide variety of phenomena occur and a whole variety of laws are required to describe them. But in the original hot Big Bang it seems that a uniformity existed, described by a single law. It is this discovery of a possible unified theory that is exciting the physicists at present and allowing them to work out models of the entire life of the Universe.

Every culture has had its favourite theory of the Universe; some of these are the foundations of whole religions. Bishop Usher even calculated the date and time in 4004 BC when, so he claimed, Genesis occurred. The important new feature in our modern theory is that it can be tested in the laboratory. If it fails, it is useless and must be discarded. So far it has stood up to the test. It may even be correct. This is what it portrays for our origins – and our future.

The Origin of Matter

The heat of the original Big Bang still survives, bathing the entire Universe in the dying embers of its glow. The Universe became transparent to this radiation some 700,000 years after the Big Bang. Since that time matter has been clumping together into stars and galaxies. Meanwhile the radiation has continued to expand and cool. It is now −270 degrees Centigrade, 3 degrees above absolute zero. This '3 degree microwave radiation' is the ambient temperature of the background Universe.

This radiation wafts on the particles of matter forming the large-scale structures in the heavens. These are built ultimately from electrons and quarks (the seeds of atomic nuclei), and little else, all of which fused in the initial heat of the Big Bang when the temperature was billions of degrees. Energy congealed into particles and antiparticles – entities with the same mass but opposite electrical charge to the corresponding particle. Thus the negatively charged electron was created along with its positively charged counterpart, the positron. Similarly quarks, which later clustered together forming protons and neutrons, were formed along with antiquarks (which make antiprotons and antineutrons). Electrons encircling protons and neutrons make the atoms of matter; positrons encircling antiprotons and antineutrons make up atoms of antimatter.

Here we meet one of the mysteries of Nature.

Gravity attracts everything inexorably to everything else. It holds our feet on the ground. That our bodies stay together, rather than falling in a pile of dust to the floor, is in part owing to the intense electrical forces within our atoms. The existence of bulk matter is the result of attractions between oppositely charged particles, in particular negatively charged electrons and positive protons in the neutral atoms.

It is an important fact of life that atoms containing the same number of electrons and protons are overall electrically neutral. The negative charge on the electron exactly balances the positive on the proton. But suppose Nature had switched the charges around such that the electrons were positive and the protons negatively charged. Atoms would still be neutral and bulk matter would appear exactly the same as it does in the real world. If we were made of this 'antimatter', physics would be identical to that in reality, where we are made of matter.

The heat of the Big Bang must have made particles and antiparticles in equal quantities – we can even reproduce the processes in the laboratory and photograph them. Matter and antimatter mutually annihilate when they meet, yet somehow an excess of matter survived this cataclysm. This now comprises the visible Universe.

If antimatter existed in bulk there would be an interface between regions of the Universe made of matter and regions made of antimatter. At this interface there will be violent annihilations going on continuously and intense bursts of gamma radiation emitted as a result. Astronomers could not fail to see these, yet none has been found. It seems that we are safe from one form of (literal) annihilation at least. Lumps of antimatter are unlikely to come raining down from the heavens, frying the Earth into gamma rays.

Here on Earth it is a slow process making large numbers of antiparticles. In several years at CERN, the European Centre for Nuclear Research in Geneva and the world leader in making antiparticles, they have made less than a billionth of a gram. So it would take several thousand years to make enough for a single antimatter bomb, even supposing you could preserve the antimatter that long in the hostile environment of matter all around it. So we can safely discount media stories of antimatter bombs – the so-called 'ultimate weapons'.

Where did all the antimatter go to?

Modern theories suggest an answer to this. While studying the behaviour of subatomic particles the physicists noticed that some particles known as 'kaons' appear to distinguish between matter and antimatter; the kaons of matter and those of antimatter behave in slightly different ways. Our understanding of this suggests that during the Big Bang the protons of matter were put together slightly faster than their antimatter images – the antiprotons. This has led to a net excess today – the galaxies of matter are the remnant of a *small* imbalance between particles and antiparticles. The Big Bang must have been very very big!

The theory of this implies that if protons were 'put together' in this way then they can also fall apart. Protons will be unstable.

Now, as the nuclei of every atom in our bodies contain protons, you might wonder how it is that we are still here. The answer is that the protons are *nearly* stable, their half life is predicted to be around 10^{32} years. This means that if you have a large collection of them, half will have decayed after that amount of time has elapsed. As the Universe has only been here for 10^{10} years – a mere ten-thousandth part of a billionth of a billionth of the proton's half life – most protons are still alive and well.

Even with this astonishing stability, physicists still hope to be able to test this theory and catch sight of the rare proton that dies before its time. In a large swimming pool filled with water there are so many protons – in excess of 10^{32} – that statistically one or two may decay in a year. Physicists have built huge tanks of water and surrounded them with detectors in the hope of catching the flash of light as a proton dies. The tanks are deep underground, away from stray influences such as the perpetual rain of atomic particles hitting the Earth's upper atmosphere which could mimic the flash of a decaying proton. There are tantalising hints but no clear evidence yet.

If they detect a decaying proton with certainty they will have gained the first sign that matter is eroding and hence seen the first glimpse of a dying Universe. In the century of your life, one or two protons may decay in your body, but you won't notice. In the deep future this erosion of the seeds of matter will become more notice-able. It is a cancer eating away at the fabric of the Universe.

If the Universe expands for long enough, then matter will begin to die off as the protons decay. However, if there is enough mass around then the Universe will slow and begin to collapse under its own weight. Either of these possibilities has consequences for our own survival prospects. The collapse into a hot rerun of the Big Bang, but in reverse, is a daunting prospect. The cool expansion into eternity with the constituents of matter eroding away looks bleak, but may be survivable!

Road to Eternity

In an open universe, or even a closed one if it lives long enough before the collapse begins, the ultimate demise of matter is a certainty. Even if protons are stable on a time-scale of 10^{32} years, they will eventually decay courtesy of the intervention of quantum mechanics. In a nutshell, quantum theory implies that if you wait long enough, anything will happen. In the case of the proton it implies that once in a blue moon a proton will spontaneously form a black hole and disappear. Blue moons occur on average every 10^{54} years – on the scale of eternity this is a small time-span.

As matter is certain to decay, we will have to change form if we are to survive. The matter that constitutes life as we know it will all die out and there will be nothing left to procreate succeeding generations. One possibility is that we discover a way of stopping or reversing the process. As this will require as yet unknown laws to be discovered, we have no idea if this is possible in principle and it is not realistic to speculate on it here.

These insights have come as a result of experiments concerned with the ultimate heat that was prevalent in the Big Bang. It is ironical that to describe the last moments of the Universe requires increasing understanding of the physical processes that governed its creation. Gravity, the framework of space and time, ruled at the outset and will step in when all else is gone.

In the first moments the heat produced a plasma of quarks, which rapidly clustered into the protons and neutrons that formed the nuclei of atoms when the temperature had cooled to a mere billion degrees. These conditions are still present in stars and have been accessible in experiments at particle accelerator laboratories for many years. These laboratory experiments have enabled us to study nuclear physics and learn about the stellar dynamics.

This symbiosis between nuclear physics in the lab and its natural realisation in stars was the first step in the unification of micro and macroscopic sciences that is currently in full swing.

Nature operates at the microscopic level and realises its aims by constructing macroscopic structures on which to play out its schemes. The human scale involves life operating at the level of cells, the chemistry of DNA working through on a large-scale host, the living being; we are complicated macromolecules. Stars are conglomerates of individual protons, neutrons and electrons working out their individual radioactive transmutations. The entire macro-universe is really a working through of beautiful fundamental interactions and laws at the atomic level, and even

beyond. The deeper we probe, so the richer becomes our awareness of the possibilities for exploitation.

We know enough about the ways that stars develop to be sure
that they will live only a fleeting existence in an everlasting
universe. The Universe is some 20 billion years old so far. In
another 20 billion years some new stars will have been born – many
are being fused in Orion's belt right now – others will die. Stars like
óur Sun will use up their supply of hydrogen fuel in another 5
billion years.

Of local concern to us is that the Sun will then contract, heat up
and expand to a red giant, evaporating the inner planets. The outgoing wind will vaporise the outer planets. The picture of the planetary nebula in the constellation Lyra shows what will remain of us.

It is to be hoped that by then we will have colonised a more
favourable planetary system, fuelled by a main sequence star. But
then the story will work through again there after another few
billion years.

This nomadic enterprise can go on for perhaps 50 billion years
as one after another 'new' main sequence stars come to their end.
After 100 billion years, however, real change is beginning to show.
Agoraphobics should quit now. The Universe has expanded so
much that galaxies are exceedingly remote. Our nearest neighbours are barely visible in even the largest telescopes. The content
of these galaxies is also changing. The stars are burning out and
nothing remains to replace them. Every star has used up its fusion
fuel and is collapsing under its own weight, a cold dark ball, a
spent fire.

Neutron stars – the remnants of heavier suns – are fairly rare;
most common are remnants of small stars – white dwarfs – balls of
electrons and spent nuclei that are the size of our present Earth.
There are black holes too; rarest of all but vastly exceeding those
today. Advanced civilisations may play Russian roulette living on
the edge of a black hole, tapping energy from it.

Some planetary systems survive. Charred remains of outer
planets could survive red giant eruptions. It depends very much
on what the planetary system consists of, and the size and distance
of the planets from their sun.

Wait long enough and even improbable events are certain. Dead stars pass close enough to one another that they will fail to hold on to their planets. The planets will detach and drift off freely through the void. Even galaxies will get pulled apart as they collide. Again, this is exceedingly rare but we've all the time in the Universe.

Some 90–99 per cent of the stars will evaporate from the galaxies and leave an homogeneous spattering of bits and pieces around the cosmos. The remaining 1–10 per cent will tug inwards and collect in the galactic centres, forming gigantic black holes. This will be what things are like after 10^{19} years – 1,000 million times longer than from the Big Bang to the present. At this time-scale neutron stars will be cooling to only 100 degrees above absolute zero – -173 degrees Centigrade. Any planets still orbiting will radiate gravitational waves and decay after 10^{20} years.

The microwave background radiation is within one ten-thousandth of a billionth of a degree above zero. The Universe is a forbidding vastness of nothing. No galaxies, only stars. Lonely stars devoid of planets. The one-time planets are themselves dead carcases outcast by gravity, roaming at random.

Aimless dead wanderers through the void. What is there left for the Universe?

The decaying protons begin to be felt a little. Enough are decaying and producing radiation that they provide a trickle of 'warmth' – a fraction of a degree above ultimate cold – and can keep the ambient temperature at this meagre level for another 10^{30} years. So there is a lot of localised warmth for our descendants to exploit. The composition of the Universe is 90 per cent dead stars, 9 per cent black holes and 1 per cent atomic hydrogen and helium.

Proton decay is now going on in earnest causing whole bodies to die out. Soon all carbon-based life forms become extinct as the carbon decays: diamonds are not forever!

The time-scale to this epoch compared to the present is as the present age of the Universe compared to a single heartbeat.

By that time our descendants will have to change into other forms. The carbon and other matter that make up *Homo sapiens* will all be dying away as the protons decay. No longer trapped by

Nature's choice materials, we must exploit natural laws to manufacture new forms and utilise what remains. Discoveries in particle physics will be put to work; new opportunities may emerge for changing the very fabric of our Universe.

If we do not manage to make new forms of matter, the end-result of decaying protons will be a Universe containing electrons, positrons, neutrinos and photons. These will be our basic toolkit for survival. Freeman Dyson has some ingenious ideas on the continuation of life and information even in these extreme circumstances (see Chapter 13).

The distance between each electron and positron will be greater than the present diameter of the Milky Way. The Universe will be 100 million trillion (10^{20}) times larger than it is now. Even this is not the end.

According to the theoretical physicist Stephen Hawking, black holes are not entirely black but radiate energy and matter. This may provide material for us if we live near the edge of a black hole – if we throw our waste into the hole it will repay us energy and matter. So there may be bizarre chances for us yet. Ultimately even the largest supercluster black holes will have evaporated by Hawking's process and any new protons produced thereby will have decayed too.

Someone calculated that, if we survive all this, our descendants (if any) will meet descendants that have developed independently on a distant planet. This will be after 10^{300} years. How can we contemplate such time-spans? If creatures still exist then, will 'today' hold any meaning for them? Will Beethoven, Mozart and Bach be encoded for that distant future?

This is too remote to be of more than intellectual interest. But modern theories suggest hazards for the make-up of matter that could threaten us now or within a few years.

Stranger than Science Fiction

Nature always seeks the most stable configuration: water flows downhill; some atoms shed radioactivity to come to more stable forms. We are made of the most stable stuff around – atoms whose electrons encircle a positively charged nucleus made of neutrons and protons.

Although this is the most stable stuff around here it might not be the most stable stuff everywhere. Some theorists suspect that there may exist 'strange matter' that could initiate a collapse of ordinary matter were it to come into contact with us.

A powerful attractive force grips the neutrons and protons, tightly building the nuclei that are at the hearts of atoms. A single proton forms the nucleus of the simplest element, hydrogen, while as many as 250 neutrons and protons cluster to form the nuclei of the heaviest elements.

Protons carry positive charge and so mutually repel one another, destablising the nucleus. Neutrons, which as their name implies are neutral, do not experience this disruption and are easier to clump. Vast quantities of neutrons can clump together forming neutron stars, which are gigantic nuclei consisting of some 10^{57} neutrons. These are the two known forms of nuclear matter: collections of up to 250 or so neutrons and protons forming the elements of the periodic table and the mega clumps forming neutron stars. For decades we have believed that all matter in the Universe is of one or other of these types. Neutron stars might be exotic given the relatively quiescent conditions around this part of the galaxy, but they are made of the same stuff as we are at heart.

The 'strange matter' that the theorists are excited about is quite different. To understand the origin of the idea we must go back to 1947 when the first clues arrived here that there are more types of matter in the Universe than had been seen to that time on Earth.

Some 10 miles above our heads the outer atmosphere experiences a continuous bombardment by photons and subatomic particles. The photons cover the whole spectrum of electromagnetic radiation – from radio waves through visible light to gamma rays. Most of the other particles are atomic nuclei. These are produced in distant stars and, accelerated by the magnetic fields in space, they smash into the atmosphere with millions of times the energy released by radioactive sources.

After the end of the Second World War there was an urgent need to understand the make-up of atomic nuclei. The cosmic rays were ideal tools in this quest: they could shatter nuclei into fragments and even leave a permanent record in photographs of what was happening. Many scientists went up mountains or sent up film in balloons to record the extraterrestrials. When the cosmic rays passed through a small chamber filled with supersaturated air (called a cloud chamber for obvious reasons), they would leave a trail of drops similar to the trails left by modern high-flying aircraft. A camera could record these trails for posterity. A more direct method was to send photographic emulsion plates up in balloons and if a cosmic ray shattered a nucleus of one of the bromine atoms in the emulsion it literally took its own picture – revealed when the emulsion was developed. As a result of many hundreds of such pictures the make-up of matter was revealed as never before.

One day in 1947 Claud Butler and George Rochester from Manchester discovered a trail in a photograph unlike anything they had seen before. Today we know that this was the first recorded example of a 'strange particle', which has no analogue on Earth. Our atoms consist of electrons whirling around a nucleus containing neutrons and protons; strange particles are like neutrons and protons but somewhat heavier and intrinsically unstable.

This glimpse of forms of matter beyond our ken came just as the nuclear physicists were building the first of the great 'atom smashers', machines that accelerated subatomic particles like protons to near the speed of light and could simulate the effects of the cosmic rays to order. When these fast-moving particles smashed into atomic nuclei in their path, a maelstrom of particles poured out. These included strange particles, materialised from the energy of the collision (Einstein's ubiquitous $E=mc^2$ at work again).

The diffuse cosmic rays had produced only a handful of examples of strange particles, but the intense collisions in the accelerators produced them in thousands. Soon they were as familiar as the conventional particles such as the electrons and quarks that make up the matter around and within us.

Strange particles too are made from quarks, but they contain a variety of quark called a strange quark, not found in the protons and neutrons of our atomic nuclei. Why it should be that Nature isn't satisfied with the minimal diet that makes the stable matter that the Earth and the stars seem quite happy with, we simply do not yet know. Whatever the reason, there is no doubt that Nature can, and does, make use of strange quarks, building up strange particles and, theorists now conjecture, conglomerates called strange matter.

Individual strange particles are heavier than individual neutrons and protons and tend not to live very long, decaying into these lighter and more stable seeds of our atomic nuclei. However, the equations describing strange quarks suggest that conglomerates containing large numbers of them may paradoxically be lighter, and more stable, than iron – the most stable of the known atomic nuclei. This 'strange matter' could be the most stable form of bulk matter in the Universe and as such could cause our atomic nuclei to change into the strange form if they meet!

Having found the quarks, which are the seeds of nuclear particles and atomic nuclei, we understand better why it is that certain nuclei exist and others do not, and can contemplate the existence of as yet unseen forms of nuclei. It is possible that out in space there are bizarre stars where the neutrons have compressed into a huge plasma of quarks where individual neutrons are not identifiable. No one is sure yet whether this happens or not; there is still a lot going on 'out there' that we are ignorant about.

If strange matter does exist, there is a consensus that the electrons surrounding the strange nuclei will shield our own atomic nuclei from the strange form. Consequently it is possible that our atoms and the strange ones might get away with 'harmless' chemical interactions involving the peripheral electrons, and the cataclysm of our nuclei being changed by direct contact with the strange nuggets thereby avoided. Any that impinge on us from outer space will stop in the Earth's crust if they weigh less than one-billionth of a gram; greater than one-tenth of a gram and they will pass right through.

Some theories of the early Universe suggest that a large fraction of the mass of the Universe survived in nuggets of strange matter with sizes between breadcrumbs and oranges. This is concentrated nuclear matter, like that in neutron stars, and a thimbleful would weigh many tonnes. It is non-luminous, not the stuff of ordinary stars, and could be responsible for some of the dark missing mass of the Universe and the Milky Way. Some astrophysicists are suggesting that some examples of what we call neutron stars may in fact consist of strange quark matter. When such stars collide, or perhaps when supernovae erupt, pieces of strange matter may be ejected to pollute the Universe.

Strange matter hitting our outer atmosphere will shine like a shooting star but with some differences that can distinguish it from conventional meteors. The most noticeable is its speed – much faster than meteors.

Meteors are pieces of gravel that are orbiting the Sun, fellow-travellers in the solar system and moving at a similar speed to us – some 20 miles a second. Any moving faster than that would escape from the Sun's grip like a car failing to take a curve. If we hit one in head-on collision, like two trains travelling in opposite directions on the same track, the net closing speed would be 40 miles per second. The added pull of the Earth's gravity might speed the rock up to 50 miles a second but no more; this is the maximum closing speed for a conventional meteor. Strange matter, by contrast, comes from all over the galaxy and will be moving much faster than this. We are all orbiting the centre of the galaxy at about 150 miles per second. Strange matter that is part of the galaxy, but not trapped by the Sun, will also be moving at this sort of speed.

Arriving with such high energies they will reach the low-lying dense atmosphere before shining out. They glow at altitudes below 10 miles, unlike meteors which burn above 50 miles. Lower and faster than meteors, their angular velocity will be much greater.

Many of them will make landfall, similar to meteorites, one estimate being that as much as 1,000 tonnes could hit the Earth annually. If so much has landed we ought to be able to find some evidence for these 'nuclearites' as they are known to distinguish them from ordinary meteorites.

These nuggets of strange matter are much denser and more compact than ordinary matter. On passing through rocks they may etch out tracks as the nuclei in the rock recoil. There could be fossil traces of nuclearites that have impinged on the Earth over the ages.

A 1 gram nuclearite could leave a trail one-tenth of a millimetre in diameter. Nuclearites of the order of 1 tonne (still smaller than a pinhead!) would pass through the Earth in under a minute, causing epilinear earthquakes whose seismic signals will be very different from those of a normal point earthquake or underground thermonuclear explosion. Maybe there is evidence for large epilinear quakes with body magnitude greater than 5 awaiting 'discovery' in existing seismic data. Some theorists suggest that such an impact could occur once a year on average.

On passing through water the nuclearite will radiate light. Any hitting the ocean could momentarily brighten the lives of deep sea fishes but the chance of humans seeing any flashes in water is of a rather different kind. The underground experiments seeking evidence of decaying protons use huge swimming pools of water and phototubes to detect light flashes. If they are lucky they might chance upon a passing nuclearite in addition to (instead of?) the purpose that they were originally designed for! Particle physicists at accelerators are looking for evidence of small strange nuclei.

The theory of quark behaviour is very delicate and it is not certain whether it implies that strange matter exists or not. But it has at least made us aware that the observed stability of the familiar nuclei such as iron, carbon, oxygen and so forth need not imply that we are made of the most stable forms of matter. Radioactivity could change our atoms into the strange forms, but extremely slowly. The transition from the 56 neutrons and protons comprising iron (the most stable nucleus) into a nucleus of strange matter takes longer than the life of the Universe. So we are safe here on Earth at present. But it would be a bizarre joke if the most stable state for Nature was not realised somewhere. And if large amounts reach Earth someday, then . . . ?

12

Beyond the Fifth Dimension

North, east and upwards: we are trapped in a three-dimensional Universe which is evolving in the fourth dimension of time. We are so used to this that it is hard to conceive of things otherwise. What would a five- or six-dimensional Universe be like? Does it even make sense to contemplate?

One's immediate reaction is to say that it is clearly nonsense to imagine more dimensions. After all, where could you 'put' them! All possible directions are 'used up', already.

All of the ones that we can easily imagine are certainly used up, but that may be a statement about our lack of imagination rather than about the nature of the Universe. Suppose that we were 'flatlanders' – two-dimensional creatures living on a flat surface and only aware of the surface 'in' which we moved around all the time. That would be the extent of our Universe; the idea of 'up' would not be in the dictionary. Then someone asks the absurd question 'could there be a third dimension?'. With our greater awareness we can imagine 'up' and so may be surprised at the difficulty the flatlanders would have in making the intellectual leap out of the paper. In turn, *we* may be unaware of extra dimensions: call them 'beyond' or 'within'.

An ultimate theory of the universe ought to answer the question of what is 'magic' about the number of dimensions in which we find ourselves. It is one of the simplest questions to ask; but the simplest questions are often the most profound and difficult to answer. It is not at all clear how you would set about it scientifically.

However the current excitement in theoretical physics centres on a theory that makes profound statements about the fabric of the Universe. It goes under the codename 'superstrings' and implies that at the time of the Big Bang there were TEN dimensions. Six of these have become hidden to our gross senses but leave their mark in giving rise to electricity, nuclear radioactivity and related phenomena. The other remarkable consequences of the theory is that it might imply that there is an entire invisible universe operating right here inside the one that we are familiar with.

We cannot see this shadow universe but we can feel it. Its weight is tugging at us via gravity. It affects the galaxies and stars in their courses. Apart from the fact that it is there, we know next to nothing about it.

What impact this has for us is only now being worked out – the theory is very new, still only poorly understood and is being studied at universities and laboratories worldwide. One Nobel Laureate has described this as the greatest advance in theoretical physics since quantum mechanics or general relativity. This is praise indeed. These are the two great pillars of twentieth-century science; to compare the superstring theory with them implies that it may well be the holy grail of theoretical physics and, if so, its implications for a hidden universe should be given due weight.

The comparison with general relativity and quantum mechanics is interesting because superstrings subsumes both of these theories. Moreover it avoids an embarrassment that physicists have kept rather quiet about for many years: the foundations of science are flawed. General relativity and quantum mechanics apply to very different situations and have never been found wanting. But one can imagine circumstances where both of these theories have something to say – and it turns out that they are mutually contradictory. Superstrings shows the way out of this paradox and shows that it is in part due to our limited imagination – there are more dimensions in heaven and earth than we had dreamed of. Until we come to grips with this we are again like primitive societies who were all too aware of the unknown.

So first, let's see where science falls apart in four dimensions, meet the superstring theory that resolves the problem, and see what it implies.

Microscopic Quantum Theory

Our immediate senses are aware of structures larger than about one-tenth of a millimetre; simple microscopes extend that awareness to the scale of microbes. In the period up to the end of the last century 'classical physics' described the known phenomena in this macroscopic universe. But hints of profound novelties occurring at short distances were already reaching into our gross senses. Hot bodies emit electromagnetic radiation and the standard theory predicted a nonsense – that there was an infinite probability to radiate ultra-violet light. This does not happen; the paradox was called the 'ultra-violet catastrophe' and signalled a major failing of the existing world view.

The great German physicist Max Planck found the solution when he invented the quantum theory. This was an extension of classical ideas into the realm of microscopic distances. Matter is made of atoms, which are extended objects, about 10^{-10} m diameter, with a detailed inner structure. Classical physics is insufficient to describe phenomena at such distances, and the behaviour of microscopic atoms causes the radiation of ultra-violet light to behave rather differently than predicted in the classical theory. The infinite probability – the ultra-violet catastrophe – was avoided once scientists appreciated the essential role of the quantum theory, which implies that the laws have to be modified at short distances.

Quantum theory gave rise to a different world view. In quantum theory there is a fundamental 'uncertainty principle', in that you cannot measure both position and momentum or energy of a system to infinite precision. The more precisely a position measurement is made, the less precisely are the momentum and energy of that system knowable. This is imperceptible for macroscopic objects but more and more striking for phenomena at microscopic and subatomic length scales.

Einstein's famous equation, $E=mc^2$, implies that energy and mass are equivalent. Energy can, in a sense, coagulate and form particles of matter; conversely matter has the possibility to change

190

form into radiant energy, as in certain nuclear reactions in the Sun for example. Now, according to quantum theory if you try to look at things at very fine distance resolution you find that the momentum and energy of the system under study fluctuate wildly – the more so the smaller the distance. The effect of the $E=mc^2$ is then that the energy fluctuations at short distances can be manifested as so-called 'virtual' particles and antiparticles (mirror images with the same amount of mass but opposite electrical charge to the particle); materialising out of the vacuum and surviving for a mere instant before they meet and annihilate.

At distances less than 10^{-13} m the fluctuations in energy are large enough that the lightest electrically charged particle – an electron – can be momentarily created along with its antimatter counterpart (the positron). As a result it is no longer possible to describe a system as containing a fixed number of particles: electrons and positrons are continuously materialising and disappearing on short time-scales. Nor is the vacuum a void – 'empty' space is a medium with an infinite number of particles and antiparticles seething within it.

All this is standard quantum theory as manifested at atomic and nuclear distance scales. It is the paradigm, essential in every theoretician's toolkit, and underwrites our theories of the fundamental forces acting on and within individual atoms. These are the electromagnetic force, which holds the electrons in the atomic periphery, the strong force, which binds the atomic nucleus, and the weak force, which is responsible for radioactivity ('beta decay') and the interactions of the ghostly neutral neutrinos. These three fundamental forces control all phenomena other than those due to the fourth great force – gravity. This force, known the longest, is in fact the least well understood. Superstring theory offers the promise of including gravity naturally in a unified theory of all forces and matter in the universe.

Gravity

Three centuries ago Isaac Newton gave the first quantitative description of one of Nature's fundamental forces with his celebrated theory of gravity. Although the force of gravity between atoms at earthly energies is feeble, *all* particles of matter attract one another gravitationally, with the result that the collective effects of many particles, such as those in the Earth, produce discernible effects, holding us on the ground, and controlling the motion of planets and galaxies.

When objects are moving very fast, the effects of gravity differ from those described by Newton's theory. One example of this is seen in the orbit of the flighty planet Mercury, whose point of closest approach to the Sun changes slightly from one orbit to the next. Einstein's theory of general relativity subsumes Newton's theory and to date agrees with all observations on gravitational phenomena.

In practice we apply the theory of gravity to eclipses, tides and the motion of satellites – namely bulk matter. What about gravity on the scale of individual atoms? The gravitational force is exceedingly feeble between individual atoms – it is overwhelmed by the electrical, magnetic and nuclear forces. When we are studying the behaviour of individual atoms and subatomic phenomena we use quantum mechanics but have no need of gravity or general relativity. Conversely, when we deal with large-scale structures that are interacting gravitationally we do not need quantum mechanics as this concentrates on the microscopic structure of matter. So in practice the two theories don't meet head on – one or other but not both are needed at any one time.

Einstein's general relativity was the first new theory of gravity since Isaac Newton's work in the seventeenth century. It includes Newton's laws and goes far beyond them, describing not just falling apples and the motion of planets and galaxies but also dealing with the evolution of the entire Universe. It makes profound statements about the relation between gravity and the nature of space and time. The best state of the art experiments cannot fault it.

The equations of general relativity show that it is *energy*, not simply mass, that gravitates. Light has energy and so gravity acts on it. The massive Sun can deflect passing light beams a little. If the Sun were much more massive it would deflect light beams a lot.

When enough mass is concentrated in a small region, the resulting gravitational forces may be so powerful that they entrap light and a black hole results.

The idea of a black hole in space is bizarre but not particularly mind stretching. It is so beloved of science fiction because of the extreme warping of space and time that occurs in its vicinity. The gravity is so powerful that space–time curl up on themselves: time, in a sense, stands still. It is here that the paradoxical conflict with quantum theory appears.

The Conflict

Quantum theory implies that energy fluctuates at extremely short distances or time-scales. We already commented that at 10^{-13} m electrons and positrons are continuously bubbling. At distances less than 10^{-35} m the energy fluctuations are so great that particles 10^{19} times as massive as a proton can form and annihilate. Such large masses concentrated in such minute distances are black holes. So quantum theory implies that very small black holes are coming and going. At very short distances, or on very short time intervals, time is standing still. Gravity is distorting the environment so much that our whole notion of space and time breaks down.

The problem is that our quantum theories of force fields ('quantum field theories') are built on the assumption that it makes sense to talk about space and time at all length scales and over as brief a time interval as you choose. Time is regarded as continuous, ever-flowing and not standing still or jerking about. Thus, general relativity (black holes) and quantum theory are fine if kept apart but must be modified in an ultimate theory.

If you ignore these conflicts and attempt to calculate numbers anyway you find nonsensical results. Quantities that should be finite in reality turn out to be infinite in the theories. For example, the gravitational force between two electrons, 10^{-22} cm apart, is predicted to be infinite.

It is not new for infinities to appear as the answers in quantum theory calculations. They occur in quantum electrodynamics (the quantum theory of the electromagnetic force) all the time but are 'harmless' in that they can be removed by a well-defined mathematical technique called 'renormalisation'. In effect the infinities disappear by a redefinition of what we mean by mass and electrical charge of the particles such as the electron. You only need to do this once and it works all the time. That this can be done consistently is profound and also practical; it provides a quantum theory of electromagnetism consistent with relativity and common sense.

Unfortunately this doesn't work in the case of general relativity. Einstein's theory implies that gravity's strength gets more and more powerful the more energy that the gravitating particles have. This turns out to undermine the theory – infinities pop up that can no longer be absorbed and we seem to be stuck with them. This is clearly a nonsensical situation and something has to be done.

For a long time people have tried one idea after another and failed. Nothing in the conventional wisdom seemed to do the job satisfactorily. Here we have an unwanted and paradoxical infinity reminiscent of the ultra-violet catastrophe that heralded the birth of quantum theory. Some new ingredient, or new theory, is called for, subsuming general relativity and quantum theory. This is what superstring theory appears to have achieved.

Just as the black body radiation paradox was the first clue to richer structures occurring at distances below our gross perception, so is this new paradox. In the case of the infinite black body radiation, atomic granularity was the answer and quantum mechanics the new dynamics. Quantum mechanics goes over into the conventional mechanics at large distances where the graininess is hidden. However, the discrete spectral lines emerging from atoms – the fact that different elements radiate characteristic spectra of colours, such as the yellow or blue of sodium or mercury street lamps – are a reminder of what lies beneath.

The paradoxes that confront general relativity and quantum mechanics are clues that there is a graininess at extremely short distances, far smaller even than the scale of the atomic nucleus. According to the new superstring theory, Nature has a complicated and detailed structure on scales millions of billions times smaller than known atomic particles such as electrons and protons. What we thought of previously as points are now regarded as extended structures vibrating like violin strings. (That is the 'string' part of superstrings. The 'super' refers to a particular property of the maths that isn't relevant to our present story.) This graininess contains six hidden dimensions that extend less than one-billionth of one-billionth part of the size of a proton.

A large-scale remnant of this deep richness is the possible existence of a dark universe. The hidden dimensions also leave an impact. In our four-dimensional perception they manifest themselves in electrical and nuclear forces.

The Fifth Dimension

The idea of a fifth dimension goes back more than 50 years to the work of Theodor Kaluza and Oscar Klein. Einstein's theory of gravity – general relativity – treats time on the same footing as space, so it is a theory of 'space–time'. Our Universe exists in 'space–time' – a total of four dimensions.

Einstein's theory is constructed in such a way that you can write its equations for mythical universes with more than four dimensions. This is a mathematical game that Nature appears not to care about since in practice we live in only four dimensions. Kaluza and Klein wrote out Einstein's theory in five dimensions and then examined what happened when the fifth dimension was siphoned out.

If you just throw it away then you are back to standard four-dimensional gravity and have achieved nothing more than a waste of paper. Somehow you have to keep the fifth dimension and yet hide it because it doesn't manifest itself in any obvious way to our gross senses. The way they did this was to suppose that the fifth dimension is curled up, compacted, existing only over very short distances (see Figure 12.1). What causes this is not known and is a question for the future. For now, just impose it on the equations and see what happens.

Well, Einstein's gravity emerges from the four dimensions that are left untouched, which is no surprise. The interesting thing is – what happens to the gravity in the curled-up dimension?

The astonishing result is that the equation describing the

A one-dimensional line

viewed in close up

is seen to be a hosepipe

with a curled-up structure - a small-scale circular dimension

12.1 Curled dimensions

gravitational forces in the fifth dimension is one that Kuluza and Klein had seen before and that is familiar to every student of physics. It is the equation that James Clerk Maxwell discovered in 1865 and that describes the *electromagnetic* force. What Kaluza and Klein's work had led to was the realisation that what we call electric and magnetic forces are in fact gravity – in the fifth dimension. When you play with magnets, or turn the starter on your car engine, you are in contact with the fifth dimension.

Today we know of other forces that act in and around the atomic nucleus. The weak force that gives rise to radioactivity is one. We know that it is intimately related to the electromagnetic force and so we expect that it, too, is gravity in higher dimensions. The modern grand unified theories imply that the weak and also the strong forces binding quarks and atomic nuclei are subtle manifestations of the electromagnetic force. The notion of higher dimensions asserts that they are all related to gravity.

The mathematics describing the weak and strong forces is more involved than that for the electromagnetic, and a total of five more dimensions is needed to bring them all together. So if the electromagnetic force is gravity in the fifth dimension, the weak and strong forces are gravity in the sixth–tenth dimensions.

There are several indirect hints that these ideas are right, that there really are more than the three space dimensions and one time dimension that we are familiar with. The theorists are now grappling with the problem of why three space dimensions grew into the macroscopic Universe while the others curled up and left their mark in other ways, such as the electrical and nuclear forces. In the first instant of the Big Bang, space and time were undergoing contortions that our mathematics is not yet able to describe. But the majority of mathematical physicists specialising in particle physics, cosmology and astrophysics are working on this problem or on closely related ones. No one has all the answers yet but pieces of mathematics are emerging from the study of superstrings and from the study of the early Universe in general that have suggestive implications.

One of these is that space and time, as we know them today, might be unstable. This is a terrifying thought but not necessarily absurd. After all, we don't know why there are the number of dimensions there are; we have clues that they are in a sense mere 'remnants' from ten, so why should they be permanent and unchanging? How guaranteed is the fabric of the Universe within which we find ourselves?

The Collapse of Space and Time

As I commented in the previous chapter, Nature always seeks the most stable configuration – the state of lowest energy. There we met the possibility of strange matter, more stable than our own, that could seed the collapse of our matter should they meet. A more dramatic possibility that has emerged from studies of the Big Bang is that the Universe as a whole might be inherently unstable. I don't mean here that its matter is eroding away on an indefinite time-scale too remote to concern us; instead I'm concerned at the possibility that the very fabric of the Universe could suddenly change somewhere *now* and spread out like a cancer at near to the speed of light, devouring everything. All the bits and pieces of matter at the deepest level remain the same but reconfigure – change 'phase' is the technical description.

The notion of matter changing phase is very familiar. Ice, liquid and steam are different phases of water; the molecules of H_2O are the same in each case but bind collectively in different ways. Which configuration they choose depends on external conditions such as temperature and pressure. You can superheat it or supercool it. For example, the water in your car radiator can heat above 100 degrees Centigrade when stuck in a traffic jam. The pressure prevents it boiling, so long as the radiator cap is efficient. Unwise motorists who start to remove the cap can receive a blast of scalding steam as a result; the superheated water has boiled as the pressure drops. Similarly water can be supercooled below freezing point, remaining liquid so long as external conditions don't change, but if they do then the water suddenly freezes. In its supercooled state we say that it is metastable, while the frozen form is stable.

A popular idea among some physicists at present is that the Universe is in a metastable state – that the cooling from the hot Big Bang left us with a supercooled rather than a frozen Universe. Stars, planets and human beings are the natural order of things given the building blocks that Nature has to play with and the way the laws of our Universe prefer them to be combined. But if the Universe is only supercooled and should freeze in the future the basic building blocks could be combined in a more energy-efficient way. You, I and everything that we've ever known would go and a new order prevail.

Already, around the cosmos, we can see examples of how basic particles form different microstructures and hence different forms of bulk matter. On Earth today electrons, protons and neutrons are bound in atoms, whereas in the Sun these same particles roam free in a plasma. In a sense matter is in a different phase here than in the hot stars; it consists of the same particles but bound tightly like ice rather than more freely as in water. The paradigm among theorists is that the Universe started very hot, hotter than any star today. In the Big Bang even the protons and neutrons melted; in those early moments their quarks were freed. Earlier still, when conditions were even more extreme, it is possible that the Universe was in some other phase; its cooling into the quarks and eventually nuclear particles could have left it in the true frozen state of lowest energy or maybe only in a supercooled state where it has remained – so far.

It is hard to imagine what a more 'frozen' form of these particles would be like as we have no intuition to guide us. All we can say is that we have no guarantee that we are the favoured end-product. If we are not, we could still be lucky – the Universe could be stuck by chance in its present phase and have no manifest way to reach its most favoured configuration.

In analogy, we are on the first floor of some cosmic cathedral, which is fine so long as there isn't a trapdoor for us to fall through, or at least, if there is, that no one opens it by mistake.

The problem is that quantum theory can 'open the door'. Tunnelling through barriers (the floor) to fall from a high-energy state to a lower one is at the root of many nuclear decay processes. So wait long enough and somewhere Nature will tunnel through from our metastable to the true ground-floor configuration. And the Universe has been around for over 10 billion years – long enough that somewhere, sometime, such a change may have or even now be taking place. This could happen at anytime, anywhere.

If a bubble of 'frozen universe' forms, it might die out or grow uncontrollably; it depends how much lower in energy this desired state is relative to the metastable one – how far above the ground level our present floor is. A growing bubble would expand at nearly the speed of light with enormous release of energy. Everything would make a big *vvarroomph*; the roar from strange matter would be a whisper by comparison.

In 1983 the distinguished astrophysicists Martin Rees and Piet Hut introduced a new feature into this debate by asking in the journal *Nature* whether modern technology might open the trapdoor inadvertently. Could a new accelerator of subatomic particles produce such a concentration of energy in one spot that it flip that part of the Universe and, like a cancer, ultimately the whole cosmos through the trapdoor – or to be more formal: 'make a spontaneous transition via quantum mechanical tunnelling'. As new particle accelerators reach into regions of energy not before probed on Earth, this awesome thought gives pause.

After some study, Hut and Rees concluded that, thankfully, we probably don't need to worry. Although it is the first time that the new accelerators will have produced such collisions on Earth, Nature is doing them all the time. Cosmic rays consist of nuclear particles at huge energies, far greater than yet produced on Earth. They are very scarce in space but even so several hundred thousand extreme collisions have occurred in the Universe in history and the Universe still survives. So Hut and Rees concluded that no particle accelerator in the foreseeable future will pose any threat to the fabric of our Universe.

But what if there are advanced beings in Andromeda who are building accelerators billions of times in excess of anything that we can even dream of? This game is the ultimate pollution – a bubble spreads and devours everything. Thankfully none is about to devour us; it travels close to but less than the speed of light, so we will have some advance warning of its arrival. I'm unsure what we could do about it if we saw one coming, but I take refuge in the hope that any people far ahead of us are advanced enough to have thought this through already and either not built the machines or surrounded them with the ultimate radiation shield!

Cannibal Universes?

Is it possible to create a universe in the laboratory? This sounds like the ultimate science fiction dream, but by 1987 understanding of the origins of our Universe had reached such an advanced state that the eminent astrophysicists Ed Farhi and Alan Guth from MIT debated the idea in the journal *Physics Letters*. They concluded, 'As you may have imagined it is rather difficult' but, within quantum theory, perhaps not impossible in principle. It is impossible in practice only given present technology and therefore, as I cautioned in the previous example, it may be accessible to advanced creatures elsewhere.

Until very recently we thought that the Universe is permanent and omnipotent. A few years ago we thought we had figured out Genesis; we argued about the long-term future, such as whether the Universe would expand and cool or suffer a heat death in collapse, but we agreed on one thing – ours is the only universe around. Catastrophic things might happen to 'the matter within our Universe, but the Universe itself – the space and time within which the drama plays out – that would go on. Now that dogma is being questioned. Andrei Linde, a distinguished Soviet theorist, even proposes that our Universe actually consists of innumerable separate mini-universes, whose laws may differ radically from the one in which we happen to exist.

Suddenly the Universe seems much less stable, less certain than it did.

Once we thought that the Earth was the centre of everything, then the Sun and finally we have become used to the idea that we occupy an insignificant outpost of an unremarkable galaxy that is but one of billions. Having had our egocentricity so rudely displaced one might have thought that that was the end of it. But no; now we are even questioning whether our Universe is the one and only – are we living in a polyverse?

The idea that we could create a new universe in the laboratory comes from the current widely held theory that in the first fraction of a second our Universe inflated drastically before settling down to the more leisurely expansion of the last 20 billion years. This 'inflationary universe' theory explains some puzzles that had plagued earlier models of the Big Bang and makes testable predictions for the present state of the Universe which have been successful so far. According to the inflationary theory, the Universe originally had a mass of under 10 kilograms in a size one-billionth of an atomic nucleus. Ten kilograms isn't much; you could check it onto an airliner without paying excess baggage charges. This is enough to start a universe, so how did it grow?

According to the theory, the interior of this region was metastable and, upon going through a phase change into the stable state that we are now in, it gained energy courtesy of a peculiar quirk of the quantum theory. The effect was like antigravity – a vast repulsion and growth of net energy until it settled in the present phase, its residual expansion being the fossil remnant of that trauma. Enough energy was generated to boost that initial 10 kilograms into the entire Universe that we see today.

So, if a universe can emerge from no more than a suitcase, might we make a cauldron in a finite region of space and arrange for it to be in the metastable state? And then, whoosh – this little region bursts out as a universe with a future evolution similar to that of our own, the whole thing starting off in the middle of the luggage check-in counter?

If someone made a new universe, what would become of our present one? Are we at risk from the experiments of some DIY enthusiast in Ursa Major? After all, can more than one universe exist? And, if it is possible to create a new one, then surely it is possible to destroy our own?

The theory that suggests this is science fact also seems to imply that we are safe if new universes are erupting. They make their own space and time without spilling into ours, so they won't destroy us. As far as we are aware, the wall of the bubble would be like the surface of a black hole.

It is hard to visualise this idea of a universe appearing apparently out of nowhere and yet being somehow disjoint from the space and time in which we exist. This is all happening in dimensions beyond our immediate experience so, as we did earlier, it may help to imagine the universe of the 'flatlander' and how this spontaneous eruption appears there.

The flatlander's universe is the surface of a sphere that is so huge that it appears completely flat, with no curvature at all. The formation of the new universe is like an aneurism on the surface where space and time suddenly bulge out and then separate from their parent into a new universe. We can visualise this, but flatlanders can say only that the new universe is 'somewhere else', as they are limited to their flat comprehension.

Someone living inside the bulge might experience conditions similar to a Big Bang. To people living elsewhere the bulge would appear as a black hole. After separating, the black hole would have appeared to have evaporated, leaving no trace of its formation. Like the flatlanders, we could say only that its bulge existed 'somewhere else'. We would say that the new universe existed in a totally separate space and time. Once gone, we and it can never communicate again. You can't get from there to here, nor can it invade our space. It could even be that our Universe split off from a host courtesy of some do-it-yourself experiment 20 billion years ago.

So the bottom line at present is that science admits the

possibility that new universes may erupt and that our present one could collapse. The former will not harm us and the latter is exceedingly improbable. In which case we are safe from these ultimate apocalypses – at least according to our current understanding. But five years ago no one would have seriously posed these ideas; today they are being worked through and the final outcome is anybody's guess.

13

Time Is Running Out

When the Sun Becomes a Red Giant

It is dawn in the Garden of Eden. The Earth spins us from the shadow of night into the bright light of day. Within a few hours the heat in the desert will be so intense that even the lizards will be seeking shade. The houses on the twentieth-century hills of Moab all have solar collectors on their roofs. They are accumulating the heat from a nuclear reactor 100 million miles away.

Solar energy – non-polluting, free of charge and permanent – utopia. But nothing comes free; there is a price to pay, even though the debt will not be called in for a long time yet. The desert heat is the end-result of the Sun consuming 600 million tonnes of hydrogen every second. So although it is free as far as we are concerned, it is a very inefficient way of providing us with fuel. Our tiny planet intercepts only one part in 1 billion of the whole; the rest goes out into space.

Several billion tonnes of hydrogen have been used up since you started reading this sentence and by this time tomorrow 100 million million tonnes will have gone for good. This is a lot, but is such a trifling fraction of the whole Sun that we don't notice it day to day, or even over a lifetime. During the entire million years of human existence the relative amounts of hydrogen fuel and its helium end-product in the Sun have changed by less than one part in 1,000. However, slowly but surely the Sun is changing, dying; wait long enough – about 5 billion years – and it will be all used up. What then?

When all of the hydrogen has gone the centre of the Sun will no

204

longer be able to resist the weight of the outer regions pressing inwards. The core will begin to collapse and in doing so its gravitational energy will turn to heat in a re-enactment of its birth from a collapsing dust cloud.

As the core collapses, its heat throws the outer regions upwards, expanding and cooling the Sun's surface. The Sun, which has risen golden over the eastern horizon for 10 billion years, begins to grow bigger and redder. Imperceptibly at first, but then gathering pace as the outer surface approaches Earth, the Sun occupies more and more of the sky. The polar ice caps melt and flood low-lying areas, altering for ever the terrestrial geography. The rising temperature evaporates the oceans, making the entire globe like a tropical rain forest covered with a perpetual cloud. Viewed from outside we would appear shrouded much as Venus looks to us today. Intense redness pervades the cloudscape until the heat boils the oceans entirely, the clouds and atmosphere evaporate into space and the barren planet is defenceless in face of the red giant that fills the whole of the daytime sky. Dante's inferno has finally brought hell on Earth.

There is no hope for Mercury and Venus, which have been consumed within the swollen Sun. If Earth lies outside it will be scorched, lifeless and desolate. Our descendants may survive underground but that merely postpones the end.

The helium that is the end-product of the hydrogen fusion can itself fuse to build up heavier elements such as oxygen, nitrogen and carbon. This is what is going on at the heart of the red giant. In doing so the Sun heats up one last time, suddenly swelling out far beyond the Earth, vaporising it and Mars too as it expands to almost the orbit of Jupiter. The Sun's atmosphere spews into space, departing the solar system; viewers from other parts of the Milky Way will see a nebulous gas, the remnants of a one-time life-giving star. Examples of such nebulae are visible to us in our own night sky; we can only guess what life forms they once may have supported.

This Apocalypse is certain, guaranteed, unavoidable, unless we learn how to intervene. It will be the end of this jewel, our home and repository of our entire accumulated culture. It signals a pivotal moment in the future history of the human species. What hope do we have? Humans have existed for a mere trifle in the Sun's time-span. In a few thousand years we have progressed from fire to nuclear power, from the Stone Age to silicon chips, from scavenging for food to chemically synthesised vitamin tablets and meal pills for space travellers. Imagine this time-span passing once more, and then again 1 million times; on that time-scale we might be able to control the evolution of the Sun and thereby postpone Apocalypse. At the very least we will surely be able to colonise other star systems.

First we must plan for survival on planet Earth so long as it exists. We will have to decide what to do if we are threatened by impacts from comets, asteroids or the many hazards that can be expected during another 250 orbits around the Milky Way. This will take us through dust clouds where new stars are forming from the debris of old ones, where some day we will find ourselves near to a supernova or have our orbit disturbed by encroaching too near some other star. Any number of things could happen before the Sun becomes a red giant.

It should be possible to prepare for such things, to leave the planet and colonise space. Flying the Atlantic would have been regarded as an impossible dream when Columbus first sailed, yet today it is part of a common vacation for millions. Colonising space in another few years seems to me to be a natural extrapolation from today. And we know that we must do so to survive.

If we colonise new worlds we will then be faced with life after our ancestral Sun has died. We will see whole galaxies of stars die out as the entire Universe moves inexorably to its own end. For the Universe is a living thing, evolving as we do, eventually to die. On that time-scale we too will have evolved into new forms. Present life has emerged from simple molecules in under 4 billion years, so after a further 5 billion our remote descendants will bear as little resemblance to us as we do the first amoeba. Indeed, the need to change our form, if not just get off the Earth, becomes increasingly important as time progresses because if the Universe survives the sudden extinctions that we have mused over, it will eventually collapse in heat or expand into ultimate cold. Flesh and bone will not survive either of these; transmogrified humans might.

206

Princeton University theorist Freeman Dyson has thought about this and I will describe some of his ideas later in this chapter.

First things first: what we can do about more immediate problems. Then we will take a look at our prospects for surviving into the deep future.

Prepare for Collision

In the short term we may have to face the prospect of being hit by an asteroid. We have been struck by moderate-sized objects in the past, even in this century. The future is likely to be no less risky. Sooner or later we are going to find ourselves on collision course with a real monster. What can we do about it?

Remarkably little research has been done into this. Perhaps it is difficult to put one's mind to work on something whose need is not immediately urgent. There are, after all, any number of problems to deal with that already threaten our species, most of them self-inflicted. If we are unable to come to terms with self-imposed Armageddon, what hope do we have of making a collective effort against natural extinction?

So, are we to give up all hope? Is the human existence to be a great joke of Nature – a brief spell of light and intelligent awareness of the cosmos between two great expanses of darkness? The politicians of the world have their contribution to make to this ultimate question. The scientists should be also addressing the question of natural catastrophe. Joseph Smith of the University of Chicago proposes that the scientific community initiate a 10-year study on the prevention of impacts with a view to examining the costs and practicalities of the task.

First of all we need to know the number and orbits of asteroids much better and detect all large ones that have paths intersecting our own. Regular satellite launches should occur carrying equipment capable of detecting large Apollo objects (Earth-crossing asteroids) and new comets. The strategy would be to scan rapidly those orbits where asteroids are most densely populated, followed by a routine calculation of their orbits. You then have to observe them again later to check that the orbits have been correctly determined. Soon you will be able to say with a good degree of precision where they are going to be and when.

Later, as experience grows, this could be extended to smaller bodies (even 10 metres across can pack a fair thump after all). It is hard to detect small objects far away in space and so an array of telescopes will be needed to cover the sky.

Forming a timetable of asteroids is well within the capabilities of present technology. It merely needs the will. The *real* concern, however, is that it first requires the awakening of consciousness. I hope this book has made clear that this *is* so. Moreover, it is a worthwhile scientific endeavour in its own right and will stimulate development of instrumentation that will find applications far beyond the original aim. Billions of dollars were spent sending a few men to the Moon; the asteroid watch is small by comparison.

This is the first step – know your enemy. Next we have to do something about it.

A world that is becoming enamoured of the 'Star Wars' defence initiative is rapidly being carried away with the omnipotence of technology. The problem of dealing with an approaching lump of rock is 'simple'. Just send up enough rockets loaded with thermo-nuclear devices and blast the rock to pieces. As we saw in Chapter 4, Hollywood chose this solution in one of its disaster movies. This is as far-fetched as the belief that we can build a shield of lasers and weapons above our heads and rely on it working 100 per cent efficiently on the day it is needed.

The Faustian proposition of sending up thermonuclear devices may be avoidable if we detect an asteroid on a looping orbit that is slowly closing in on our own on successive circuits. We would have many years to settle on a course of action – a small deflection could be enough to make us safe.

Another area of ignorance concerns the make-up of asteroids and comets. The Giotto mission to Comet Halley has shown us more of comets than we ever knew. They are tenuous and less likely to be of concern than asteroids. Although bits of asteroids have landed, our knowledge of asteroids in pristine condition is minimal.

We need a systematic mission of flybys to both asteroids and comets. We have sent robots to Mars, so we can land on an asteroid. This is essential if we are to determine their properties. For example, we need to know if they are solid and hard or crumbly. Is there a lot of flaky rubble on the surface? Are they fragile and susceptible to artificial break-up? Is it easy to fly around an asteroid or is there a cloud of debris that would create a hazard for a team of astronauts intending to deal with it?

This is the most likely natural global catastrophe, and we can begin to tackle it with relatively unsophisticated means. We need not sit around passively awaiting extinction if we have prospects of developing the technical means to deal with the problem. Some of the plans that attempt to survive nuclear holocaust may have lessons for a global catastrophe of the sort I have been discussing. Some of the effects of a huge collision will be like those from global nuclear war. The nuclear winter, caused by smoke from burning cities, may well have its analogue in the dust cloud sent up by an asteroid disrupting the atmosphere. It takes more than two years for the atmosphere to clear itself of aerosol spray particles, so this is the period that we need to contemplate surviving. The Swiss have a national plan which is a good example of where to start. It is compulsory to have underground shelters for all individuals per-manently stockpiled with two years' supply of food and other essentials.

However, nuclear war is a more likely bet, in the short term, than an asteroid impact; and, as very few are seriously planning to outlive nuclear war, there is not much hope of these ideas being put into action. I am merely reporting the facts in the hope that people will eventually become concerned enough to act on them.

New Worlds

We may learn how to deal with asteroids, comets and other natural catastrophes but sooner or later we will have to quit the planet. The Sun will eventually become a red giant and we must take ourselves beyond its range of destruction. If we continue to live near the swollen Sun we will have to adapt our energy supplies to the new conditions. We may have to go and colonise another star system, or even leave the galaxy as the stars die out or collapse inwards to form a great black hole. The chances are that we will have destroyed ourselves in thermonuclear war or industrial pollution before we have the chance to see what are the limits of technological achievement.

None the less, we have to make a start. It is unrealistic to plan far ahead but the first step was already taken when Neil Armstrong stood on the Moon. Many people still alive today were born before commercial aircraft existed; now they see us venture into space. Within a decade of marvelling at Yuri Gagarin and John Glenn in their pioneering orbits of the planet, we had reached the point where trips to the Moon ceased to be media events. By 1986 private citizens were being seated on the space shuttle as if the new frontier were already conquered.

The Challenger disaster made many people question science and technology, as if humans are preordained to remain earth-bound and are tempting fate to try to fly. Yet in the same month we saw the success of the Voyager mission, which flew past Uranus on cue, sending back pictures of an outpost of the solar system, something that would have been thought impossible 20 years ago. And for the first time international collaboration sent a team of rockets out to meet Halley's comet.

The technology for space exploration and development certainly exists already. Is the best motivation for future research really to put lasers and mirrors in space for military purposes? So far refugees from war have been able to flee to other countries. Where will a refugee from thermonuclear world war be able to hide? When car exhausts have polluted the air, trees been destroyed for cigarette papers (and books!) and life in the industrial environment become utterly impossible, where do we go? At some point, and very soon, we have to start thinking seriously about this.

The science fiction writers know the answer: they have us populating other planets, asteroids and purpose-built space stations. The idea of building space colonies has been looked into seriously by some scientists, notably Gerard O'Neill of Princeton. He started the project in 1969 as a stimulus to a physics course that he was teaching at the university. Gradually it became clear to him that the idea was feasible and that the required technology is for the most part already available.

He has written about his ideas in some detail in the magazine *Physics Today* (September 1974) and in *The High Frontier* (Jonathan Cape, 1976) so I will review his ideas only briefly.

People need air and water, land, gravity and energy to keep going. We could have all of these if we lived inside huge cylinders, several miles long and a few miles diameter. The cylinders rotate, so we would be pressed to the ground as in a centrifuge – though we would experience it like gravity. Solar radiation provides the power, enough to satisfy our needs ten times over at present consumption. In cylinders of this girth it is possible to build towns, fields, forests, even mountains to give an Earthly perspective and minimise psychological 'home sickness'.

A major barrier to space travel is getting off the ground. Compare the huge rockets that sent the Apollo astronauts on their way with the small craft that later lifted them from the surface of the Moon. The Moon's gravitation is so weak that anyone can be a high jump champion there. It is an ideal launchpad for space ventures. Moreover, the Moon is full of minerals, which could be mined and lifted into space to build the colony. In the longer term the asteroids could also be mined.

Using materials from outer space is the big jump. So far, space missions have relied totally on supplies brought from home, like early voyagers on the seas. Then they arrived in new lands, discovered new things and exploited the discoveries. So it can be in space. Mining in the solar system will be the great liberator.

So, how to get started?

It should already be feasible to build a prototype of 100 metres radius and half a mile long. This could support a population of a few thousand people! Rotating every 20 seconds it would reproduce the Earth's gravity. Present technology could accommodate a cylinder of 4 miles radius and 20 miles long, which could house 1–20 million people as the upper ecological limit. The atmosphere would be like the Earth's at a height of 2 miles, so it takes a little acclimatisation but is quite healthy as mountaineers will testify. The clouds will be similar to those on a summer's day.

In fact if you have two parallel cylinders rotating in opposite senses they can maintain their orientation as they orbit the Sun. The surface of each cylinder is divided into land areas and windows. As the axis of the cylinder points towards the Sun, you can't directly see sunlight through the windows. There is no external atmosphere to scatter light and make blue sky so you need to have mirrors outside reflecting the sunlight in through the windows.

The mirrors rotate with the cylinders. By opening or closing covers on the mirrors you can increase or decrease the amount of light. So night and day can be controlled in length to set the average temperature within the cylinder and reproduce the seasons.

Solar power stations are placed at the sunny end of the cylinder, so as to receive the maximum unshielded radiation. These will produce enough power for the inhabited cylinders and also the agricultural cylinders that accompany them.

Agricultural areas encircle the main cylinder. Their climates can be distributed through the seasons so that there is always a fresh supply of different crops. The design of these cylinders can be more functional; there is no need to include 'psychological' aids such as mock Earth features.

The early chapters in this book dealt with the hazards of collisions. The space colonies will be more vulnerable as they have no external air shield to burn up the stones; on the other hand, they are a much smaller target than the Earth. Most meteors are cometary, more snowballs than rock. The chance of being hit by a 1 ton lump is one in 1 million years. A piece of 100 grams will hit once in three years on average but well-designed craft should be able to deal with that.

Travelling inside a cylinder could be by bicycle or by electrically powered pollution-free vehicles; with an extent of a few miles only there would be no need for more than this. Travel between cylinders involves power-free craft using the natural spin of the surface to speed them on their way. The surface is moving at nearly 400 miles an hour. Unlock a craft on the outer edge and it will fly off tangentially across the intervening space at the speed of a jetliner. By swinging under the other cylinder it will be able to dock at zero

212

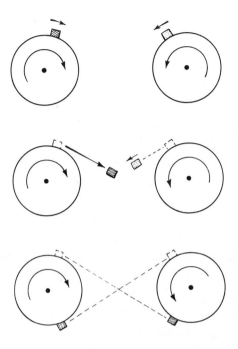

13.1 Travelling between two rotating cylinders The cylinder on the left is rotating clockwise. The vehicle (the box on the top) departs at zero relative velocity to the surface, which is very fast relative to the centre of the cylinders. It arrives at the other cylinder, which is rotating anticlockwise, and is captured, again at zero relative velocity.

relative velocity – like the passage of the ball between two lacrosse sticks (see Figure 13.1).

A series of cylinders 100 miles apart could support a total population larger than that of the present Earth. Different cultures could occupy different cylinders if desired – the possibilities for social experimentation are beyond present evaluation. O'Neill hopes that the 'need' for conflict and war would be reduced. The pressure for land and better lifestyle would be less than on Earth certainly, though I somehow doubt that human society is that straightforward. There may be insuperable unexpected psychological problems. For example, in the 1950s high-rise tower blocks were thought to be a utopian solution to slum clearance. The problems that they generated were unforeseen; many occupants would have preferred to remain in the unsanitary conditions from which they had been 'released'. Will we be rediscovering the isolation of the high-rise apartments? We understand human nature poorly enough on Earth that it is hard to extrapolate to an entirely new environment.

Cable cars could transport people among the cylinders in a few hours. There are no constraints of aerodynamics and so the craft could be roomy and comfortable, quite unlike the cramped conditions on modern airliners. The external vehicles that are whipped from the surface of one cylinder to another are so simple to operate that family trips to distant communities should be feasible. Polluting sports such as motor racing can take place in special venues. New sports may emerge such as manpowered flight. The effective gravity inside the cylinders comes from the rate of spin and decreases as you go up from the surface towards the axis of the cylinder (at which point it has vanished). So you get lighter as you climb the mountains and can fly at altitude.

In principle we could build the craft and place them where we like. In practice it is obvious that they should be within easy reach of Earth and the Moon. This is also at our 'natural' distance from the Sun. We must avoid being eclipsed by these natural bodies too often as our power supplies depend on sunlight. The craft must be stable against displacements in three dimensions. The Sun and Moon raise significant tides on Earth; bring the Earth into the system as well and there will be a complicated mix of forces on the spacecraft. The solution to the equations was recently worked out and it is possible to park the craft at various special locations in our vicinity where they will orbit the Sun with us while making excursions of some tens of thousands of miles. In the long term it would be possible in principle to put several colonies in such orbits.

So let's start building.

If we get lunar material we can exploit the Moon's low gravity to get things easily up to the construction site. Indeed, components could be pre-assembled on the Moon. There are plentiful oxides on the lunar surface which can be used to provide oxygen for water.

The total mass of a prototype station is around 500,000 tonnes.

We need aluminium, titanium, silicon and oxygen; 98 per cent of this can be obtained from the Moon. Add nitrates and trace elements to lunar soil and you have a viable agricultural base. This leaves some 10,000 tonnes of material to be brought from Earth, which is a major undertaking but not necessarily impossible.

The scale of the enterprise in relative terms is not essentially different from the circumnavigations of the globe in the Middle Ages and the great colonisations of the seventeenth and eighteenth centuries. It is technically feasible given a commitment similar to the Moon programme of the 1960s. To me the main problem seems to be a psychological one. Who will decide who should go and colonise the space cylinders? Will no one want to go or will everyone want to quit polluted Earth, causing a waiting list and divisive decisions on priorities? I suspect that the former is likely to be nearer the truth, at least initially. But this may not be a bad thing. In the first instance the prototype will hardly be habitable other than by committed specialists; 'real' colonies will follow from the experience gained.

O'Neill's article in 1974 projected that the prototype station could be under way by 1988. That time has now arrived and there is no sign of action so far. All that we have to stimulate high technology is the so-called 'big science' – which Britain at least is beginning to question its ability to afford – and military extravaganzas such as the Star Wars strategic defence initiative.

Surely we can do better than this. We *have* to!

Future Life

The Universe has existed for 20 billion years so far. The human species has developed in just 1 million years, a trifling one twenty-thousandth part of the whole span. If the time-span from the Big Bang to the present is likened to a cosmic year, then human life developed during the last half an hour on New Year's Eve.

The whole genus, of which we are the pinnacle, began only during the last afternoon; the first primates arrived only during the last day; the first mammals emerged during the last week; the first insects began only during the final fortnight. No life at all on Earth through the whole spring, summer and autumn. The first single-celled organisms only began to emerge in November and then in the last days of the winter an explosion of hierarchies and forms.

When we look at the Universe in this compacted time-frame we see dramatically the exceedingly rapid emergence of complicated biological structures. If we now look to the future we might just be able to imagine what possibilities there are for life forms yet to come.

The Universe is evolving, expanding and cooling. If it continues to do so then various disasters begin to occur after 10^{11} years (see page 180 above). Eventually matter itself may be expected to erode away, probably on the time-scale of 10^{30} years. Suppose that the Universe has a life of that length; where are we now?

If we liken the entire life of the Universe to a human scale of 100 years, then the life to the present corresponds to a fraction of a second after conception.

Suppose that all we knew of life was the existence of the newly formed egg. Would we imagine the foetus, baby, adult? Surely our imagination would not generalise so far. *Homo sapiens*, in the cosmic scale, is like that barely formed egg. Assuming that we get through the next few nuclear decades, what forms will develop aeons from now? On such a scale, and bearing in mind how rapid the evolution has been so far, I think we can assume that whatever is possible in principle will occur in practice. Where does that lead us?

Even to think about this in any serious fashion presupposes that we know that 'life', consciousness, actually is. If it is no more than a complicated collection of molecules then it may become possible to transmute life forms in the future.

Imagine a future where biological science and technology are sufficiently advanced that a complete map could be made of you at the molecular, or even atomic level. Your exact constitution in terms of atoms of carbon, calcium, oxygen and so forth would be known. The way that they fit together, everything that defines 'you' in terms of the organic molecules comprising your brain, all of these would be listed in some super computer.

So there is a blueprint for building 'you'.

Now we need an intricate machine that can go to a chemical bank and select a few thousand billion billion carbon atoms, a similar number of nitrogen and so forth and assemble them according to the blueprint. In fact it might be less complicated than this, in that banks would store pre-assembled molecules rather than the constituent atoms. Eventually the machine will fit all of these together in exactly the same combinations as exist in the real you. Would this new collection of molecules think it was you? If consciousness is entirely a result of chemical structures, then presumably the collection would, at that instant, have the same memories and thoughts as you had when the blueprint was made.

If this is true, we could vaporise a person into their constituent molecules and reassemble them at a later stage. If we combine the jigsaw pieces faithfully as they were immediately prior to vaporisation then we will have the same jigsaw, the same person existing again – presumably unaware that anything untoward has taken place.

Once *Homo sapiens* is able to store and reconstruct the essential biological molecules it will be freed from the human body form. It can adopt whatever form best suits it. In an ageing, cooling Universe, as the stars die out and energy supplies are exhausted, the surviving life forms will be those that can best adapt themselves to low energy demands.

Freeman Dyson has thought a lot about the realities of this, and has shown that there is nothing that violates any known laws of Nature. Nature may well allow it in principle; given time-scales billions of epochs longer than we have existed, is it unreasonable to suppose that the technology will turn it into a practicality? As Dyson says, 'We could not imagine the architecture of a living cell of protoplasma if we had not seen one'. In similar vein, we could not imagine the new born baby if all that we have seen was the undivided egg. Nor can we foresee the forms life will take on in another billion billion years.

This brings us back to the question 'What is life?'. I don't mean what gives life its 'vital force'; rather, what *defines* life? After all, we recognise whether things are 'alive' so we have some intuitive

217

feeling for what life is. More relevant for our contemplation of the long-term future is the survival of *intelligent* life.

Computer scientists are currently developing so-called 'intelligent' machines. To know whether a machine is intelligent or not we subject it to the 'Turing test'. (Alan Turing was a mathematical genius who died in 1954 when only 41 years old. He played a leading role in the development of modern computing and was the inventor of the test named after him.)

Imagine that you are sitting at a terminal in one room and use it to communicate with another terminal which is operated by an unseen individual in another room. You pose questions at your terminal and receive responses from the next room. Can you tell from the responses whether it is a real person – an intelligent being – or a machine in the other room?

If you play chess with it and if you are a reasonable player you might quickly decide it is a machine – or a poor player! But now that chess-playing computers operate at a sophisticated level, it may prove hard to decide. If it is impossible to decide by interrogation whether you are interacting with a computer or a person, then the other room contains an intelligent source. A machine that passes this test is said to be intelligent.

These ideas from computing can be turned around and taken over into the realm of biological systems; we can imagine a living creature as a type of intelligent computer. In computing jargon, the computer is the hardware and the program is the software. In the biological example, a human is a *program* that has been designed to run on a particular type of hardware – namely the human body. The data are encoded in a special type of store, namely DNA molecules and nerve cells. 'Life' then becomes equivalent to 'information processing'.

If we are no more than an intelligent program, capable of passing the Turing test, then it is possible that this program could run on a different type of hardware. To some extent this is a technical way of stating what we have already discussed, namely, whether we could reassemble the essential biological molecules into new, non-humanoid forms? However, the Turing way of posing the problem goes far beyond this. Implicitly it raises the question of whether we even need the carbon atoms and the molecules at all. Our culture and life itself may be able to continue, in the sense of information processing, using quite different forms of matter from those we are used to. Indeed, if carbon and the constituent protons erode away, as Chapter 11 discussed, there will come a time when the Universe no longer contains these essential ingredients. So, even if our descendants invent the necessary technology, there is the question of whether 'we' will be able to survive *in principle*.

First, to build the system we will need to exploit whatever matter there is remaining in the dying universe. There must also be enough energy around to run it. If an unlimited amount of information can be processed in the future, then 'life' can exist for ever.

In an expanding cooling universe it may indeed be possible to satisfy all the constraints and survive.

The unit of computer storage is called the 'bit' (the term is shortened from 'binary digit', and is applied to the computer's ability to store the result of a choice between two alternatives). The processing of information involves manipulating 'bits per second'. The laws of physics, in particular thermodynamics, limit the rate of information processing. At room temperature it is impossible to exceed 10^{21} bits for every watt of power in a second. Modern computers are well within this constraint – an IBM personal computer has 10^8 and a CRAY supercomputer still only 10^{10} bits per second per watt.

Now consider the human machine. A human thought, a moment of consciousness, lasts about 1 second. Each of us dissipates about 200 watts of power at room temperature (similar to a light bulb). So we are at most 10^{23} bits (the 10^{21} bits multiplied by 200 watts). To maintain an intelligent society of 1 billion individuals, some 10^{33} bits are required. That is the target that we have somehow to meet.

The act of processing information generates waste heat. More is metabolised the more bits are involved and the higher the temperature. We live at room temperature; future life forms may be able to choose what temperature is optimal for them. The lower the temperature, the less waste heat there will be. But you mustn't get too cold; you must be above the ambient temperature of the universal microwave background radiation (currently −270 degrees Centigrade) and you must be able to radiate away the waste heat generated by metabolism.

The most likely long-term surviving particles of matter will be electrons. Electrons radiate electromagnetic energy – light, heat and radio waves. Nature limits the rate at which this can occur. So for life to continue the creature must metabolise less waste heat than the maximum it can radiate away. Hibernation can help it keep within bounds. Life may metabolise intermittently while continuing to radiate away waste heat during hibernation.

A creature's subjective awareness of time depends upon its metabolic rate. This subjective time may have little relation to 'real' time. Freeman Dyson has analysed the effect of this hibernation and concludes that, although biological clocks would be slowing down, going on and off as the Universe expands and cools, subjective time may go on forever. Moreover, a *finite* amount of energy is needed for indefinite survival. Between now and the end of never, a society with the complexity of the human species will use only as much energy as the Sun radiates in 8 hours. So the problem of energy reserves is trifling. The reserves in a galaxy can sustain a society a billion billion times more complex than ours.

Thus in principle there is nothing yet known in physics that prevents this. The technology and the architectures of life forms are less certain. One feature that will be needed is memory – to be immortal with a finite memory would be undesirable. Dyson has ideas on how we might store information by ordering the remaining electrons – little magnets oriented up or down – like a binary code.

A philosopher wrote that there is one certain truth, namely that life has no purpose. Yet there is a great psychological urge to seek purpose in it all. Preservation of the human species and development of awareness and culture are threads that link the generations, hence the interest in extinction: you and I will surely die some day but others will continue in the human relay race. The possibility that the race will end does concern us.

When I think of what has happened in the last 50 years I wonder whether we can survive the next 50 let alone worry about natural extinction. Scientists are evaluating the prospects for surviving a nuclear winter. Now we suddenly discover that aerosol sprays are ripping a hole in the protective ozone layer over the poles; this will let in solar radiation that could be lethal. These are man-made problems amenable to immediate political solutions.

Then there are threats that we may or may not be able to deal with. We are in an ecosystem along with a complex microbiology. Viruses and other disease-spreading organisms nutate. Nature always keeping one step ahead of our efforts. A cracked container in a germ warfare laboratory has been a favourite life-threatening scene in some novels, but Nature could do it itself – I know of no general principle saying that human science can necessarily combat every mutation, at least in the time-scale required.

For example, when I started writing this book AIDS was little known by the general public; now it is perceived as a potential threat to the species. In an extreme, the human race could contract, dominated by ascetics, unmarried virgins and a percentage of monogamous pairings. The population might fall by a fraction of a per cent or by a large amount. In the latter case there would be a profound change in our socio-economic structure until the virus died out with no hosts to propagate it. Humans would reflower, however.

The chances of a natural catastrophe in the short term are small and, though guaranteed in the long term, there is plenty that we can do to prepare. In the great extinctions of the past, many life forms survived and next time around we should be intelligent enough to make it with the ants.

The most dangerous things in the Universe may well be humans. We are currently in a critical period where we have to elevate our moral stature to match our rapidly increasing scientific and technological development. If ever we meet advanced creatures from other worlds it would be encouraging to know that those societies have proved that it is possible to do this. If there is a message in this book it is this: we are not omnipotent. We are much more vulnerable to external circumstances than we would like to admit. If we can humble ourselves to realise that, then maybe we can begin to face our self-made dangers with more responsibility and urgency. If we don't, then we will wake up one morning and find we're not here!

Suggestions for Further Reading

I have listed here some source material (with an arbitrary restriction to being post-1982 except in a few classic cases) together with articles that may help you probe further into some of the themes in this book. The list is by no means complete or authoritative; it simply contains articles that I found useful at some stage or other. In many cases they contain references to earlier works which should enable you to research topics in depth. By its very nature, the frontier of research is often controversial and I have chosen a personal perspective. Many of the issues are still being argued over and these articles will help give a flavour of some of the disputes.

Impacts, Meteorites and Comets

R. Harrington and T. van Fladern, *Icarus*, vol. 39 (1979), p. 131.

R. Grieve and P. Robertson, 'Earth craters', *Icarus*, vol. 38 (1979), p. 212.

W. Napier and V. Clube, 'A theory of terrestrial catastrophism', *Nature*, vol. 282 (1979), p. 455.

R. Kerr, 'Impact looks real, the catastrophe smaller', *Science*, November 1981, p. 896.

D. Hughes, 'The first meteorite stream', *Nature*, September 1982, p. 14.

R. Ganapathy, 'A major meteorite impact on Earth 34 million years ago: Implications for Eocene extinctions', *Science*, May 1982, p. 885.

'Close encounters in Space', *Sky and Telescope*, June 1982, p. 570.

D. J. Michels, 'Observation of a Comet on collision course with the Sun', *Science*, vol. 215 (1982), p. 1097.

R. Ganapathy, 'Tungusku: Discovery of meteorite debris . . . ', *Science*, June 1983, p. 1158.

R. Grieve, 'Impact craters shape planet surfaces', *New Scientist*, November 1983, p. 517.

'Geological rhythms and cometary impacts', *Science*, December 1984, p. 1427.

D. Hughes, 'Meteorites from Mars', *Nature*, October 1984, p. 411.

R. Knacke, 'Cosmic dust and the Comet connection', *Sky and Telescope*, September 1984, p. 206.

I. Halliday *et al.*, 'Frequency of meteorite falls on Earth', *Science*, March 1984, p. 1405.

D. Steel and W. Baggaley, 'Collisions in the solar system – Impacts of the Apollo asteroids upon the terrestrial planets', *Monthly Notes of the Royal Astronomical Society*, vol. 212 (1985), p. 817.

E. Marshal, 'Space junk grows with weapons tests', *Science*, October 1985, p. 424.

'Voyager 2 at Uranus', *Sky and Telescope*, November 1985, p. 42.

M. Waldorp, 'Voyage to a blue planet', *Science*, February 1986, p. 916.

A. P. Boss, 'The origin of the Moon', *Science*, January 1986, p. 341.

'Io spirals towards Jupiter', *New Scientist*, January 1986, p. 33.

'Giotto finds a big black snowball at Halley', *Science*, March 1986, p. 1502.

'Are cometary nuclei primordial rubble piles?' *Nature*, March 1986, p. 243.

Extinctions

L. Spencer, *Mineralogy Magazine*, vol. 295 (1939), p. 425.

J. Laurence Kulp, 'The geological time scale', *Science*, vol. 133 (1961), p. 1105.

S. Durrani, *Physics of the Earth and Planets*, vol. 4 (1971), p. 251.

N. Snelling, 'Measurement of the geological time scale,' Talk at British Association of Science, 1987; editor of *Chronology of the*

Geological Record, Geological Society of London, Memoir No. 10 (published by Blackwell, Oxford, 1985).

H. Urey, *Nature*, vol. 242 March (1973), p. 32.

A. W. Alvarez *et al.* 'Extraterrestrial cause for the Cretaceous – Tertiary extinction', *Science*, June 1980, p. 1095.

R. Ganapathy, 'A major meteorite impact on Earth 65 million years ago: Evidence from the Cretaceous–Tertiary boundary clay', *Science*, August 1980, p. 921.

R. Ganapathy, 'A major meteorite impact on Earth 34 million years ago: Implications for Eocene extinctions', *Science*, May 1982, p. 885; for an opposing opinion see G. Keller *et al.*, *Science*, vol. 221 (1983), p. 150.

P. J. Smith, 'The origin of tektites – settled at last?' *Nature*, November 1982, p. 217.

'Extinctions and ice ages – are comets to blame?' *New Scientist*, June 1982, p. 703.

C. Officer and C. Drake, 'The Cretaceous Tertiary transitional', *Science*, March 1983, p.1383.

'Extinctions by catastrophe?' Five articles in *Nature*, April 1984, pp. 709–20, and commentary p. 685.

'Periodic impacts and extinctions', *Science*, March 1984, p. 1277 (Report of a workshop on comet impacts and their effect on evolution).

'Mass extinctions in the ocean', *Scientific American*, June 1984, p. 46.

'Geological rhythms and cometary impacts', *Science*, December 1984, p. 1427.

'Ammonoids and extinctions', *Nature*, January 1985, p. 12 and pp. 17–22.

The dinosaur controversy: *Nature*, June 1985, pp. 627 and 659; *Science*, March 1985, p. 1161; *New Scientist*, November 1984, pp. 9 and 30.

'Extinctions ARE periodic', *New Scientist*, March 1986, p. 27.

R. E. Sloan *et al.*, 'Gradual dinosaur extinction', *Science*, May 1986, p. 629.

C. B. Officer *et al.*, 'Cretaceous and paroxysmal Cretaceous–Tertiary extinctions', *Nature*, vol. 326 (1987), p. 143.

The Sun

J. Eddy, 'The Maunder Minimum', *Science*, vol. 192 (1976), p. 1189.

F. Close, 'Is the Sun still shining?', *Nature*, vol. 284 (1980).

J. Gribbin, *The Strangest Star*, Fontana, 1980.

'100 to 200 year solar periodicities', *Nature*, September 1982, p. 14.

S. Sofia *et al.*, 'Solar radius change between 1925 and 1979', *Nature*, August 1983, p. 520.

J. Parkinson, 'New measurement of the solar diameter', *Nature*, August 1983, p. 518.

'Chasing the missing solar neutrinos', *New Scientist*, January 1984, p. 20.

R. A. Kerr, 'The Sun is fading', *Science*, January 1986, p. 339.

Hans Bethe on solar neutrinos, *Nature*, April 1986, p. 677.

G. Williams, 'The solar cycle in Precambrian time', *Scientific American*, 1986, p. 80.

R. Bracewell, 'Simulating the sunspot cycle', *Nature*, vol. 323, (1986), p. 516.

F. Paresce and S. Bowyer, 'The Sun and the interstellar medium, *Scientific American*, September 1986, p. 89.

'600 million years of solar cycles', *New Scientist*, October 1986, p. 29.

W. Haxton, 'The solar neutrino problem', *Comments on Nuclear and Particle Physics*, vol. XVI (1986), p. 95.

J. Bahcall, G. Field and W. Press, 'Is solar neutrino capture rate correlated with sunspot number?', Princeton University report, 1987.

The Galaxy

F. Hoyle and R. Lyttleton, 'The effect of interstellar matter on climate variation', *Proceedings of the Cambridge Philosophical Society*, vol. 35 (1939), p. 405.

W. H. McCrea, 'Ice-ages and the galaxy', *Nature*, vol. 255 (1975), p. 607.

L. Blitz *et al.*, 'The new Milky Way', *Science*, June 1983, p. 1233.

'The Earth's orbit and ice-ages', *Scientific American*, February 1984, p. 42.

'A black hole at the galatic centre', *Nature*, vol. 315 (1985), p. 93.
'The galactic centre: Is it a massive black hole?' *Nature*, September 1986, p. 1394.

Stars and Supernovae

E. Norman, 'Neutrino astronomy: a new window on the universe', *Sky and Telescope*, August 1985, p. 101.
D. Patterson, 'A supernova trigger for the solar system', *New Scientist*, May 1978, p. 361.
A. Burrows and T. Mazurek, 'Signatures of stellar collapse in electron-type neutrinos', *Nature*, January 1983, p. 315.
M. G. Edmunds, 'Upper limit on the mass of a star (The decline of a superstar)', *Nature*, December 1983, p. 741.
'Dead Stars', *Nature*, March 1984, p. 142.
S. Chandrasekhar, 'Stars: their evolution and stability' (Nobel Lecture), *Science*, November 1984, p. 497.
'Supernova sets limit on neutrino mass', *New Scientist*, March 1987, p. 24.

The Nature of Matter

F. Close, *The Cosmic Onion*, Heinemann Educational, 1983 (American Institute of Physics, 1987).
F. Close, M. Marten and C. Sutton, *The Particle Explosion*, Oxford University Press, 1987.
C. Sutton, *Building the Universe*, Blackwell, 1985.
M. Turner and F. Wilczek, *Nature*, vol. 298 (1982), p. 633.
M. Rees and P. Hut, *Nature*, vol. 302 (1983), p. 508.
E. Farhi and A. Guth, *Physics Letters*, vol. 183B (1987), p. 149.
E. Witten, 'Strange matter', *Physical Review*, vol. D30 (1984), p. 272.
M. Green, 'Superstrings', *Scientific American*, September 1986, p. 44.

Dark Matter and the Missing Mass

'Dark matter in spiral galaxies', *Scientific American*, June 1983, p. 88.

V. Rubin, 'The rotation of spiral galaxies', *Science*, June 1983, p. 1339.

L. Blitz *et al.*, 'The new Milky Way', *Science*, June 1983, p. 1233.

J. Silk, 'The black cloud', *Nature*, September 1983, p. 388.

'New light on dark matter', *Science*, June 1984, p. 971 (Report on a workshop at Fermi Laboratory, Chicago).

P. Hut and S. White, 'Can a neutrino dominated universe be rejected?' *Nature*, August 1984, p. 637.

'Candidates for cold dark matter', *Nature*, October 1984, p. 517.

'Tracking down the missing mass', *New Scientist*, January 1986, pp. 32, 37–40.

J. Bahcall and S. Casertano, *Astrophysical Journal*, vol. 293 (1985), p. 1–7.

'New clues to galaxy formation', *New Scientist*, January 1986, p. 34.

M. Rees, *Monthly Notes of the Royal Astronomical Society*, vol. 218 (1986), p. 25.

M. Waldrop, 'In search of dark matter', *Science*, September 1986, p. 1386; October 1986, p. 152.

The Future

F. J. Dyson, 'Time without end', *Reviews of Modern Physics*, vol. 51 (1979), p. 447.

G. K. O'Neill, 'The colonisation of space', *Physics Today*, September 1974.

J. Barrow and F. Tipler, 'Eternity is unstable', *Nature*, vol. 276 (1978), p. 453.

'Thermodynamics of a closed universe', *Nature*, March 1984, p. 319.

Glossary

alpha particle   A nucleus of helium comprising two *protons* and two *neutrons* tightly bound to one another. May be emitted in the radioactive decay of a *nucleus (fission)*.

antimatter   For every variety of fundamental particle there exists an antiparticle with the same mass but with the opposite sign of the electrical charge. When a particle and its antiparticle meet they can mutually annihilate and liberate energy.

asteroid   Small rocky objects orbiting the Sun. Most orbit between Mars and Jupiter but several have trajectories that cross our own. Remnants of *comets* and the debris from collisions between a handful of small bodies that condensed between Mars and Jupiter during the formation of the solar system. Also known as minor planets or planetoids.

atom   System of *electrons* orbiting a *nucleus*. Smallest piece of an element that can still be identified as that element.

aurora   Display of diffuse light seen high in the atmosphere mainly in extreme polar regions. Caused by charged particles trapped in the Earth's magnetic field.

beta decay   Decay of a radioactive *nucleus* with production of an electron (*beta particle*). The underlying process is the transmutation of a *neutron* into a *proton* with *electron* and *neutrino* emission. This process is controlled by the *weak interaction* and was its first known manifestation.

beta particle   *Electron* emitted in radioactive decay of a *nucleus* (*beta decay*).

229

Big Bang   The galaxies are receding from one another: the Universe is expanding. The Big Bang theory proposes that this expansion began 10–20 billion years ago when the Universe was in a state of enormous density.

black hole   A region where gravity is so powerful that light cannot escape. Hypothesised to be formed when some stars collapse. The gravitational influence of the collapsed star can be felt but no information escapes from within the black hole.

comets   Members of solar system travelling around the Sun on elongated orbits. Thought by many astrophysicists to be akin to mile-sized dirty snowballs. So tenuous that the *solar wind* blows material from them and gives rise to long tails of gas and dust that is their familiar manifestation in the sky.

cosmic rays   High-speed particles and nuclei coming from outer space.

deuteron   *Nucleus* comprising one *proton* and one *neutron*. Sometimes called heavy hydrogen. Produced at an intermediate stage of stellar *fusion*.

electromagnetic force   One of the fundamental forces of Nature. Attraction of oppositely charged particles traps negatively charged *electrons* around a positively charged *nucleus* in *atoms*.

electromagnetic radiation   Energy emitted by electrically charged objects. Familiar examples include light, radio waves, microwaves, X-rays and *gamma rays*.

electron   Negatively charged elementary particle constituent of *atoms*. Carrier of electricity through wires.

electronvolt (eV)   Unit of energy. 1 eV is the energy gained when an *electron* is accelerated by a potential of one volt.

fission   Break-up of a large *nucleus* into smaller ones.

fusion   Combination of small nuclei into larger ones.

gamma ray   Photon. Very high-energy *electromagnetic radiation*.

ion   *Atom* carrying electrical charge due to its being stripped of *electrons* (positive ion) or having an excess of electrons (negative ion).

230

meteor   The streak of light seen in a clear night sky when a small particle of interplanetary dust or stone burns itself out in the Earth's upper atmosphere.

meteorite   A *meteor* that makes landfall; remnants of *meteoroids* found on the ground.

meteoroid   Collective term applied to meteoric material in the solar system.

molecule   Cluster of *atoms*.

nebula   Gas or a collection of stars that appear as a bright mist in the clear night sky.

neutrino   Electrically neutral elementary particle, with little or no mass. Most abundant particles in the universe. Only takes part in *weak interactions*; produced in radioactive processes and as a by-product in stellar *fusion* and *supernovae*.

neutron   Electrically uncharged partner of the *proton* in atomic nuclei.

nucleus   Dense centre of *atoms* built from *neutrons* and *protons*. The latter give the nucleus a positive electrical charge by which *electrons* are attracted and atoms formed.

photon   Bundle of *electromagnetic radiation* and carrier of *electromagnetic forces*.

plasma   A gas of *ions* and *electrons* moving freely. A plasma is in effect an ionised gas.

positron   Antiparticle of *electron*. Carries positive electrical charge. Stable until it meets an electron, at which point the pair may mutually annihilate into *electromagnetic radiation*.

proton   Positively charged constituent of the *nucleus* that give it electrical charge. Built from three *quarks*.

protostar   An early stage in the formation of a star. It has fragmented from a gas cloud and started to collapse but nuclear reactions have not yet begun.

quark   Believed to be one of the fundamental constituents of matter. Clusters of quarks comprise the *neutrons* and *protons* in the atomic *nucleus*.

quasar   A contraction of the name Quasi-Stellar Object. A compact extragalactic object that looks like a point of light but emits more energy than hundreds of galaxies combined.

They are among the most distant objects that we have observed in the Universe.

radioactivity Spontaneous decay and transmutation of *nuclei* with emission of particles comprising alpha, beta or gamma radiation.

shooting star Another word for a *meteor*.

solar flare Sudden short-lived brightening of the Sun's visible surface caused by an explosive release of energy in the form of particles and radiation.

solar wind Flow of electrically charged particles, mainly *electrons* and *protons*, from the Sun into the solar system.

strange matter Hypothesised form of matter whose atomic *nuclei* contain a substantial percentage of *strange particles* in addition to the *quarks* that comprise the *neutrons* and *protons* of normal nuclei.

strange particles Variety of particles that are not stable under normal conditions on Earth but may stabilise within *strange matter*. They have been seen fleetingly in *cosmic rays* and produced in particle accelerators.

sunspots Comparitively dark regions on solar surface, their number varying on roughly an 11-year cycle (the sunspot cycle).

supernova Sudden appearance or brightening of a star caused by an explosion that blows off most of the star's outer material accompanied by collapse of the remainder into a dense ball of *neutrons* (neutron star) or *black hole*.

weak interaction (force) One of the fundamental forces of Nature. Most famous manifestation is in *beta decay*, also involved in some radioactive decays of *nuclei* and *neutrino* interactions.

WIMPS Acronym for Weakly Interacting Massive Particles, hypothesised particles that are more massive than *protons* and which take part in the *weak interaction*. They may have been formed soon after the *Big Bang* and still occur in the centre of stars like the Sun. If so, they may affect the internal fuel cycle in the Sun.

Index